Exceptional Children

EXCEPTIONAL CHILDREN

James H. Bryan
Northwestern University

Tanis H. Bryan
University of Illinois, Chicago Circle

Distributed by:
Mayfield Publishing Co.
285 Hamilton Ave., Palo Alto, CA 94301

Our thanks to these individuals and organizations for the permission to reproduce their photographs in this text.

Figure 1–1 used by permission of Tom Stanfield.

Figures 1–2, 5–1, and 12–1 courtesy of the Chicago Early Childhood Education Project.

Figures 3–1, 6–1, 8–1, and 11–1 used by permission of Allan Grant Productions.

Figure 5–2 courtesy of Jane T. Hotchkiss.

Figure 11–2 used by permission of Justin Schwartz.

Figure 13–1, a *Los Angeles Times* Photo, used by permission of the California Special Olympics and Ernie Breedlove.

Figures 13–2, 13–3, and 13–4 courtesy of P. J. Lang, B. Melamed, and the *Journal of Abnormal Psychology*.

Alfred Publishing Co., Inc.
15335 Morrison Street
Sherman Oaks, California 91403

Current printing last digit: 10 9 8 7 6 5 4 3 2

Library of Congress Cataloging in Publication Data

Bryan, James H.
Exceptional children.

Includes index.

1. Exceptional children. I. Bryan, Tanis H. joint author.
II. Title.
HQ773.5.B72 155.4'5 78-32119
ISBN 0-88284-078-9

Only fools and villains need to devalue
what they understand, and only they will
withdraw compassion from human suffering. . . .

From Perry London, *Behavior Control*

Contents

ix   Contents

Preface

This is a book about exceptional children, or at least children with one or more exceptional conditions, and those concepts, issues, and procedures we feel are important to understanding them. In writing the book, we have focused upon what we consider to be relevant research findings, from whatever theoretical source they may have sprung. The book has no underlying theoretical position; neither of the authors is a Skinnerian, Freudian, or Piagetian. This is not to say that our biases do not show; they do. Rather, we wish to emphasize that the book does not structure its material from a particular theoretical perspective. We present research findings that are important in understanding the topics discussed.

The book is organized in three sections. In the first section we introduce the reader to some of the laws, professional developments, historical influences, and current controversies and concerns that seem germane to understanding the field of exceptional children. Chapters 2 and 3 introduce the reader to some topics that are important in how we think about and act towards children. Thus, our notions of intelligence and our theories and practices concerning socialization affect the ways we define, assess, and educate the exceptional child. Whether one is a parent, teacher, or mental health expert, it is important to be aware of ideas and facts concerning intelligence and personality development.

In Section II we present various forms of exceptionality. Handicapping conditions like learning disabilities (Chapter 4) and mental retardation (Chapter 5), as well as such nonhandicapping forms of exceptionality as giftedness (Chapter 10) and prosocial behaviors (Chapter 11), are examined. Depending upon available information, we discuss definitions, incidence, characteristics of the condition, and some of the factors that might affect it. In addition, we describe some of the typical measurement devices applied to these conditions and the problems associated with measuring them. The particular emphasis of the chapters, however, will vary according to the "state of the art" of the field. For example, there is a relatively strong emphasis upon the development and measurement of the sensory systems of hearing and vision. On the other hand, relatively little attention is paid to the assessment of behavior problems, or how the "normal" child behaves. The reason for this difference in stress is simple. We know a lot about the assessment and development of sensory systems, while our knowledge of social development and how to assess it is scant.

The introduction of a chapter on prosocial behavior within a book addressed to the problem of exceptional children deserves special mention. There is no category of exceptionality called prosocial children. That does not mean to say that some children are not exceptional in their concern for others and their willingness to help and cooperate. Rather, what we mean is that such children have not often been studied, and thus a corpus of information about them is not available. We are suggesting that prosocial behaviors in children be considered as a form of exceptionality just as, traditionally, giftedness and creativity are. Some individuals may reasonably believe that such material should not be included in the book. To our knowledge it has not been done before. Moreover, it is understandable that some readers might feel that the chapter is misplaced, that since there is little information concerning exceptionally prosocial children, perhaps the material should be placed in the book's early sections. Without belaboring these issues, we would like to explain our decision to retain the chapter within the section pertaining to exceptional children. First, as stated, we believe prosocial behavior should be considered a new category of exceptionality. Second, there is a substantial body of information concerning the development of children's prosocial behavior, and we are relatively knowledgeable concerning those factors that might produce such children. Third, to our knowledge, little of this information has been incorporated into basic psychology or education courses, although this failure may well be remedied in the future. Finally, almost all of us are concerned with producing not only the "well-behaved" child, but one who will also show compassion for the needy, and cooperation and honesty when dealing with others. Most parents and teachers hope their children will conduct themselves with more than the minimal conformity required in a situation. We hope that this chapter, then, will provide some useful information as to how this aspiration might be fulfilled.

The final section of the book, Section III, concerns techniques for remediation and service. Although we occasionally mention treatment strategies while discussing particular exceptional conditions, we have generally left them for Chapters 12 and 13. We have postponed presenting much of this information as many of the techniques employed by specialists, particularly in psychological treatment, are generally applicable to a wide range of exceptional children. Chapter 12 presents educational service and corrective techniques while Chapter 13 examines psychological remediation strategies.

We realize that you will spend considerable time and effort in studying this book. We hope that when you have finished, you will have a better idea as to the complexities, characteristics, and problems of exceptional children that challenge the adults involved with them. We also hope that you will have retained and even enhanced your compassion for all children.

Finally, no book is written without the help of others. We wish to express our appreciation to the many reviewers who spent much time and, obviously, much thought in helping us prepare this text. While not all of their suggestions were followed, many were, and all were given considerable attention. Their constructive comments were of considerable help to us. Moreover, no manuscript goes to the publisher written in longhand. Several secretaries spent many hours in making sense of illegible copies and placing correct translations upon paper, and did so with apparent good cheer. To Sue Evangelist, Pat Czaszar, and Lorraine Nelson we owe many thanks. Thanks also to Abby Fisher and Richard Sherman for their hard work during the proofreading stages of the book production process. Finally, special thanks to Justin Schwartz, who was responsible for some of the photography used in this book.

A Note on the Selection of Key Terms

We have included at the end of each chapter a brief list of special terms introduced in that chapter. At their first usage these terms have been set in boldface type in the text. It is our intention that these brief glossaries will aid the student in more quickly grasping key concepts. We fully realize many important terms and concepts have been omitted, but these lists, by necessity, were largely based on our personal choice and were not meant to unduly emphasize one concept over another.

James H. Bryan
Tanis H. Bryan

I

FOUNDATIONS

**INTRODUCTION AND
CRITICAL ISSUES**

INTELLIGENCE

**SOCIALIZATION AND
BEHAVIOR CONTROL**

FIGURE 1-1

CHAPTER 1

Introduction and
Critical Issues

There are millions of children who need special help, thousands of people helping them, and hundreds of professors training people to help them in the future. Like any field, that of **special education** is a dynamic one with its own technical vocabulary, debates over issues, and fights over legislation. This chapter will introduce you to some of the characteristics of the field. In it we discuss the nature and numbers of children served by special education, recent legislation that is critical to the treatment of exceptional persons, and the provision of services to them. We will outline the issues and facts characterizing the services and research aimed at the **exceptional child**. First, we discuss the nature and numbers of children served by special education to indicate to you the scope of the problem and associated services. We then present some of the more important recent laws and court rulings that have had a profound impact upon the definitions, perspectives, and services affecting the handicapped child. Next, a brief historical overview of the treatment of children, particularly exceptional ones, is offered to give you some idea as to how our society reached its present point in its attempts to help children. This overview is followed by a discussion of some of the major problems confronting today's workers in the field of special education. Finally, we briefly define categories of exceptionality.

Scope of the Problem

Millions of children are, have been, or should be receiving some form of special education. If one defines handicapped children as individuals up to nineteen years of age who suffer from mental retardation, visual impairments, neurological or orthopedic difficulties, speech defects, or some form of learning disabilities, estimates of the number of handicapped children exceed seven million (Hobbs, 1975). The Bureau of Education for the Handicapped (BEH), the major federal agency responsible for such individuals, has estimated that there are 7.08 million handicapped children. This does not include at least one type of exceptionality, intellectual giftedness. It is also unfortunate, but BEH has estimated that more than half of the children who suffer from some sort of problem do not receive appropriate educational services. In essence, there are about 3.5 million children in the United States denied an adequate education.

While there are many handicapped children going without needed services today, the government has recently shown increasing concern that this group receive appropriate and equal educational opportunities. Part of this concern is reflected in new laws, part in the provision of new money. Laws may, and money certainly will, stimulate the growth of special education as efforts are increased to provide services to children who are currently inadequately served or not served at all. Let us look at some of the critical legislation and court decrees.

THE COURTS

If one were to dramatize some of the most important current events in special education, our heroes or villains would have among them lawyers, judges, and legislators. Whether one views them as saviors or sinners depends upon one's particular perspective, but there can be no doubt that they have been enacting critical roles in this field in recent years. Court decrees and legislation have drastically changed the nature of education services designed for the handicapped and reflect society's changing attitudes toward exceptional children.

One effect of the current thrust by lawyers and legislators has been to establish that neglect of handicapped persons by the educational establishment will no longer be tolerated. For example, one landmark case is the *Pennsylvania Association for Retarded Children v. The Commonwealth of Pennsylvania*, 1972. In this suit the court ordered the Pennsylvania State Department of Education to identify all children who had been excluded from the public school system because of mental retardation. Once the excluded children were located, the schools had to provide them with medical and psychological evaluations and place them in appropriate, *free* public education programs. That was not all. The court also ordered that all children currently enrolled in classes for the mentally retarded were to be reevaluated to determine whether they were receiving suitable education. The State Department of Education was ordered to submit a report on the number of children who were receiving special services, and the nature of the financing of these programs. Two masters (apparently "person watchdogs") were appointed by the court to ensure that the department complied with the court decrees.

A second notable court case was *Mills v. The Board of Education of the District of Columbia*, 1972, which led to the ruling that no child can be excluded from a regular public school unless the District is prepared to finance the child's education within special classes, private schools, or with tutors. The court decreed that prior hearings and periodic assessments of both the child's status and the educational program were a necessary part of the schools' responsibilities toward these children. No matter how severely handicapped the child, the public school system must provide educational services and must demonstrate their adequacy.

These court decisions have had far-reaching effects on educational programs throughout the land. In their wake, however, have come some unfortunate problems. First and foremost is the lack of money; the states did not have the means to comply with the court decrees. There were insufficient funds to hire personnel to perform the initial diagnoses and periodic reviews of the children's progress and not enough classroom resources, including teachers. In addition, the definition of adequate and appropriate educational services is vague and leaves considerable latitude in interpretation and, thus, in compliance with the court's intentions. More-over, compliance must sometimes be won through political clout, often lacking in many districts. Evidently there is an active, organized parents' association in the state of Pennsylvania that pressured school districts to comply with the court decree. Unfortunately, many communities lack cohesive, powerful organizations. It is clear, nonetheless, that the courts have played increasingly active and important roles in the field of special education. In doing so they have reiterated that handi-capped children cannot be the victims of educational discrimination, and that adequate and appropriate learning opportunities are their right. Unhappily, one can only agree with Cruickshank's statement that for the judicial system to have to specify for educators what is good and bad is an "awful indictment of educational leadership at the local level" (1972, p. 387).

LEGISLATION

Indictments like Cruickshank's have not only goaded indifferent edu-cators to take real responsibility for teaching the handicapped; they have also spurred legislators to act. As will be indicated in Chapter 2, there have been attempts, some successful, to prohibit legally the use of intelligence tests in the schools. The law that is having great impact upon special education and education in general and that has generated great concern and controversy is the *Education for All Handicapped Children Act* of 1975, commonly referred to as Public Law 94-142 (PL 94-142).

This important act appears to be the outcome of the current move-ment to ensure civil rights for all citizens. The handicapped apparently have bene-fited from the efforts of the Blacks to lay claim to their legitimate rights. Once black persons obtained the right to drink coffee, milk, or water in public places or sit wherever, whenever, and with whomever they wished, the door was opened for other minorities, whether ignored or oppressed, to demand their rights from a negligent and often indifferent majority. Through the legislation that allows Blacks their rights of citizenship, the voices of the handicapped were heard and heeded. Thus

President Carter declared: "The time for discrimination against the handicapped is over" (*Chicago Sun-Times*, May 24, 1977). The president's attitudes have been reflected in actions. Joseph A. Califano, Secretary of Health, Education, and Welfare, has signed regulations implementing the Rehabilitation Act of 1973, which requires that any recipient of funds from any federal agency must guarantee that its programs do not discriminate against the handicapped (*Chicago Sun-Times*, May 24, 1977). Words are being translated into deeds and PL 94-142 is the biggest deed of all.

Education for All Handicapped Children Act of 1975

PL 94-142 is likely to have great impact on the nation's treatment of handicapped children. This law has many provisions whose implications are likely to affect handicapped and nonhandicapped alike. The provisions include definitions, allocations of money, procedures to be followed at all levels of the educational system, and statements regarding personnel. The measure explicitly recognizes that it is in the public interest that all handicapped children receive not only an appropriate education but that it be a free one as well. The law assumes that we now have the technology to provide a more adequate education to such children, given that ample funding is provided to the states. The law states that teaching the exceptional child is not the domain solely of special education, but also must involve parents as well as professionals from related education and health fields. In addition, the law specifies that the procedures used to evaluate children must be non-discriminatory against either the child or the child's family, and such procedures must be open to public scrutiny. Moreover, education for the handicapped child is to be conducted in the **least restrictive environment.** That is, continual efforts must be made to integrate these children into the mainstream of the educational community.

Carrots and Sticks: The Carrots

As is usually the case, the law offers both carrots and sticks to the states. The biggest carrot is money. The statute indicates that each state may count up to 12 percent of its children, ages five to eighteen, as eligible to receive federal funds in support of their education. The 12 percent figure is not capricious but reflects the general estimate that approximately that proportion of the nation's children are handicapped. In addition, the law mandates that by 1978 all children between the ages of three and eighteen years, and by 1980 all those between three and twenty-one, who are eligible for services will receive a free and appropriate public education.

The federal government is authorized by this legislation to pay the states for the excess costs of providing these services and can spend up to $200 million in 1977, $387 million in 1978, $1.2 billion in 1980, $2.32 billion in 1981, and $3.16 billion in 1982 to assist the states in educating handicapped youngsters. The

FIGURE 1-2 Children participating in a program designed for their special needs

help the federal government offers the states in implementing PL 94-142 is critical because it costs more to provide a handicapped child with an educational opportunity equal to that offered the nonhandicapped. It has been estimated that the basic cost per year to educate a normal child is $655 while that for a handicapped child is more than double, approximately $1376 (Hewett and Forness, 1977). While the authorization of funds is one thing and the actual release of appropriations another, the law does state that the federal government is committed to ensuring that equal educational opportunity for the handicapped becomes a reality.

The Sticks

Now, what are the sticks involved? We mentioned that it was found that court decrees were more likely to be implemented if there were some clout to enforce them. There is considerable clout in PL 94-142. The federal government can withhold funds for a variety of programs to any state or local agency that is not in compliance with the statute. Those who violate this law risk the withdrawal of federal funds for programs quite unrelated to handicapped children. Obviously, a state may opt not to file for federal funds under this law. It makes no difference with regard to the stick. The state must still comply with the provisions of this act because it was written to be consistent with other civil rights legislation. Seeking funds or not, the state will be in violation of other laws if it fails to implement PL 94-142. The federal government thus can withhold money under a number of banners to ensure the implementation of this particular piece of legislation. More-over, compliance with the law is also demanded of private schools, although if such schools are not receiving any federal funds, the stick is not nearly as stout as for public schools. In effect, for almost all forms of education, whether or not one tries for the carrot, the stick can still be applied.

Assessment of the Individual

Assuming that the state opts to apply for federal funds through PL 94-142, it must develop a plan describing how it is going to meet the specifics of the legislation. Let us look at these specifics. The law clearly defines special education. It is *instruction designed to meet the individual needs of the handicapped child.* First, the child must have a nondiscriminatory, multidisciplinary assessment. Nondiscrim-inatory means that if the child speaks a language other than standard English, or has some physical or sensory deficit, the assessment procedures must take these factors into account.

State and local education agencies must show that none of the proce-dures or material used in evaluating the child is radically or culturally discriminat-ing. Assessments are conducted in the child's native language. Parents must also be informed of the school procedures and their rights in their native language.

Multidisciplinary means that the team analyzing the child must include specialists in various components of the child's handicap (for example, psychologist, special education teacher, speech pathologist, physician). The assess-ment must result in an individual education plan (IEP) for the child. The IEP must include short- and long-term educational objectives, a description of the specific services the child will be provided, their anticipated duration, and the evaluative procedures determining whether educational objectives are being met. In addition, the law demands that during the first year of services, the child is to be evaluated at least twice so as to ensure that the objectives, and procedures for achieving them, are adequate. Thereafter, the child is to be reevaluated yearly.

Local education agencies are further required to keep records on handicapped children within their geographic domain even if the children attend private schools or schools outside the agencies' boundaries. School authorities are to maintain records of IEPs and to establish procedural safeguards to ensure that handicapped children are educated in the least restrictive environment. That is, the child is to be maintained in the most common educational setting possible that still meets his or her educational needs. This means that children cannot be removed from regular classrooms or community school placements without justification. If the child is withdrawn from traditional school settings, the educational institution must justify the move.

Scope of PL 94-142

The assessment's procedures and its product, the IEP, are thus well outlined. In addition, PL 94-142 specifies the scope of the program it mandates. Special education services are not to be limited to classroom activities or special education teachers. The schools must have available facilities and personnel needed for the wide range of services often necessary to help handicapped children. Transportation must be provided to bring the child to school. Trained personnel within the district are to include psychologists, audiologists, speech therapists, and social workers. There must be physical and occupational therapy suited to the child's needs. The law thus demands of the school the broad spectrum of services needed by handicapped children; no wonder the program is expensive.

According to the law, state educational plans and programs for the exceptional must be visible to the public. State education agencies are required to hold public hearings and to consult with handicapped persons, their parents, and teachers before implementing or changing their offerings or policies. Screening programs are to be public, with school authorities notifying parents in the district of the services available and their right to use them. Parents and guardians of the handicapped may inspect their child's records and must be notified in advance of contemplated changes in the child's school placement. If the parents or guardian object to the school's assessment or placement of their child, there are procedures for lodging their protests. PL 94-142 specifies grievance procedures to be followed by those parties unhappy with the educational system's treatment of their handicapped child. If either the school district or the parents request a grievance hearing, a hearing officer not employed by the school district adjudicates the conflict. At this inquiry, aggrieved parties may be accompanied by a lawyer or other advocate, and special education experts. There is a right to present evidence, demand the presence of witnesses, confront and cross-examine them, and to record the proceedings in writing or electronically. If the hearing fails to solve the dispute, the aggrieved may seek redress in the courts.

Summary of PL 94-142

In summary, the important components of PL 94-142 are:

1. Each handicapped child, age three to twenty-one, will be given nondiscriminatory testing and evaluation by a professional multidisciplinary team. The product of the evaluation will be an individual education plan.

2. The program must be implemented in the least restrictive environment possible for the child.
3. Parents and guardians shall be consulted regularly prior to evaluation and placement of the child in any school program. Parents and guardians shall be consulted and informed in their native language of the policies and procedures relevant to their child. School records shall be available to parents.
4. The child's education plan will be reviewed annually to determine the effectiveness of the program.
5. Children and parents or guardians have the right of due process.
6. The state education agency is responsible for the implementation of a policy that provides a free, appropriate public education to the handicapped child.

Some Concerns

While the passage of a law does not guarantee public acceptance and conformity to it, this measure appears to have a good deal of public support. The day President Ford was to sign PL 94-142 into law, the White House reportedly got more telephone calls and telegrams urging his support than had ever before been received there for any pending bill. Certainly the intention to improve the educational status of the handicapped child is admirable, and the goal of non-discrimination against people reflects a basic principle of our country. In spite of good intentions and public support, however, concern has been voiced over the impact of this legislation. Some educators have referred to PL 94-142 as the "Lawyers Full Employment Act of 1975," expressing their fear that the law will stimulate adversary relationships between parents and schools as well as increasing bureaucratic red tape and stretching out delays in obtaining services. Others are concerned with the degree to which the law specifies assessment procedures as this has been traditionally the prerogative of the particular specialist. Yet others see the law as a possible intrusion by the federal government into what has been the responsibility of the individual states, reflecting an undesirable trend toward a national educational plan. Others, not so concerned about the goals or procedures outlined in the law, fear that compliance will not be possible with the funds being made available.

As of now, it is not known just how the personnel of school districts and state education agencies will respond to the law in their professional activities. There are hints, however, that a professional rebellion may be brewing. The teachers in at least one school district have insisted that their contract with the district contain the provision that the teachers have no handicapped children in their classrooms! Irrespective of our objections and concerns, PL 94-142 outlines what special education should be and enlists our conscience to provide equal opportunities for the handicapped. It may provide the carrots and it certainly does provide the sticks to facilitate our good faith and action. Whether these goals can be accomplished through these means remains to be seen.

PL 94-142 is the most contemporary legislation relevant to handicapped children in the United States. Evident in this law is a humanistic philosophy by which we try to implement constitutional guarantees of equal treatment for all citizens, including those with disabilities. With this legislation, and the attitudes and dollars associated with it, it is hoped we can solve the problems of the handicapped and grant them those civil rights enjoyed by other citizens. While it is encouraging that our hopes can be translated into the law of the land, it is sad to think that it was necessary to produce such laws, and court actions, to gain civil rights for any group. The struggle to make being different acceptable has been a long one, one in which progress has crept rather than run.

A BRIEF HISTORY OF EXCEPTIONALITY

There is evidence dating from 3000 B.C. that handicapped individuals existed. For example, cave people during the Stone Age, apparently practiced "psychiatry" by chipping away at the skulls of those whom we would think of as mentally ill (Hewett and Forness, 1977). Lacking systematic studies, we do not know how effective this form of psychiatry was. Throughout history the treatment of the handicapped has reflected the surrounding social and economic conditions. By and large, explanations advanced to account for various handicapping conditions have been shaped by people's religious or mystical beliefs, while the treatments received by the handicapped have been affected by both religious and economic conditions.

Childhood in the Ancient World

In ancient times life was harsh for everyone and survival of the fittest was indeed often the rule. Ancient Sparta and Greece practiced infanticide, killing deformed babies or leaving them to die. Since more babies died than survived during this time, the destruction of handicapped newborns may have served to further hasten early death. While preliterate societies sometimes protected the weak and deformed, the harshness of life and the absence of modern medicine limited the assistance that could be provided. During this period the life span of people was regarded differently than it is today. There was no separate world of childhood (Plumb, 1976). Children were treated as infants until about age seven years. Then, following intricate and sometimes painful rituals, they became adults. Spartan boys, for instance, were flogged, while Arabian boys were circumcised without benefit of anesthesia. Once they entered adulthood, they engaged in adult activities, save making love and war. Until children entered adulthood, they were not likely to be regarded as important (Plumb, 1976). Since so many infants died, there was a certain indifference to death.

Treatment of the Handicapped

For those who survived and became handicapped, religious beliefs dominated thinking about the cause and treatment of their disability. Primitive people invoked demons and gods to explain many of life's uncontrollable events; hence, a person acting strangely was believed to be inhabited by demons or to have lost favor with the gods. Religious ceremonies to exorcise the demons or to invoke the benevolence of the gods were ancient people's attempts to help handicapped persons. The early Hebrews used exorcism in the form of prayer, beatings, and starvation to drive away evil spirits. (Hewett and Forness, 1977).

Through the Middle Ages the treatment given to handicapped persons varied among different periods and geographic locations. With religion as a dominating force, handicapped persons were viewed at different times as witches, fools, or innocents to be protected (MacMillan, 1977). It should not be believed, however, that the treatment of the handicapped showed slow but continuous improvement over time. For instance, while it was true that during the sixth to eleventh centuries in Western Europe, the mentally ill were considered possessed by the devil, it was only much later that the therapeutics applied to such people included torture and execution (Hewett and Forness, 1977).

The treatment of the handicapped varied considerably from region to region even during the same time period. While the mentally disturbed residents of Western Europe saw devils and were treated by torture, those of the Arab world were helped according to the scientific philosophies advanced by the Greeks. In the eleventh century, there were rather enlightened programs for the blind in Egypt, Japan, and France. Most blind people, however, were not fortunate enough to be treated in such programs; they were subject to a beggar's existence and viewed by others as sinners. Perhaps, however, their plight was not so unusual since for much of history people were kings or serfs, beggars or exploiters, and life and survival were difficult for almost all. Most people were illiterate and those whom we now view as minimally handicapped (for example, the educable mentally retarded) were probably not much different from anybody else (Crissey, 1975).

During the sixteenth and seventeenth centuries, religious dogma continued to monopolize people's view of the handicapped, who fared none too well. For example, this was the era that spawned the Spanish Inquisition and launched the attack against witchcraft. While such a movement was hardly likely to benefit many ordinary citizens, it must have been especially difficult for the handicapped. There are several reasons why they were particularly likely to suffer under the Inquisition. First, their handicaps made them more visible. Some forms of disability, such as mental illness, may have been seen as evidence of witchcraft, while mental retardation would reduce one's ability to convince jurors of one's lack of demonic qualities. Incidents of torture and death may have been most frequent among the handicapped population. But even during this period, some improvement in the treatment of the handicapped was evident. The first teachers of the hearing impaired appeared on the scene and attempts were made to refine diagnosis of mental retardation and to separate these individuals from others suffering from mental illness (Hewett and Forness, 1977).

Children in the Modern Era

It was in this same period that children in Western Europe won some sort of recognition as people. At least this was the first time that they were represented on their parents' tombs (Plumb, 1976). But even then, there was no world of childhood as we now view it. In fact, children lived much like adults, sharing their games, dances, liquor, and, if capable, their sexuality. It was not until the 1600s, with the appearance of the cult of the Christ child, that we begin to see children holding status different from that of adults, and this was true only if the parents were wealthy. Books primarily for children were developed, separation of the sexes and ages came about, and the notion that the child was an individual worthy of respect was advanced. By 1700 juvenile books were being written with an eye towards moral education and the child was viewed as a being to be protected from the various forms of sinning.

Around the eighteenth century, education underwent a revolution in attitudes and practices and many of the assumptions underlying this revolution remain with us to this day. It was decided during this time that educational programs should follow the developmental stages of the child; reading should be taught first, followed by writing and increasingly complex matter (Plumb, 1976). These changes were adopted first only by the wealthy. It took many more decades for their influence to reach the poor. In the meantime, the children of the poor kept the status of adults, enjoying and suffering the various benefits and evils this brought. Such children did not receive special protection, at least not for a time.

During the eighteenth century, there were two separate, and unequal, forms of education, one for the poor, another for the rich. During the Middle Ages, the poor had received their education, if at all, from priests or monks in the local neighborhood monastery. The age at which matriculation occurred was dictated by the family's labor needs. If the child's labor was needed, his education might begin as a teenager or young adult. If labor was plentiful, education began at an earlier age. Wealthy children, on the other hand, began their studies sooner, experienced a more disciplined academic and social life, were often placed in academic institutions away from home, and finally, had the opportunity for advanced education.

With the advent of the Industrial Revolution, the lives of children of the poor did not improve. Fulfilling the labor demands of that revolution, many were often the victims of factory accidents and abuses. Moreover, this was a period with a stricter code of discipline. Children who misbehaved were shipped off to prisons or other centers of detention. The plight of the young during this period is perhaps best summarized by statistics presented by Hewett and Forness (1977). According to these authors, 64 percent of the children born in the countries undergoing the

Industrial Revolution died before reaching the age of ten; 80 percent of the 32,000 children entrusted to the Paris Foundling House between 1771 and 1777 died within a year after their admission. Deformity and death of children, either through accidents, murder, or suicide, aroused public indignation. The general public's call for reform in the treatment of unfortunate persons, whether slaves, prisoners, or the handicapped, led at last to the accumulation of funds and properties to support charitable undertakings (MacMillan, 1977).

Perhaps partly because of the excesses of the Industrial Revolution, the foundations for contemporary philosophies and treatments of handicapped persons had their start in Europe and the United States about 200 years ago. During this time political reforms were initiated in those countries that focused on individual rights and freedoms. The individual, except for Blacks and American Indians, was given the right to expect some measure of freedom and dignity. The individual, relative to the state, rose in status. Simultaneous with the shift to political individualism, a humanitarian reform movement emerged. People were becoming increasingly conscious of the obligation to nurture the helpless, the handicapped, and the dependent. We now turn our attention to some of the pioneers in this humanistically oriented revolution. Their contributions to the handicapped were significant, and their courage in the face of public rejection and ridicule was great.

Pioneers

Who were the pioneers in improving the lot of the handicapped? Certainly one of them was Philippe Pinel, a French physician of the 1800s. Pinel treated the mentally ill and his views concerning them were a radical departure from those of his contemporaries. He rejected the then common notion that the cause of mental illness was brain damage at best, or inherent evil at worst, and that the treatment should be restraint and punishment. His view of the mentally ill was that they were medically, not spiritually, afflicted and should be treated as such. His ideas led him to medical innovations that, while mundane today, were outright radicalism in his time. First, he removed the chains from the mentally ill. In taking this giant step, he tested the possibility that more humane treatment of patients would not result in homicide or suicide. This was not his only contribution, great as it was. He also introduced the method of psychiatric case studies, looking not for demons but for antecedents to the patient's illness. His empirical efforts finally led him to develop a taxonomy of mental illness, classifying it into four categories: mania, melancholia, dementia, and idiocy (Hewett and Forness, 1977).

Pinel was not alone in his struggle on behalf of the impaired. Benjamin Rush, the director of the Pennsylvania Hospital, introduced more humane care for the mentally ill in the United States and wrote the first textbook on psychiatry published in this country. In France, the Abbé de l'Epée organized and opened a school for the hearing impaired, the National Institute for Deaf Mutes, while Boney and Pereira developed systems by which the deaf might learn language through finger spelling and lip reading. Programs for the visually impaired were also being initiated in Germany and Switzerland. Wax tablets for writing and methods to guide pencil movements on paper were created at this time and Valentino Huay started the first school for the blind in France.

The belief that the deaf and blind were able to benefit from education marked the beginning of the field of special education. Following this the impact of education upon the mentally retarded was explored. The most dramatic attempt, depicted in the French film *The Wild Child*, was undertaken by Jean Marc Gaspard Itard. Itard, a French physician working at the Institute for Deaf Mutes in Paris, was brought the "wild boy." The boy, subsequently named Victor, had been captured by hunters in the forest. He was believed to be about eleven or twelve years of age and apparently looked and behaved more like an animal than a child, even an under-socialized one. Victor had no speech, but uttered gutteral sounds, made peculiar body movements, lacked modesty in his toilet habits, and had the unfortunate habit of biting people (Hewett and Forness, 1977). Itard set about civilizing the boy, setting goals to develop his speech and to instill appropriate social behaviors. The physician devoted five years to this enterprise, but it fell far short of his hopes. Victor never developed language, although he did master a number of words and sounds. He was able to read somewhat insofar as he could act out words written on the blackboard. Victor's social behavior did improve, although at the onset of puberty he became a serious management problem. At this point, Itard terminated his training and allowed Victor to live with his governess, free of tutorial interruptions, until his death at age forty.

While Itard was personally disappointed in his accomplishments with Victor, apparently others were not. He received public recognition for his efforts and achievements from the French Academy of Sciences, probably the most prestigious scientific organization in the world at that time. Itard's legacy was impressive. He gave hope to those aspiring to train the handicapped, demonstrating that such aspirations could be partially fulfilled even in a case as extreme as Victor's. He indicated a possible prototype for such treatment and developed basic ideas about sensory training that are still respected.

Edward Seguin, another French physician and a protégé of Itard, was largely responsible for initiating reforms on behalf of the mentally retarded. Like Itard, his legacy was great, both in stimulating philosophical commitments to and a belief in the capability of retarded persons, and in the methods that he developed for diagnosing and teaching these individuals. Seguin firmly believed that all human beings, including the retarded, have a universal right to education. "While waiting for medicine to cure idiots," he declared, "I have undertaken to see that they participate in the benefits of education" (Crissey, 1975, p. 801). The teaching method he proposed was based upon the diagnosis of the affected party and thus could be directed towards specific disabilities. Unlike many of his contemporaries, Seguin focused on the individual's behavior rather than upon physiological or anatomical pathologies associated with mental retardation. He introduced the notion that diagnosis of the mentally retarded must include assessments both of their problems and strengths, that it must take into account not only the physiological but the psychological as well.

Seguin migrated to the United States in 1848, where he was instrumental in changing views about the mentally retarded and their treatment. Here, at least in the Northeast, he began establishing schools especially designed to house and help the mentally deficient. The long-standing tradition of housing such people in institutions for the mentally ill and the blind was broken by his work. Partially because of Seguin's efforts, public interest in the plight of the retarded was stimulated so that by 1876 the Association of Medical Officers of American Institutions for Idiotic and Feeble-minded Persons was formed. Before long the organization began publishing its own newsletter, the *American Journal of Mental Deficiency*. Distinctions between the mentally retarded and other handicapped persons were rapidly being achieved, and with them would come increasing knowledge concerning mental retardation.

To some degree, what Seguin did for the mentally retarded, Dorothea Dix did for the mentally ill. Preaching a philosophy of benevolence toward these sufferers, this retired schoolteacher was able to establish 32 hospitals for the mentally ill between the years of 1841 and 1881.

During this period, other major developments in the field of exceptional education were unfolding. Louis Braille, blind since boyhood, developed a system enabling the blind to read. Interestingly, his embossed symbols were based on a method of "night writing" developed to allow Napoleon's soldiers to exchange information in war zones during the night without exposing their position by lights (Hewett and Forness, 1977).

Samuel Howe and Thomas Gallaudet were activists in seeking support for the deaf, and in the case of Howe, the blind as well. For both men education of the handicapped was the goal. Indeed Gallaudet opened one of the few colleges for the deaf that exists in the world today, a college bearing his name and located in Washington, D.C. Howe demonstrated the feasibility of educating the handicapped with his most spectacular success, the training of Laura Bridgman, a deaf-blind-mute.

The most famous success in educating the handicapped is Anne Sullivan's work with Helen Keller during the late 1800s. Anne Sullivan, herself a visually impaired woman who had benefited from Samuel Howe's work, modeled her treatment of the blind and deaf child after that of Laura Bridgman. Helen Keller eventually became one of the nation's intellectuals. She graduated from college, wrote several books, and became an eloquent spokeswoman on behalf of the deaf-blind. The title of the play and movie based on her life, "The Miracle Worker," reflected many people's views of Anne Sullivan's accomplishment.

The achievements of these pioneers in the field of special education cannot be underestimated; they were truly revolutionaries in their days. Like most revolutionaries they withstood much public condemnation and embarrassment. Howe, for example, was caricatured as a Don Quixote riding against windmills and a report of his was described as ". . . one for idiots as well as concerning them" (Hewett and Forness, 1977, p. 39). It is useful now to turn to some of the principles and developments that facilitated the successes of these pioneers and dictated the direction and methods of treating the handicapped.

CHANGING PERSPECTIVES

Up to and including the 1800s, the conditions under which the mentally ill, the retarded, and other disabled individuals lived could only be characterized as dreadful. The form of restraint was often chains; the form of discipline, brutality. Pioneers like Dix and Howe proposed an upgrading of physical facilities and initiation of educational programs tailored to the individual needs and assets of the afflicted individuals. They urged that both academic and vocational skills be formally taught and that continuing research be conducted as to the efficacy of various educational approaches. Their hope was that the child could be educated at home during early years and, when older, taught in a day school located at special institutions, eventually becoming an independent and contributing member of society (Crissey, 1975). Unfortunately, what they proposed and what we got were not the same.

Retarding Influences

Two developments in the late 1800s and early 1900s affected prospects for the handicapped. One, whose influence is still being felt, was the **eugenics-**heredity-genetics movement. Proponents of this movement argued that we are what our genes determine we will be; genes not learning, biology not environment determine our character. This theory led to the belief that mental illness, retardation, criminality, poverty, parliamentary government, as well as salmon fishing were rooted in the instincts of the human being. Indeed, the use of instincts as an explanation for behavior became so popular that one enterprising psychologist determined that there had been postulated by 1924 some 504 separate instincts (Hall, 1961). While those who fished for salmon were probably unaffected by theorizing concerning their instincts, many others were not.

The Case of the Kallikaks

Presumably the "proof positive" concerning the role of genes was a study conducted by Goddard in 1910. Goddard traced the descendants of a man named Kallikak. Kallikak had at least two loves, one his legal wife, the other a retarded barmaid. His legitimate children were of normal ability and apparently produced normal offspring. The story of the illegitimate children, however, contains an altogether different scenario as they eventually contributed to society several hundred mentally retarded citizens. The fact that, in addition to their disparate gene pools, the two sets of offspring also experienced different life styles vis-a-vis health, child care, education, and community status was by and large ignored. The explanation of genes and instincts was simply too popular. Associated with this belief was the erroneous notion that if a problem is genetic, educational attempts to correct it will fail. Obviously such a set of faiths would not foster support for the proposed educational programs for the handicapped; rather it is more likely that these programs were seriously crippled.

Disappointments in Early Special Education

Unfortunately, it was also at this time that the original optimism concerning the training and education of the handicapped waned. The rosy expectations of the early pioneers concerning the benefits of special education to the handicapped were not fulfilled. While Itard had made great strides in his work with Victor, Victor did not resemble the usual French boy or man. While Seguin, Howe, and Sullivan achieved remarkable results with the handicapped, their followers fell short of these accomplishments. We do not know whether these pioneers failed in their attempts to teach teachers, whether their followers simply were not good students, or whether the educational technology was incorrect from the beginning. Whatever the cause, early hopes for educating the handicapped were not realized. As a result, the initial goal of providing day schools for teaching these children was forsaken for full-time residential care. Moreover, since it was believed that the handicapped shared a defective gene pool with social deviates, the notion sprang up that they too were likely to be socially or psychologically deviant. The stereotype lumped the blind, deaf, and mentally retarded with the criminal, the "sexual sinner," the dangerously crazed. People feared the handicapped. Segregated institutions, designed originally to provide a benevolent and intellectually stimulating environment, were reduced to convenient warehouses for the storage of exceptional persons (Crissey, 1975).

It would be misleading to suggest that most or all of the handicapped children were shunted aside to state institutions. In the early 1900s special classrooms were provided within the public schools where children who were deaf, blind, orthopedically handicapped, epileptic, or behavior-disturbed were taught. With the introduction of intelligence tests, classes were developed specifically to serve the mentally retarded, or at least children with low IQ scores. The numbers of children in special education classrooms increased until the onset of the Great Depression in the 1930s, only to show a rapid increase following World War II (Crissey, 1975). The number of special classrooms for the exceptional child equaled 87,000 in 1948, and had climbed to 390,000 by 1963 (Hewett and Forness, 1977). Moreover, various private agencies such as the National Easter Seal Society for Crippled Children and Adults and the American Foundation for the Blind were established.

Post–World War II

The era following World War II ushered in new attitudes and technologies. By 1950, the popularity of the eugenics movement had waned and experience had demonstrated that the mentally retarded were not likely to become criminals or even sex-crazed perverts; that given suitable education they did not have to be economic parasites nor swell the ranks of the unemployed. By and large the educable mentally retarded appeared very much like everyone else. The many wounded soldiers who returned home clearly physically handicapped were not seen as a threat to public safety. The nature of their experiences, the price they paid for the war effort, elicited more public sympathy than antagonism. In addition, the war forced the medical profession to look more closely at the treatment of handicaps, and psychologists to rethink the treatment of the mentally or emotionally ill. Indeed, it was from the impact of World War II that the field of clinical psychology was born.

Civil Rights Fallout

During the past 30 years, a variety of social events have markedly influenced the outlook for exceptional children. The civil rights movement has benefited not only Blacks but the handicapped as well. Parents, determined to obtain better education and treatment for their children, have learned to organize, fight institutional lethargy and bureaucratic red tape, and to influence Congress. The early demands of the Blacks for equality in public schools and public places led to demands for equal education for handicapped persons. Institutions today are expected to be equally accessible to all citizens, not just those with intact bodies. While social activism was largely carried out by the parents of the handicapped during these early years, now the handicapped themselves are bearing their own torch in lobbying efforts and demonstrations. The handicapped have become litigious. When schools and institutions are unresponsive to their needs and rights, these groups now turn to the courts for redress, and they obtain it.

Work of Presidential Committee

While "progress" moves in spurts, there have been some notable recent accomplishments on behalf of the exceptional child. In 1961, President Kennedy appointed a committee to study mental retardation. The panel's report set the framework for a national plan that provided the guidelines and goals for subsequent programs (Crissey, 1975). The report made three major recommendations: (1) The panel suggested the establishment of research centers for the study of mental retardation, particularly its causes and prevention. This recommendation was implemented, with the help of federal funds, through the building and staffing of twelve centers and twenty university affiliated facilities that provide interdisciplinary training and clinical services (Hobbs, 1975). Since their inception some of these research centers have broadened their base of interest to include other forms of exceptionality. (2) The panel also suggested that a greater number of professional and service personnel be trained to work with handicapped persons, particularly at the higher professional levels. The outcome of this recommendation was Public Law

91-230, which authorized federal funds to some 300 universities and colleges to pay for such training. These programs enroll about 40,000 students each year in addition to providing in-service training to teachers (Hobbs, 1975). (3) A third recommendation was that the country upgrade the welfare, health, and social conditions of the needy. Thus, in 1963, the National Institute of Child Health and Human Development was established, followed by the Office of Child Development, which has been responsible for such important programs as Head Start, Home Start (like Head Start but for younger children), and parent-child centers (Hobbs, 1975).

SOME CONTEMPORARY PROBLEMS

In the initial section of this chapter, we discussed Public Law 94-142, perhaps the most comprehensive law addressed to the education of the handicapped yet advanced. It is essentially a prescription for dealing with the exceptional child, and demands that all these children receive appropriate free public education. We then reviewed the history of the treatment of the handicapped, including some of the pioneers and major events that shaped it. However, old problems may still exist, and new ones may now have been created. There are some critical issues that await solution, and in the following section, we will discuss some of them.

The Severely and Multihandicapped

One contemporary problem in the field of exceptional children is how best to serve the severely and multihandicapped. Generally, these children, if they are to be served, receive aid through state agencies rather than public schools. However, many state agencies are organized around a particular problem or handicap, and are often unable or unwilling to serve those falling outside of their specialized domain. A state might have one agency responsible for the mentally ill, another for the mentally retarded, and yet another for the physically handicapped. Unfortunately, such an organizational structure may deprive children with multiple handicaps of needed services. To the degree to which the agencies' personnel rigidly limit their services to only those whose handicaps lie within a narrow category, children with many disabilities can be legitimately denied service on the basis of falling outside of the agency's responsibilities. That such problems may arise is suggested by a study by Friedman and MacQueen (1971). They found that of 195 children who were crippled or had chronic health problems, 37 percent had speech difficulties, 43 percent obtained intelligence test scores within the range typically viewed as reflecting mental retardation, and 25 percent were defined as maladjusted. Thus many impaired children will have several problems, and whether they are served by any specialized agency may well depend more on the benevolence of the administrators than on the children's rights to state services.

An additional point concerning organizational structures for rendering services: Assigning services to state agencies has tended to result in treatments more medically than educationally oriented. With the advent of PL 94-142, increased responsibility for schooling severely and multihandicapped children is being assumed by educational agencies which naturally give teaching very high priority. The educational status of these children is expected to change with anticipated federal support for learning programs, but as yet, these programs are in their early stages of development.

The Labeling Controversy

The second major problem revolves around the use of labels in dealings with the handicapped. For years children have been diagnosed and categorized according to various special education labels; university programs have trained teachers to meet certification requirements according to these labels; research and policy issues, parents groups, and professional organizations have all been structured around these labels. Thus we have an association for children with learning disabilities and an association for the mentally retarded, to name but two of the many categorically structured associations. Several developments triggered dissatisfaction with, disavowal of, and reorganization of our current thinking about special categories. These developments were shifts in theories concerning social deviance: increasing recognition among social scientists of the impact of expectancies on the behaviors of others; and finally the practical, and mostly negative, side effects of the use of labels.

Changes in Theory

Let us look at the theoretical shift. It has long been recognized that people become social deviants not simply because of their behavior but also because someone defines the term and applies it to particular persons. It takes at least two people to make a deviant, the person who is labeled deviant and the person doing the labeling. Moreover, sociologists have long felt that much of human conduct is determined not so much by the personalities of those involved as by the roles they assume, or to which they are assigned by others. This idea was evaluated and publicized by an eminent sociologist, Howard Becker (1963). His work on the sociology of deviance emphasized the role of the labeler in affecting and maintaining others' deviance. This corresponded in time to psychology's disenchantment with theories of human conduct that relied upon notions of personality and generally neglected situational and social forces. It was perhaps this disillusion that led to increased interest in the role of the labeler and situational factors determining who was to be cast in the role of a social, emotional, or mental deviant. In effect, the question was posed: If the label reflects not its "victim" but rather its assigner, of what use is it?

During the same period, Robert Rosenthal, a Harvard psychology professor, was conducting laboratory research on the role of expectancies in affecting behavior. His findings (Rosenthal, 1966) demonstrated that even where elaborate precautions are taken to avoid possible biasing of results, the expectancies of the experimenter will make a difference! Conceivably, expectancies that spring from a label might well markedly affect how one treats the handicapped. In terms of the practical effects of the employment of labels, other challenges have arisen. Educators have failed to demonstrate that placement in programs organized according to special education categories benefits the child either educationally or socially. Studies have generally not found that children placed in segregated facilities achieve more than those remaining in the regular classroom. It is argued that labels produce, or at least are associated with, the general public's rejection of the labeled child. These categories are thought to imply a wide variety of negative personal attributes that may not, in reality, exist. Now it is not altogether clear that all of the negative expectations concerning the affected child are simply the result of the label. Exceptional children can misbehave as well as others. What results from what has yet to be carefully sorted out, but there is concern that the label itself increases social rejection of the child (Dunn, 1968; Lilly, 1970). It is believed that through the labeling process children are shunned, excluded from opportunities, deprived of their liberty through commitment to institutions (Hobbs, 1975).

States Change Categories

In response to these concerns, states are beginning to change their categories of special education. Instead of classifications like mental retardation, learning disabilities, and behavior disorders, rankings of mildly, severely, and sensorily handicapped are being used. University programs are likewise starting to shift away from training programs based upon specific categories to those based upon the newer system.

Unfortunately, the problem is that we really do need labels, maybe not those to which we are accustomed, but certainly some terms that convey specific information concerning the attributes of the individual. Labels help us communicate, guide us in the formation of programs, help advance our theoretical and practical knowledge concerning people. For instance, one state uses the term "mentally handicapped," which covers morons, imbeciles, and idiots. But the state's law fails to define these terms, thus rendering them almost meaningless (Gearheart, 1972). The ultimate purpose of the label is to convey information about a cluster of people who share certain features not shared by individuals without such a label. The greater the degree of such separation of groups of people, the more useful the label. It is our belief that the reversion to a less informative labeling system, one based on the severity of the problem, will confuse rather than clarify our conceptions concerning handicaps. Does it make sense to lump into one category the severely psychotic child with the severely brain damaged? It may be appropriate for the practical purposes of organizing state agencies' services but it does not advance our conceptualizations or further our knowledge concerning the cause, prevention, and treatment of handicaps.

Labeling and Minority Children

An important current issue in labeling and categorizing children has been attitudes toward minority children undergoing special education evaluation. Of late these attitudes have been greatly affected by the work of Jane Mercer (1968, 1971, 1973), who found that the proportion of Spanish surname children within classes for the mentally retarded greatly exceeded what would be expected on the basis of their representation in the general population. Their numbers within such classes were simply too great. Mercer coined the term "six-hour retardate" to describe children who were in classes for the retarded while in school but led normal lives the rest of the time. Studies conducted in other parts of the country have also reported that minority children are more likely than Whites to be labeled as mentally retarded. To correct this, PL 94-142 requires that children whose families do not speak English must receive their communications from the schools in their native languages. Additionally, such children must be tested in their primary language. Accompanying these requirements is public antipathy of such magnitude that efforts have been made to ban all intelligence testing from various state school systems.

The issues and complexities involved in our notions about intelligence and the tests used to measure it are numerous and are discussed in chapter 2. There is little question, however, that professionals working with the exceptional are becoming increasingly sensitive to the problems of labeling children, particularly those from minority cultures. One danger associated with this sensitivity is that school officials will become reluctant to attach any labels to minority group children and therefore might deprive them of needed special services. To our knowledge there is at least one school district in which special service is being given white children who have achievement scores considerably higher than many black children for whom no special tutoring is provided. While this may reflect racial discrimination, it appears to be more an outgrowth of the school personnel's desire to avoid the accusation of racial discrimination via the labeling process.

Least Restrictive Environments

Among the contemporary goals for the handicapped is that of providing them living and educational experiences within the home and regular classroom. There is the goal and the hope that the handicapped will be allowed to conduct their lives within the same environments as the nonhandicapped. Many handicapped persons have been removed from segregated institutions and relocated within their home communities. Responsibility for their care has become increasingly that of the school, less that of institutions. Buildings are to be altered to allow the physically handicapped access to them, and elevators redesigned so the blind can push the correct floor button. The back-to-the-community movement, however, has received a mixed review. First, not all parents are happy to have the institutions closing their doors. One group of parents is suing the Association for Retarded Children for its role in effecting the closing of an institution. Second, families and communities who have the task of integrating and caring for the handicapped child are not necessarily receiving the support needed to carry out their task. To place great burdens on these families and their communities may result in a very short-lived popularity for the least restrictive environment policy.

The schools face similar problems. Exceptional children are increasingly being mainstreamed. This means they receive their education in regular school classrooms or, at least, in classrooms located in regular school buildings. If classroom teachers are expected to integrate exceptional children into the regular school programs in the absence of special services support, they will be frustrated at best, rebellious at worst. As previously mentioned, the integration of handicapped children into regular classrooms has already become an issue in some teacher contract negotiations. Additionally, there is concern that a current budget crunch faced by many school districts may result in the dismissal of special education teachers under the rationale of the **mainstreaming** movement. While some segregated classes will no doubt continue to be needed, the special education teacher's role is changing from a special classroom teacher to a resource person for the classroom teacher.

As our concern for and consciousness of the handicapped increases, some old problems remain and some new ones demand attention. Hobbs (1975) has summarized a number of contemporary assumptions concerning the handicapped that underly some of these problems.

1. Children are a national resource worthy of respect and care.
2. We must have some structure for organizing and providing services and evaluating their outcomes.
3. Handicapped children should be educated in ways that permit them to participate in the mainstream life of their communities.
4. While classifying children is necessary for the organization of services, these classifications should use measures and terminology least likely to be harmful to children.

DEFINITIONS AND THE EXCEPTIONAL CHILD

There are many ways of classifying exceptional children. Before we discuss one classificatory system, let us examine the purposes of classification for diagnosis.

Functions of Diagnosis

There are three primary functions of diagnosis as it is practiced: scientific, therapeutic, or moral. In a scientific enterprise, it is important that events, objects, or persons be categorized with specified dimensions so as to stimulate further knowledge. Thus, for study purposes children may be diagnosed as retarded, normal, or gifted in order to further our understanding of one or more of these groups. The scientific goal for categorizing is to increase our knowledge about persons who share characteristics implied by the label. In the therapeutic enterprise, a diagnosis may be directed toward grouping a person with a larger population in order to determine suitable **remediation** efforts. The goal in this instance is to provide information that dictates which of several therapeutic approaches would be most appropriate for the child. Finally, and unfortunately, diagnosis and categorizing may be a case of name calling in which the professional seeks to propagandize the desirability or undesirability of particular behaviors. Often the propaganda follows establishment lines, but uses technical-scientific jargon rather than the more traditional religious rhetoric (London, 1964). An example is the recent debates among psychiatrists and between psychiatrists and representatives of the Gay Liberation movement as to whether homosexuality reflects mental illness or a moral judgment by heterosexuals.

Each rationale for diagnosis is relevant and important. Science has progressed through the taxonomies (classifications) that have been developed in various mental health fields; people have benefited from diagnostic links with therapies and education; and perhaps, with the decline of the theologian, we need a new spokesperson for morality. At issue is the particular hat, scientific, therapeutic, or moralistic, that the professional diagnostician chooses to wear. While the public may be confused about the differences among these enterprises, the evaluator cannot afford to be. It is of critical importance that the expert discriminate among these functions in his or her own diagnostic efforts.

Judging Diagnostic Schemes

The criteria used to judge the adequacy of a diagnostic scheme will vary according to the function the diagnosis serves. A classificatory scheme within the scientific framework whose purpose is the advancement of knowledge must meet contemporary standards set for good science. The method used and the evidence it yields determine the worth of such a scheme. To evaluate diagnostic procedures within the therapeutic domain, we must weigh the treatment the diagnosis specifies. If the treatment reduces troublesome behaviors or increases the child's happiness or competence, the diagnostic procedures can be rated as effective. Like the scientific enterprise, however, we must have empirical evidence before we can say the diagnosis has been evaluated. Perhaps the moral enterprise is reducible to political or persuasive criteria. If the diagnostic proclamations inhibit bad ("pathological") behavior or facilitate good ("normal," "adjusted") behavior in large segments of the population, diagnosis may be adequate to its purpose.

The essence of a diagnostic or category system within the scientific and therapeutic functions in special education is that such systems deal with *deviations in behavior* that are deemed to be of considerable *social significance*. Thus, the term *exceptional* explicitly refers to deviations and implicitly suggests deviations of social importance. The exceptional child is one who is different from others with whom he or she is being compared, usually different in some socially important way.

The definition of exceptional children should not be taken to imply that all labeled children differ from their peers in a socially undesirable fashion. For example, the child with a very high IQ score would be considered exceptional because such a score is a statistical rarity and, it is presumed, reflects behaviors or potentials for behavior that are of social moment. By and large, however, most forms of exceptionality do reflect a condition that most people would view as undesirable and that require some form of special treatment.

Exceptionalities vary in type and degree; they are summarized below according to their traditional classifications. These conditions are defined more completely in later chapters, where specific kinds of exceptional conditions are discussed. For the moment the following brief descriptions set the stage for the reader. It should be noted that there are efforts currently afoot in various states to eliminate the categories listed. As yet, the movement does not appear to have succeeded, nor do we feel that if it does, it will last.

Categories

Categories indicate how children deviate from normal or nonhandicapped youngsters in sensory intactness (hearing, vision), neuromuscular or physical characteristics (cerebral palsy), mental characteristics (mental retardation), communication skills (speech defects), and emotional or social behavior (emotionally disturbed). The definitions and categories that follow are partially adapted from the Rules and Regulations for Special Education of the state of Illinois and do not appear to violate in significant ways those categories traditionally presented in textbooks across the land.

Visual Impairment   A deficit in vision that prohibits the child from achieving educational potential without special services and materials. Visual impairments are defined on the basis of one's visual acuity across distance and of one's field of vision. There are many kinds and degrees of visual impairment. Some children may have mild problems correctable with glasses. Others may have considerable sight loss even with the use of vision aids, while the most severely impaired are blind and must be educated through senses other than vision.

Hearing Impairment   Residual hearing that is not sufficient to allow the child to understand the spoken word or to develop language. It results in extreme deprivation in learning and communication. Children vary considerably in degree and type of hearing loss. The less the hearing loss (all other things being equal), the better able the child is to develop communication skills. Severe deafness may seriously impede acquiring academic skills while a mild hearing loss may require minimal environmental adaptation. Like the visually impaired, the hearing impaired require educational techniques that do not use this primary sense.

Physical or Health Impairment   Refers to either temporary or permanent physical or health problems that require adaptation of a physical facility so that the child may receive adequate education. There are physical problems caused by **cerebral palsy,** bodily malformations, muscle and blood diseases, and chronic problems such as diabetes, arthritis, and cardiac conditions that affect the type of educational facilities, schedules, and placements needed by the child. The child who is seriously or chronically ill may require a home or in-hospital program or may simply need reduced activities within the regular classroom.

Learning Disability   A problem in one or more of the processes essential to learning. These processes include perception, conceptualization, language, memory, attention, impulse control, or motor functions. The most frequently mentioned characteristics of learning disabled children include hyperactivity, short attention span, perceptual motor problems, emotional outbursts, clumsiness, speech and language problems, disorders of thinking and memory, impulsivity, specific learning disabilities, and equivocal neurological signs (Bryan and Bryan, 1978). In essence, these are children with normal intelligence who should be achieving in school but who, for no apparent reason, are not.

Behavior Disorders   Affective (emotional) or behavior problems that interfere with the child's learning and/or social functioning. Such problems include overt action, like excessive and inappropriate aggression, and inaction, like excessive and inappropriate withdrawal. Extreme cases of behavior disorders include various types of psychoses, such as **schizophrenia** and **autism.**

Mental impairment   Two or more mental problems severe enough to affect significantly the child's ability to benefit from standard educational programs. Mental impairment is the more benign term for mental retardation, and, as with other handicapping conditions, it varies in degree. Retardation is detected by scores on intelligence tests and, more recently, by estimates of the child's adaptive behaviors.

Multiple Impairments   Two or more serious impairments that limit the child's ability to benefit from educational programs. For example, the cerebral palsied child who may hear or see poorly, or the retarded child who is hearing impaired.

Educational Handicap   A term describing the problems of children whose difficulties in school seem to be the result of social or cultural circumstances. The child's background may be so different from that required for competent school performance that special help is required.

Speech and/or Language Impairment   Deviations in a child's speech and/or language that are greater than would be normally expected and that interfere with the child's educational or social growth. Like other handicapping conditions, speech and language problems vary from the slight to the very severe. The condition's severity is related to the degree to which it interferes with the child's educational and social development. Speech and language problems are often associated with other difficulties, such as learning disabilities, mental retardation, cerebral palsy, and physical impairments.

Developmental Disabilities A rather new category consisting of cerebral palsy, epilepsy, or other neurological conditions that are related to, or require treatment similar to, mental retardation. The disability develops before the youngster is eighteen and is expected to continue indefinitely (Hobbs, 1975). The important feature of this grouping is not the particular nature of the ailment, but the fact that it will require lifetime support services. Thus the type of services needed rather than the type of problem determines the classification.

While the terminology employed and the specific definitions of handicaps vary from time to time and among states, categorizing is important as it affects who receives which type of services. The terms used to describe handicapping conditions alter as philosophies and perspectives shift. New categories develop as society changes. For instance, while not currently included as categories to define exceptionality, juveniles who use drugs and commit crimes are receiving growing recognition as a social problem. It may be that these problems will represent new categories of exceptionality.

SUMMARY

The Bureau of Education for the Handicapped (BEH), the major federal agency responsible for handicapped children, has estimated that there are about 7.08 million handicapped children in the United States and that half of these are not yet receiving appropriate educational services. In the wake of the civil rights movement, there have been court cases and legislation aimed at improving rights and opportunities of handicapped persons. With respect to children, the courts have ruled that all, no matter how handicapped, have the right to a free public education. When school districts are unable to provide appropriate educational programs, they are responsible for paying another institution to do so.

The most important legislative act for the handicapped child is PL 94-142. Its most critical provisions include nondiscriminatory testing by multidisciplinary teams; parent consultations; implementation of the program in the least restrictive environment; annual review of the child's education plan; the right of due process; and implementation by the state education agency of free, appropriate schooling for all handicapped children.

There have always been handicapped persons, at least dating back to 3000 B.C. Throughout history treatment of the handicapped has varied from the humane to the brutal. When religious beliefs dominated people's perspectives of the handicapped, religious dogma might dictate that one treat the handicapped as devils or as saints. Only 200 years ago political reforms in Europe and the United States laid the foundations for granting all persons inalienable rights and freedoms. To translate these concepts into help for the handicapped, however, took considerable effort from many pioneers on both continents. There were courageous, insightful men and women who worked diligently to change the ways in which handicapped persons were treated and to develop effective treatments for them. Their efforts were slowed a bit by the eugenics movement, which implied that handicapping conditions were irremediable. A second retarding influence during this period was the failure of pioneers to effect miracles; they could not eliminate problems associated with severe handicapping conditions.

Nineteenth century programs for the handicapped were located within residential institutions. In the early 1900s in this country, education classes for handicapped children were set up in public schools. Such school programs subsequently grew rapidly with significant changes in attitudes toward the handicapped fostered by the two world wars. Today we see enormous advances in providing special education programs suited to the many kinds of conditions handicapping children.

While great strides for helping the exceptional child are being made, certain problems must not be overlooked. Currently there is considerable concern for the severely and multihandicapped. Although small, this population is quite heterogeneous. Rigidly structured education agencies have found it difficult to provide services for these persons and efforts are underway to eliminate present oversights and inadequacies in this area.

A second problem has to do with labeling children as members of a special education category. At the current time the labels seem to be necessary as they are used to divide resources among programs. There are fears, however, that the labeling process not only stigmatizes the labeled but is actually a self-fulfilling prophecy. One possible solution to this problem would be to label and fund programs rather than children; as yet we have not managed this. There is a particular concern that labeling has negative consequences for children from minority or other disadvantaged groups. This has resulted in radical changes in testing procedures. Additionally, through the mandate of PL 94-142, children and their families who speak other than English as their first language must receive communications in their preferred language. The danger now is that through fear of overlabeling children from minority cultures, those with special needs will be overlooked rather than "labeled" and thus not receive needed special services.

A third problem concerns the integration of handicapped persons into community programs, a development mandated by recent laws. To what degree funds will be available to help restructure the environment to maximize integration remains to be determined. In addition, handicapped persons may well receive rejection from the nonhandicapped public rather than acceptance.

REFERENCES

Becker, H. *Outsiders.* New York: Free Press of Glencoe, 1963.

Bryan, T., & Bryan, J. *Understanding learning disabilities.* Sherman Oaks, Calif.: Alfred Publishing Co., 1978.

Crissey, M. S. Mental retardation: Past, present, and future. *American Psychologist,* 1975, *30,* 800–808.

Cruickshank, W. M. Some issues facing the field of learning disability. *Journal of Learning Disabilities,* 1972, *5,* 380–388.

Dunn, L. M. Special education for the mildly retarded: Is much of it justifiable? *Exceptional Children,* 1968, *35,* 5–22.

Friedman, R. J., & MacQueen, J. C. Psychoeducative considerations of physical handicapping conditions in children. *Exceptional children,* 1971, *37,* 538–539.

Gearheart, B. R. *Education of the exceptional child.* Scranton, Pa.: Intext, 1972.

Hall, J. F. *Psychology of motivation.* Chicago: J. P. Lippincott Co., 1961.

Hewett, F. M., & Forness, S. R. *Education of exceptional learners.* Boston: Allyn & Bacon, 1977.

Hobbs, N. *The futures of children.* San Francisco: Jossey-Bass, 1975.

Lilly, M. S. Special education: A teapot in a tempest. *Exceptional Children,* 1970, *37,* 43–49.

London, P. *Modes and morals of psychotherapy.* New York: Holt, Rinehart & Winston, 1967.

MacMillan, D. L. *Mental retardation in school and society.* Boston: Little, Brown & Co., 1977.

Mercer, J. R. *Sociological perspectives on mild mental retardation.* Paper delivered at Inaugural Peabody-NIMH Conference on Socio-Cultural Aspects of Mental Retardation. Nashville, Tenn., 1968.

Mercer, J. R. Who is normal? Two perspectives on mild mental retardation. In E. Gartley Jaco (Ed.), *Patients, physicians and illness* (rev. ed.). New York: The Free Press, 1971.

Mercer, J. R. *Labeling the mentally retarded.* Berkeley, Calif.: University of California Press, 1973.

Plumb, J. H. The great change in children. *Readings in education: 76/77,* Guilford, Conn.: The Dushkin Publishing Group, 1976.

Rosenthal, R. *Experimenter effects in behavioral research.* New York: Appleton-Century-Crofts, 1966.

Rowitz, L. Socioepidemiological analysis of admissions to a state-operated outpatient clinic. *American Journal of Mental Deficiency,* 1973, *78,* 300–307.

KEY TERMS

autism Defined in Chapter 6.

cerebral palsy A neuromuscular disability caused by brain injury that is characterized by involuntary motor control disturbances.

exceptional child A child who is deviant along some developmental dimension that influences adjustment to common social, physical, or academic demands.

least restrictive environment A stipulation of Public Law 94-142 that requires educational placement that is most common while still meeting the individual's educational needs. The person may not be segregated without appropriate legal safeguards or clear evidence that it is necessary.

mainstreaming The practice of integrating exceptional children into regular school programs whenever possible, depending on the severity of the handicapping condition and available resources.

remediation The attempt to restore to a normal or sound condition; to improve, overcome or remove a defect.

schizophrenia Defined in Chapter 6.

special education The provision of instructional activities and supportive services for exceptional students.

CHAPTER 2

Intelligence

For many years psychologists and educators have been arguing, researching, publishing about and enjoying some economic bounty from the nature and measurement of intelligence. Very recently, controversies about intelligence and the tests that are presumed to measure it have spread from professionals who deal with such material and the parents whose children they affect to legislators and concerned citizens. The administration, uses, and interpretations of intelligence tests have become a matter of national concern. Should intelligence tests be given to minority children? If so, which tests and by whom? Should test results be open to public scrutiny and be made part of the child's permanent school record? And what do the test results mean anyway? These questions have been posed by persons concerned about the uses and abuses of intelligence tests and are germane to our study of the exceptional child. Indeed, the intelligence test is one of the most important tools used by professionals working with handicapped children in their attempts to differentiate and understand them. For instance, intelligence test scores serve as a basis for determining whether a child is retarded, learning disabled, or able to benefit from a normal education. The answers to these questions have varied, but the consensus is that professional testers must not be islands unto themselves; intelligence testing must be under the control, at least to some extent, of nonprofessionals. Public Law 94-142 makes this point quite explicit.

Controversy over Intelligence Testing

There has always been controversy among professionals concerning the nature and assessment of intelligence, but public skepticism over the methods used in measuring it has probably never been so great. Why is there such a controversy now?

There are no doubt many factors that have caused the public to raise a critical eyebrow. Intelligence testing has always been a handmaiden to practical affairs so the public was destined to become involved with the movement. After all, there is hardly a man, woman, or child schooled in the United States who has not taken some standardized test of intellectual abilities, capacities, or skills. At the same time, awareness of several factors about intelligence test usage has been sharpened during the last several decades. First, it has become increasingly clear that intelligence test scores are not constant. One person may receive scores that vary considerably from one test administration to another. Since this is frequently the case, the wisdom of using test scores for identification and school placement of individuals is questionable. Additionally, there is concern that intelligence tests may somehow penalize or underestimate the "true" intelligence of members of minority groups, and thus become instruments for denying minority individuals equal opportunities. Finally, some have argued that the controversy about intelligence is a reflection of an underlying change in our basic values. Professor Cronbach has written, "The controversy over tests was a symptom of the shift of forces. The world view entrenched before World War II is now under attack, and an alternative scheme that cherishes pluralism, affiliations with local communities, and fulfillment rather than 'perfection' is taking shape. . . . It is this struggle for the minds of men, and not concerns for specifics such as mental tests, that has generated the recent controversies" (1975, p. 12).

To understand intelligence tests requires understanding their history, which we will consider first, following that with a description of the most commonly used intelligence tests and the problems associated with them.

HISTORY OF INTELLIGENCE TESTING

Concern for differences among the intellectual capacities of individuals is a recent development. While the Greeks used terms to mean reason, they were more preoccupied with differentiating people from beasts, not one person from another (Tuddenham, 1962). Reflections on separating and distinguishing human beings from lower animals persisted until the late 1800s. Consideration of how people differ from other people in mental ability has occupied scholars only for the past 200 years.

Early Influences

Several developments in the 1800s played an important role in affecting subsequent test development and the accompanying controversies. One was the work done by Wundt in his laboratories in Leipzig, Germany. It was found there that an individual's reaction time was affected by many, apparently trivial, events. The intensity of the stimulus, the instructions given to the subject, and the **sensory system** concerned were found to affect the speed of a subject's response to a stimulus. Tuddenham writes, "Their discovery that small-appearing differences in experimental conditions could lead to large differences in results sensitized the intelligence testers of a later day to the necessity of providing for their instruments the most complete specification of test materials, instructions, and scoring standards" (1962, p. 473).

A second early influence upon the subsequent development of intelligence tests was the work of Mesmer in France. Mesmer's efforts to study and perhaps exploit his "animal magnetism" helped to arouse interest in hypnosis and abnormal psychology. While he failed to "mesmerize" the professional community with his demonstrations and explanations of hypnotic states, he did influence others to examine individual differences among people, and especially raised interest in abnormal conditions of behavior.

Perhaps the grandfather of the testing movement was England's Francis Galton, a cousin of Charles Darwin. Galton, evidently influenced by his cousin, became interested in how genetic mechanisms produce differences among people. Indeed, Galton has been called the founder of eugenics (Tuddenham, 1962). An empiricist rather than an armchair philosopher, he began his study of individual differences in a laboratory at the South Kensington Museum. For a fee of three cents, Galton would measure the head size, arm span, imagery, color vision, hearing acuity, and a multitude of other sensory and physical functions of voluntary subjects (Cronbach, 1960; Tuddenham, 1962). Galton not only tested about 10,000 paying customers but also introduced a concept that became extremely important in measuring intelligence. This was that a person can be meaningfully measured in terms of his position relative to other people. The person's standing relative to others was thus perceived as providing meaningful data for both theory and practical affairs. To this day, intelligence test scores reflect individual's rankings relative to others of comparable age.

The Next Phase

The term "mental testing" did not appear in an American journal until 1890. Even then the topic was not a popular area of research. Psychologists in the United States were primarily preoccupied with determining the structure of the average mind, not individual differences in how people use their minds. However, one psychologist, J. M. Cattell of Columbia University, was interested in individual intelligence in the framework developed by Galton. Cattell focused on measuring uncomplicated, basic processes of human behavior. Among his carefully garnered measures were tests of an individual's ability to detect sensations, quickness in responding to a stimulus, accuracy in estimating ten-second intervals, and speed in naming colors. His work generated considerable enthusiasm among his colleagues, thus awakening American interest in individual differences and intelligence testing.

Two subsequent studies, however, greatly altered the course of this interest. In 1899, Stella Sharp found that the measures employed by Cattell failed to correlate with or predict more complex intellectual performances. In 1901 Wissler found that Cattell's measures were unrelated to college students' grades and that his tests were not correlated with one another. Whatever Cattell was measuring, the tests were not related to the same thing, and they were not assessing ability important in practical achievement, such as school grades.

The Work of Alfred Binet

The major figure in measuring intelligence was Alfred Binet. This Frenchman was an eminent scientist long before he became involved in the development of intelligence tests. His interests ranged from studies of the psychic life of insects to chess players, and his research methods ranged from head measurements to inkblot tests. His intellectual range was vast, his reputation as a humanitarian and scientist excellent. Like many French physicians and social scientists who were his contemporaries, Binet's curiosity turned toward the study of individual differences in general, and intellectual functioning in particular. His view of intellectual functioning differed markedly from that of Galton and Cattell. According to Binet, intellectual functions were not reflected by simple sensory processes, but rather by performance on complex tasks. While he never defined the concept of intelligence, he stressed fairly complex mental operations in his discussions of it. Early in his career, Binet emphasized the roles of memory and mental imagery; later he focused more upon the importance of attention and adaptation to the demands of novel environments. Still later he suggested that mental ability is tied to one's power to understand and to reason. Binet urged scientists to shift their attention away from simple sensory tests of hearing acuity and color vision toward the study of more complicated mental processes (Tuddenham, 1962). His suggestion was followed.

Binet's contributions were not limited to preaching. It was he who devised the first test of intelligence, a test whose format and approach have not been radically changed to this day. His test has had a profound impact upon scientists, practitioners, and the public. The circumstances surrounding its development are also important. In 1904, the Minister of Public Instruction in France created a commission to study ways of improving public education for defective children. The commission decided to start special schools for defective children but their concerns about instituting special schools anticipated those of today. Tuddenham quotes Binet as saying, "[The commission] decided that no child suspected of retardation be eliminated from regular school and admitted to a special school without having undergone a pedagogical and medical examination attesting that his intellectual state renders him unable to profit in the ordinary measure from the instruction given in regular schools" (1962, p. 482). In our current terminology, mainstreaming, retaining children in regular classrooms, was a major consideration of the commission.

They were also concerned with how to measure the child's intellectual status and were particularly worried about the problem of the biases of those persons making judgments about that status. The commission fully recognized that "special" school placements were likely to carry social stigmas. Tuddenham again quotes Binet: "It is necessary to guard against the judges who will compose [judgments] getting into the habit of leaving decisions to luck, based on subjective and hence uncontrollable impressions, which will be sometimes good, sometimes bad, and will give too large a part to the arbitrary, the capricious. . . . It will never be to one's credit to have attended a special school" (1962, p. 483). Thus Binet implied that the commission wanted to eliminate testers' biases and the damaging consequences of misdiagnosis. Binet and a coworker, Simon, then developed a test that could help detect those children in need of special services but that would prevent children not needing them from being the victims of arbitrary decisions. Their efforts were guided by two factors. One was a goal more practical than theoretical. They wished to help public education serve children better. Second, their approach was empirical. In their attempts to determine what measures might best fulfill this goal, they sampled a wide variety of measures, ranging from palm readings and the size of the child's cranium to his or her ability to deal with complex problems (Cronbach, 1960). Palmistry did not pay off, but the problem solving activities, memory tests, and reasoning tasks were found to be promising.

In sum, Binet and Simon developed a measure to predict schoolroom performance; they did not undertake to develop a measure of adjustment, general competence, social skills, or future success as a doctor, butcher, or thief. Quite sensibly, many of the test items were devised to measure skills directly related to school activities; indeed some were adaptations of French teachers' classroom materials. As a result, many items in the original and in subsequent revisions of the scale assessed verbal skills. Competencies in arenas of life outside the classroom were not included. Skillfulness in hunting, lovemaking, survival in the streets of an urban slum were not issues. The mission dictated the method and the method had a pervasive, enduring influence upon intelligence testing that is felt to this day.

The intelligence test devised by Binet and Simon and its subsequent revisions had limited impact upon institutions of higher education in the United States. It was not long, however, until the scale was discovered by clinicians, educators, and social reformers. It was they who picked up the baton and led the march of the intelligence testing movement in this country. Mental testing was adopted across the country in institutions that had programs for the mentally retarded, and by numerous state teachers' colleges. The test was advertised by its American proponents as the royal road to solving virtually all the country's social problems. Whether it was from the enthusiasm of its proponents, the popularity of its use, or some unknown factors, the test ultimately did become an acceptable object for study in prestigious American universities. Lewis Terman, a professor at Stanford University, became one of the most important American scientists to be involved with the test. It was he who produced the 1916 *Stanford-Binet Intelligence*

Test (SB), the prototype of a series of similarly titled tests periodically revised. Terman translated the test into English and made it suitable for use with American children, carefully standardizing it to account for the idiosyncracies of United States culture.

The original Binet-Simon test and the Terman revision were constructed to yield a single score, an intelligence quotient that would allow educational decisions to be made about individual children free from the personal biases of the decision makers. Intelligence was summarized by a single score through a standardized, objective procedure.

The devising of a group test of intelligence was another milestone in the testing movement, a development that sprang from a national crisis. During World War I the nation needed an easily administered test to screen men entering the military services. Eminent psychologists devised group tests, the Army Alpha and Beta, which the armed services used on more than 1.75 million men. The successful development of group tests for adults led, unsurprisingly, to similar tests for children. Within thirty months of their publication, about four million children were given group intelligence tests (Cronbach, 1975).

Since the pioneering work of Binet, Simon, and Terman, the history of the testing movement has been marked by practical problems. These tests were intended to increase objectivity in decision making procedures so that child and adult could enjoy maximum educational, and subsequently social, benefits. However the test creators construed intelligence, the notion was reduced to a single score that became, in the hazy translations of laypersons and professionals alike, a single entity or thing. The score, which was designed for practical purposes, came to be seen as an attribute of the person tested. As their popularity grew, the tests were administered to virtually all children and adults who had contact with public institutions. It is not then surprising that anxiety about the tests also increased (Cronbach, 1975). At this time, at least one city has banned the use of intelligence tests (Bersoff, 1973) and they are being subjected to public scrutiny elsewhere across the country. We now turn our attention to contemporary views of intelligence, how it is measured, and the usefulness of these measurements.

PERSPECTIVES OF INTELLIGENCE

The concept of intelligence has played an important role in attempts to understand and help children and adults alike. People are often categorized according to their presumed intelligence, and their behaviors are often explained on the basis of it. We now focus on how this concept has been viewed by professionals involved in the development of intelligence tests and the theories associated with them.

Definitions

There have been wide variations in definitions of intelligence among theorists since the early 1900s. Indeed, in a famous symposium held by distinguished psychologists in 1921, the number of definitions of intelligence matched the number of participants. Binet's view of intelligence, as mentioned earlier, shifted during the course of his work. He eventually settled on the idea that intelligence is the power to reason and to understand (Tuddenham, 1962; Sattler, 1974). Terman believed intelligence is reflected in one's ability to carry on abstract thinking. Goddard, another early pioneer and enthusiastic supporter of the intelligence testing movement, suggested that intelligence is a single underlying faculty or function of the brain, determined by the genetic composition of the individual. This underlying faculty was assumed by Goddard to control most human conduct of social or personal significance (Tuddenham, 1962). Wechsler, a more recent leader in the testing movement, has defined intelligence as "the capacity of an individual to understand the world about him and his resourcefulness to cope with its challenges" (1974, p. 139). Wechsler further argues that intelligence cannot be equated with intellectual ability or capacity since it includes motives, persistence, and awareness of one's goals, as well as reasoning processes. Tuddenham suggests that intelligence is "not an entity, nor even a dimension in a person . . . [but rather] . . . an evaluation of a behavior sequence from the point of view of its adaptation adequacy" (1962, p. 517). Similarly, Cleary, Humphreys, Kendrick, and Wesman view intelligence as the "entire repertoire of acquired skills, knowledge, learning sets, and generalization tendencies considered intellectual in nature that are available at any one period of time" (1975, p. 19).

It is thus seen that the definitions of intelligence range from general adaptiveness to cognitive skills, knowledge, and specific reasoning abilities. There is some consensus among professionals as to what constitutes intellectual operations. Most psychologists appear to exclude from the definition the consideration of temporary motivational, social, or situational factors that might affect behavior. The consensus appears to be closer to the perspective of Binet, Simon, and Terman than that proposed by Wechsler. Controversies about the definition are not the only disputes that surround the field of intelligence. The nature of intelligence, the role of heredity, the meaning of intelligence test scores are also controversial; we turn now to these disputes.

General versus Specific Abilities

Questions about the nature of intelligence represent one of the most long-standing issues among those theorizing about intelligence. This debate revolves around whether intelligence is: (a) many different and separate abilities, (b) a single overriding capacity that underlies each individual ability, or (c) a single entity in combination with a few specific abilities. Goddard was perhaps the first to argue that a single underlying factor accounted for an individual's performance on many tasks, and that it alone best described intelligence. On the other hand, Spearman believed that a general factor plus a specific factor best accounted for the pattern of results based upon measures of the intellect. Thurstone, however, argued that intelligence was composed of many separate elements, each reflecting an ability. In this vein, Guilford (1966) has proposed a model of intelligence that hypothesizes some 120 factors that reflect intelligence.

The current trend is to conceptualize intelligence as a cluster of some number of partially independent abilities or operations rather than as a general single factor (Reese and Lipsett, 1970). On the one hand, it does seem reasonable to look at the relationships among various measures of intellectual operations and group them according to whether they correlate or are associated with each other. This is essentially the approach taken in factor analysis and it frequently yields results that reflect the operation of specific abilities rather than one ability governing the individual's performances on a variety of tasks. On the other hand, the view that intelligence reflects a multitude of separate abilities does not appear to lead to better predictions of a person's later performance than does the use of tests designed to assess general intelligence. Often the predictions are worse (McNemar, 1964). Tests designed to measure specific abilities do not yield results that fulfill practical goals. Additionally, many of the discovered specific abilities do not appear stable. Tests measuring complex functions rather than specific abilities still remain the most popular measurement devices for evaluating intelligence.

Genes

Perhaps no other topic in psychology has produced such violent controversy in recent years as the impact of genetic mechanics upon intellectual functioning. It is a reflection of our times that the hypothesis that genes may be important in intellectual functioning has become so controversial, since the hypothesis has been advanced almost from the time the Binet test was published. A popular early conception of intelligence was that abilities are primarily if not exclusively determined by the person's genes. Indeed, during the early 1900s, such conceptions were so widespread and held by so many distinguished psychologists that legislation was enacted limiting the immigration of various supposedly genetically inferior ethnic groups to the United States (Kamin, 1973). The notion that there is a genetic influence upon intellectual functioning was used then, as it occasionally is now, to justify ethnic and racial discrimination.

But this use was not the only unfortunate application of early theorizing. A second notion associated with the genetic hypothesis was that any attribute resulting primarily from one's biology could not be changed through remediation techniques. It was assumed that genes set the limits of an individual's behavior and, alas, when those limits were reached, so was one's fulfillment of hopes and dreams. It was further assumed that intelligence tests measured this innate capacity (McNemar, 1964).

It is our belief that this notion concerning genes, limits, and tests is still prevalent among the laity, if not among professionals. There really seems to be little reason to assume that the biological foundations of humans are not somehow involved in the operations of their intellectual functions. We agree with Cleary et al. (1975) that such a faith is warranted by many studies on lower animals that have demonstrated the importance of selective breeding in a variety of behaviors (Fuller and Thompson, 1960). Activity level, aggression, sexual behavior, specific learning ability of lower animals, to name but a few, have all been shown to be affected by genes. However, belief in the importance of biology in determining intelligence does not necessarily mean agreement with the implications often drawn from this position. It is increasingly realized that the impact of genes upon behavior is determined by the individual's specific environment. While there is certainly no learning without genes, conversely, there cannot be genetic influences in the absence of an environment. And apparently the influence of genes changes across environmental settings. We do not yet know how to assess the effect of environmental-genetic interaction upon people; thus it is not yet possible to gauge the role of each in affecting intellectual functioning. Knowing little about how environments may alter intellectual functioning, we cannot determine when any individual has reached this hypothetical limit (Liverant, 1960; Zigler, 1968). Finally, there is no reason to assume that genetic influences on intelligence follow racial or ethnic lines. Until we are able to determine just how environments interact with specific genes affecting intellectual abilities, any notions that races or ethnic groups differ in mental capacity because of genetic sources cannot be reasonably defended.

Popular View of Intelligence

Whatever the definitional and theoretical disputes among professional researchers, the public seems to believe that intelligence has two properties. First, laypersons think that intelligence is the capacity to act in all those ways necessary to have a meaningful, acceptable, and enriching life and to make all the decisions necessary for maintaining that life. Secondly, the general public also evidently assumes that intelligence is a fixed attribute of an individual, something that characterizes the person and remains fairly stable from early infancy to old age. McCall, Hogarty, and Hurlburt nicely summarize this view of the popular conception of intelligence. Many believe, they write, that intelligence is "an unchanging characteristic that governs nearly all of the individual's mental performance at every age" (1972, p. 728). Finally, many people think that intelligence tests measure this capacity. These assumptions concerning the breadth, stability, and measurement of this "thing" called intelligence are now being challenged.

Uses of Intelligence Tests

To understand the uses of intelligence tests, it is necessary to remember the history of the intelligence test movement. Binet's original goal was to help provide special education for intellectually defective children. He was aware that providing such special services to children might well result in stigmatizing them and hence was eager to eliminate faulty diagnoses resulting from the biases of teachers or other judges. He hoped to reduce biases by providing a measurement procedure that was objective, would yield reliable scores, and would predict the likelihood that children would benefit from ordinary classroom experiences. Binet's test and its current offspring of intelligence measures are far removed from theories concerning intelligence. Rather, we have several good instruments that can be used to assess present academic performance or predict it for the near future. Many people, however, do not conceive of or use intelligence tests with these limited goals in mind. Results of these tests are presumed to provide information beyond predictions about school grades. But what do such tests tell us? Do they predict behaviors, and if so, which ones? Is the information they yield reflecting a stable phenomenon not subject to significant changes? Is this information useful for distinguishing those children who need diagnosis, special classroom assignment, tutoring, or psychotherapy? Can an analysis of an individual's responses to various parts of the examination help describe his or her personality and personal difficulties? How are the tests administered and of what do they consist? The remainder of the chapter is addressed to these questions. First, we will discuss the standards used to evaluate tests, examining the concepts of reliability and validity. This is followed by a discussion focused upon several of the infant and childhood intelligence tests that have gained some measure of popularity.

RELIABILITY AND VALIDITY

Any form of assessing differences among people must be evaluated according to its reliability and validity. **Reliability** "means the dependability of the assessment you are making" (London, 1975, p. 317). The question is whether the results obtained from the test are likely to be obtained again.

Determining Reliability

There are several ways to determine the dependability of the measure. One way is to ask the same questions of an individual at different times. This method, called **test-retest**, is simply giving the subject the same test on two different occasions. If the person's answers to many of the questions are the same the second time as the first, the test will be judged reliable, that is, dependable. A second method for establishing reliability is to determine whether the test-taker answers the question in the same way when its phrasing is somewhat different. If the individual's answers are consistent, the test question will be judged reliable. This second method for determining reliability is often referred to as the **split-half,** or **alternative form, method.** If the results of tests are not reliable, then they cannot be used for predicting the test-taker's future behavior.

Validity

Reliability, however, does not establish the truthfulness of the test; it says nothing about what you are measuring but simply that whatever you are assessing, you are obtaining dependable answers. As London points out, "All sane observers, using the naked eye alone, can agree that the earth is flat and the sun goes around it—the observation is perfectly *reliable,* and perfectly *untrue*" (p. 317). Thus reliability is not enough to establish the adequacy of a test. A test must also be *valid.* For a test to be considered adequate, the scores it yields must be useful in predicting something other than how the individual will answer the same questions again. **Validity** refers to the test's predictive powers, and it can be established by various methods.

Predictive Validity

One form of validity is called **criterion** or **predictive validity.** This refers to how well test results will predict something. Thus, one method of validating an intelligence test would be to determine if such tests accurately predict subsequent performance in school, in learning tasks, or in creativity. The validity of the test is determined by how well the results can predict some behavior other than that of the same test.

Construct Validity

The second type of validity is **construct validity,** which refers to how well the test correlates with behaviors dictated by some theory. Validation requirements for construct validity are more rigorous than other kinds of validity checks. A single prediction will not suffice to establish construct validation. Rather, a network of predictions between the test and the behaviors the theory suggests as relevant must be demonstrated. "A test with high construct validity approaches the concept from many different angles which should be logically related to each other . . . and tries to see empirically if the logical relations are supported by the facts of behavior" (London, 1975, p. 321). "Construct validity is evaluated by a complex combination of logical and empirical operations in which the test and the theory underlying it are subjected to simultaneous scrutiny" (Cleary et al., 1975, p. 25).

Incremental Validity

Sechrest (1967) has proposed employing another type of validity when evaluating a test. While his recommendation has not been generally accepted or applied, it is our belief that it is an important one. Sechrest has proposed that tests be evaluated as to their incremental validity. Given that a test has some form of validity, Sechrest suggests that it also be evaluated as to whether it demonstrates "efficiency over the information otherwise easily and cheaply available" (p. 369). It really does not make sense to spend a great deal of time and money to administer lengthy tests to answer a question that can be answered at considerably less cost.

False Positives and False Negatives

Yet another important consideration concerning tests is their use for individual diagnosis. Teachers and parents working with exceptional children are fundamentally concerned with aiding particular students to achieve particular goals. Their interest is with the individual rather than with the possible benefits to groups of children. All currently available psychological tests, however valid, are not perfect. Some are better than others, but none can yield perfect measures. Whenever a test is given to a child, errors of measurement will be made. Sometimes the test score of a particular child will lead to the inference that the youngster has an attribute that in fact he or she does not. Hence, some children may be labeled as anxious, hyperactive, normal, aggressive, or intellectually dull, when, in fact, they are none of these. Pseudoscores lead to incorrect labeling of a child. Such inaccuracies are referred to as **false positives.** On the other hand, children's scores on any particular test may be inaccurately low. In these cases, children may be viewed as not being anxious, hyperactive, or aggressive when in fact they are. These instances of misdiagnosis are called **false negatives.**

All psychological tests will yield some false negatives and false positives. Since this is so, professionals diagnosing and treating individuals are often faced with a critical question: How many false negatives and false positives yielded by a particular test will be acceptable? The answer will have important implications for the children with whom the professionals deal. Tests simply must be viewed in light of these false instances, and testers should be aware that reliance on one or even a multitude of tests will yield misdiagnoses. Just what standards concerning these instances should prevail in good clinical practice? A study by Huelsman (1970) nicely illustrates these points. In the field of learning disabilities, there is a prevalent hypothesis that discrepancies of performance on particular parts of intelligence tests can be used for individual diagnosis. There is some evidence that children who fail to read can be differentiated, as a group, from children without such difficulties on the basis of subtest discrepancies. However, if one were to use this evidence as the basis for diagnosing individual children's reading capabilities, 39 percent of the reading failures and 38 percent of the reading achievers would be misdiagnosed! That such error rates in diagnosis would be acceptable to most clinicians is doubtful.

Finally, you should be aware that the publication of a test does not guarantee that the test is reliable or valid. Publication is not a reflection of the test's adequacy. Meeting the minimal standards of reliability and validity as indicated by the book, *Standards for Educational and Psychological Tests and Manuals,* published by the American Psychological Association, is voluntary on the part of the test constructor. Many tests are published that do not meet these standards and appear to be valuable only in producing healthy incomes for their constructors. Before putting faith in a test, one should be aware of its dependability and accuracy. An excellent source of such information is the Buros *Measurement Yearbooks* (1972).

Let us now turn to a description of some of the more popular tests of intelligence and relevant research findings. We first discuss some of those measures often used in testing infants; then move on to those more frequently employed with the preschool and school-age youngster.

INFANT INTELLIGENCE TESTS

The development of infant intelligence tests has a long history. The first test still frequently used to assess the mental abilities of infants, was proposed by Gesell in 1925 and called the *Gesell Developmental Schedules.* Since Gesell's pioneering work other scales, such as *Cattell's Mental Test for Infants and Young Children* and the *Bayley Scale of Infant Development,* have been offered. Cattell's test hit the market in 1940, while Bayley's initial version was first produced in 1936. Infant tests have been around awhile and, because of their availability, have been the objects of considerable research and refinement. The assumption of a number of early theorists was that intelligence might be inherited, or at least was not easily influenced by environmental forces. If these assumptions were correct, then it should be possible to devise a measure of an infant's intellectual capacity.

One of the major aims in this area is the development of methods to detect potential learning problems in preschoolers and kindergarteners. The employment of tests of infant intelligence for such purposes are predicated upon the supposition that detection and intervention at this stage of the child's development will prevent failure in the elementary school years. To detect and intervene requires a gauge that will predict school failure at some future time. Discrepancies in the growth of critical areas, such as language and motor skills, are assumed to foreshadow subsequent failure in reading, writing, and arithmetic. The faith in early detection is a faith in our ability to discover inadequacies in very young children. This confidence is based upon the notion that a child's development proceeds in a regular and predictable fashion, that delays in defined developmental areas are linked critically to skills the child needs to progress, and that measures of these important developments can be devised for very young children. A further assumption underlying the efforts at early detection is that intervention provided children experiencing developmental delays will eliminate or ameliorate later problems. If problems are dealt with early, special services may not be required later. This assumption has been based in large part upon longitudinal studies of high-risk infants in whom birth traumas have been linked to (1) conceptual and behavioral problems that appeared later, (2) analyses of parents' accounts of their disabled children's development, and (3) studies of language development in normal children and in children with speech problems.

The Nature of Some Infant Tests

Because infant tests are used frequently, the reader should be aware of the particular behaviors that are important in evaluating the child. Some of these behaviors were identified by Gesell.

The Gesell scales, first reported in 1925 and revised several times since, give norms for critical ages beginning at four weeks and ending at thirty-six months. Thus, the scales span the first three years of a youngster's development. The behaviors that are assessed at each age level are divided into four categories: motor, adaptive, personal-social, and language (Bayley, 1970). There are several categories that do not appear to reflect the operation of mental function. For example, the category of motor behaviors includes assessment of body control, manual coordination, creeping, walking, and jumping while the personal-social items refer to such behaviors as feeding oneself, toileting, and dressing. According to Bayley (1970), the tested mental responses fall into the categories of adaptive and language actions. Adaptive behaviors refer to the child's looking at, reaching for, and manipulating an object such as a rattle or cube; building a tower from blocks or placing blocks into a form board. Language items include cooing, being alert, saying and understanding simple words.

The *Cattell Infant Intelligence Scale* employs many of the language and adaptive category items from the Gesell scales. Test items are available for use with two- to thirty-month-old infants. At the older levels, items from the *Stanford-Binet Intelligence Test* are intermingled with those drawn from the Gesell scales. Unlike the Gesell scales, which yield a developmental age score, the Cattell scales are scored to produce an intelligence quotient (mental age/chronological age x 100).

Bayley's mental and motor scales are suitable for use with children ranging in age from one to thirty months. Like the Cattell scales, the *Bayley Scales of Infant Development* has borrowed many items from previously published infant scales. Thus the Motor Scale includes holding the head up, creeping, standing, turning over, and sitting, as well as manual skills like throwing a ball. The mental scale consists of items referring to adaptive behaviors; for example, responding to visual stimuli, shaking a rattle, cooing, smiling, imitating, following instructions, and showing memory for an object no longer in view (Bayley, 1970). The mental and motor scales are scored separately to yield a Mental Development Index and a Psychomotor Development Index. The final form of the test is based on observation of more than 1200 children's responses. The care taken in developing this test and providing normative information concerning children's responses to the items makes it the best developed of the three infant tests discussed.

Accuracy of Infant Tests

The original hope of the authors of infant tests was to devise an assessment procedure suitable for infants and permitting fairly accurate predictions concerning their later intellectual development. This hope carried with it some assumptions. With respect to such aspirations and measures, Kagan has written:

> "Much of the research on infant mental development has been guided by two related—and essentially unproven—hypotheses. The first posits a hypothetical entity, called intelligence, which can be measured by noting the rate of development of those response systems that are emerging at the moment. . . . There are neither adequate data nor persuasive theory to support this axiom. . . . A second assumption guiding work with infants presumes that early cognitive structures are derivative of **sensori-motor** actions, a view usually attributed to Piaget. The significance of sensori-motor coordination for adaptive functions is readily acknowledged, but their necessary causal connections to cognitive development are, we believe, still open to debate" (1971, 177–178).

Kagan directly challenges the usefulness of current concepts of infant intelligence and, by implication, the usefulness of tests resting upon these concepts.

The traditional method for determining the validity of an infant intelligence test is to administer it to a group of infants, wait several years, and then give another test of intelligence, usually the Stanford-Binet, to the same group of children. The validity of the infant test is indexed by the degree to which scores on it prove to be predictive of scores on the second test. But most reviewers of research on infant intelligence tests have generally concluded, with varying degrees of pessimism, that infant tests are of little use in predicting later intelligence test scores. Bayley (1970) has written: "The findings of these early studies of mental growth of infants have been repeated sufficiently often so that it is now well-established that test scores earned in the first year or two have relatively little predictive validity (in contrast to tests at *school age or later*), although they may have high validity as measures of the children's cognitive abilities at the time. . . . The lack of stability in the first three years cannot be attributed to poor reliability of the measuring instrument" (1970, p. 1174). McCall et al. write: "It is something of an overstatement to say that there is 'no prediction' from the infancy period to childhood IQ. There are correlations that attain statistical significance between certain ages from some tests, but the size of the relationships is not particularly impressive and certainly not adequate for clinical application" (1972, p. 729).

Infant Intelligence Tests Generally Not Valid

By and large, it is safe to say that there are no genuinely valid infant intelligence tests, if this is meant to imply that some test given to an infant under two years of age will predict the child's scores on intelligence tests given years later. As early as 1939, Anderson failed to find correlations between infant test scores and those obtained by five-year-olds on the *Stanford-Binet Intelligence Scale*. In 1972, the picture had not appreciably changed. McCall et al. (1972) summarized the results of nine separate studies analyzing the repeated testing of children over a long period of time. These authors indicated that none of the studies reported consistent findings that would suggest that very early intelligence test scores correlated with those obtained from the same children some years later.

Validity of Tests

It would be misleading to suggest that all aspects of the infant scales fail to be predictive, nor is the total score useless for all children. One particular feature of the infant scales that may be predictive of subsequent intelligence test scores is that pertaining to vocal behaviors and language development. McCall et al. (1972) reported a number of studies that suggest that there is some hope for the utilization of infant scales, but indicated that we need to reexamine what leads to what and for whom. In one study, infants who had been given the Gesell scale at six, twelve, eighteen, or twenty-four months were subsequently given the Stanford-Binet at three and one half, six, or ten years of age or the Wechsler scale at a later time. It was found that items on the Gesell scale which involved vocalizations best predicted later IQ scores, particularly for female infants. McCall et al. also referred to other investigations suggesting this relationship between vocalization and later IQ scores. A study conducted in England, for example, showed that the speech quotient obtained on the *Griffiths Infant Scale* by eighteen-month-old children was somewhat predictive of general IQ scores achieved when those children were eight years of age. However, this relationship held only for females. "In summary, three studies indicate that vocalization in infancy may have special salience for females that it does not for males with respect to predicting later mental performance" (McCall et al., 1972, p. 735). Three studies do not make a complete test, but clearly the results are suggestive of a new direction in infant intelligence testing.

Evidently, the total scores on infant intelligence scales are not necessarily devoid of all meaning. While total scores are not helpful in predicting subsequent test scores for most youngsters, there is a category of children to whom these tests might be usefully applied. Children who score abnormally low on the infant tests are likely to obtain low scores on subsequent intelligence tests. In effect, "It has been possible to make fairly good predictions of future low intellectual status, especially when organic damage was apparent in infancy, but it has not been possible to make good predictions within the normal or superior ranges" (Reese and Lipsett, 1970, p. 536). This finding is not surprising since one purpose of developing these scales was to detect which children might have severe dysfunctions. Apparently such tests can be useful in the early detection of children who are likely to have severe problems in their intellectual development. The validities of infant tests in predicting subsequent IQ scores may be increased by limiting testing to babies who are physically or developmentally abnormal, especially when such test scores are combined with the observations of pediatricians (Werner, Honzik, and Smith, 1968).

Sechrest (1967) has suggested, as indicated earlier, that tests need to be evaluated on the basis of their power to increase knowledge over that gained by more economical procedures. Tests should be judged as to their incremental validity. After reviewing many studies in which infant tests were compared with other sources of information, McCall et al. concluded: "These results imply that parental education may be a better predictor of childhood IQ than an assessment on the child during the first two years of life" (1972, p. 733). For the child of average or rapid development, the parents' socioeconomic status is a better indicator of subsequent intellectual development than are the results obtained from infant intelligence tests. When there is suspicion of defective development, however, such as mental retardation or brain damage, the infant scale may usefully be employed.

It is possible that many of the infant scales reflect errors of both commission and omission. First, most of the items comprising such tests are directed to sensory and motor skills, skills not assessed by childhood IQ tests such as the Stanford-Binet or the *Wechsler Intelligence Scale for Children*. These scales primarily tap linguistic or verbal skills. Bayley has suggested that the "lack of consistency over time in mental test scores reflects a series of changes in the nature of mental processes as they progress from simple sensori-motor adjustments to increasingly complex forms of adaptations, generalizations, abstractions, and their accompanying reasoning processes" (1970, p. 1177). On the face of it, it would be surprising if simple sensorimotor abilities were correlated more than minimally with the verbal skills developed by the child as he or she matures. These tests, then, do not measure the same abilities continuously across ages.

There is another possible reason why scores on infant tests are not good predictors of subsequent scores on childhood intelligence tests. Some evidence suggests that perceptual and attentional factors may be an important basis for intellectual development (Maccoby, Dowling, Hagen, and Degerman, 1965; Kagan, 1969; Lewis and Goldberg, 1969). Specific items designed to assess these factors have not been included within the popular infant tests. Hence it would appear that the tests of infant intelligence might well be measuring the wrong behaviors and overlooking the appropriate ones, at least if one's goal is to predict infants' subsequent IQ scores on the Stanford-Binet or the WISC. There is little to indicate that the use of these tests with very young children is justifiable, with the exception of infants who may be severely disabled. In these cases, the assessment should lead to differential diagnosis and intervention, such as would occur if it were established that the child was hearing impaired rather than severely retarded. At the same time, concern must be voiced for the children who are misdiagnosed as either pathological or normal. There is no compelling evidence to suggest that *false positive* and *false negative* misdiagnoses are so rare that we can feel comfortable in applying infant tests for individual diagnosis. We do not know that such tests give more information than ratings or observations made by parents, pediatricians, or other sensitive and experienced child watchers. If there is a slight increment in knowledge, we must ask whether such knowledge is worth depriving other children of the scarce and costly time of a psychologist or psychometrician.

Other Approaches to Infant Testing

The discouraging results obtained in infant tests have led researchers along two somewhat different empirical paths. Some are attempting to refine the psychometric approach, eliminating items that are not predictive and adding items that may be more useful in forecasting later scores. An example of such efforts is the work of Cameron, Livson, and Bayley (1967) on the relationships of infant vocalizations to subsequent intelligence scores.

A second approach is to emphasize the study of cognitive processes rather than the development of better test items (Zigler, 1968; Kagan, 1971). Correlates of attention, such as heart rate deceleration and inhibition of motor activity, are types of responses studied in this approach. When the emphasis is upon cognitive processes, researchers focus on how infants receive, organize, and respond to new information.

Except in the case of the severely handicapped child, it is no longer possible to assume that infant intelligence tests, loaded with measures of sensorimotor skills, yield useful information about subsequent IQ scores or academic success dependent on verbal skills.

CHILDHOOD INTELLIGENCE TESTS

By now almost everyone in this society has had some type of test of their intelligence. It is a booming business, albeit a controversial one. In the remainder of this chapter, we hope to familiarize you with the two most popular gauges of children's intelligence, the Stanford-Binet (SB), and the *Wechsler Intelligence Scale for Children* (WISC). Following the description of these two important tests, we look at some of the findings concerning influences upon test scores and what these scores have been interpreted to mean. We hope that you will get a sense of the complexity and the ambiguity surrounding the notion of intelligence as it is usually measured.

Stanford-Binet

This test, originally published in France in 1905, has undergone five revisions. Its latest form was published in 1960 by Terman and Merrill (1960), while the test norms were updated as recently as 1972 (Terman and Merrill, 1973). The test is designed to assess individuals ranging in age from two to eighteen years, but its use is mostly limited to children. Items that were irrelevant to scholastic aptitude were eliminated in the 1960 scales (Cronbach, 1960). In the test's latest revision, little new material has been added and there have been no changes in the format, but word knowledge is emphasized more than in the 1937 version. There are 142 test items that are presented to the subject in order of difficulty, defined by the percentage of subjects who passed the item. The difficulty of each item is well established as more than 4000 individuals were recently tested to ensure that items had not changed in this regard. As you can well imagine, the contents of any test that assesses individuals ranging in age from two to eighteen years would have to vary widely. To describe the nature of the items, we have adopted the analysis of the SB made by Anastasi (1961) and Freeman (1963).

> *Years 2–5.* At these age levels, the subtests require manipulations of objects (placement of pieces in a simple form board, block building), recognition of body parts, the recognition of objects referred to by name and function. Rote memory, the use of words in combination, verbal comprehension, and word knowledge are also assessed.
>
> *Years 6–12.* The child is tested for form perception, visual motor skills, rote memory, word knowledge, number concepts, and arithmetical reasoning.
>
> *Years 13-Superior Adult III.* At this level, visual analysis and imagery; visual motor skills; rote memory for digits, words, and sentences; word knowledge; and problem solving are assessed.

Memory, spatial orientation, numerical concepts, and language skills are tapped at scattered age levels throughout the test, using increasingly difficult items. For example, tests of memory may require the child to recall objects or the content of written passages, numerical tests start with simple counting and proceed to complex reasoning problems. The reliability of items within each age level seems adequate, with the lowest reliability occurring at age three and the highest at the Superior Adult II (Terman and Merrill, 1973). The final IQ score is a deviation IQ. That is, the IQ score indicates the amount by which a person deviates from the average performance of individuals in his or her own age group. An IQ score of 100 reflects the average score for subjects within that particular age range. The **standard deviation** of the IQ score is approximately 16 points. This means that given a random sample of children, approximately 68 percent will achieve scores on the SB between 84 and 116, while an additional 14 percent will score between 116 and 132. By the same token, another 14 percent will obtain scores between 84 and 68. Thus 96 percent of the children tested would be expected to obtain IQ scores between 68 and 132.

The test is administered individually to the child. The procedure is to start the test at the highest level in which the child is likely to pass all of the items and proceed to the age level where the child fails all of the items. The subject has to have adequate vision, hearing, and oral speech for proper administration of the test. Sensory or language defects can seriously affect the score.

Limitations of the Stanford-Binet Test

The 1937 and 1960 forms of the SB are heavily weighted with questions that assess verbal abilities. Anastasi (1961) reports that **correlations** between scores on the vocabulary test and the mental age of the child range from .71 to .83

for children eight to fourteen years old. Stormer's study of the 1960 revision of the SB indicated that the upper-year levels contained items calling primarily for verbal abilities (Sattler, 1974). Ramsey and Vane (1970) also found similar results in their analysis of test items for years four to six. There is little debate that the SB consists of many items measuring children's verbal abilities. It also appears that other abilities are assessed at different age levels and that similar items at various age levels do not necessarily measure the same abilities (Sattler, 1974).

The 1960 version of the SB has been cited for a variety of defects as well as virtues. Cronbach has written that this scale and its 1937 predecessor are "an instrument efficiently designed for one particular function, namely, providing a single score describing the child's present level of general intellectual ability. It is interesting to the child, precise, and well standardized. The large amount of research on the scale gives a basis for interpreting results which no newer test can offer" (1960, p. 188). On the other hand, the test has been criticized for ignoring the child's creativity, emphasizing verbal abilities, assessing very superior students inadequately, and placing various items at particular age levels (Sattler, 1974). In addition it should be noted that adequate test performance requires, at the minimum, some experiences common in an urban culture. As Cronbach (1960) has written, the test "is of dubious value for comparing culture groups" (p. 184).

Clinical Uses: Scatter

Finally, mention should be made of the clinical uses of the SB test. For many decades, the hypothesis has been entertained that one can make inferences concerning emotional or pathological conditions of the test-taker on the basis of his or her SB scores. Such hypotheses have served to stimulate research and to substantiate clinicians' diagnostic reports. The notion is that if an individual shows a wide range of *unexpected* successes and failures on the SB, the **scatter** or **variability** reflects the presence of some abnormality. The reasoning is that if the child shows the capability of successfully performing one intellectual operation, subsequent failures on items that require this operation reflect a kind of "mental block." Clinicians, psychologists, or special educators often attend to and attribute importance to variability, or scatter, in a test-taker's performance on the SB.

There are a number of ways in which scatter can be indicated. For example, it may be evidenced by a subject "failing a test at a given year level and passing a test at higher year levels" (Sattler, 1974). Indeed Harris and Shakow (1937) were able to evaluate research that used nine different methods for determining scatter.

By and large, research attempts to validate clinical hypotheses concerning scatter have not been successful, and probably for good reason. A scattered performance by an individual may well reflect factors other than emotional disturbances. Scatter can be the result of factors intrinsic to the test, such as the unreliability of the items comprising the scatter. Or it can be related to characteristics of the person that are not reflections of pathological states. Examples are momentary lapses in the subject's cooperation with the examiner or the not-so-momentary condition wherein the subject has acquired particular skills. Indeed, Liverant (1960) has pointed out that scatter in intellectual performances may be the rule rather than the exception for most of us. While clinicians may well be obligated to report that which they observe and to speculate on the meaning of variations in test performance, it is clear that they must do so at considerable risk of error and should do so with considerable humility. The analysis of scatter on the SB might provide some interesting ideas about the child that need further exploration, but scatter in itself does not adequately demonstrate any personality attribute of the individual being tested.

The Wechsler Intelligence Scale for Children

The WISC is the Stanford-Binet's chief competitor. "The chief differences are in organization, in greater precision of the Binet at low mental ages, and in the greater variety of tasks in the Wechsler scale" (Cronbach, 1960, p. 189). The WISC is widely used for the assessment of intelligence in children ages five to fifteen. There is also a form available for testing adults, the *Wechsler Adult Intelligence Scale* (WAIS), and one for children ages four to six, the *Wechsler Preschool and Primary Scale of Intelligence* (WPPSI). The scale consists of twelve subtests, two of which are optional. Of the ten required subtests, five form the basis for the Verbal Intelligence score, while the remaining five comprise the tests yielding the Performance Intelligence score. The two IQ scores can be combined to yield a Full Scale IQ score.

The Verbal Scale subtests, and items similar to those used, include:

1. General Information: From what animal do we get milk?
2. Comprehension: What are some reasons we need fire fighters?
3. Arithmetic: If I cut a peach into thirds, how many pieces will I have?
4. Similarities: In what ways are a tree and bush alike?
5. Vocabulary: Tell me what rainbow means.
6. Digit Span (optional): Repeat the following numbers, 5-8-3-2-6.

The Performance Scale subtests of the WISC include:

1. Picture Completion: The child is shown drawings and is asked to indicate which part of the drawing is missing (for example, a nose left out of the drawing of a face).
2. Picture Arrangement: The child is presented with several pictures which, when arranged properly, will depict a meaningful story.
3. Block Design: The child is asked to arrange a set of red and white blocks so as to match the pattern in a picture.
4. Object Assembly: The child is given a jigsaw puzzle to assemble into a meaningful product, such as a face.

5. Coding: There are two coding tests, one appropriate for five- to seven-year olds, the second for children eight to fifteen. The version suitable for the younger children presents them with pictures of various shapes, such as a star and a circle. Inside the shape is another symbol: a vertical line, a horizontal line, a circle, or so on. Below this presentation are five rows of shapes that have not been filled in. The child is shown how to match shapes to symbols and, during the test proper, is given two minutes to complete the task. The version of coding for the older child is essentially the same, but the visual stimulus is a set of boxes divided in two, the top half containing a number between one and nine, the bottom half, geometric shapes. The child is given two minutes to complete this task also.

6. Mazes (optional): The child completes a series of mazes that increase in difficulty.

Like the SB, the WISC was recently revised. The first form of the WISC was published in 1949 and altered somewhat in 1974 (Wechsler, 1974). The newer version is referred to as the *Wechsler Intelligence Scale for Children—Revised* (WISC-R). Test revisions were based upon the responses of more than 2200 children who were fairly representative of all children in place of residence, family's socio-economic status, and race. There were three major changes in the revised test. The first was to raise its age range. While the WISC was suitable for testing children five to fifteen years of age, the WISC-R is appropriate for children from six to sixteen years. In addition, the new group of subjects tested to develop norms of performance included a proportional representation of nonwhites, thus correcting a serious shortcoming of the WISC. Finally, the content of items was changed to give them a more contemporary ring than the 1949 test items. By and large, however, the format and the subtests are similar to those of the WISC.

WISC-R Reliability

The reliability of the test is quite good, whether judged by the split-half or the test-retest method. The reliabilities of the Verbal and Performance IQ scores, as well as the Full Scale IQ score, are quite high, and all are higher than the reliabilities associated with the subtests of the WISC-R.

Like the SB, the IQ score achieved on the WISC-R is a *deviation* score, with the average score being 100 and the standard deviation 15. Hence, about 84 percent of children tested will obtain an IQ score no greater than 115. The highest 1 percent of individuals at any age level will have scores over 135 and the lowest 1 percent will have IQs of 65 or below.

Insofar as the WISC-R is a relatively new test, research pertaining to it is sparse. However, given its similarities to the WISC, it is likely that the findings relative to that earlier test might also characterize the WISC-R.

Research on the WISC

There have been a number of hypotheses generated about the significance of particular subtests for revealing components of intellectual and emotional functioning. These hypotheses are quite popular in spite of failure to verify them empirically. The following discussion is based upon Sattler's (1974) review of these ideas.

The general information subtest is considered a reflection of the child's cultural background and ability to remember what he or she has seen and heard. The comprehension subtest is thought to measure the child's social judgments and ability to use facts in a social and emotionally relevant manner. The arithmetic subtest is considered a good index of reasoning ability plus "numerical accuracy in mental arithmetic" (Sattler, 1974, p. 189). The similarities subtest is thought to reflect verbal concept formation and logical thinking, while the vocabulary subtest is related to a variety of mental operations based on language ability and general information. The digit span subtest is linked to attention and short-term memory while the picture completion subtest is thought to assess ability to separate the trivial from the important in the environment. The picture arrangement subtest is seen as a measure of nonverbal reasoning ability and the ability to plan ahead, although there is some question of whether any reasoning tasks are entirely free from verbal processes (Bryan and Bryan, 1978). The block design subtest is linked to visual-motor coordination and capacity to organize perceptually, or make sense of the environment. The object assembly test is also considered a good estimate of perceptual organization. The coding subtest is thought to measure the child's visual-motor coordination, speed of mental operation, and short-term memory; and the mazes subtest is believed to reflect planning ability and perceptual organization.

While these clinical interpretations of subtests are popular, there is not much empirical support for their validity. Factor analytic studies of the WISC find that the test taps some five different abilities (Sattler, 1974). Sattler suggests tht the WISC measures two types of verbal abilities. One is verbal knowledge, which is the result of formal education. The second is the ability to apply judgments following some intellectual reflections. The third and fourth factors are related to attentional abilities and to interpreting and organizing visually perceived information within a limited period of time. The fifth factor appears to have no psychological interpretation.

WISC as a Test of Nonintellectual Functions

There have been attempts to employ the WISC as a diagnostic test of other than intellectual functions. Wechsler (1958) and Rappaport (1946) suggested that a person's emotional and mental states might be diagnosed from the pattern, or scatter, of subtest scores. Differences between verbal and performance IQ scores or between sets of subtest scores form the basis of scatter analysis. Since there are twelve subtests and three additional scores, scatter analyses take many forms.

By and large, the use of scatter analyses have not increased our ability to predict the emotional or social state of the individual. It has been found that individual subtest scores are not sufficiently reliable to yield information based on scatter analyses (McNemar, 1957). It is also apparent that even if groups can be discriminated using scatter analyses, the number of false positives and negatives are sufficient to preclude the use of a scatter analysis for individual diagnosis. In a strong statement against the use of this type of analysis, Cronbach wrote: "No objective treatment of the Wechsler scores has proved able to classify individual patients with a useful degree of accuracy. Indices representing 'scatter' of subtest scores—e.g., the range from highest to lowest subtest score—are worthless as diagnostic signs" (1960, p. 201).

So far we have presented the contents of the SB and the WISC. The format of the test, the types of test items and the relationships among them, and the subgrouping of test items to form judgments about the test-taker have been described. Now we turn to critical questions about the use of these tests. For instance, questions have been raised about what these tests predict, the stability of test scores, factors that make test scores unreliable, and the tests' applicability to groups of children, particularly those from minority backgrounds.

USES OF CHILDHOOD INTELLIGENCE TESTS

One of the questions asked is: What behaviors do intelligence tests predict? It is clear that scores on one intelligence test do predict scores on other intelligence tests (Littell, 1960; Sattler, 1974). If you want to predict how well a person will score on the SB, you might as well test the person with the WISC. Most of the time we are not interested in how one performs on different intelligence tests, however.

Correlates of IQ Scores

"The man in the street, and often the unwary psychologist, thinks of intelligence as something really existing 'out there'; something which the psychologist may or may not recognize successfully, and measure with more or little success. In these terms it would make sense to argue about whether a particular test 'really' measures intelligence. Such reification is utterly mistaken; there is nothing 'out there' which could be called intelligence . . . concepts only exist in the minds of scientists." (Eysenck, 1973, p. 1). The conceptualization of the nature of intelligence and what intelligence tests actually measure are two very different things. Many people believe that there is a "true intelligence" or a "potential intelligence," a relatively constant ability, perhaps genetically influenced, that is pervasive in determining the child's behavior in a wide variety of situations. The search for culture-fair, culture-free tests of intelligence reflects the belief that there is a "potential intelligence" within the body that can and should be separated from cultural influences and experiential history (Liverant, 1960). When we examine the definition of learning disabilities (chapter 1), we see that potential intelligence is a benchmark in the definition against which academic failure is assessed. However, intelligence "is not an entity, nor even a dimension in a person. . . . (Intelligence is) an evaluation of a behavior sequence from the point of view of its adaptive adequacy" (Tuddenham, 1962, p. 517).

Intelligence may also be defined on the basis of what tests of it predict. It is important to note that a concept can be defined through the tests that measure it, that is, on the basis of the behaviors the test results predict. Cleary et al. suggest: "Intelligence and other ability tests are useful to the extent to which they are correlated with socially relevant and important criteria, not whether they measure someone's conception of innate capacity" (1975, 23). Which behaviors do children's intelligence test scores predict? These measures tell us something about the child, such as social class and parents' attitudes (Bayley, 1970; Reese & Lipsett, 1970; McClelland, 1973); but is that what we mean by the concept of intelligence? Surely we do not administer intelligence tests to assess parental education level, parental achievement demands, or other cultural influences. We can obtain this kind of information from parents themselves. But these variables are important correlates of intelligence test scores.

Children's intelligence test scores do provide us with information about who is likely to do well in school and on academic achievement tests (McNemar, 1964; McClelland, 1973). Anastasi writes: "The Stanford-Binet is primarily a measure of scholastic aptitude" (1961, p. 208). The same can be said of the WISC. There is some evidence that intelligence tests are helpful in predicting future occupational success, although the degree of their power to do so is open to debate (McClelland, 1973; Sattler, 1974). There is some evidence that intelligence tests are useful in predicting performance on some laboratory tests of learning that involve verbal content, although it has by no means been shown that these tests measure learning ability in all tasks (Stevenson, 1970).

In sum, intelligence test scores are good predictors of performance in schoolwork, learning tasks with high verbal content, and other intelligence tests and of parental social class and perhaps future occupational success. It should not be surprising that intelligence test scores predict these particular variables. Middle-class parents emphasize the importance of schoolwork and verbal skills, verbal skills are in high demand in the performance of schoolwork, intelligence tests measure verbal skills, and occupational success may depend upon school experiences that in turn depend upon verbal skills.

There is general agreement as to what intelligence tests do *not* measure. They do not measure "inborn capacity" (Cronbach, 1960; McNemar, 1964), or learning ability (Stevenson, 1970). They are not culture-free, and they do not assess potential (Cleary et al., 1975). The scores are not constant, nor are they free from influences in the immediate situation.

Constancy of Intelligence Test Scores

Intelligence test scores are often used in planning for a child's educational placement both in the immediate and distant future. People who employ these tests hope that the test scores will help them read the murky crystal ball of future events. We thus ask about the stability of intelligence test scores across a long period of time. Does the intelligence test score of an individual's standing relative to peers change much over the course of three, five, or twenty-five years?

Evaluating Constancy of Scores

Constancy of intelligence test scores is assessed in two ways. The most frequently employed method is to correlate the scores obtained by the child at two or more distinct points in life. A **correlation** indicates the degree to which the child maintains his or her rank relative to others. If the highest to lowest scoring children are the same on two testings, the correlation between the two tests is said to be perfect. The second means of judging the constancy of intelligence test scores is to examine the change in a child's score across two testings. The interest in this method is in absolute scores rather than relative rankings. Table 1 illustrates the difference between these two methods.

Studies of the constancy of intelligence test scores during childhood indicate that the correlations of test scores obtained by children are very high, particularly when children are more than five years of age. For instance, Bayley (1949) found that tests given to children older than six years were closely related to scores at age eighteen. The closer in time the administration of the two tests, the higher the correlation; such correlations are likely to be .80 or higher. Correlations between tests administered at ages fifteen and eighteen were .96 (Bayley, 1949). Bradway, Thompson, and Cravens (1958) found correlations above .55 between two administrations of the SB after a lapse of 25 years. Even the scores obtained at ages four and twenty-nine showed rather high correlation. "In terms of group trends, the long-range predictive validity of a Stanford-Binet IQ, especially when obtained with school-age children, is remarkably high" (Anastasi, 1961, p. 206). MacMillan writes: "It is safe to draw these conclusions from the longitudinal data: Intelligence is a relatively stable human characteristic; as age increases, this characteristic becomes increasingly more stable; the correlations of IQ at two points in time increase as the age of initial testing increases and as the interval between testings decreases" (1977, p. 177).

Note that Anastasi refers specifically to *group trends*. People studying intelligence testing are making predictions on the basis of groups of people, but those determining school placements are making predictions about individuals. While there are high correlations across time in IQ scores for groups, the perspective is considerably different when we examine the constancy of IQ scores over long periods for individuals. The evidence is abundant that there are frequent and

TABLE 1 Constancy of IQ Scores

Child	IQ at Age Six	IQ at Age Ten
Gail	175	160
Lisa	160	110
Ara	150	109
Cara	110	108
Lynne	100	95
Donna	90	92
Justin	80	85
Danny	70	73
Peter	69	72
Sheri	65	68

Notice that the ten hypothetical children maintain the same relative rankings when tested at age six and at age ten. The correlation between the two tests would equal 1.00, or a perfect correlation.

marked changes in intelligence test scores for individuals. Honzik, MacFarlane, and Allen (1948) reported that more than half of their sample of children showed changes in intelligence test scores greater than 15 points and that 9 percent changed more than 30 points between six and eighteen years of age. McCall, Appelbaum, and Hogarty (1973) investigated the stability of intelligence quotients and test profiles of 48 males and 66 females who had had at least 12 assessments of intelligence between the ages of three and thirteen years. The results were that the "average individual's range of IQ between two and a half and thirteen years was 28.5 points; one of every three children displayed a progressive change of more than 30 points; and one in seven shifted more than 40 points. Rare individuals may alter their performance as much as 74 points" (1973, p. 70). Baker, Sontag, and Nelson (1958) found that 62 percent of a sample of fifty children changed more than 15 points in their Stanford-Binet IQ scores between the ages of three and ten years. It is quite clear that individual IQ scores are subject to marked shifts and that absolute scores are not constant.

What Do Variations Mean?

The variations found in the absolute scores of individuals have important implications. An examination of Table 1 reveals that a single testing of Lisa and Ara might be very misleading if educational and social decisions made for these children at age six determine their placement at age ten. If one is to use intelligence tests for the purpose of individual diagnosis, it is critical that the test be repeatedly administered to the child. This has been legally recognized in PL 94-142, which mandates annual testing.

There are many factors that may contribute to the rise and fall of an individual's IQ scores. Some moderate shifting is likely due to errors of measurement. A child's high score may reflect good guessing on a particular day; a low one may be the result of poor rapport with the test-giver. On retesting, a child's score is likely to drop if it was high on the first evaluation and to rise if it was low. Additionally, IQ score shifts have been linked to a number of personal and social characteristics of the test-taker. McCall et al. reported that boys are more likely to show increases in IQ scores with age than girls, while girls who are "relatively more favorably disposed to traditional masculine roles tend to increase in IQ more than girls who are less so" (1973, p. 70). Low-income groups are less likely to show shifts than middle- or upper-income groups and are also likely to achieve decreasing scores with age.

Personality characteristics of both children and parents have been associated with shifts in IQ scores. Children who are independent and competitive appear to be more likely to show shifts upward than those who are less so. Youngsters whose parents encourage them in their intellectual tasks and use moderate and rational discipline techniques are likely to show increases in IQ scores (McCall et al., 1973). Thus, a host of factors have been found to be correlated with changes in an individual's IQ scores across time.

Uses and Abuses

Whether the current controversy over the use of intelligence tests in public schools reflects a more fundamental change in the public's values (Cronbach, 1975), or whether the controversy is simply limited to the technology of testing, there is no question that public concern over testing is now very great. Professional journals are examining the issue, and apparently many of the problems are being resolved only in the courts. While controversy about intelligence testing is not new (Cronbach, 1976; MacMillan, 1977), the hostility toward it is.

Intelligence tests and their cousins, aptitude tests, are used for at least two broad purposes: to determine the best educational and remedial program for individual children; and to limit an individual's subsequent opportunities to participate in particular kinds of educational programs. The original goals of the French commission that mandated Binet to devise a test was based on the former goal. Binet was aware of the need for special education as well as the potential stigma attached to the receipt of such schooling. He was concerned that decisions about school placements be as objective and free of capricious factors and personal biases as could be humanly possible. In this country, however, with limited resources allocated to colleges and universities, aptitude and intelligence tests have served to deny people the opportunity to obtain whatever bounty may result from higher education. The latter use of intelligence tests has fed the belief that they are another method to propagate prejudice and prevent equal opportunities, thus incensing those barred from the colleges. Organizations who share these beliefs have pressured legislators to take action against the use of intelligence tests. For example, the California State Legislature has voted twice against the use of group intelligence tests within the schools, only to have the governor veto the bill each time. Nonetheless, the courts have prohibited use of an intelligence test for the purpose of identifying mentally retarded children. In addition, there have been several court decisions declaring it illegal to give minority group children intelligence tests that have been standardized for children from the majority culture. Finally, PL 94-142 demands that tests used to evaluate individuals for diagnostic purposes must be administered in the child's native language.

Criticisms of Intelligence Testing

Criticisms of testing have taken a number of forms. First, it has been argued that the tests were constructed without adequate representation of minority group children. It is believed that intelligence tests are inappropriate for use with children not represented in their construction. Second, it has been claimed that the content of the test items are culture-bound, that is, children from minority groups have not had as much exposure to the experiences reflected in the items as children from the white middle class. Third, language differences among children and between the minority group child and the examiner are said to yield underestimates of the minority group child's intelligence. There has been concern that the examiner may be swayed by his or her stereotypes of the minority group so as to under-evaluate seriously the child's responses. Finally, there is concern that the minority group child interacting with a white middle-class examiner might feel fear, anger, or anxiety, any of which could adversely affect the youngster's test performance.

Responses to Criticisms

Happily, there have been a variety of responses to these charges, some taking the form of research, others the attempt to develop alternative methods of assessment. As mentioned, in its restandardization the revised WISC test did include an appropriate proportion of minority children, at least black children. The attempts to produce a culture-free test have not been successful, nor are they likely to be and still yield useful predictions concerning future academic performance. Additionally, some limited research has suggested that some of these charges may not have a basis in reality. Research comparing the scores of black children given an intelligence test in black dialect with those given the standard test has failed to demonstrate significant differences (Sattler, 1974). More disturbing, there is at least one study showing that intelligence tests given in Spanish to Mexican-American children yielded lower scores than the same tests given in English (MacMillan, 1977). The problems associated with the examiner's interpreting a test given in the child's native language, as required by law, may be quite serious (Sattler, 1974).

While there has been speculation that black children tested by white examiners may experience considerably more stress during the examination, the evidence on this point is somewhat mixed. There seems little doubt that negative interactions between the examiner and the child will tend to reduce the child's IQ score. However, in the research that found such effects the test was administered in a nonstandard way, employing procedures that are highly, and probably unusually, **aversive** (Sattler, 1974). The concern that the examiner's stereotypes and expectancies may affect the performance of a minority child has received mixed support from studies of actual intelligence testing situations (MacMillan, 1977). But, studies of these factors in interview and laboratory settings do suggest that examiner stereotypes and expectancies would have an impact on intelligence testing results (Hyman, 1954; Rosenthal, 1966).

There is little doubt that intelligence tests are discriminatory if you define intelligence as anything other than an estimate of performance in academic and verbal tasks. If intelligence means a child's ability to survive on the streets, be creative, be socially or interpersonally sensitive, act appropriately in many different situations, be clever, or to earn money, then one should not use intelligence tests. If one uses intelligence tests to predict these skills, then the general finding that minority children obtain lower scores than white middle-class children produces a series of false, misleading predictions.

However, if intelligence tests are perceived as estimates of the likelihood of success in a school program emphasizing verbal skills and abstract ideas, there is little question that the IQ is useful in making accurate forecasts. In spite of the admitted difficulties in using intelligence tests today, they are among the best predictors of school performance. It is perfectly reasonable to challenge school policies on the basis of contemporary educational practices. One might question, however, whether attacks upon an instrument that predicts the child's success given these educational practices will ultimately serve the child. We appear to have come full circle in our uses, or abuses, of intelligence tests. These measures were originally developed to provide a basic evaluation of a child's mental abilities in order to minimize the biases of teachers and the excessive influence of parental status and power. By denouncing and legally prohibiting the use of these tests, we now appear to be opening the door once more to such biases and influences. "The fact that any scientific instrument is popularly misused, however, does not in itself render it useless for the purposes for which it was intended. It simply underscores the fact that many test users have not been adequately trained" (Reese and Lipsett, 1970, p. 555).

SUMMARY

Intelligence tests were originally developed in hope of facilitating more sensitive and more valid assessments and decisions concerning the educational programs suitable for children. The goals of the test developers were to produce objective, practical, and empirically based instruments that would permit detection of children who might not have the intellectual abilities to succeed in the traditional classroom.

While intelligence tests are often useful for predicting academic achievement, both the concept of intelligence as well as the tests themselves have been the subject of controversy. These disagreements have arisen from changing ideas of the nature and assessment of intelligence and from the abuses resulting from the use of intelligence tests. To understand the foundation of much of the debate over intelligence, one must recognize that the public holds a number of beliefs about intelligence and the ways it is measured. One commonly held belief is that intelligence is a capacity to act in all ways necessary to have a good life. Second, it is generally thought that a person's intelligence is an attribute that remains constant across the life span. Finally, many assume that intelligence tests assess this very important and stable attribute. While people may construe intelligence in a variety of ways, it is clear that intelligence test scores are not perfectly constant across time. Intelligence tests do help in predicting a child's academic performance, but may be insensitive in predicting his or her performance on a variety of other intellectual or social tasks.

In assessing the worth of any measuring device, one must know its reliability and validity. Reliability is defined as the dependability of measurement. Essentially this means that if one tests an individual on the same or comparable items, his or her responses to those items should be similar. But reliability is not enough. Tests must also demonstrate that they have some kind of validity, that they predict some important activity.

In reviewing infant intelligence tests, we see that such tests are not generally good predictors of the child's subsequent intellectual development. That is, scores on infant intelligence tests do not generally correlate highly with scores that the child will obtain on other intelligence tests given during the school years. Very low scores on such tests may, however, be useful in detecting children likely to have serious intellectual problems, perhaps resulting from physiological damage.

The most popular children's intelligence tests are the *Stanford-Binet Intelligence Test* and the *Wechsler Intelligence Scale for Children.* Childhood intelligence tests are good predictors of classroom success. Scores on these tests are related to or predictive of the child's ability to learn tasks that require verbal skills. In addition, the test scores predict performance on other intelligence tests. However, the tests are not culture-free; they do not assess fixed and unchanging capacities and do not measure some ability or capacity that is resistant to all forms of environmental influences.

While tests yield scores, people interpret them. Much of the current controversy concerning intelligence revolves around how such test scores should be or are interpreted. Test scores help one predict the likelihood of a child's success in school. Thus, they may be helpful in determining the educational placement that will best facilitate the child's development. However, scores are often interpreted as reflecting the child's ability to learn in any setting and thus may be used to deprive the child of potentially beneficial educational opportunities. Because of the abuse of intelligence tests, particularly in the treatment of minority group children, authorities have attempted to prohibit or control the use of such tests.

REFERENCES

Anastasi, A. *Psychological testing.* New York: The Macmillan Co., 1961.

Baker, C. T., Sontag, L. W., & Nelson, V. L. Individual and group differences in the longitudinal measurement of changes in mental ability. In L. W. Sontag, C. T. Baker, & V. L. Nelson (Eds.), *Mental growth and personality development: A longitudinal study.* Monographs of the Society for Research in Child Development, 1958, *23*, No. 2., 11–83.

Bayley, N. Consistency and variability in the growth of intelligence from birth to 18 years. *Journal of Genetic Monographs.* 1949, *75*, 165–196.

Bayley, N. Development of mental abilities. In P. H. Mussen (Ed.), *Carmichael's manual of child psychology* (Vol. 1). New York: John Wiley & Sons, 1970.

Bersoff, D. N. Silk purses into sow's ears: The decline of psychological testing and a suggestion for its redemption. *American Psychologist,* 1973, *28*, 892–899.

Buros, O. K. (Ed.). *The seventh mental measurements yearbook,* N.J.: Gryphon Press, 1972.

Bradway, K. P., Thompson, C. W., and Cravens, R. B. Preschool IQs after 25 years. *Journal of Educational Psychology,* 1958, *49*, 278–281.

Bryan, T., & Bryan, J. H. *Understanding learning disabilities.* Sherman Oaks, Calif.: Alfred Publishing Co., 1978.

Cameron, J., Livson, N., & Bayley, N. Infant vocalizations and their relationship to mature intelligence. *Science,* 1967, *157*, 331–333.

Cleary, T. A., Humphreys, L. G., Kendrick, S. A., & Wesman, A. Educational uses of tests with disadvantaged students. *American Psychologist,* 1975, *30*, 15–41.

Cronbach, L. J. *Essentials of psychological testing.* New York: Harper & Row, 1960.

Cronbach, L. J. Five decades of public controversy over mental testing. *American Psychologist,* 1975, *30*, 1–14.

Eysenck, A. J. *The measurement of intelligence.* Baltimore: Williams and Wilkins, 1973.

Freeman, F. S. *Theory and practice of psychological testing.* New York: Holt, Rinehart & Winston, 1963.

Fuller, J. L., & Thompson, W. R. *Behavior genetics.* New York: John Wiley & Sons, 1960.

Guilford, J. P. Intelligence: 1965 model. *American Psychologist,* 1966, *21*, 20–26.

Harris, A. J., & Shakow, D. The clinical significance of numerical measure of scatter on the Stanford-Binet. *Psychological Bulletin,* 1937, *34*, 134–150.

Honzik, M. P., MacFarlane, J. W., & Allen, L. The stability of mental test performance between two and eighteen years. *Journal of Experimental Education,* 1948, *17,* 309–324.

Huelsman, C. B., Jr. The WISC subtest syndrome for disabled readers. *Perceptual and Motor Skills,* 1970, *30,* 535–550.

Hyman, H. H. *Interviewing in social research.* Chicago: University of Chicago Press, 1954.

Kagan, J. On the meaning of behavior: Illustrations from the infant. *Child Development,* 1969, *40,* 1121–1134.

Kagan, J. *Change and continuity in infancy.* New York: John Wiley & Sons, 1971.

Kamin, L. J. *Heredity, intelligence, politics and psychology.* Paper presented at the meetings of the Eastern Psychological Association, 1973.

Lewis, M. Infant intelligence tests: Their use and misuse. *Human Development,* 1973, *16,* 108–118.

Lewis, M., & Goldberg, S. Perceptual cognitive development in infancy: A generalized expectancy model as a function of the motor-infant interaction. *Merrill-Palmer Quarterly,* 1969, *15,* 81–100.

Littell, W. M. The Wechsler Intelligence Scale for Children: A review of a decade of research. *Psychological Bulletin,* 1960, *57,* 132–156.

Liverant, S. Intelligence: A concept in need of re-examination. *Journal of Consulting Psychology,* 1960, *24,* 101–109.

London, P. *Beginning psychology.* Homewood, Ill.: The Dorsey Press, 1975.

Maccoby, E., Dowling, E., Hagen, J. W., & Degerman, R. Activity level and intellectual functioning in normal pre-school children. *Child Development,* 1965, *36,* 761–770.

MacMillan, D. L. *Mental retardation in school and society.* Boston: Little, Brown & Co., 1977.

McCall, R. B., Appelbaum, M. I., & Hogarty, P. S. Developmental changes in mental performance. *Monographs of the Society for Research in Child Development,* 1973, *38,* No. 3, 1–84.

McCall, R. B., Hogarty, P. S., & Hurlburt, N. Transitions in infant sensori-motor development and the prediction of childhood IQ. *American Psychologist,* 1972, *27,* 728–748.

McClelland, D. C. Testing for competence rather than for "intelligence." *American Psychologist,* 1973, *28,* 1–14.

McNemar, Q. Lost: Our intelligence? Why? *American Psychologist,* 1964, *19,* 871–882.

Ramsey, P. H., & Vane, J. R. A factor analytic study of the Stanford-Binet with young children. *Journal of School Psychology,* 1970, *8,* 278–284.

Rappaport, D. *Diagnostic psychological testing.* Chicago: The Yearbook Publishers, 1946.

Reese, H. W., & Lipsett, L. P. *Experimental child psychology.* New York: Academic Press, 1970.

Rosenthal, R. *Experimenter effects in behavioral research.* New York: Appleton-Century-Crofts, 1966.

Sattler, J. M. *Assessment of children's intelligence.* Philadelphia: W. B. Saunders Co., 1974.

Sechrest, L. Incremental validity. In D. N. Jackson & S. Messick (Eds.), *Problems in human assessment*. New York: McGraw-Hill Book Co., 1967.

Stevenson, H. W. Learning in children. In P. H. Mussen (Ed.), *Carmichael's manual of child psychology* (Vol. 1). New York: John Wiley & Sons, 1970.

Terman, L. M., & Merrill, M. A. *Stanford-Binet Intelligence Scale: Manual for the third revision*. Boston: Houghton Mifflin Co., 1960.

Terman, L. M., & Merrill, M. A. *Stanford-Binet Intelligence Scale*. Boston: Houghton Mifflin Co., 1973.

Tuddenham, R. D. The nature and measurement of intelligence. In L. Postman (Ed.), *Psychology in the making: Histories of selected research problems*. New York: Alfred Knopf, 1962.

Wechsler, D. *Wechsler intelligence scale for children: Manual*. New York: The Psychological Corporation, 1949.

Wechsler, D. *The measurement and appraisal of adult intelligence* (4th ed.), Baltimore: Williams & Wilkins, 1958.

Wechsler, D. *Manual for the Wechsler intelligence scale for children— Revised*. New York: Psychological Corp, 1974.

Werner, E. E., Honzik, M. P., and Smith, R. S. Predictions of intelligence and achievement at 10 years from 20 months pediatric and psychologic examinations. *Child Development*, 1968, *39*, 1063–1075.

Zigler, E. Mental retardation. In P. London & D. Rosenhan (Eds.), *Foundations of abnormal psychology*. New York: Holt, Rinehart & Winston, 1968.

KEY TERMS

alternative form method A measure of reliability obtained by correlating scores yielded from two forms of a test. If the scores from the same student on the two forms are highly correlated, it can be assumed that the tests are measuring the same construct or set of characteristics.

aversive Defined in Chapter 13.

construct validity The process of establishing that a particular test is valid by multiple predictions based upon a psychological theory.

correlation Numerical expression of the degree of relationship or correspondence between two variables or sets of measures.

criterion (predictive validity) Process used to determine if measures taken at one point in time predict some different aspect of behavior or performance later in time.

false negatives The occurrence of a score that indicates that an attribute, problem, or characteristic of an individual is not present when, in fact, it is. Thus children actually needing special services are not identified.

false positives The occurrence of a score that indicates that an attribute, problem, or characteristic of an individual is present when, in fact, it is not. Thus children may be identified, labeled, and segregated for special services when it is not necessary.

reliability The dependability or consistency of a measure, observation, or finding.

scatter (variability) The range of performance(s) on some measure or across measures.

sensorimotor skills Pertains to the growing control and coordination of sensation and motor movements, abilities that are associated with normal development during the first two years of life.

sensory system The network of organs that receive or experience external stimulation and begin the transmission of that information to the brain.

split half method A measure obtained by using half the items of a test to produce one score and the other half to yield another, independent score for the same student. The scores are correlated, and that correlation provides an estimate of the reliability of the total test.

standard deviation A measure of the variability or dispersion of a set of scores around their mean (average) value.

test-retest (reliability) The correlation between scores achieved by the same student on two administrations of the same test.

validity The degree to which a test measures what it was designed to measure.

CHAPTER 3

Socialization and Behavior Control

This chapter is concerned with how children learn acceptable behavior, and how adults view their actions and try to change them. It examines ways in which children are influenced to do what does not necessarily come naturally to them, to act in ways that are required of them. Much of **socialization** is related to teaching children to do and, it is hoped, like doing that which they may initially have no inclination to do. An extensive discussion of socialization is warranted for several reasons. First, most people are, or will be, responsible for one or more children. While the major task of the parent is to keep the child alive, a parental role almost equally important is to socialize the youngster, to induce him or her to act in socially acceptable ways. Secondly, for a variety of reasons, many exceptional as well as ordinary children have inadequate or inappropriate socialization experiences. Among exceptional children are many in special need of social training. For those readers who become parents, or who are likely to work professionally with handicapped children, an adequate understanding of socialization practices is a necessity. Thirdly, it is recognized that parents are not the sole influence in the socialization process. Television, teachers, even politicians, have been named as important socialization agents. It is likely that teachers consistently underestimate, just as parents probably overestimate, their influence on the social training of children. Whatever the estimates of influence, most of us are apt to be involved in socializing children. Finally, there is an ever-increasing use of behavior control techniques in institutional settings. Techniques to induce behavior change are becoming increasingly sophisticated and efficient, and their applications quite widespread (London, 1969, Bootzin, 1975). The educated person, whether parent, teacher, lawyer, or psychologist, should be aware of the development of these techniques. The chapter begins with a discussion of socialization, focusing on the main perspectives that are particularly important in determining how one views and influences a child's personality formation. It then goes on to explore some principles of training that may determine how efficiently the child is socialized.

PERSPECTIVES ON SOCIALIZATION

All parents realize that their offspring will require guidance in order to become a socially acceptable and competent person. However, parents often differ with regard to their particular goals for their child and the methods by which they hope to accomplish these goals. It is important to realize that both parental goals and the methods associated with these goals are influenced by the work of psychiatrists and psychologists. In the remainder of this chapter, we will describe the nature of socialization, some important theories concerning it, and finally some research findings that seem particularly germane to it.

What Is Socialization?

Socialization generally refers to the training of a child to conform to interpersonal and/or social customs considered important by those persons doing the training. The study of how to help a relatively primitive being to act without supervision in ways that it does not wish to act, ways that often go contrary to its own biological and social needs, has been quite challenging (Aronfreed, 1968). A mother's major tasks might thus be to help the child use a toilet, delay eating, play nondestructively, like others, and to like being liked by others. Similarly, among the teacher's major responsibilities are getting the child, by hook or crook, to attend to tasks that may be boring and pass up activities that may be more interesting or fun. In effect, the socialization of young children often calls for the suppression of strongly motivated behaviors, inducing the child to give up something he or she wants, pass up a satisfying experience. In addition, socialization involves teaching children to behave themselves even under circumstances where external rewards for appropriate behavior and external sanctions for poor behavior are apparently absent.

Goal of Socialization

Often then, the goal of socialization is to train the child to act in a socially appropriate way even when not afraid of punishment or seduced by promises of immediate rewards. The child's behavior, it is hoped, will become relatively independent of immediate influences within the environment.

Internalization

It is hoped that the child will **internalize** the appropriate behavior. When behavior is relatively independent of immediate sanctions and rewards, that behavior is considered to be *internalized*, that is, governed by some need, motive, value, or thought within the child. It is unlikely that the process of internalization is ever complete, that the child, or the adult, ever becomes entirely free of environmental forces. (Aronfreed, 1968; Mischel and Mischel, 1976). However, it is also clear that some individuals do show more internalized conduct than others; some die for their principles, while others often fail to resist forces in their immediate environment. Because internalization is rarely total does not mean that it cannot be encouraged with adequate guidance. In summary, important features of the socialization process are the inhibition of strongly motivated but undesirable behaviors, the fostering of weakly motivated but highly desirable ones, and the production of desirable conduct in the absence of immediate rewards or in the face of immediate obstacles. This is clearly a challenging task.

FREUD, SKINNER, AND BANDURA

The systematic socialization of children is critically dependent upon the "change agent's" (that is, parent, teacher, psychologist) view of personality development. The implicit personality theory adhered to by the responsible adult is crucial in determining the nature of the child's problem, the methods used to remedy it, and the goals one holds for the child. The theory determines the way we attempt to interact with children to influence their social development. Many individuals have contributed to our notions of personality development, but the work of three men, Freud, Skinner, and Bandura, is particularly important. Their ideas have had an important effect on our view of children's personal and social development. Let us examine how these men have influenced our perspectives on socialization.

Sigmund Freud and Psychoanalysis

Sigmund Freud, the founder of psychoanalysis, is the grandfather of a variety of therapies that emphasize insight as the road to solving problems of living. Freud's theory of human behavior is the most comprehensive ever advanced. Within this theory, he attempted to account for a multitude of human and social conditions ranging from love to war, perversions to politics, instincts to intellect, and the sane to the insane. Freud hypothesized about the structure and processes of the human mind and about interactions among these processes that he believed to be important. He advanced ideas about the relationship between the developing biological organism and the environment. Of special importance to this chapter, he attempted to explain the development of moral judgments and behavior through his notions about parents and the young child's biological gratifications. His work was an eloquent and grandiose attempt to account for human behavior and led to an enormous amount of experimentation and study. Freud has had a great impact upon our conceptualizations of personality development and human conduct. He changed our fundamental notions of the human condition (Rieff, 1959).

While many parts of Freud's theory have lost favor among today's scientists, it is important to recognize his influence upon our ideas of raising children. While some of his notions may be incorrect, the legacy he left us is pervasive. For decades his ideas have influenced child-rearing methods as well as those for the treatment of a variety of human ills. Diagnosis and interventions for young and old, whether play therapy or parental counseling, often carry assumptions he laid down.

Socialization through Identification

According to Freud (1933, 1940, 1959), a child becomes socialized primarily through a process of identification with parents. The child adopts the characteristics, values, and trivial behaviors demonstrated by his or her parents. The adoption of the parents' values is of particular importance in socialization as such values were believed to inhibit future transgressions by the child or to produce guilt in the wake of a misbehavior. Several features of the identification process as postulated by Freud should be noted. First, the process was presumed to occur unwittingly and to be a defensive act by the child (Rieff, 1959). He or she does not think about and select which of the parents' characteristics or values to adopt; rather, the youngster identifies without forethought or conscious selection. Indeed, this process was thought to occur during that period of life when forethought is not likely to be characteristic of the child. Identification reflects neither systematic learning by the child nor conscious training by the parent. Rather, it is believed to spring automatically from the child's experience of anxiety or fear (Rieff, 1959). The process of identification is rooted in two of the child's concerns. One is that the parent will withdraw love; the second is the fear of physical assault. It is through these circumstances children adopt values that guide their behavior into socially appropriate actions.

While Freud felt that the children's adoption of their parents' values is a necessity if society is to survive, he also felt that such identifications might serve as a mainspring for subsequent personal suffering. This is likely to happen if an individual's values are such as to define biological striving as excessively offensive. When such is the case, the individual may repress these biological strivings and the thoughts they engender and become unconscious of them. Thus, according to Freud, values lead to the suppression of acts but not to the elimination of the need they reflect. The need simply becomes inaccessible to conscious processes. Psychological problems were thought to be the result of a continuing need to express motives that are morally offensive to the individual but of which that person is unaware.

It is trite to say that Freud attributed great importance to unconscious processes. He felt that much of human behavior is governed by impulses of which the person is unaware. Moreover, Freud believed that the expressions of unconscious needs are never obvious, but rather take the form of subtle behaviors, like slips of the tongue and dream states. As these expressions are subtle and less open to intellectual scrutiny, difficulties associated with such needs are less open to easy remedy. Hence values, and by implication, behavior suppression, while necessary for society, may actually bode ill for the child. In effect, socialization was conceived as being fraught with dangers (Rieff, 1959). The moral was that one has to be careful that the child does not embrace too many values attached to too many strongly motivated behaviors. Additionally, identification and the adoption of values are seen as hinged more upon **affective** than intellectual states; values are embraced from states of fear, either of assault or love withdrawal.

In summary, Freud believed:

1. Parents are the critical socialization agents.
2. The effects of parents upon children are primarily the result of an automatic process rather than a product of tutoring or behavioral example.
3. The values held by parents are critical guides to behavior.
4. Children must incorporate these values for adequate socialization to occur.
5. While adoption of values is necessary, they can also result in conflict, misery, and neurosis.

Freud's Influence on Child-Rearing

How Freud "really" affected our child-rearing practices is anyone's guess but his influence does show in several ways. First, we still see Freud's mark in our definitions of which environmental factors affect children. We continue to focus primarily upon the family as the major source of socialization. Our choice of the period we deem critical in fitting children for communal life is also reflective of Freud's influence. Important events in this process are often believed to be completed while the child is still very young. There is a narrowing of our view of environmental events that may be significant in socialization, that is, a focus upon parents and their interactions with their children during a relatively brief span of time.

Secondly, through notions of the unconscious, Freud made us particularly sensitive to subtle and mysterious forms of behavior. Since he believed that much of human conduct arises from unconscious motives, he elevated the importance of such phenomena as slips of the tongue, dreams, and memory errors. As Rieff

(1959) has argued, Freud endowed behavioral trivia with great significance. But more important, the emphasis on the unconscious propagates the belief that everyday behavior is really a reflection of something else. For example, many readers have no doubt heard that you can tell what a person is "really like" when he or she is drunk, implying that when one is sober, that isn't the "real" person. It is as if Freud convinced us that what is obvious about a person is of little matter; what is hidden is of considerable importance. We are thus led to believe that overt behaviors are not important; that they are reflective of something else, like needs or instincts, and thus should not be the focus of training efforts. If the reader agrees with this argument, then altering the child's behavior through praise, candies, or punishments will seem fruitless.

Finally, Freud believed that the most efficient mode of treatment was to focus upon the individual rather than upon the environment. This last position has affected the way we identify and treat children who demonstrate deviant behavior or inadequate learning. It has propagated a system of diagnosis and treatment that resides, to a great extent, within the treater's office, if not upon a couch in that office, rather than one that is concerned with the children's interactions within classrooms or on the streets.

B. F. Skinner: Behaviorism

Skinner (1960) introduced a perspective of socialization that was a radical departure from the one developed by Freud. Skinner proposed that theories about human behavior have to be tied to observable behaviors or conditions. Notions that are not linked to explicit environmental events or behaviors are to be avoided as they would be misleading, at best. Concepts of the conscious and unconscious, needs and motives, guilt or egos should be dropped. In effect, you are as you behave. The focus is upon behaviors, not inferences about unobservable happenings within the head or the psyche.

Role of Reinforcements

While the empirical work related to Skinner's influence is vast and important, in this section we focus upon how his perspective may have altered our views of socialization. In addition to escalating the importance of behavior, Skinner expended considerable energy in theorizing about and studying the role of **reinforcements** in governing human conduct. A reinforcement is an event that increases the probability that the behavior that immediately preceded it will be repeated. Many believe reinforcements account for most of our behavior and are the primary determinants of our actions. Several features concerning reinforcement should be noted. First, its definition does not involve explanations or concepts concerning presumed motives or needs of the child. In fact, the child does not "need" reinforcements; he or she just gets them. Second, reinforcing events are not limited to those that may satisfy biological needs or social motives. They are simply events that increase the probability of behavior. To understand reinforcements and, by implication, much of human conduct, one should focus upon determining what is reinforcing, the effect of giving reinforcements more or less frequently, their timing, their development, and the impact of their disruption.

Because the determinants of conduct are located in reinforcing events outside the person, the importance of the environment in determining behavior is emphasized. Look not to inner motives and dynamics, but to reinforcements and environments, so the Skinnerians argue. Nor do reinforcements come from parents alone; they spring from many sources and events. Parents are not seen as the only major parties involved in the control of behavior; they are not the sole agents of socialization. Reinforcements can be received from peers, parents, teachers, strangers, lower animals, and events not related to another person's actions. Behavior control can come from many sources.

Skinner's Effect on Education

Skinner's work has had a profound effect on education. He and his followers developed a technology that produces predictable effects in relatively controlled environments. While this technology is limited in its scope by virtue of being applicable only to changing observable behaviors, it has proven effective in its application to many different behaviors. The two best-known educational developments associated with the Skinnerians are the introduction of **behavior modification** techniques and the teaching machine into the classroom. While teaching machines have not fulfilled the hopes originally held for them (White, 1970), the use of **token economies** in schools and other institutional settings has been both frequent and controversial. The most basic contribution of this approach, however, is Skinner's mandate to look at the child's behavior and at the environment in which it takes place. This fundamentally altered our orientation from one focused exclusively on the individual and presumed inner psychological events to one considering the situation's impact upon the individual.

Difference in Freudian and Skinnerian Perspectives

The two perspectives of socialization derived from the works of Freud and Skinner yield profound differences in approaches that parents or teachers might take in influencing children. We now highlight a few of these differences. First, Freud disdained examining behavior per se, seeing it as important primarily for purposes of understanding unconscious processes. The Skinnerian perspective reverses these priorities, arguing that the behavior itself is critical, while denying unconscious processes. Which view you assume will influence your response to a child's behavior. For example, should aggression, bed-wetting, or shyness be treated as reflecting a simple problem of an unwanted behavior or a "more serious" underlying problem, a symptom perhaps of poor parenting, sibling conflict, or incestuous desires? How one views a "symptom" is critical in determining how one responds to it. Does one directly train a new and better response, or attempt to produce "insights" concerning the unwanted behavior?

Second, the Skinnerian and Freudian perspectives differ considerably in their view of the consequences and operations of socialization. Skinner appears to be more optimistic than Freud. Freud believed that when the socialization processes are seriously amiss, important, long-standing, and relatively intractable consequences are the likely results. Long-term therapeutic efforts by specially trained (and expensive) personnel are required for cure. The Skinnerian, on the other hand, argues that with the reordering of reinforcements, and with some patience, cures may be obtained. And insofar as anybody can give the reinforcements, therapeutic agents may be more available, efficient, and less expensive than when treatment is based upon the Freudian perspective.

To summarize the Skinnerian perspective:

1. Behavior is emphasized for itself, rather than as a reflection of something else.
2. Reinforcements are seen to be the primary determinants of conduct.
3. External events, not internal needs, motives, or processes, are of critical importance in affecting behavior.
4. Children are influenced by many people and events, not simply by parents, throughout their course of life.
5. Errors in training can be corrected through a proper reordering of reinforcements.

A. Bandura: Social Learning Theory

The work of Bandura (1969a, b) is presented here not so much because he has developed a radically different perspective for viewing socialization, but because he has brought to our attention a feature of learning that has been heretofore relatively neglected by many concerned with socialization.

While Bandura did not invent or discover imitation, he has certainly contributed to our understanding of it. More than any other theorist, he has demonstrated the importance of the child's observations of others in affecting conduct. Thus, the major focus of Bandura's work is upon learning through observation.

There are some additional points advanced by Bandura that should be noted. He argues that all learning is not controlled by reinforcements, that the child can and does learn behaviors in their absence. Under many everyday conditions, children will learn from what they see and hear. This does not mean to say, incidentally, that Bandura disdains the role of reinforcements in governing behavior. Indeed, he argues that they are a primary factor in eliciting the behavior once it has been learned by the child. Children learn by listening and looking, but apparently many will not demonstrate this learning until some bounty is likely. Like Skinner, Bandura emphasizes the role of the immediate environment, particularly people within it, in affecting children's learning and performance. Important influences are not limited to parents, but can include teachers and television, peers and parent substitutes, strangers and loved ones. Additionally, like Skinner, Bandura believes that many problems arising from socialization can be corrected efficiently and at less cost through direct behavior training than through the various forms of "insight" therapies. Finally, while Bandura's perspective includes notions concerning the child's inner states, it also includes concern with behavior. Atypical behavior is not, however, viewed as a reflection of something amiss in the unconscious; rather, it is perceived as something amiss in the learning history of the boy or girl.

Bandura's ideas about observational learning and imitation will be presented in some detail at the end of this chapter. We include his work because it is a well-researched theory that has been neglected in the field of education despite its profound implications for parents and teachers.

In summary, Bandura's Social-learning Theory:

1. Emphasizes the importance of the child's observing others in affecting learning.
2. Views reinforcements as particularly important in eliciting behavior but not in affecting learning.
3. Stresses the immediate environment, especially people within it, in influencing children's learning and performance.
4. Views deviant behavior as a breakdown in learning.

These three men, Freud, Skinner, and Bandura, have had an important influence upon how we view and implement the socialization of young children, whether in the classroom or the home. Freud postulated that behavior was only important as a reflection of something else. Skinner introduced the environment and the operation of reinforcements within it, while Bandura reintroduced the impact of behavioral examples in shaping our youngsters. Their theoretical positions are often in conflict; their emphases upon inner states, reinforcements, and the mechanisms of learning are very different. Our views of how to rear children have nonetheless been affected by each.

As Freud's prestige within the community of educators and psychologists has dwindled, there has been increasing study and implementation of varying techniques and methods for altering behavior. Growing numbers of professionals responsible for aiding those in distress have shifted their concerns from uncovering unconscious dynamics to using procedures designed to help their clients rid themselves of specific behavior patterns. These modifiers of behavior do have a technology that can aid others, and their approach will have an increasing effect on the ways in which parents deal with children. The intelligent parent, not to mention the various specialists who earn their living helping exceptional children, can ill afford to remain ignorant of this technology or the principles upon which it is based. It is now time to turn to some of the ideas and research findings that are important in behavior modification and socialization. Many of these are based upon studies of rats and pigeons, while some are founded on the study of boys and girls themselves. Whether based on mouse or human, the results have important implications for the socialization of children. We first discuss the topic of positive reinforcement, then consider punishments and the role of observational learning as they may affect behavior control.

POSITIVE REINFORCEMENT AND BEHAVIOR CONTROL

It is probably much more appealing ethically to control children by providing them with a positive rather than a punitive experience. Punishment violates the principles of many people who believe that control must be exerted through positive practices rather than through terror or intimidation. Parents and teachers generally hope that the necessary task of socialization can be implemented with a minimum of offensiveness.

Everyone generally agrees that positive reinforcements play a critical role in governing children's behavior. Children often engage in acts because they have been reinforced in the past or because they anticipate that they will be in the future. Youngsters learn all sorts of behaviors, good and bad, desirable and undesirable, because of their association with positive reinforcements. It is important for the teacher and parent to realize that it is the witting employment, the systematic use, of reinforcements that maximizes the effectiveness of the socialization procedures. Since much behavior is believed to be controlled by positive reinforcements, let us consider factors that are significant in a program of positive behavior control.

What Can Be a Reinforcement?

One critical factor is understanding what is reinforcing for the particular individual for whom such a program is desired. While positive reinforcement is defined as any event that increases the likelihood that the response immediately preceding it will be repeated, there is no end to things that can be reinforcing. Verbal praise, money, tokens, bottle caps, baseball hats, parakeets sitting on one's head, viewing complex stimuli, the opportunity to do something you frequently choose to do all have been found to serve as reinforcements. We do not yet know which reinforcements are biologically derived and which are learned; we do know that there are a myriad of events or objects that can be used as positive reinforcements to control the conduct of child. But the study of reinforcements does not stop with a list of all the various forms they can take. Matters are much more complex.

Not all reinforcements are biologically derived or traceable to the genes. Many things and events become reinforcing; they are learned. When reinforcements are learned, they are referred to as **conditioned, secondary,** or **acquired**

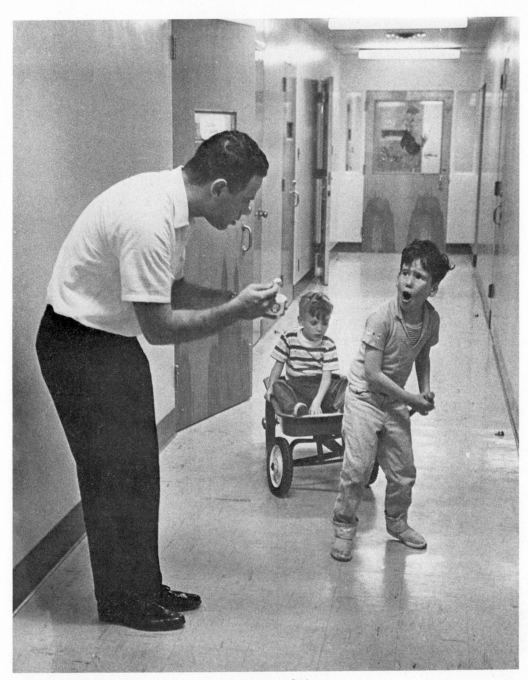

FIGURE 3-1 A demonstration of a reinforcement technique

reinforcements (Gewirtz, 1969). It is believed that learning occurs as a result of repeated associations between an event and a reinforcement. For instance, the pairing of smiles and verbal approval with a known reinforcement, such as food, will transform smiles and praise into reinforcements. Eventually, through pairing, the event—smiles and praise in this case—which was originally neutral in its impact on the person, becomes reinforcing. This process is particularly important for persons who work with handicapped children. It is believed that some disturbed children, at least those who are severely socially retarded or deviant, have difficulty in learning conditioned reinforcers. These children, like others, obtain reinforcements from events that satisfy their needs. It is believed, however, that the socialization process breaks down when these children fail to be reinforced by means of social approval. To help such children, attempts are frequently made to expand their reinforcement horizons. The intervention strategy involves helping them learn some secondary or conditioned reinforcements (Bandura, 1969a). It does require some ingenuity to determine just what forms of reinforcement will bring the child's behavior under the appropriate social controls.

The reader should recognize that the reinforcement value of an event is not an absolute property of a stimulus or response; it is relational in nature (Bandura, 1969a). Thus, a thing or event that was reinforcing in one context may lose its appeal and effectiveness in another. In yet another situation the same reinforcement may obtain greater impact than it had at first. When we discuss contrast effects, we shall return to this point. The impact of reinforcements depends on situational factors and factors related to the person's history. As these change, so will the influence of reinforcements.

The Administration of Reinforcements

The effectiveness of positive reinforcement is also related to the "when" of its administration. Just what circumstances indicate the proper time to give a reinforcement? As will be discussed, various schedules will produce various behavioral results. First and foremost, however, positive reinforcements should be provided when the desired response is demonstrated. That is, reinforcements should be given *contingently*. Unconditional love and generous displays of affection no doubt have their desirable outcomes, but the control of behavior through positive reinforcements requires that they be given following the desired behavior.

This consideration is particularly important for persons working with handicapped children. Many people in this field believe it is very important to communicate to the child their acceptance and love. Admirable as these sentiments are, several problems can result from unconditional love. First, when the caretaker's positive responses are unrelated to the child's performance, the child is deprived of one important source of information concerning the appropriateness of his or her behavior. If reinforcements are given willy-nilly, it may be harder for the child to discriminate suitable from unsuitable actions. Second, if social approval or other reinforcements are used unconditionally and in abundance, they, like the inflated dollar, will lose their effectiveness. Thus a great many noncontingent or unqualified, positive reinforcements will likely produce a situation where any particular one will fail to direct the child's attention to a desired behavior or to promote a steady improvement in performance.

The Role of Perspective in Reinforcement

The perspective of the change agent is critical in establishing which behavioral response is to be corrected. It is in defining the problem that the varying perspectives play such a crucial role. If one believes that undesirable behaviors are symptoms reflecting underlying problems and that insight is critical for personal problem solving and self-control, one will approach remediation in a quite different fashion than if one believes the behavior itself defines the problem. The Freudian perspective then would generally lead one to support expressions of presumed need states, to have the child "get it off his chest," and to relate these difficulties to the home environment. Reinforcements would be directed toward those expressions that are thought to best resolve the obscure and complicated underlying problem. Those taking the behavioristic approach, on the other hand, will define their target conduct not on the basis of underlying dynamics, but rather on whether encouraging particular actions would resolve the child's problems.

As an example of the importance of these two perspectives in determining the target behaviors to be reinforced, let us take the case of a school-phobic child. The Freudian approach would emphasize the underlying reasons for the child's unreasonable fears, encourage and reinforce the youngster's expressions of sexual and aggressive fantasies and feelings about his or her important interpersonal relationships. In effect, and perhaps unwittingly, those of the Freudian perspective would be reinforcing those behaviors that are believed to reveal something hidden from awareness. The behavior modifier, on the other hand, would give reinforcement for those behaviors that are required for attending school, while withdrawing them from conduct that interferes with going to school. In effect, this perspective leads to the question: What is reinforcing the child's avoidance of school, and what behaviors might be reinforced in order to encourage the child's school attendance?

Using Reinforcement to Solve Socialization Problems

Problems in socialization are really of several types. Sometimes children display inappropriate behaviors, sometimes they attempt to perform the correct behavior but do so poorly, and sometimes they fail to perform the behavior at all.

In regard to the first problem, that of the control of inappropriate behavior, several methods have been recommended with regard to the use of positive reinforcements. First, it is important to determine what reinforcements are maintaining the inappropriate response. Once such reinforcements are determined, they should be withdrawn. For example, children's disruptive behaviors within the classroom are often being reinforced by the attention, and even the reprimands, that they receive from teachers or peers. If the undesirable behavior is being maintained by such reinforcements, then clearly attempts should be made to ignore it. Behaviors that are not reinforced will eventually cease and are said to be *extinguished*. The withdrawal of positive reinforcements of the behavior is part of the **extinction** process. A second method, not mutually exclusive from the first, in dealing with inappropriate behavior, is to give positive reinforcements for behaviors that are incompatible with the undesirable ones. For example, the child who is reinforced for sitting quietly at a classroom desk will be less likely to commit disruptive behaviors. Thus, it is often recommended that reinforcements for *incompatible alternative responses* be employed in an attempt to eliminate a child's transgressions.

The second problem, that of the child not committing the desired response or of doing so only poorly, reflects problems of response deficiency. When response deficiency is the problem, it is often recommended that the responsible adult initially give the child reinforcements for the crudest approximations of the desired behavior. As time and training progress, reinforcements are given only as the behavior becomes increasingly like that deemed desirable. Finally the child is given rewards only when the correct behavior is exhibited. This process is called **shaping** (Gewirtz, 1969).

Amount, Timing, and Scheduling of Reinforcements

The impact of positive reinforcements is determined by the amount of reinforcement, the timing of it, and the schedules with which it is administered.

Amount

In general, the greater the *magnitude* of reinforcement, the more efficient the learning or performance. Magnitude of reinforcement can take many forms. It can refer to amount of weight or volume, to the number of units of reward, or to the amount of activity involved in consuming or enjoying a particular reinforcer. Apparently the relationship between the reinforcer and performance is maintained irrespective of whether magnitude means quantity or time.

The magnitude of reinforcement has to be defined relative to previous experiences rather than by some absolute physical property of the reward. We have known for some time that reinforcements show a *contrast effect*; reinforcement effects can be influenced by the magnitude of reinforcement previously experienced by the child. The child who is accustomed to a small amount of reward and suddenly receives a much larger one is likely to perform better than if he or she had been receiving a large bounty all along. This is a **positive contrast effect**. If the child is accustomed to great amounts of reward and suddenly receives much less, performance is likely to be depressed more severely than if the reward had remained consistently small throughout the proceedings. This is a **negative contrast effect** (Flaherty, Hamilton, Gandelmann, and Spear, 1977). Adults interested in using positive reinforcers to affect children's performance should be alert to the relational properties of reinforcements as indicated by these contrast effects. When teachers and parents initiate a program of behavior control with substantial dividends, they may be forced into maintaining this magnitude throughout the program.

Timing of Reinforcement

The effectiveness of reinforcement is also determined by its *timing*. The sooner the reinforcement follows the target behavior, the greater the impact. Delays in the receipt of reinforcement impede learning a new task and performance on one already well learned. A time gap between performance and reinforcements, however, is often unavoidable. Parental approval for good academic performance can hardly be expressed in the schoolroom, nor can the teacher be ever alert to all the accomplishments of every pupil. There is a way to bridge this gap, however, and that is through the use of words. It is likely that describing in words the child's pleasing conduct while giving the reinforcement will strengthen that conduct.

Scheduling of Reinforcement

There are a number of *schedules* of reinforcement, and these have different results on performance. In *continuous* reinforcement a reward is bestowed each time the child behaves in the desired way. This schedule does not appear to produce greater learning than when a less generous reinforcement schedule is used. In addition, the effects of continuously rewarding behavior are likely to disappear rather quickly, to show relatively rapid extinction, once the reinforcement is stopped. The child rather quickly stops that behavior once the reinforcements cease. Behaviors only occasionally reinforced are more likely to continue, to show resistance to extinction, once reinforcements are terminated, than behaviors that have been continually rewarded.

Four types of schedules for reinforcing behaviors on an occasional basis have been well studied. These are the *fixed* and *variable ratio* schedules and *fixed* and *variable interval* schedules. The fixed ratio schedule is a procedure in which reinforcements are given, for example, after every third, fifth, or tenth response. It is similar to paying a person for piece work. So many pieces, so many coins. This schedule results in a frequent rate of responding which is occasionally interrupted by a lapse in the behavior being fostered following the reinforcement. The variable ratio schedule also bestows rewards following a certain number of responses, but the exact number of responses varies from one reinforcement to another. In this schedule the child might be rewarded after three responses, then after five, two, and so on. Like the fixed ratio schedule, this produces a high rate of responding, but does not appear to result in the frequent lapses seen with fixed ratio schedules.

In the interval schedules of reinforcement, the reward is given following selected periods of time. In a fixed interval schedule, once a reinforcement is given, it is not given again until a set period of time has elapsed. Then, when the appropriate behavior occurs again, reinforcement is administered. The time period can be seconds, minutes, or hours. This schedule usually produces an initial pause in the behaviors immediately after each reinforcement, followed by a gradual increase in the rate of responding. The longer the time interval between reinforcements, the lower the rate of responding.

The variable interval schedule is similar to the fixed interval but the time separating the reinforcements vary. The variable interval schedule is likely to produce a consistent rate of responses.

In general, the ratio schedules produce higher rates of performance than interval schedules, and the variable schedules seem to produce more regular patterns of response. In setting up reinforcement programs in the classroom then, whether for exceptional or normal students, one is not limited to a continuous reinforcement schedule and one should be aware that particular procedures will yield particular effects.

Some Limitations

Before we conclude this section on positive reinforcements, the reader should be aware of certain dangers in the planned use of positive reinforcement programs. Some schools, for instance, have instituted token economy systems, in which children earn tokens for certain behaviors. These tokens can be exchanged by the child for reinforcements. Recently it has been observed that the use of token economies may decrease an individual's intrinsic interest in the task being rewarded. Levine and Fasnacht (1974) cite several investigations which found that if individuals, including children, receive token rewards for engaging in activities previously appealing to them, their interest in the task diminished when the reinforcements were withdrawn. These authors provide several possible explanations for this finding. One hypothesis is based on **attribution theory,** a theory suggesting that "how we attribute the causality of our behavior will in turn determine future behavior" (p. 816). That is, when children receive rewards for a performance, for example, completing a math assignment, they will attribute their interest in the task to the reward rather than to the math itself. Subsequently, in the absence of the token, children will think they are less interested in the task than if they had not received reinforcements in the first place! A second explanation for a task's possible loss of appeal following reinforcement is that the token focuses the child's attention on the reward rather than on the task. The child presumably is then deprived of the opportunity to explore the potentially absorbing components of the task. Levine and Fasnacht caution against the implementation of token economies unless there is no alternative.

There is a second danger associated with the use of positive reinforcements. Sometimes, social approval may be aversive rather than pleasing to the child. In these instances, the positive reinforcement may inhibit rather than cultivate the target behavior. Midlarsky, Bryan, and Brickman (1973) conducted a study in which an adult praised a child's act of generosity when that adult would not act charitably. They found that under such circumstances, the grownup's praise served to dampen rather than to increase the child's subsequent willingness to be generous. Praise actually curtailed the behavior being reinforced. The message is that if you want a child to do something you do not do and that the child probably does not want to do, it is better not to use praise as a means of getting the child to do it.

A third problem associated with the use of positive reinforcements to affect behavior change is that the targeted conduct is often not demonstrated in other appropriate situations or in the same situation following a lapse of time or rewards (Kazdin and Bootzin, 1972; Bootzin, 1975). Behaviors instilled in one situation are not frequently or automatically generalized or transferred to other situations. If one wishes to inculcate behavior that will be demonstrated in other places at other times, special efforts may be required. Generalization of behavior to other places and times might be facilitated by conducting training sessions in various locales with various instructors. Or, generalization may be aided by thinning out reinforcements, by gradually reducing their frequency while cultivating the behavior. While it is hoped that once a behavior has been established it will be reinforced in other, spontaneous settings, it is probably wise to build a systematic program to sustain behavior across time and space.

We have spent some space in describing the positive control of children's behavior. There is no doubt that children's behavior in many situations can usually be controlled through the judicious use of positive reinforcements. But there are occasions when other methods of behavior control are needed. For example, it is not possible to reinforce an alternative response unless the child exhibits it, and shaping such behavior can be very tedious. One may not have the time or patience to allow the extinction of offensive behaviors following the removal of positive reinforcements. If a child runs into the street after an ice cream vendor, extinction procedures might well result in extinguishing the child. In group settings children's offensive behaviors may be very taxing, costly, or potentially destructive to themselves or others. Techniques for immediate behavior suppression may be necessary. It is not surprising, then, that many adults use physical and verbal assaults, spankings and scoldings, to control children's behavior. These techniques do appear to be rapid and efficient in suppressing unwanted behavior (Holtz and Azrin, 1963; Aronfreed, 1968). We turn now to consideration of punishment as a means of behavior control.

PUNISHMENT

While it may sometimes be necessary, punishing children is certainly controversial. Punishment offends our humanistic inclinations and is often as aversive to the giver as the recipient. As the saying goes: "This hurts me as much as you." Punishment is considered by some to be a dangerous practice, one to be avoided at all costs. It is ironic that objections to punishment revolve around contradictory assumptions. Returning to the perspectives of Freud and Skinner, we see that Freudians object to punishment on the grounds that the excessive suppression of inappropriate behaviors may lead to unconscious states and dynamics that stifle personal growth and produce severe psychological trauma. Skinnerians argue that punishment should not be used because it is ineffective. On the one hand, punishment is deemed too effective; on the other, too ineffective. Regardless of perspectives, punishment is apparently used. In fact, recently the United States Supreme Court declared it a legal tool for the classroom teacher. Whether one philosophically endorses or abhors the use of punishment to control children's behavior, one should be aware of its forms, factors that influence its effects, and the dangers it carries.

What Is Punishment?

Punishment is defined as "the presentation of an aversive stimulus contingent upon the occurrence of a particular act" (Flaherty et al., 1977, p. 153). The term aversive has a very broad meaning, so punishment can take many forms. In addition, to qualify as punishment the aversive event must be contingent upon the commission or omission of some action. When it is applied without a reason, the aversive event simply reduces to brutality, not punishment.

There is little doubt that the use of punishment is probably necessary with the younger child and that it will work, at least under certain circumstances. There is little doubt that the improper use of such techniques can produce highly undesirable side effects. Before going into those conditions that make punishment effective, and the undesirable side effects it may create, we need to mention the role of warmth and love in affecting its impact. For punishment to be effective in the long run, that is, to suppress behavior for an extended period without serious side effects, the disciplinarian probably needs to have a basically benevolent relationship with the child (Hoffman, 1970). Continual punishment in the absence of such a relationship will most likely lead the child to escape, withdraw, or become excessively aggressive. A barrage of punishment without offsetting interpersonal rewards will probably cause many problems for both the child and the adult involved.

THE FORMS OF PUNISHMENT

There are many forms that punishment may take. Physical assaults, such as spankings and whippings, are one form. Punishments may also be given through verbal assaults. Thus, the parent or teacher may scream or yell, may say that the child has lost his or her affection, or may point out the implications of the transgression for the child and others involved. Generally research psychologists have grouped the various forms of punishment into several categories. For example, Aronfreed (1968) indicates that punishing actions can be grouped according to their reliance upon the power of the punishing agent. Hence, verbal and physical assaults, screamings and spankings, are examples of the use of *power assertive* techniques in disciplinary efforts. Verbal punishments that withdraw love, express disappointment, or threaten the child with a nonviolent disruption in an important interpersonal relationship are frequently referred to as *love withdrawal* procedures (Hoffman and Saltzstein, 1967; Saltzstein, 1976). Another form of verbal discipline, called **induction,** emphasizes to the child the consequences of the transgression upon the lives of others. As will be discussed shortly, these various forms of discipline appear to yield important and different results (Saltzstein, 1976).

There are, however, other forms of punishment. Disrupting a pleasant activity, like turning off the television while the child is watching, may be punishing. Or the adult correcting the child may withdraw reinforcers, for example, take away an allowance or isolate the child in a room and so cut off the rewards associated with social interaction. Thus, punishments may take the form of physical assault, explicit disapproval, disruption of a pleasant act, and withdrawal of a reward (Aronfreed, 1968).

Factors That Influence Punishment

What are some of the important factors in determining the effectiveness of punishment? One primary consideration is the behavior that is being punished. The more highly motivated the behavior is, the more likely it is to be difficult to suppress. Moreover, if the response to be suppressed is frequently, immediately, and highly rewarded, it will be increasingly difficult to suppress or eliminate (Aronfreed, 1968; Flaherty et al., 1977). One eye must always be focused upon reinforcements and the level of motivation in the transgressions. Punishments must fit the response to be inhibited.

Intensity

A second consideration is *intensity.* Generally speaking, the greater the intensity of the punishment, the greater its suppressive effects (Church, 1963; Parke and Walters, 1967). But generally speaking is not specifically speaking, and there are considerations that should be noted with regard to punishment intensity and its relationship to behavior.

There is at least one important circumstance where the intensity of punishment is inversely related to its effectiveness, that is, where the suppression of a response is better accomplished with a relatively mild rather than strong level of punishment. We have such a case when the child is confronted with learning difficult standards of conduct in situations where the cues are complex or subtle. For example, while we generally condemn violence, we also generally condone self-assertiveness. The situations demanding the suppression of aggressive actions may be difficult for the child to differentiate from those calling for self-assertiveness. When the basis for being a saint or a sinner is subtle, and thus difficult for the child to determine, it is likely that high intensity punishment will be less effective than low intensity in inhibiting the naughty activity (Aronfreed, 1968; Flaherty et al., 1977). Ample evidence from a variety of sources suggests that high levels of emotional arousal may well interfere with learning. Thus, when the child is expected to learn to make difficult discriminations, high intensity punishment may interfere with rather than facilitate learning.

There is another important point to be made concerning intensity. Any punishment must be of sufficient strength to ensure that the behavior is in fact suppressed. A failure to suppress behavior through punishment may produce several untoward effects. First, if the transgression is not immediately stopped, it may well be subsequently reinforced. For example, suppose a little girl is caught sneaking into the cookie jar. If the punishment is ineffective, she may continue to be a cookie thief and subsequently get rewarded for this. Additionally, it has been shown that if ineffective punishments are repeatedly applied before a reinforcing event, punishments may then serve as cues to elicit the behavior (Flaherty et al., 1977). In our example, the cookie thief who is ineffectively disciplined may then believe, or at least act as if she believes, that subsequent raids on the cookie jar are permissible. Under such circumstances weak punishments may increase rather than inhibit transgression.

Finally, the strategy of gradually increasing the intensity of punishment is probably not a good one. There is good reason to assume that with such a strategy, the child may well become adapted to punishment and thus able to tolerate levels he or she could not stand if punishment were strong enough at the beginning of the training (Flaherty et al., 1977). The problems associated with the cue function of discipline and the adaptation to discipline suggest that initial intensity should be strong enough to ensure the inhibition of the transgression.

Duration

Yet another determinant of the effectiveness of punishment is its *duration*. In general, the longer the punishment lasts, the greater the subsequent suppression of the behavior (Flaherty et al., 1977). Clearly there is a limit to how long punishment should continue before it loses its effectiveness; it is possible that, like high intensity punishment, prolonged penalizing may inhibit the child's learning difficult tasks. Nonetheless, given an easy learning task for the child, the longer the punishment within the bounds of reasonableness, the more effective the subsequent inhibition of the act.

Consistency

Another important element in the efficacy of punishment in suppressing behavior is the consistency with which it is administered. Psychologists have often suggested that consistency in discipline is a critical factor in successful socialization (Feshbach, 1970; Gewirtz, 1970). Parents, teachers, or whoever enforces standards of conduct, should do so in a consistent manner to produce better socialized and better behaved children. In fact, it has been generally found that the greater the consistency of punishment, the more effective the behavioral suppression (Flaherty et al., 1977). There are several good reasons for this. First, the more consistently the behavior is punished and suppressed, the more unlikely that such behavior will be reinforced. Second, it is generally believed that punishment is effective, in part, because it produces fear or anxiety that becomes conditioned to (paired with) the child's acts or thoughts associated with transgression. Whether anxiety becomes conditioned to thoughts or motor acts is a matter of theoretical debate (Aronfreed, 1968; Bandura, 1969a, b; Flaherty et al., 1977), but the fact is that consistent pairing of anxiety or fear with the transgression will tend to inhibit the misdeed.

Before leaving the topic of consistency of punishments, an additional point needs to be made. The reader may recall that when positive reinforcements are given occasionally rather than continuously, the reinforced behavior will be more likely to persist when reinforcements subsequently stop. The reader might wonder, then, whether occasional punishments might not have a similar effect. If such were the case, then inconsistently administered punishments might be more effective in inhibiting behavior than consistent ones once they are withdrawn. Generally, however, this partial reinforcement effect (that is, the behavior shows greater resistance to extinction following occasional rather than continuous reinforcements) does not appear to be nearly as pervasive or strong for punishments as for positive reinforcements. In effect, unwanted behavior is more likely to be suppressed when consistency of its punishment is also increased.

Timing

The *timing* between a behavior and punishment is important, just as in the case of positive reinforcement. *Delay of punishment* affects the effectiveness of it. As might be expected, the closer the punishment is to the time of the transgression, the more likely it is to stop the behavior (Parke and Walters, 1967; Aronfreed, 1968; Flaherty et al., 1977). However, most mischief is not immediately detected, much less nipped in the bud. Children are often unsupervised and, even if supervised, most of them typically take great pains to hide their misconduct. Delays between the occurrence of misbehavior and the punishment of it are probably unavoidable in many cases, and in the lives of most children are probably the rule rather than the exception. As with positive reinforcements, it is also possible to bridge these delays with words (Burton, 1976). The guiding adult must somehow get the child to think about the transgression and influence him or her to feel bad (that is, anxious, guilty) about it in hopes that these aversive feelings will inhibit future repetitions of the behavior. Just what techniques may be employed?

Approaches to Discipline

Several approaches to such discipline have been studied. As previously discussed, there are inductive verbal techniques that stress to the child the effects of the naughtiness upon the lives of others. Another procedure is for the disciplinarian to withdraw love and affection from the child. Thus, the adult may act hurt, markedly reduce the frequency of interaction between them, and indicate disappointment in the child. A third procedure, referred to as power assertion, is to scold and spank. The use of these techniques leads to different outcomes for the child and caretaker (Hoffman, 1970; Saltzstein, 1976). In general, children of parents who withdraw love tend to adhere to rules and regulations with a rather uncritical acceptance and deference to authority. These children are described as developing a conventional or conformist morality. Rules are followed because they exist, because they have been publicly sanctioned, not because they are important to the welfare of others or oneself. Children of parents who employ induction techniques are likely to judge a transgression on the basis of its impact upon others. Their children are characterized as having a humanistic, moral orientation; they are less rule bound and more people oriented than children exposed to either power assertion or love withdrawal procedures. Adults who frequently use power assertion in disciplining produce children who evaluate a transgression on the basis of its immediate reinforcement contingencies; that is, the likelihood of punishment or rewards following the act. The frequent use of power assertion retards the internalization of morality (Saltzstein, 1976). When external surveillance is absent, this child has little reason not to transgress.

Another distinction between verbal approaches to discipline has been proposed by Olejnik and McKinney (1973). They compare parents who use a **prescriptive approach** with those who use a **proscriptive approach.** In a prescriptive approach the child is told what he or she should do, while in a proscriptive approach the child is told what he or she should not do. The virtue of the prescriptive approach is that it provides children alternate behaviors that would be acceptable to those around them. Olejnik and McKinney found that children were more generous to others following prescriptive than proscriptive guidance.

There is no question that speaking to the child about the nature and consequence of transgression is important in the socialization process. Words serve as a link between punishment and a misdeed committed long ago. They provide children with the concepts that help them perceive situations and their behavior appropriately so that they can govern their conduct correctly and independently. They also suggest to the child suitable alternative responses. Finally, verbal inputs provide the child with a set of principles from which he or she can develop a moral posture to guide future behavior.

Some Dangers: Need for Alternative Responses

The provision of alternative behaviors is an important consideration in punishment. If a child has but one technique to obtain a goal, and this technique is prohibited, then more intense and frequent punishment may be required to root out unwelcome behavior. If the child has acceptable alternative routes to a goal, everyone will benefit. There is another reason why we should be sensitive to the need to develop other acceptable responses when administering punishments. Punishment, whether in the form of power assertion, induction, or love withdrawal, is likely to arouse anxiety. It is never pleasant to be disciplined. Following a punishment, most children's anxieties diminish; they "cool off." "Cooling off," or anxiety reduction, serves as an important reinforcement to any behavior occurring during this period. For example, if the child is required to apologize or be self-critical during the cooling-off period, the child is reinforced through anxiety reduction for apologizing or being self-critical (Aronfreed, 1968). If, on the other hand, the child spends the cooling-off period spitting, body rocking, withdrawing, or avoiding, these actions are also reinforced and for the same reason. The cooling-off period can be used to inculcate acceptable behaviors, including expressions of guilt, acts of redemption, or other routes to the goal. It is also possible that the cooling-off period can result in a child's learning, by chance, to behave neurotically, peculiarly, and otherwise self-destructively.

Learned Helplessness

There is another danger associated with punishment, at least when it is unavoidable, and that is that the child may learn to act helplessly. *Learned helplessness* refers to those circumstances where one learns that one cannot avoid punishment and therefore must accept it (Flaherty et al., 1977). This effect has been demonstrated in lower animals, college students, and children. It occurs when punishment, either alone or in conjunction with positive reinforcements, is uncontrollable by those receiving it. In studies of lower animals, the use of punishments that the animal can neither control nor avoid ultimately puts an end to its escape attempts. Even when the circumstances change and the animal can control and avoid punishments, it still will fail to learn those behaviors that will alter its treatment. In studies of college students, both uncontrollable positive reinforcements and punishment experiences reduced the subjects' performance on what was considered an important task. Dweck and Reppucci (1973) in their study of children found that those who experience repeated failure stop trying to succeed even when they have the ability to do so. When boys and girls fail and believe this to be the result of their not being in control of the situation, they learn helplessness. These children do not think they have the capacity to succeed. Thus a child who continually experiences punishment may attribute the punishment to being incompetent and learn to act helplessly. The belief that one is in control of what happens to oneself is evidently an important determinant of behavior and there is no question that disciplinarians should be sensitive to training alternate forms of behavior.

Imitating Aggression

Another difficulty associated with discipline may arise from power assertion. It has been frequently demonstrated that children will imitate the aggressive behaviors of others (Bandura, 1969). We are not sure about the reasons for this imitation, but the fact of it has been well established (Aronfreed, 1968; Bandura, 1969a, b; Gewirtz, 1970). Some believe that children who are scolded and spanked learn through their experiences how to aggress against others and come to prefer aggression as a solution to interpersonal conflict (Bandura, 1969a, b). Others maintain that generally the child will be too terrified for such learning to occur (Aronfreed, 1968). Whether the disciplined youngster will adopt or imitate the aggressive actions of another is therefore debatable. What does seem reasonable, however, is the assumption that children who are not the object of the hostility themselves will learn such behaviors from the disciplinarian if they witness them as a third party. The teacher who screams at Johnny in the classroom may be training Mary in the art of screaming. In effect, then, the frequent use of verbal and physical abuse may well teach the young observers in the home or classroom how to aggress against others.

Generalized Inhibition

Finally, inappropriate use of discipline may produce a child who is too frightened to take any action, even acceptable ones (Bandura, 1961; Bootzin, 1975). The effect of such *generalized inhibition* can be offset by providing the child with alternate responses or verbal signals of safety and security. But generalized inhibition is a danger of which we need to be aware.

In our discussion of the determinants of punishment, we included the factors in its effectiveness as well as the dangers in its use. To summarize the dangers, if the punishment is not intense enough, the child may learn that punishment is a signal to misbehave. Second, if the punishment is too intense, the child may be too upset and frightened to learn appropriate standards of behavior and the circumstances that govern those standards. Third, in discussing various forms of punishment, we indicated that different kinds of discipline lead to different kinds of morality. Power assertion techniques result in children who are externally oriented, children whose behavior is governed by the likelihood of detection, who are concerned with whether the reward is worth the risk of punishment. This is hardly a basis for controlling conduct in the absence of supervision. Fourth, if punishment is unavoidable, the child may, in future situations, not try to avoid punishment. The child learns helplessness. Fifth, the behaviors the child engages in during the "cooling-off" period that follows punishment may be reinforced by anxiety reduction. In the absence of appropriate behaviors during this period, the child may commit inappropriate behaviors and thus learn peculiar or other maladaptive actions. Sixth, if the disciplinarian and child do not share a warm interpersonal relationship, the punished child may withdraw from the disciplinarian and be deprived of an important source of learning.

We hope you have gained some appreciation of the technical complexities involved in the use of punishment, its applicability, and its limitations. While it is desirable to avoid it when possible, punishment is probably necessary including, for the very young child, spankings and scoldings. Methods for socializing children need not be limited to handing out punishments and rewards. There are other means to train and teach children. One approach we believe to be particularly important for parents and teachers is that implicit in Bandura's social learning theory. We now turn to this topic.

OBSERVATIONAL LEARNING

One of the most commonly stated justifications for including exceptional children in regular school classrooms is that they will imitate and learn from nonhandicapped children (Snyder, Appolloni, and Cooke, 1977). The evidence concerning children's imitative behavior in the classroom is sparse, but there are many studies indicating that models play an important role in affecting children's learning and performance and that they can serve as a useful therapeutic tool (Bandura, 1969b).

There are many investigations that demonstrate that a variety of children's behaviors are affected by their observations of others, and that this is true whether the observations involve live people or persons seen on television. Behaviors such as aggression, courage, altruism, social assertiveness, moral judgments, self-administered positive reinforcements, rule abstractions, rescue behaviors, to name but a few, are response classes affected by models. Observational learning is a powerful influence upon children's everyday behavior. Since this is the case, there is no reason why models cannot be exploited in teaching and corrective efforts.

Controlling Observational Learning

According to Bandura (1969a, b) there are four processes important in controlling observational learning and performance. These are: *attentional processes, retention processes, motor reproduction processes,* and *incentive* and *motivational processes.* We shall now discuss these processes in some detail.

Attentional Processes

It seems obvious that children have to pay attention to the model and his or her actions in order to learn from that model. What is not so obvious are the factors that may affect the child's attention. Bandura has suggested that certain personal characteristics of the model are likely to direct the child's attention to that person. For example, characteristics signalling the likelihood that the model receives or controls a relatively large amount of positive reinforcement will affect the child's imitation. Models who are "powerful" or who have high status are likely to be imitated more frequently than those with little power or status. Those who are similar to the child are more likely to be imitated than those who are not. Individuals who are "warm" and attentive rather than indifferent or "cold" to the child are more likely to be imitated when such imitation does not require self-sacrifice (Bryan, 1975). Thus, a host of model attributes are thought to affect imitation by their hold on the child's attention to the model. A child's attention is also dependent upon certain characteristics of the child. Among the most important is whether he or she has had a history of being reinforced for imitating others. Children who have been reinforced for such behavior are likely to show more observational learning and imitation than those who have not been so rewarded. Additionally, children who are emotionally aroused, either physiologically or psychologically, are likely to demonstrate more observational learning than children not aroused (Bandura and Rosenthal, 1966). Properties of the model's actions are also important in affecting children's attention. A behavior that is novel or distinct will increase the likelihood that children will attend to it. A loud model will be more attention getting than a quiet one, a novel one more so than a familiar one. There are, then, many factors connected with the model, the model's actions, and the observers of the model that are thought to affect the child's attentional processes.

Retention Processes

It is one thing for a child to attend; it is another for the child to learn. While attention is necessary, it is not sufficient to produce learning. The child must retain what has been observed. The next factors important in affecting observational learning are retentional processes. According to Bandura (1969b), the child's retention of what has been observed is fortified either by rehearsal operations or symbolic coding procedures. Rehearsal operations refers to the child practicing, either mentally or explicitly, the behavior he or she has viewed. The child focuses upon a visual image of the behavior witnessed and openly or covertly practices it. A second operation that may aid retention of the observed material is symbolic coding. Here, the child attaches appropriate verbal labels to the observed behavior. Words rather than images are used to retain the modeled behaviors. Explicit instructions to the child to rehearse or to code the observed behavior will increase the observational learning that takes place.

There are events, however, that interfere with the child's rehearsal or coding operations. If the behavior is presented too rapidly, or is too difficult or complex, the child will be unable to code or rehearse it and learning will be attenuated. If the child lacks verbal skills or an adequate vocabulary, symbolic coding operations may be ineffective.

Motor Reproduction Processes

Attentional and retentional processes are presumed to underly the learning of the observed behavior. The child sees and remembers. These processes then produce a scheme that guides the child into the correct movements. Another condition affecting such imitation is the child's capacities to make the correct movements. Imitative behavior that is new to children requires that they have all the necessary capabilities to act; they must put these capabilities into the correct order so that they can respond in an unaccustomed fashion. The child's motor imitation can be hampered in several ways. Simple physical limitations will prevent many actions. While many a little leaguer will imitate the tantrums, yells, and joys of the major league star, they simply do not have the strength to hit the ball 400 feet. Additionally, some motor actions require very fine and subtle bodily cues for their proper executions, and to the degree that this is true, imitative actions may be crude at best. As an example of such a difficulty, Bandura (1969b) cites the instances of voice training. Insofar as the voice coach must rely on hidden muscles and other physiological elements to demonstrate technique, the aspiring singer is hardly in a position to watch all the motor components necessary for perfect imitation. In such situations, simple demonstrations in the absence of verbal instructions would be a relatively ineffective teaching procedure. Finally, some motor acts are heavily influenced by correct internal feedback, and hence may be difficult to learn through observation. Flying toward a basketball hoop in the face of a team of opponents or learning to ride a bicycle may require many bodily cues not available to the observer. Again, observational learning would be limited by the subtleties of necessary cues.

Incentive or Motivational Processes

Assuming that the child pays attention, remembers what he or she has seen, and has the motor capacities to perform the act, why should the child do it? Bandura suggests that incentives are the primary factor determining whether or not the observer will perform. The child will perform the act if there is clearly some probability that there will be reinforcement for so doing. Bandura (1969a, b) argues that incentives are important then for eliciting, but not necessarily for learning, behavior. But it would be misleading to assume that incentives play no role in governing learning since the performance of the act will provide in itself additional practice and thus may allow the child to better retain it through rehearsals (Bandura, 1969b).

There is another important point concerning incentives. The child who is observing need not always be reinforced for imitating, nor be the one to whom hints of future reinforcements are given. If the child sees what happens to a model as a consequence of the latter's actions, the disposition to imitate that model will be affected. The child who sees the model receive a positive reinforcement following an action is more likely to imitate than one who does not view such a consequence (Bandura, Ross, and Ross, 1963b). By the same token, a model who draws down punishment is less likely to be imitated than one who does not (Parke and Walters, 1967). Thus, the teacher's or parent's reinforcements or punishments of a particular child's actions will have predictable effects upon other children who happen to be privy to the scene.

It has recently been recognized that incentives for imitation of others do not have to be material or social reinforcements. It is not critical that the model receive some reward; incentives operate in other ways. One of the most important forms of incentives may be the model's own responses to his or her actions. An incentive to imitate may be provided to the child by the model's own affective responses to his own behavior. For example, models who express positive affect, who appear to be happy, following a particular behavior are more likely to be imitated than those who are trying it and not liking it (Bryan, 1971; Lerner and Weiss, 1972; Midlarsky and Bryan, 1972). Hints of future self-generated pleasure can serve as incentives. This point is particularly important for several reasons. First, it is unlikely that most parents or teachers give social approval or M&M candies in response to many of the child's appropriate behaviors. Such routine administration of approval or candies would soon be tiresome for the donor and fattening for the child. It is our belief that much observational learning and imitation is inspired by teachers' or parents' affective responses to their own conduct. The administration of positive affect is certainly less taxing than endlessly bestowing candy or praise. Teachers and parents should be aware of this important source of incentives. Many of our own affective expressions come so naturally they are unwitting, but they provide incentives for the child to act in ways that may or may not be socially appropriate. Consciousness raising about this phenomenon make us better able to socialize our charges.

The Impact of Observational Learning

In summary, social learning theory has led us to focus upon the important influence of others' behavior upon children and adults who observe it. Observational learning is an important influence in the socialization of children. Learning is now no longer viewed as simply the result of giving positive rewards or punishment; it is also a product of observation. Training children is not limited to words and reinforcements, but includes examples of worthy behavior.

The work and theorizing of Bandura have led to the accumulation of considerable knowledge concerning factors that affect observational learning. Characteristics of the model, such as power, nurturance, social status, affect, and similarity to the child have all been implicated in affecting imitative behavior. The child's characteristics, such as verbal skill and attentional and motor capabilities, have been shown to be relevant to the child's learning through observation. The nature of incentives has been further studied and consequently better understood. Finally, the range of behaviors that appear to be affected by observing others is extensive, indicating that observational learning may well have a pervasive influence upon the everyday training of children. Teachers and parents should be aware of modeling effects.

SUMMARY

Socialization refers to how we influence children to conform to interpersonal and/or social customs. This requires inducing the child to suppress strongly motivated behaviors, give up things, and act appropriately even when rewards and punishments are absent. The goal is to get the child to internalize appropriate behaviors and to commit those actions with no external pressure to do so.

In this chapter we reviewed three dominant perspectives on how the child's personality develops, the various means whereby children become socialized, and the training procedures that follow from these perspectives. One perspective reviewed was that of Sigmund Freud, who believed parents are critical socialization agents, that much of human conduct springs from unconscious motives, that the most efficient mode of treatment is to focus on the motives and unconscious processes of the individual. A second perspective significantly different from Freud's is that of B. F. Skinner. His approach emphasizes behavior and those external events that affect it. Agents of influence include not only parents but may also include other persons who can reinforce the child and, thereby, influence his or her behavior. Skinner's work has generated enormous amounts of research and has had great impact on educational and psychological training programs. The work of Bandura was also included as he expands upon a behavioristic approach by demonstrating that children learn in the absence of reinforcements; they learn by observation and imitation of others. Like Skinner, Bandura believes that interventions should be focused upon changing behavior and that there are many important agents in the child's life in addition to parents.

The chapter then presents definitions of reinforcements, stressing that they can take many forms for individuals. To be effective, reinforcements have to be administered at the proper time and in the proper amount. They must be given contingently to be effective in cultivating behavior; the closer in time the administration of the reinforcement is to the behavior, the more likely it is to enhance the behavior.

There are various schedules of administering reinforcements, including the continuous, the fixed and variable ratio, and the fixed and variable interval schedules.

While reinforcements have been shown to be very effective in influencing children's behaviors, there are certain limitations in their use. Token economy systems, which have been used in classrooms, may decrease children's interest in the task when reinforcements are withdrawn. Second, reinforcements from an adult who does not model the behavior being fostered may be quite aversive to children; adult praise can then inhibit rather than increase children's commitment of certain behaviors. Third, once reinforcements are stopped it has been found that the child may not continue the reinforced behavior, and that conduct reinforced in one situation may not generalize to others. Thus, while behavior modification procedures are very effective for a wide range of problems, they should not be used unless necessary to resolve specific problems.

It is sometimes necessary to punish children, although this often offends our ideas about child rearing. Punishment is "the presentation of an aversive stimulus contingent upon the occurrence of a particular act" (Flaherty et al., 1977). We see that for punishment to suppress behavior for an extended time without serious side effects requires a benevolent relationship between the disciplinarian and the child. We also see that continual punishment will lead to maladaptive behaviors in the child such as withdrawal or aggression.

Punishment can be physical, verbal, the interruption of a pleasant act, or the withdrawal of a reward. There are different forms of discipline and they have different outcomes. The gratifications in the behavior to be punished, the intensity of the punishment, its duration and consistency, as well as its timing, all count in the effectiveness of punishment.

Parents who use inductive verbal techniques in disciplining emphasize to the child the effects of transgressions upon others. Other parents use love withdrawal, act hurt, and reduce the frequency of interaction with the child. Adults may also use power assertion techniques, that is, scoldings and spankings. It has been found that love withdrawal produces children who adhere rather uncritically to rules and regulations; they become conventional or conformist in their morality. Parents who use inductive verbal techniques tend to produce children who judge transgressions on the basis of how they affect others, while those using power assertion develop children who act appropriately primarily because they are frightened of punishment for not doing so.

Certain dangers associated with the use of punishment were reviewed. It was pointed out that with punishment, children may learn helplessness, a situation in which the child comes to believe that punishment is unavoidable and efforts to succeed are fruitless. Another problem is that children may come to model the aggressor and thus become aggressive toward others. Finally, it was indicated that some children become too frightened to do anything, that is, they experience generalized inhibition.

Another method of influencing children is through modeling the desired behavior. For a child to learn through observation requires attention, retention, motor reproduction, and incentive and motivational processes. The child must pay attention to the model, and remember what he or she has observed. The child must have the motor capacities to reproduce the act, and finally, must want to imitate the model. Observational learning exerts much influence upon children.

REFERENCES

Aronfreed, J. *Conduct and conscience: The socialization of internalized control over behavior.* New York: Academic Press, 1968.

Aronfreed, J. Moral development from the standpoint of a general psychological theory. In T. Lickona (Ed.), *Moral development and behavior: Theory, research and social issues.* New York: Holt, Rinehart & Winston, 1976.

Bandura, A. Social-learning theory of identificatory processes. In D. A. Goslin (Ed), *Handbook of socialization theory and research.* Chicago: Rand McNally, 1969a.

Bandura, A. *Principles of behavior modification.* New York: Holt, Rinehart & Winston, 1969b.

Bandura, A., & McDonald, F. J. The influence of social reinforcement and behavior models in shaping children's moral judgments. *Journal of Abnormal Social Psychology,* 1963, *67,* 274–281.

Bandura, A., & Rosenthal, T. L. Vicarious classical conditioning as a function of arousal level. *Journal of Personality and Social Psychology,* 1966, *3,* 54–62.

Bandura, A., Ross, D., & Ross, S. A. Vicarious reinforcement and imitative learning. *Journal of Abnormal and Social Psychology,* 1963, *67,* 601–607.

Bootzin, R. R. *Behavior modification and therapy: An introduction.* Cambridge, Mass.: Winthrop Publishers, 1975.

Bryan, J. H. Model affect and children's imitative behavior. *Child Development,* 1971, *42,* 2061–2065.

Bryan, J. H. Children's cooperation and helping behaviors. In M. E. Hetherington (Ed.), *Review of child development research* (Vol. 5). Chicago: University of Chicago Press, 1975.

Burton, R. V. Honesty and dishonesty. In T. Lickona (Ed.), *Moral development and behavior: Theory, research and social issues.* New York: Holt, Rinehart & Winston, 1976.

Church, R. M. The varied effects of punishment on behavior. *Psychological Review,* 1963, *70,* 369–402.

Dweck, C. S., & Reppuci, N. D. Learned helplessness and reinforcement responsibility in children. *Journal of Personality and Social Psychology,* 1973, *25,* 109–116.

Feshbach, S. Aggression. In P. H. Mussen (Ed.), *Carmichael's manual of child psychology* (Vol. 2). New York: John Wiley & Sons, 1970.

Flaherty, C. F., Hamilton, L. W., Gandelman, R. J., & Spear, N. E. *Learning and memory.* Chicago: Rand McNally & Co., 1977.

Freud, S. New introductory lectures on psychoanalysis. (W. J. H. Sproutt, trans.). New York: Norton, 1933.

Freud, S. An outline of psychoanalysis. *International Journal of Psycho-analysis,* 1940, *21,* 27–84.

Freud, S. *Collected Papers* (Vols. 1–5). New York: Basic Books, 1959.

Gewirtz, J. L. Mechanisms of social learning: Some roles of stimulation and behavior in early human development. In D. A. Goslin (Ed.), *Handbook of Society for Research in Child Development,* 1967, *32* (1, Serial No. 109).

Hoffman, M. L. Moral Development. In P. H. Mussen (Ed.), *Carmichael's manual of child psychology* (Vol. 2). New York: John Wiley & Sons, 1970.

Hoffman, M. L., & Saltzstein, H. D. Parent discipline and the child's moral development. *Journal of Personality and Social Psychology,* 1967, *5,* 45–57.

Holtz, W. C., & Azrin, N. H. A comparison of several procedures for eliminating behavior. *Journal of Experimental Analysis of Behavior,* 1963, *6,* 399–406.

Kazdin, A. E., & Bootzin, R. R. The token economy: An evaluative review. *Journal of Applied Behavior Analysis,* 1972, *5,* 343–372.

Lerner, L., & Weiss, R. L. Role of value of reward and model affective response in vicarious reinforcement. *Journal of Personality and Social Psychology,* 1972, *21,* 93–100.

Levine, R., & Fasnacht, G. Tokens may lead to token learning. *American Psychologist,* 1974, *29,* 816–820.

London, P. *Behavioral control.* New York: Harper & Row, 1969.

Midlarsky, E., & Bryan, J. H. Training charity in children. *Journal of Personality and Social Psychology,* 1967, *5,* 408–415.

Midlarsky, E., & Bryan, J. H. Affect expressions and children's imitative altruism. *Journal of Experimental Research in Personality,* 1972, *6,* 195–203.

Midlarsky, E., Bryan, J. H., & Brickman, P. Aversive approval: Interactive effects of modeling and reinforcement on altruistic behavior. *Child Development,* 1973, *44,* 321–328.

Mischel, W., & Mischel, H. N. A cognitive social-learning approach to morality and self-regulation. In T. Lickona (Ed.), *Moral development and behavior: Theory, research and social issues.* New York: Holt, Rinehart & Winston, 1976.

Olejnik, A. B., & McKinney, J. P. Parental value orientation and generosity in children. *Development Psychology,* 1973, *8,* 311.

Parke, R. D., & Walters, R. H. Some factors influencing the efficacy of punishment training for inducing response inhibition. *Monographs of the Society for Research in Child Development,* 1967, *32,* (1, Serial No. 109).

Rieff, P. *Freud: The Mind of the moralist.* New York: The Viking Press, 1959.

Saltzstein, H. D. Social influence and moral development: A perspective on the role of parents and peers. In T. Lickona (Ed.), *Moral development and behavior: Theory, research and social issues.* New York: Holt, Rinehart & Winston, 1976.

Skinner, B. F. Pigeons in a pelican. *American Psychologist,* 1960, *15,* 28–37.

Snyder, L., Apolloni, T., & Cooke, T. P. Integrated settings at the early childhood level: The role of nonretarded peers. *Exceptional Children,* 1977, *43,* 262–269.

White, S. The learning theory approach. In P. H. Mussen (Ed.), *Carmichael's manual of child psychology* (Vol. 1). John Wiley & Sons, 1970.

KEY TERMS

affect Moods, feelings, or emotions.

affective Having to do with moods, feelings, or emotions.

attribution theory A theory concerned with the processes by which individuals interpret events or behavior as being caused personally or by part of the environment.

behavior modification An approach to changing behavior involving a variety of techniques based on learning principles such as conditioning and reinforcement.

extinction A reduction in the probability that a response will occur due to a change in the environmental events associated with the response.

induction A form of verbal punishment in which the consequences of inappropriate behavior on the lives of others are made salient.

internalize To incorporate guiding principles within the self as a result of learning or socialization.

negative contrast effect The depression of performance due to the reduction in amount of reward relative to prior experiences.

positive contrast effect The improvement in performance due to the increase in amount of reward relative to prior experiences.

prescriptive approach A method of verbal discipline in which the emphasis is upon the appropriate or desired behavior.

proscriptive approach A method of verbal discipline in which the emphasis is upon the inappropriate or unacceptable behavior.

reinforcement The presentation of an event (positive) or the removal of an aversive stimulus (negative) which increases the probability that a certain behavior will be repeated.

acquired, secondary, or conditioned reinforcement A stimulus becomes reinforcing as a result of its association with an unconditioned stimulus or a primary reinforcer.

response induction The attempt to elicit some form of responding so that behavior modification procedures may be applied. (Typically used in situations of response deficiency.)

shaping The reinforcement of small changes in behavior that are increasingly close approximations of the desired behavior.

socialization The process of growing into a society in which individuals acquire the behaviors, attitudes, values, and roles expected of them.

syntax The structural principles of a language; the ways that words are arranged to form sentences.

token economy A behavior modification technique in which reinforcement for appropriate behavior is in the form of symbols or tokens that can be exchanged for desired objects or privileges.

II

TYPES OF EXCEPTIONALITY

LEARNING DISABILITIES

MENTAL RETARDATION

**EMOTIONAL AND
BEHAVIORAL DISORDERS**

THE HEARING IMPAIRED CHILD

**SPEECH AND
LANGUAGE DISORDERS**

**LOW INCIDENCE HANDICAPS:
VISUAL IMPAIRMENTS AND
PHYSICAL HANDICAPS**

THE GIFTED CHILD

PROSOCIAL BEHAVIOR

CHAPTER 4

Learning Disabilities

Learning disabilities are the newest category of officially recognized child deviance. It has been only within the past fifteen years that learning disabilities have been given official credence through federal and state legislation supporting expenditures to train teachers and to develop school programs focusing on this problem. This is not to say that learning disabled children have not existed, by one definition or another, as long as there have been schools. Rather, it is only recently that the educational systems have been given explicit responsibility, as well as the funds, for helping the learning disabled child. The field is very young, and our knowledge of the problems very primitive.

Extent of the Problem

Despite the field's newness, its growth has been rapid. For example, the number of college graduates pursuing a career in learning disabilities expanded so much that the number of professionals in one major professional organization, the Division of Children with Learning Disabilities (a chapter within the Council for Exceptional Children) more than doubled in two years (*Division for Children with Learning Disabilities Newsletter*, 1973). At least 29 states now have certification requirements specifying the courses and number of hours that must be completed at the college level in order to obtain employment as a learning disability specialist (Bryan and Bryan, 1978). Congress authorized, through Public Law 94-142 (PL 94-142), the spending of millions of dollars for learning disabilities programs. The Bureau of Education for the Handicapped was funding 38 Child Service Demonstration Centers for learning disabled children as of January 1977 (Kukic, 1976).

The number of children believed to have learning disabilities is considerable. Estimates of the number and percentages of such children vary, since definitions and standards for counting children vary among the states and from one study to another, and the figures have ranged from 1 percent to 28 percent (Clements, 1966; Bruiniks, Glaman, and Clark, 1971). While a precise count of learning-disabled children awaits the results of epidemiological studies, Senator Ralph Yarborough, Chairman of the Senate Committee on Labor and Welfare, has indicated that between 500,000 and 1.5 million children are in need of intervention programs for learning disabilities.

One can only speculate what precipitated the development of this new field. Three forces seem to be particularly relevant: (1) rapid advances in technology in the United States; (2) the advances in educational technology during and after World War II; and (3) recent medical advances.

Causes of Awareness of Learning Disabilities

Since 1947, economic success in the United States has become increasingly dependent upon one's ability to adapt to technological change. Learning to use new home appliances or how to analyze a computerized bank statement can present problems if one is illiterate or poorly educated. Employment requirements have become increasingly tied to educational degrees, even though many job functions probably do not require advanced education. The college diploma, whether relevant or not to job performance, has become a prerequisite for many jobs. Perhaps for this reason, the percentage of Americans 25 years or older who have completed four years of high school more than doubled during the decade of the sixties, jumping to 52.5 percent of the population. Moreover, the proportion of this age group who completed four years of college also more than doubled, rising from 4 percent to 10.7 percent. A child who fails to acquire academic skills cannot be viewed with equanimity by parents. The future in this society of a boy or girl who cannot read, write, or compute is dim. A child's school difficulties represent a serious problem for conscientious parents.

Technological developments in education and changes in educational perspectives are additional sources nourishing the field of learning disabilities. The national crisis of World War II brought new techniques for teaching complex skills to soldiers already in service and basic skills to illiterates so they could join the armed services. Since the war, the results of those training programs have filtered down to the general education system in the forms of individualized and programmed instruction and behavior modification. This developing technology stresses principles of learning and task analysis, however, rather than personality. This prohibits our saddling children with global judgments of laziness or stupidity and encourages our understanding the individual's specific abilities to meet the demands of the learning task at hand.

Advances in medical technology have led to the appearance of increased numbers, and perhaps types, of developmental disabilities. Infants who once might not have survived gestation, or who suffered anoxia (oxygen deficiency), low birth weight, birth injury, or maternal infections like rubella are now more likely to survive such ordeals. These infants become "high risk" children as they are more apt to experience developmental and learning problems than those who escape these traumas (Graham, Ernhart, Thurston, and Craft, 1962; Werner, Honzik, and Smith, 1968). These conditions and factors have all probably contributed to the rapid growth of the field of learning disabilities.

DEFINITIONS OF LEARNING DISABILITIES

Definitions serve several important functions in the field of exceptional children. They help us conduct research on homogeneous groups, render specific treatment to particular children, and anticipate future education and service needs of persons within such groups. By using definitions we can delineate the boundaries of services to be rendered, winnowing out the children both eligible and ineligible to receive special services from a wide assortment of available professionals. Although, as discussed earlier, there are many dangers involved in labeling children, the dangers of stigmatizing without implications for treatment (Scheff, 1966; Seaver, 1973) and of overlooking the great heterogeneity among individuals who share a label, some type of classification system is necessary to set limits to populations to be assisted and studied.

What is meant by the term learning disabilities? The answer depends in part on when the question is asked. As we examine definitions that have been developed, we see how they have changed as the dominating theoretical perspectives in the field have changed. Early definitions emphasized brain damage and brain processes, while the later ones emphasize learning and products of learning. Let us look at these definitions.

Task Force I, 1966

The first formal definition, underwritten by a committee organized by the Office of Education, explicitly linked learning problems with minimal cerebral dysfunction to describe a group of children who presumably shared the common characteristics of minimal, often physiologically undetectable, brain damage and school failure. This definition reads: "The term 'minimal brain dysfunction syndrome' refers in this paper to children of near average, average, or above average general intelligence with certain learning or behavior disabilities ranging from mild to severe, which are associated with deviations of functions of the central nervous system. These deviations manifest themselves by various combinations of impairment in perception, conceptualization, language, memory, and control of attention, impulse or motor function" (Clements, 1966, pp. 9–10). Specialists were unhappy with this definition because, while gross brain damage may be easy to detect, minimal brain dysfunction is not. The problem is that the educational diagnostician is always limited to the evaluation of intellectual and social behavior, behaviors that can be observed and measured. The stronger the direct evidence for brain damage, such as the presence of seizures or paralysis, the less likely the diagnostic conclusion is to be "minimal" brain damage. The linkage of minimal brain damage with specific learning disabilities through strong and direct evidence is currently impossible. We do not have the technology to determine the link between the brain and learning. In addition, this definition tended to emphasize the processes presumed to underlie learning rather than the products (acquired skills) of learning. Hence, processes such as problems in attention, memory, and conception were stressed while difficulties in reading and arithmetic were not mentioned.

Children with Specific Learning Disabilities Act, 1969: The Discrepancy Definition

The 1966 definition of learning disabilities was found unacceptable. A national advisory committee to the Bureau of Education for the Handicapped recommended an alternative definition that subsequently was incorporated in federal legislation funding services for learning disabled children. The *Children with Specific Learning Disabilities Act of 1969* defined the target children thus: "Children with special learning disabilities exhibit a disorder in one or more of the basic psychological processes involved in understanding or using spoken or written language. These may be manifested in disorders of listening, talking, reading, writing, spelling or arithmetic. They include conditions which have been referred to as perceptual handicaps, brain injury, minimal brain dysfunction, dyslexia, developmental aphasia, etc. They do not include learning problems which are due primarily to visual, hearing, or motor handicaps, to mental retardation, emotional disturbance, or to environmental disadvantage" (*Children with Specific Learning Disabilities Act of 1969*, PL 91-230, *The Elementary and Secondary Education Amendments of 1969*.)

The development of the *Education for All Handicapped Children Act of 1975*, PL 94-142, triggered organized efforts to improve upon the definition of learning disabilities. Many voices of dissatisfacton were heard and many suggestions for changes were made. There were complaints that the 1969 definition was too vague (Hammill, 1974). Others were unhappy that the law did not count among the learning disabled children from disadvantaged environments and thereby minority groups, as well as children with other handicapping conditions (Kirk, 1974). In spite of the complaints about, the unhappiness with, and the efforts to change the definition of learning disabilities, no changes were produced. It apparently was felt that insofar as there was no hard research data collected on a large enough sample to state with any certainty that there are characteristics commonly shared by children called learning disabled, changes in definition would be premature. The one point of agreement among professionals is that learning disabled children show a major discrepancy between achievement and presumed potential ability, a discrepancy not caused by known handicapping conditions or circumstances. Thus it came to pass that the 1969 definition of learning disabilities was incorporated into PL 94-142.

Problems with the Definition

There are a number of important features in this definition. First, there is less emphasis upon the role of minimal brain dysfunction than heretofore. While learning disabled children may have minimal brain dysfunction, proof of dysfunction is not necessary for a child's inclusion in this category. Second, there is an explicit recognition of the academic nature of this handicap. The definition mentions reading, writing, and other products of education. The rules and regulations proposed for implementing PL 94-142 further stress the importance of the discrepancy between the child's potential and academic achievement. The rules indicate that for a child to be defined as learning disabled, he or she must not be achieving commensurate with age and/or ability levels in one or more of eight areas of academic performance. These areas are: oral expression, reading comprehension, written expression, basic reading skills, listening comprehension, mathematics calculation, mathematics reasoning, and spelling (*Federal Register,* 1976, p. 52407).

There are several problems with the discrepancy definition of learning disabilities. One arises from the concept of potential. When one argues that a child has potential ability, does it mean the child can master the particular material being taught at that moment, material in related areas, or any material the school deems necessary? One must also examine how potential is assessed. Typically it is measured by the child's performance on an intelligence test. As we discussed in chapter 2, performance on intelligence tests is quite variable for individual children. The scores are affected by the testing atmosphere, the nature of the tester, the child's motivational state, as well as other external and basically irrelevant factors (Masland, 1969). While intelligence test scores are reasonably stable for many children, some youngsters show wide variations from year to year. Given the variations in motives and interpersonal relationships that might raise or lower a child's score on an intelligence test, prediction of an individual child's school potential would seem subject to considerable error and so rather hazardous. In addition, since the definition of learning disabilities excludes children who have learning problems due to "environmental disadvantage," the assessment of potential relative to achievement is apparently intended for youngsters from the middle or upper socioeconomic classes.

In spite of the definitional problems, both stereotypes and research concerning characteristics of learning disabled children have been generated. The research has moved ahead by defining learning disabled subjects on the basis of **reading deficits** (Bryan and Bryan, 1978). Stereotypes, some correct and some incorrect, have been generated by clinical observations. We turn our attention to the personal characteristics associated with learning disabilities. We cannot stress too strongly that these characteristics are based on attempts to describe children with

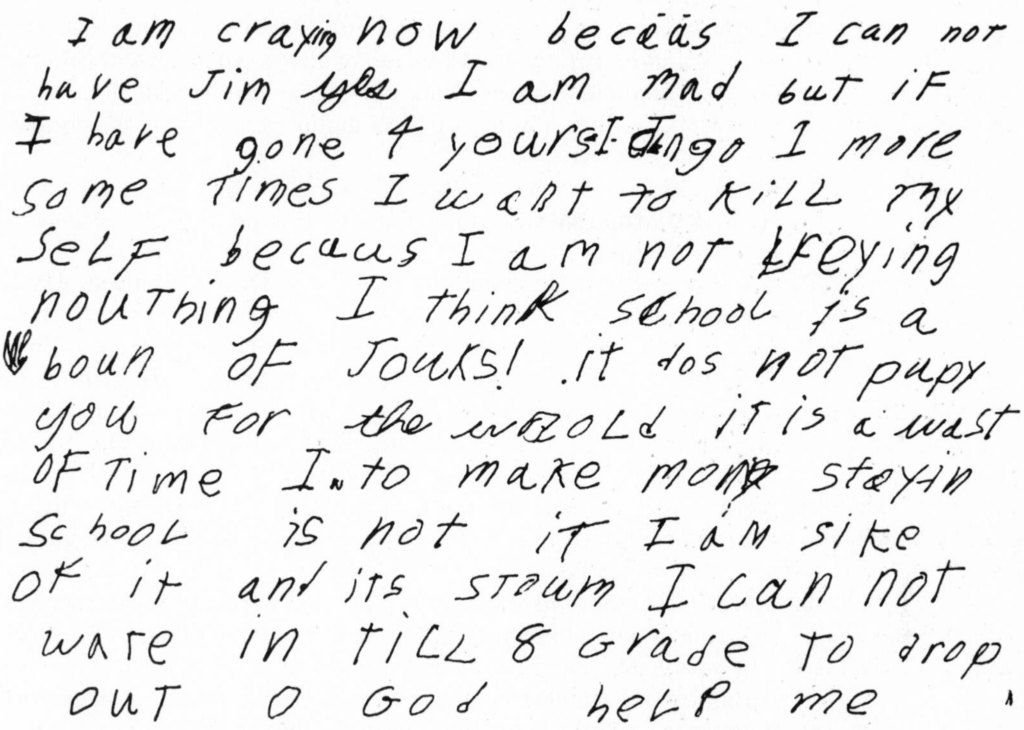

I am craying now beceus I can nor have Jim yles I am mad but if I have gone 4 yoursf tingo I more some times I want to kill my self becaus I am not preying nouthing I think school is a boun of Jouks! it dos not pupy you for the weold it is a wast of time I to make mony stayin school is not it I am sike of it and its staum I can not ware in till 8 grade to drop out O god help me

FIGURE 4-1 A learning disabled child tells what it's like to have trouble in school

learning problems. These attempts have been undertaken by persons with varied training and interests, and are based on descriptions gathered from children across the country who are as likely to be dissimilar as similar. In other words, the group called learning disabled are very heterogeneous; the characteristics associated with this label are not likely to be present in all, or even many, learning disabled children; and there is great diversity among the persons doing the labeling. At this time, the characteristics associated with this category are useful for developing questions about learning problems. They do not represent a syndrome of dysfunction, nor even a set of characteristics that have been empirically demonstrated as actually describing learning disabled children. They serve as a point of entry to understanding learning disabilities and to developing an educational technology for such children.

Characteristics of Learning Disabled Children

There have been a variety of characteristics, virtually all socially or educationally undesirable, attributed to learning disabled children. These are the ten most frequently cited:

1. **Hyperactivity,** or motor behavior not demanded by the situation or task and disruptive to the group or the expectations of others.
2. **Perceptual-motor impairments,** or difficulty in coordinating a visual or auditory stimulus with a motor act, such as is required in copying letters of the alphabet.
3. **Emotional lability,** or emotional outbursts that observers consider unreasonable in light of the situation or the child's immediate past history.
4. General coordination deficits, in other words, clumsiness or awkwardness.
5. Disorder of attention, either (a) distractibility or paying attention to what one should not, or (b) **perseveration,** concentrating on something too long.
6. Impulsivity, or behavior suggesting little reflection on the part of the child.
7. Disorders of memory or thinking, such as difficulty in recalling materials that should have been learned or in understanding abstract concepts.
8. Specific learning disabilities, such as an inability to learn reading, remember what one has read, or learn arithmetic or spelling.
9. Difficulty in understanding or remembering spoken language, deficits in articulating speech, or poor linguistic habits.
10. Equivocal neurological signs, or signs that are not clearly associated with particular neurological problems but that are also not clearly within the normal range of functioning. (Bryan and Bryan, 1978).

These characteristics have been derived more from clinical observations than from systematically gathered information. By and large, they emphasize problems in **processing** rather than deficits in **products.** That is, the first seven characteristics are process problems; they are describing problems in the way children try to do things. Thus they portray children who do not pay attention when they should, appear to act too quickly for their own good, or cannot remember what is expected of them. It is only in the category of specific learning disabilities that we pay attention to the deficiency of the products, or skills, acquired by this kind of child.

MODELS OF LEARNING DISABILITIES

Frequently, people borrow certain ways of viewing a problem from other professions. When this happens, the individual will often assume that the difficulties and remediation procedures faced and employed by one group of professionals are analogous with those confronting his or her own group. In effect, the individual will take those assumptions and procedures that apparently work for one set of problems and try to apply them to his or her activities. There are two models that have been used by professionals dealing with exceptional children, including those working with the learning disabled: the medical and the psychometric models.

The Medical Model

While there are many different medical models (London, 1972), the medical disease model has had the greatest influence upon psychologists and educators. Historically, the medical disease model developed as a conceptual tool to interpret the processes of a biological disease in order to cure persons afflicted with it. Historically and legally, physicians are concerned with the elimination of abnormal functions. Their emphasis is upon the study, detection, and cure of abnormalities. In the medical model perspective, normal is defined as that which has no "abnormal" signs. The patient is viewed in terms of a bipolar continuum in which placement at one end represents being normal and at the other, abnormal. Emphasis is on the identification and cure of abnormal characteristics, not upon the identification and facilitation of normal functions. Persons are labeled by what is wrong, not by what is right, with them. In addition, the medical disease model focuses upon biological explanations for problems. Biological functions deemed important are those intrinsic to the patient's condition. Social and cultural factors that may contribute to the ailment are ignored in this framework; organic malfunction is primary. The disease model regards its methods and findings as transcending social or cultural systems (Mercer, 1968). This model has provided a useful perspective for the physician.

Application to Learning Disabilities

The initial explanations for learning disabilities were nested in the idea that these children were suffering from some sort of minimal brain dysfunction, and/or that the problem was inherited. Given this notion, various paths were followed in an attempt to understand learning failures. One focused upon children's genetic backgrounds, their perceptual and perceptual-motor problems, possible language deficits, and possible attentional difficulties. There were various explanations of just how the brain might be going wrong. Some hypothesized that systems in the brain were out of synchronization, that some parts unexpectedly matured faster than others. Such ideas suggest that *maturational lags* in brain growth are important in understanding learning disabilities. Other theorists suggested that the problems were linked to heredity and genetics and pointed to studies of families whose members across generations had problems of reading. Others felt that the learning disabled child had probably experienced damage to a particular part of the brain and cited studies of adults who had suffered brain damage (Bryan and Bryan, 1978).

Objections to Medical Models

While the ideas concerning the relationship between the brain and learning disabilities have provided important stimulation, direction, and results to workers in this area, virtually all of the assumptions underlying the medical model have been challenged. Justified or not, here are several of the objections to applying this model to personality and educational problems. There is little evidence to relate specific biological structures or processes to many personality characteristics or educational achievements. Although it has been demonstrated that a virus produces syphilis, it has not been demonstrated that a virus, or a particular set of genes, produces reading difficulties, hyperactivity, or suicide. There are many known causes of allergies, but the relationship of allergies to personality and academic functioning remains to be established. At this time we do not have the medical technology to show that specific brain structures or processes are related in specific ways to particular skills and behaviors. Even if we could establish a physical basis for whatever ails the student, the disease model is much less likely to provide hints for cures. This is to say, even if we establish that allergies are related to reading disabilities, the cure for reading disabilities is still reading instruction. Furthermore, within the medical disease model some theorists have emphasized the role of heredity. The incidence of reading problems in families has been used as evidence that such problems are genetically linked. Again, even if genes are somehow involved, the cure is more likely to be educational than medical.

Concern with the application of the medical model to psychological and educational problems is not limited to the fear that this perspective will lead special educators astray. There is also the fear that such a viewpoint may create more problems than it cures (Scheff, 1966). This anxiety is based upon two factors, the conservative strategy demanded by the medical model and the stigma often associated with diagnostic labeling.

The medical disease model causes its practitioners to focus on the elimination of abnormality. The professional's safest strategy in dealing with a patient is to assume that there is something pathological somewhere. If a practitioner is to commit an error of diagnosis, it is best to commit a safe one, to diagnose illness which is not there rather than to discern health when there might be pathology. In other words, it is better to predict a false positive than a false negative. If the diagnostic error is on the safe side, all a patient might lose is a little time and a lot of money. On the other hand, if the practitioner commits a diagnostic error and concludes the patient is healthy when really ill, the patient may lose both a lot of money and his or her life. Hence the medical model tends to favor a conservative strategy, one that dictates an assumption of illness until proven conclusively otherwise. This particular strategy is reasonable when dealing with a matter of life and death, but is it reasonable when applied to academic, social, or emotional problems? The answer to this question is critically dependent upon the laws and stigma attached to the particular problem. To be labeled as mentally ill by a physician will frequently, and with appalling rapidity, result in a citizen's loss of freedom and civil rights (Scheff, 1966). To label a youngster learning disabled will mandate a school system to enroll the child in a special educational program, sometimes in a separate classroom. This will considerably alter important aspects of a child's life. Adoption of the conservative strategy is based upon a diagnosis that in itself stems from rather primitive guesswork, yet it can have significant life consequences for the labeled individual. In addition, the degree to which a label is associated with stigma, as is certainly the case with the diagnosis of mental illness (Goffman, 1961; Nunnally, 1961) and mental retardation (Christoplos and Renz, 1969; Jones, 1972), is the degree to which the conservative strategy may inflict enduring damage on the individual.

Perhaps because of these objections, a second model or perspective concerning learning disabilities has gained popularity. This is the psychometric model.

The Psychometric Model

In the psychometric or statistical model, the definition of normal is based upon the statistical concept of the normal curve. Whether one is considered normal or abnormal depends upon where a person's score falls in the distribution of scores from a population. Both ends of the curve are abnormal as the scores there occur infrequently. The score that falls toward the middle or the mean of the distribution is not abnormal because it occurs most often. Just what degree of "differentness" or "deviation" is thought to be abnormal is an arbitrary decision and depends upon the goals, resources, and whims of those doing the defining. What is clear, however, is that "differentness" or abnormality can be traced back and defined on the basis of that person's score or scores relative to other people's on a particular test or tests. Unfortunately, professionals often transpose the score to the person. To be defined as abnormal under this model means that the abnormal person stands out, has visibility because of being different. The normal person is one who cannot be differentiated from most members of the group, who has, in effect, become invisible. This model is presumed to be nonevaluative. But tests are given to determine the status of some function or trait of an individual deemed important to the person or to society. Tests are employed to assess functions that are socially valued. Thus evaluations become impossible to avoid. It is bad to have a low IQ score and good to have a high one, even though both scores may be equally deviant from the average IQ score. While descriptive statistics operate in a moral vacuum, individuals cannot.

Mercer (1968) has suggested that these two models, the psychometric and the medical, have become fused into the "clinical perspective." Practitioners who apply the clinical perspective to troubled persons use the psychometric model to define the existence of a problem and the medical model to diagnose and understand it. Children who obtain a score that is infrequent and which reflects a state or trait deemed undesirable are then examined as if the score were symptomatic of some underlying physiological malfunction. The transposition of a low, undesirable score into a sign of pathology carries with it all of the implications of the medical disease model.

Children's difficulties in school achievement are often thought to emanate from the child rather than from the environment. In the field of learning disabilities, poor teaching and parenting are relatively neglected as important sources of school failures, and problems in learning that may arise from environmental disadvantage have been specifically excluded from the legal definition of learning disabilities. However, with increasing emphasis upon diagnosis and treatment of school-acquired skills, or products, such as reading and mathematics, perhaps the focus will broaden from exclusive assessment of the child to include the various social and institutional forces that generate and sustain academic failure. In the following review of the findings concerning learning disabilities, you will see how each of these models has guided research into the causes and characteristics of learning disabled children.

PROCESS PROBLEMS

In this section we present major constructs that have been used to study the processes underlying learning disabilities. These include notions about perception and information processing, attentional problems, and language development and deficits. In discussing these constructs, we define the behavior to which they refer, assess the construct, examine findings relevant to that idea and explain why people feel that the construct is important in understanding learning disabilities. We shall see that the learning disabled child appears to have difficulty in a multitude of process functions and that each of these constructs refers to complex rather than simple behaviors.

Perceptual Handicaps and Information Processing

There are a number of theorists and researchers who feel that a primary problem of learning disabled children is their perception of the world about them (Kephart, 1963; Barsch, 1967; Cratty, 1969; Cruickshank, 1975). Such learning problems are viewed as a breakdown in the brain's systems governing the person's ability to distinguish between the foreground and background, that is, the important from the unimportant, the necessary from the trivial. The term perceptual handicap was defined by a blue-ribbon committee as an inadequate ability "in recognizing the fine differences between auditory and visual discriminating features underlying the sounds used in speech and the orthographic forms used in reading; retaining and recalling those discriminated sounds and forms in both short- and long-term memory; ordering the sounds and forms sequentially both in sensory and motor acts; distinguishing figure-ground relationships; recognizing spatial and temporal orientations; obtaining closure; integrating intersensory information; relating what is perceived to specific motor functions. . . ." (Wepman and associates, cited by Hobbs, 1975, p. 82). It is also believed that children with perceptual handicaps frequently are hyperactive, easily distracted, and impulsive. The theorists of this school of thought believe that minimal brain dysfunction is the cause of the perceptual handicap and that this dysfunction is related to the development of fine and gross motor skills. These theorists, by and large, derived their ideas from observations of very young children's development. During this time children's perceptual skills are reciprocally related to their development of motor skills. For instance, the ability to walk and run may affect the child's freedom to explore the environment; the ability to use crayons (that is, develop fine motor skills) affects the likelihood the child will experiment with drawing shapes and pictures. Hence, the child's gross and/or fine motor skills are presumed to affect perceptual development, which in turn governs his or her academic performance.

Visual Perception

Many assessment techniques have been developed to test children's perceptual adequacies; most of these evaluate visual perception. The best known is probably the *Bender Visual Motor Gestalt Test* (Bender, 1938). This test consists of nine designs, one of which is shown in Figure 4-2. These designs are presented one at a time to the test-taker, whose task is to reproduce each design. Performance is evaluated by the accuracy of the reproduction. For instance, rotations of the design or failure to connect its components are noted. The test was originally devised to determine brain damage in adults, but is now commonly used in clinical assessments of children (Koppitz, 1964).

There are several subtests in the *Illinois Test of Psycholinguistic Abilities* (ITPA; Kirk, McCarthy, and Kirk, 1968) that are also employed to assess visual perception. In the Visual Reception subtest the child is briefly presented a picture, the picture is then removed and the child has to choose that same class of item from a series of items. For instance, the child may be shown a picture of a tennis shoe and then have to select a picture of a saddle shoe from among several alternative items. In the Visual Association subtest the child must select the item that best fits a scene. For instance, the child has to indicate that a picture of a man's hat goes with a picture of a man; a picture of high-heeled shoes with a woman. In the Visual Memory subtest the child has to reconstruct in correct order a series of geometric forms, while the task in the Visual Closure subtest is to locate all of the stimulus items within a complex stimulus array.

Other popular tests of visual perceptual processing include the *Developmental Test of Visual Motor Integration* (DTVMI; Beery and Buktenica, 1967), the *Frostig Developmental Tests of Visual Perception* (DTVP; Frostig and Horne, 1964), and the *Purdue Perceptual-Motor Survey* (Roach and Kephart, 1966). This last test, unlike the others, includes a variety of physical motor activities such as walking on a balance beam, jumping, and hopping.

These tests have been used for the diagnosis of children's educational and, in some cases, emotional problems. In addition, intervention programs have been developed based upon the child's performance on these tests. The idea is

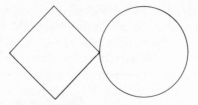

FIGURE 4-2 An example of a design from the Bender Visual Motor Gestalt Test

Source: Bender, L., "A Visual Motor Gestalt Test and Its Clinical Use," American Orthopsychiatry Association Res. Monograph, 1939, No. 3. Reproduced by permission.

that if a child does poorly on one of these tests or subtests, the processes measured must be improved upon before the child will be able to master school subjects.

The various tests used to assess perceptual processing appear to be rather primitive. They treat complex behaviors simplistically and unidimensionally and yield a high number of false positives and negatives. At least one reviewer suggested that the *Purdue Perceptual-Motor Survey* not be used at all (Jamison, 1972), while another indicated that the information available concerning the test construction (for instance, the reliability and validity of subtests) is so sparse that the test is not suitable for frequent use (Landis, 1972). The ITPA and the Frostig tests have been criticized for failing to measure the abilities their authors assumed they assess (Carroll, 1972; Chissom, 1972). Indeed Newcomer and Hammill (1975) conclude that the subtests of the popular tests of visual perception do not assess independent processes and lack validity, particularly when used with other than white middle-class children. Newcomer and Hammill suggest that these tests are of little value for assessing a child's deficits, for making predictions concerning future deficits, or for developing remediation programs that revolve around the child's test performance.

Perception versus Visual Acuity

Before presenting the data on perceptual handicaps in learning disabled children, it might clarify matters to make the distinction between perception and visual acuity. Visual acuity refers to how well we see, how well our eyes work singly and in unison. There is no evidence that the problems of learning disabled children have anything to do with their vision; that is, visual acuity problems have not been found to be more evident among learning disabled children than among the nondisabled. Refractive defects involving the adjustment of the lens of the eyes, which may produce near- or farsightedness, are not significantly more prevalent in the learning disabled. Severe binocular problems, difficulty in getting the two eyes to work together to attain proper focus, are also unrelated to the presence of a learning disability. While common sense would dictate that many of the phenomena associated with reading difficulties, such as reversal of letters and mirror writing, are related to problems of vision, research has demonstrated that common sense is wrong. All in all, studies do not support the early guesses that reading problems are linked to visual acuity (Lawson, 1968). Given the early belief, however, that the two were related, it is not surprising that a variety of remediation programs to improve visual acuity appeared. Studies of the effectiveness of optometric training (for example, eye exercises), neurological organization training (such as practice walking on a balance beam) have generally failed to find that such training improved children's academic performances (Helveston, 1969). While these programs were popular, they did nothing to upgrade the learning disabled child's academic skills.

Studies of Processes

With respect to visual perception, we find that the tests used to measure perceptual functioning appear to be crude and the intervention strategies based on notions of perception, ineffective. Thus, we turn our attention now to laboratory studies of perceptual processes since in the laboratory there can be better control and finer measurements of perceptual responses. The tests of visual perception administered in laboratory settings are similar to the tests described above. Sometimes children are shown pictures for a short time and asked to match the picture with one of several presented afterwards. At other times children are asked to remember what they have seen or to reconstruct a series of pictures from memory.

The studies on visual perceptual processing are primarily based on groups of children with reading deficits. The results of these studies show that older reading disabled children do not differ from nondisabled children in perceptual competencies. Differences are found, however, when comparing younger learning disabled and nondisabled children in their perceptual performances. Learning disabled children in the primary grades appear to perform less adequately than their peers in visual perception tasks (Lyle and Goyen, 1968; 1974; Goyen and Lyle, 1971a,b; Vellutino, Steger, and Kandel, 1972; Kinsbourne, 1973). Young poor readers seem to be inefficient in noting the critical details of the visual stimulus, although such deficiencies are not observed in older poor readers. It may be that younger retarded readers experience perceptual difficulties while older children with reading problems may differ from competent readers in verbal and/or intellectual skills. It should be noted that learning disabled children are frequently described as having difficulties on these various perceptual processing tasks that are not directly related to perception. They are seen as making more errors in following instructions and as more impulsive in responding than other children. It is therefore possible that the perceptual difficulties found in young retarded readers are a reflection of basic problems in following instructions and generally poor problem solving strategies.

Auditory Perception

While some theorists and researchers have been concerned with processing of information by visual perception, others have focused upon learning disabled children's auditory information processing, the ability to interpret correctly what is heard. Auditory processing is differentiated from hearing acuity, the ability to detect the auditory signal. In everyday activities it is sometimes difficult to distinguish between problems in hearing acuity and auditory processing failure. It is sometimes difficult to discriminate between the child who does not hear and the child who hears but does not understand. In the former case, the child is hearing impaired; in the latter the problem is presumably related to learning disabilities. It is wise to pay attention to these differences because many children with hearing acuity problems are misdiagnosed as mentally retarded, emotionally disturbed, and learning disabled (DiCarlo, 1960; Reichstein and Rosenstein, 1964).

Auditory perception is essential in classroom activities since teachers use speech as a major instructional tool. The child has to listen to the teacher's words, respond appropriately, and do so quickly (Rosner, 1973). The child has to perceive the verbal message, select the relevant information from it, and respond on the basis of his or her understanding of it. The difficulty a youngster may have with the verbal input depends upon a variety of factors, including the length and sense of the message and the nature of the response demanded of the child. It is relatively easy for a little girl to respond to the direction to get her coat. It is considerably more difficult to react to a long string of instructions given in complex sentences requiring the child to perform a sequence of intricate motor acts.

There are a number of assessment devices frequently employed to measure children's auditory perception and information processing. Parts of standardized tests of achievement and intelligence, such as subtests on the WISC or the Stanford-Binet, are frequently used for this purpose. Additionally, some tests have been designed specifically to tap auditory processing. For example, on the ITPA, the child is asked questions like "Do policemen signal?" and "A dog says bow-wow, a kitty _____?" Children are also tested for their ability to remember a string of verbally presented numbers.

Assumptions and Challenges

In developing tests of auditory processing and employing them for diagnostic purposes, researchers have made a number of assumptions. First, they assume that these various tests tap parts of the auditory perception system and that the results are indicative of performances on other tasks requiring auditory processing. For instance, if a child does not remember a series of sounds well, it is expected that the child will also do poorly in discriminating between sounds, ordering in proper sequence the sounds heard, and in understanding words that he or she has heard. It is further assumed that such deficits are significantly related to school performance. Finally, it is believed that training that improves performance on such tasks will also generalize to strengthen the child's academic performance.

All of these assumptions have been challenged. It is not at all clear that a child who performs incompetently on a subtest evaluating one specific type of auditory processing will in fact perform poorly on another test requiring auditory perception. Moreover, tests used to assess auditory processes are not pure tests; that is, they may be tapping verbal and other skills as well as auditory processing abilities (Bryan and Bryan, 1978). Likewise, the relationship of each of these behaviors to the child's school achievement is not clear. For example, some children may have difficulty indicating whether two words sound the same or different but have no problems in communicating with others. Newcomer and Hammill (1975) have argued that these tests do not predict children's difficulties in reading, spelling, or arithmetic. Finally, evidence is quite sparse that remediation programs to improve auditory processing affect children's subsequent school performance. Ross and Ross (1972) did find that a group of educable mentally retarded children taking part in a training program to improve their "listening skills" performed better on several tasks than did similar children not given this help. The group receiving the training performed better on tests that included story comprehension, following directions, remembering a series of digits, and repeating sentences. While the results of this particular study suggest that listening can be taught, it is important to note that the training program employed many techniques, such as reinforcements and activities commonly used in classrooms, that may have helped elicit better performance and increase the likelihood of generalization to school activities. On the other hand, Newcomer and Hammill (1975) reviewed the data on the efficacy of perceptual training programs and challenged the notion that training auditory processing skills is effective in improving children's academic achievement.

Laboratory Research

As with visual perceptual processing, investigators studying auditory information processing have turned to the laboratory as the setting for research, where they use a variety of measures and tasks. Sometimes children are asked to detect sounds that are masked by noise; sometimes they are presented partial words and asked to complete them; or they are presented similar sounds and asked to indicate whether or not the sounds are identical. Finally, in a **dichotic** listening task the child is given two messages simultaneously, one to each ear, and asked questions concerning the messages' content.

Laboratory results, based upon varying samples and procedures, have been fairly consistent in indicating that learning disabled children may have difficulties in discriminating sounds when the relevant information is given in a complex way. If the sounds are made within a noisy context, consist of words rather than single sounds, or are embedded in irrelevant stimuli, learning disabled children can be expected to perform less competently than the nondisabled. Additionally, learning disabled children do not improve with practice as rapidly as do nondisabled children (McReynolds, 1966; Doehring and Rabinovitch, 1969; Dykman, Ackerman, Clements, and Peters, 1971; Senf and Freundl, 1971). Whether such deficits reside only or primarily within the auditory processing systems or reflect other factors as well has not yet been determined. As of now, however, there does appear evidence that a significant number of learning disabled children may have particular difficulty in coping with complex verbal information.

Cross-Modal Integration

One popular notion is that learning disabled children may have particular difficulty in integrating information that is presented through more than one sensory modality. In this case, the child's problem is not believed to be due to visual perceptual or auditory perceptual deficits, but rather to an inability to integrate auditory and visual information when they are presented simultaneously. Thus it is believed that the learning problem stems from the child's difficulty in **cross-modal integration.**

As there are no individualized tests assessing such problems, work in this area has been limited to laboratory-based experiments. Measures and tasks employed in these experiments vary. For example, children may be presented with a series of long and short sounds and asked to match the sounds with printed dots and dashes. Or, children may be given auditory and visual stimuli and be asked to recall the information in the order in which it was given, or by the specific modality in which it was received. The findings of several studies of retarded readers have shown that they perform less adequately in these tests than nonretarded readers. Whether compared as to their competence in matching auditory to visual inputs, ordering the presentation of the material, or responding quickly, poor readers do not fare as well as adequate readers (Birch and Belmont, 1965; Senf and Freundl, 1971; Freides, 1974).

There are several points that should be noted about this area of investigation. First, studies often fail to rule out the possibility that one or another of the information processing systems may be deficient. That is, if the child has trouble coping with auditory stimuli, then failure in a task requiring cross-modality integration may stem from this deficiency and not from a difficulty in integrating the materials presented to two modalities. Second, difficulties in cross-modal integration have been found in a number of deficient populations and thus are not uniquely associated with the learning disabled child. Such problems have been demonstrated in children diagnosed as emotionally disturbed and in adults labeled schizophrenic (Freides, 1974).

Problems of Attention

A frequent characteristic of the learning disabled child is the inability to pay attention. Attentional problems were among the first characteristics to be associated with the learning disabled and to this day teachers and other professionals working with such children indicate that attention is a major difficulty (Keogh, Tchir, and Windeguth-Behn, 1974; Bryan and Bryan, 1978; Hallahan and Reeve, in press). Moreover, one prominent group of theorists not only believe that attentional problems are central to learning disabilities but have linked them to malfunctioning of the brain, specifically **the reticular activating system** (Dykman et al., 1971).

Components of Attention: Alertness

Attention is a complex behavior consisting of at least three major components: *alertness* or *orienting behaviors, focusing* or *selection* actions, and *vigilance.* The first component, alertness or orienting responses, is pretty primitive as it can be evoked in most lower animals, as well as in children, at an early stage of development (Kessen, Haith, and Salaptek, 1970). Any radical stimulus change in the environment, such as when the teacher admonishes "Pay attention!" is likely to elicit a child's orienting response. As most teachers realize, this arousal state lasts but a brief time. While not much research or theorizing has been done on the role of orienting responses in learning disabilities, there have been a few speculations. Strauss and Lehtinen (1947) have suggested that learning disabled children over-react to external stimuli. On the other hand, Keogh and Margolis (1976) hypothesize that hyperactive children often fail to engage in a task, indicating that perhaps such children underreact to radical changes within the environment. As yet, we do not know whether learning disabled children fail to attend because they are not adequately aroused, because they are aroused by too many irrelevant but competing stimuli, or because of factors that have nothing to do with the orienting response. What is known is that they do fail to come to attention. Let us now look at the information relevant to the actions of focusing or selecting that to which to attend and to the maintenance of that attention.

Focusing

Once a child is aroused and presumably willing to attend, attentional problems still may be evidenced. Two difficulties may crop up. First, the child may not be able to organize adequately what he or she sees. The child may be distracted by irrelevant features of the stimulus array, and is then unable to determine the critical features of the task and respond to them appropriately. The child cannot get his or her act together. The second problem occurs when the child believes that the act is together, but it isn't. The first problem is referred to as **field dependence** (Keogh, 1973) or difficulties in selective attention (Hallahan and Reeve, in press); the second is impulsivity (Kagan and Kogan, 1970). To make matters more complex, field dependence has been associated with impulsivity (Messer, 1976). Thus children who are field dependent, who are strongly affected by irrelevant features of the perceptual field, may also be somewhat impulsive, that is, may be inclined to make quick and wrong judgments.

There has been considerable research into the relationship of field independence or dependence to learning disabilities. Keogh has hypothesized that learning disabled children are likely to have difficulty organizing perceptual inputs, and are apt to focus on the irrelevant features of inputs. She argues that such children have relative difficulty in separating the figure (that is, the important) from the ground (that is, the unimportant). Keogh (1973) reports the results of several unpublished studies supporting the hypothesis that weaknesses in perceptual organization might characterize children who do, or will, experience academic difficulties. Watson found in a study that reading skill was correlated with the ability to ignore immaterial features of a stimulus display. Becker found that high risk kindergarten children were less able than low risk children to ignore extraneous aspects of a task. Finally, Keogh and Donlon (1972) compared the performance of severely and mildly learning disabled boys on a variety of tasks, one of which was for assessing field dependence. There were no differences in the performance of these groups, but the authors compared the scores of both groups with those of nondisabled children studied by other investigators and found the expected differences. More recently, Hallahan and Reeve (in press) have reviewed the literature concerning the learning disabled child's ability to focus attention upon relevant rather than irrelevant features of the tasks. They cited many studies indicating that the learning disabled child is less able to focus attention on relevant matters than the nondisabled child. There seems little question that learning disabled children do suffer from selective attention difficulties.

It has also been hypothesized that learning disabled children are impulsive, that they fail to reflect upon the possibilities of several explanations or responses in situations where the correct one is uncertain. Before examining how impulsive behavior may be related to attentional problems, let us consider how impulsivity is most frequently measured. The most popular test of reflectivity-impulsivity is the *Matching Familiar Figures Test* (MFFT: Kagan, Rosman, Day, Albert, and Phillips, 1964). The test requires the child to study a picture of a familiar object (the standard) and then indicate which of six other pictures is identical with that standard. Figure 4-3 illustrates items from this test. Impulsive children are defined as children who make their choices very quickly and/or make errors. Reflective children take their time and/or make few errors. Studies of impulsivity are related to questions of attention since many investigators have focused upon the scanning or visual strategies children use as they attempt to match the figures to the standard. In summarizing these studies, Messer (1976) indicates that impulsive children are less systematic or more global in viewing the test items than are the reflective children. He writes: "In particular they do not scan the distinctive features as systematically as reflectives" (p. 1037). The relationship of scanning strategies to academic failures has not been directly studied, but comparisons of reflective and impulsive children find the impulsive child has less adequate short-term auditory memory, less adequate short-term visual memory, less competency in solving mazes, and even less skill in playing the card game, Hearts (Messer, 1976).

Given the possible relationship between impulsive behavior and learning, are learning disabled children more likely than other children to demon-

FIGURE 4-3 Sample items from the Matching Familiar Figures Test

Source: Psychological Monographs, 1964, 78 (1, Whole No. 578) "Information processing in the child: Significance of analytic and reflective attitudes," Kagan, J.; Rosman, B. L.; Day, D.; Albert, J. and Phillips, W.; reproduced by permission.

strate impulsive behavior? There is some evidence to suggest that the answer is yes. Keogh and Margolis (1976) reported that learning disabled boys made a greater number of errors on the MFFT than achieving boys. Studying first grade children's impulsivity, Kagan (1965) found that impulsive first graders were less skilled than reflective children at oral reading one year later, and were less able to match the experimenter's spoken word with one of five visually presented words. Although the evidence is sparse it does suggest that impulsivity may contribute to a child's learning disability.

Vigilance

The third major component of attention is the child's ability to sustain effort upon a task. Until a task is completed or a problem solved, the child's resistance to external distractions (such as noise) or internal distractions (such as boredom) has a significant effect on the child's learning. Vigilance is typically assessed by measuring the quality of the child's performance on an easy but monotonous task. Usually, but not always, the child is asked to respond to easily distinguished signals presented at irregular intervals and without forewarning. Measures of the child's vigilance include noticing the signal, responding to an incorrect signal, and the time the child takes to react to the correct signal.

There is some evidence that learning disabled children may have difficulties in maintaining vigilance. For example, poor readers have slower reaction times to correct signals than competent readers (Noland and Schuldt, 1971). Keogh (1973) reports that Margolis, in an unpublished study, found children's vigilance scores related to both reading achievement and teacher ratings of students' academic achievement. Finally Anderson, Holcomb, and Doyle (1973) and Doyle, Anderson, and Holcomb (1976) found that learning disabled children, particularly the hyperactive among them, had difficulty in sustaining vigilance on a boring task.

In summary, there is increasing evidence that many children with learning disabilities may suffer from attentional problems, at least in focusing and maintaining their attention.

Language Deficits

In the early investigations of learning disabilities, professionals drew an analogy between adults who had suffered brain damage and subsequently lost their speech (aphasics) and children who failed to develop language in the expected manner. Since there was evidence that adult aphasics suffer damage to the left hemisphere of the cerebral cortex, it was thought that the same areas of the brain were impaired when language failed to develop properly in children. Indeed, children's language problems were categorized using terms originally applied to adult aphasics. For example, Johnson and Myklebust (1967) divided language and reading problems into receptive (understanding that which is heard) and expressive problems (writing and talking). Growing from this context was the idea that since learning disabled children might have brain damage, they might also have language problems. While the logic was hardly perfect, the idea did bear fruit. There is a good deal of evidence that many children with learning disabilities frequently have problems using and understanding language.

A variety of tests and methods are employed to assess children's language. The ITPA (Kirk, McCarthy, and Kirk, 1968) has a number of subtests that presumably measure various dimensions of communication. The Peabody *Picture Vocabulary Test* (Dunn, 1959) is a test of children's receptive language vocabulary in which the child has to indicate, in a series of questions, which of four pictures represents the examiner's spoken word. Another test popularly employed is the *Auditory Discrimination Test* (Wepman, 1958), in which the child indicates whether a pair of spoken words sound similar or different. The ability to distinguish among sounds is thought to be important by specialists in speech and learning disabilities.

A number of tests are more linguistically oriented. In linguistic analysis, language is divided into three major components: syntax, phonology, and semantics. Syntax (or grammar) refers to the rules that govern joining words in the construction of sentences. Phonology deals with the production of single sounds (that is, "p," "b," "sh") and the rules for combining sounds the language uses. Semantics refers to the meaning of language, which is in turn related to the acquisition of concepts (that is, acquisition of vocabulary and the ability to categorize and classify objects and events).

Insofar as language development has been well studied and mapped according to developmental stages (Bryan and Bryan, 1978), it is not surprising that there are standardized tests and the clinical procedures to study the language of individual children. One test is the *Northwestern Syntax Screening Test* (Lee, 1970, 1974), which assesses receptive and expressive language in children up to age 8. In examining receptive language, the child is asked to point to the pictures depicted by the sentences: "This is the father's dog" . . . "This is the father dog." To assess expressive language, the child is asked to discuss a picture and the specialist makes a linguistic analysis of the response. Lee (1974) has also proposed a clinical procedure, The Developmental Sentence Analysis, for assessing children's expressive language. She proposes that the examiner record enough of the child's conversational speech to gather fifty complete sentences. The linguistic features of these sentences are then scored with reference to the child's use of various parts of language, such as pronouns, main verbs, negatives, and conjunctions.

Historically, language problems have been thought to characterize many learning disabled children, and these problems can take many forms. For example, Semel and Wiig (1975) found that learning disabled children were weaker than nondisabled children in their understanding of syntax and expressive use of syntactic structures as assessed by the *Northwestern Syntax Screening Test*. Fry, Johnson, and Muehl (1970) found that poor readers used less complex sentences than good readers and were less skilled in organizing, integrating, and telling an original story of their own. Vogel (1974, 1977) found poor readers were less competent than adequate readers in detecting whether a sentence heard was a statement of information or a question, in repeating sentences, and in supplying missing words from a spoken paragraph. Moreover, Wiig, Semel, and Crouse (1973) found that 8- to 10-year-old learning disabled boys have difficulty in forming sentences varying in tense, and misuse singulars and plurals, skills usually developed by the 3- to 4-year-old. Finally, Wiig and Semel (1975) found that learning disabled adolescents were less able than nondisabled adolescents to name verbal opposites, formulate sentences, define words, and retrieve words descriptive of pictures. They were less accurate and much slower in responding verbally to test questions, less likely to detect incorrect responses, and more likely to use simpler phrases and sentences in conversation.

These problems appear to be pervasive and serious. It seems that children who have language deficiencies are not just slower in their language development, destined eventually to catch up to others. Rather, many learning disabled children appear to have language deficits that endure (Menyuk, 1963). Thus, in studies of learning disabled adolescents, it has been found that their language is considerably deficient relative to nondisabled peers and indeed is not comparable to that of many 8- to 9-year-olds (Wiig and Semel, 1976). Additionally, their language problems are not simply reflected in academic tasks or formalized or standardized tests, but mark their social communications as well (Bryan and Pflaum, 1978).

The evidence does indicate that many learning disabled children are likely to have pervasive language problems. Many of these children are less competent in understanding words and voice inflection, have more difficulty in defining words, creating sentences, and recognizing their linguistic errors than do nondisabled children. It is important to realize that most of the research on language problems has studied the productions and responses of learning disabled males, not females. One study specifically concerned with sex differences in the language skills of learning disabled children found that the learning disabled males were less adequate linguistically than nondisabled males (Bryan and Pflaum, 1978). This was not true, however, of learning disabled females. It is possible then that the reported language difficulties of learning disabled children are traceable to the language problems of disabled males, while these difficulties may not be typical of learning disabled females.

PRODUCT PROBLEMS

Product problems refer to deficiencies in the school achievements, or products of the child. A product problem orientation directs one's attention to deficiencies in reading, arithmetic, writing, and spelling rather than toward brain functions, attentional deficits, or perceptual problems. Since professionals have primarily concentrated on the product problems of reading and arithmetic, the discussion within this section of the chapter will be limited to these two areas.

There is an increasing tendency to define the learning disabled child as one who shows a product deficiency relative to what might be reasonably expected. Products rather than processes are becoming more important in delineating those children who will be treated as learning disabled.

Reading Problems

There is little question that reading problems are widespread. Sartain (1976) has estimated that 13 to 15 percent of the population of the United States is illiterate, and if the criterion of literacy is the ability to understand federal income tax directions, one could say that 20 percent of all Americans are inadequate readers. Sartain has also stated that approximately 10 percent of all children have difficulty in learning to read. It is important to note that not all reading problems have been traditionally within the domain of the learning disability specialist. There is, after all, a field of reading with its own history, perspectives, and experts. The relationship between specialists in the two fields is somewhat controversial since both lay claim to expertise in helping the child with a reading problem.

Learning disability specialists have historically linked reading difficulties to brain pathology. Customarily, reading problems that were the result of teaching ineptness or motivational or situational influences have been outside the learning disability specialists' domain. These professionals have concentrated on children who demonstrated reading problems, but who also might have suffered physiological trauma or dysfunction. In their view children with reading deficits were those who had some difficulty associated with their internal state, whether physiological or intellectual. The reading problem is called **dyslexia** and children with severe reading problems were considered *dyslexic*. When the learning disabilities field shifted away from the medical to the psychometric model, several new criteria were introduced to define reading problems as the legitimate concern of learning disability specialists. Children who have *severe* and *enduring* difficulties in the acquisition of reading skills are now considered dyslexic. A psychometric definition is often used. A child in the primary grades who is six months below grade level on a standardized reading test and the child in the upper elementary grades who is two years below grade level are considered to have severe reading problems that fall within the sphere of the learning disability specialist. As we noted, approximately 10 percent of school-aged children have reading problems; among these, about 2 percent have dyslexia (Sartain, 1976).

Since children's reading difficulties take various forms, there have been attempts to subcategorize these problems. First, it is important to note that children with reading problems, specifically, dyslexia, are not found to have any particular syndrome of characteristics. Earlier descriptions of dyslexics attributed to them difficulties with space and directions, learning to tell time, and soft neurological signs (these are minor abnormalities which neurologists believe suggestive of minor dysfunctioning or delayed neurological development). However, there is little empirical evidence to support the notion that children with severe reading problems are more likely than others to experience these difficulties. No doubt some do sometimes, but as a group there are no particular characteristics outside of having a hard time reading that can be attributed to all the children termed dyslexic. What does appear clear is that such children do have problems not only in reading but in writing and spelling. These boys and girls commonly make reversals, omissions, and substitutions of letters; have difficulty in arranging symbols in their proper order; and this is so whether the task involves reading, writing, or spelling.

Taxonomies of Reading Problems

As there are many degrees and types of reading failures, attempts have been made to subcategorize children with varying problems. Rabinovitch and Ingram (1962) have suggested dividing reading retardation into three categories: *primary reading retardation; brain injury with resulting reading retardation; secondary reading retardation.* Children with primary reading retardation are assumed to have a multitude of symptoms including spatial and time confusions, language problems, and difficulties in processing auditory and visual information. The brain injured child with reading retardation is presumably like the adult aphasic in having trouble producing or understanding speech. The secondary reading retardation group is thought to be the most common and results from environmentally induced causes such as poor teaching or poor motivation.

Boder (1971) has also attempted to develop a taxonomy of reading problems. She proposed that one type of problem is *dysphonetic dyslexia*, where the child can read only a small number of words that he or she has previously learned by sight. A child with this problem has learned to connect a word with a particular array of letters, and does not possess phonic or word analysis skills. According to Boder, a second type of reading problem is *dyseidetic dyslexia*. In this case the child has difficulty remembering the appearance of letters or words. Apparently, this type of child has trouble recognizing the whole word and infers the letter or word from analysis of its component parts. These children read analytically by sounding out familiar and unfamiliar combinations of letters. The third group proposed by Boder is *mixed dysphonetic-dyseidetic dyslexia*. A child with this problem has neither the visual nor the auditory means to decipher the written word and may remain a nonreader unless given intensive help. Even then, remediation may be very slow and painful.

Johnson and Myklebust (1967) divide reading retardation into two major categories, *visual* and *auditory dyslexia*. Visual dyslexia consists of visual discrimination difficulties and causes the child to confuse letters or written words that appear similar. Many of the children appear to make spatial and orientation errors by reversing and inverting letters. Shortcomings of visual memory are presumed to limit the child's ability to follow and remember sequences of symbols. Auditory dyslexia shows up in errors in discriminating sounds and in making the association between the printed symbols and the sounds heard. For children with such a problem, thinking of rhymes or listening for parts of words are very difficult tasks.

We have reviewed some of the proposed taxonomies for viewing and understanding children with dyslexia. But actually children can be categorized in an infinite number of ways. In evaluating taxonomies, it is important to realize that good ones differ from poor ones primarily on the basis of whether members grouped together bear important similarities with one another and important differences from others outside their group. Whether a proposed taxonomy does in fact accomplish this is a matter for observation. The auditory-visual taxonomies do seem to have some empirical support; that is, children do appear to have difficulty in one or the other type of tasks (Lyle, 1969). It is for future researchers to determine if the remaining proposals for such categorizations will be useful. As of now, these proposals reflect hypotheses, not empirically validated groupings.

Hypothesized Causes of Reading Problems

Notions concerning the etiology, or causes, of reading problems depend in part upon one's professional affiliation. Two professional groups are addressing themselves to the problem of reading retardation, the learning disability specialists and the reading specialists. For the expert in learning disabilities, definitions of dyslexia are embedded in the framework of the medical model, and attempts to discover those personality and physiological correlates associated with reading difficulties occupy much of the specialists' time. The focus then is upon the child. The reading expert, on the other hand, emphasizes the role of events external to the child that might be generating reading problems. Sartain (1976), for example, indicates that the most common cause of reading disability is simply poor teaching. Likewise, Boyd (1975) cites poor teaching or radical changes in instructional methods as reasons for reading problems. The reading experts' focus then is more likely to be the environment.

Within the field of learning disabilities, much of the work concerning causes of dyslexia has been addressed to auditory and visual information processing, and the role of language. Thus, many of the presumed process problems of the learning disabled child have become the causes investigators have hypothesized as producing this particular product problem, dyslexia. We will now briefly discuss the research findings on the association of information processing with reading retardation.

Difficulties in Visual Processing

There is some evidence that dyslexic children, at least at certain ages, do have problems associated with visual information processing. Lyle (1969) found that retarded readers below 8 years of age were especially baffled by tasks demanding perceptual skills. For example, these young children had problems in tasks requiring letter reversals and those involving designs. This visual perceptual problem among young retarded readers has generally been supported by other research (Lyle and Goyen, 1968, 1974; Goyen and Lyle, 1971a,b; Kinsbourne, 1973). It would be a mistake, however, to assume that all poor readers have problems in visual processing tasks as these weaknesses have tended to be found mostly with young subjects. When preadolescent and older children with reading problems are compared with peers who are fluent readers, differences in perceptual and visual processing appear to be less extensive or even nonexistent (Lyle, 1969; Vellutino, Steger, and Kandel, 1972; Vellutino, Pruzek, Steger, and Meshoulam, 1973; Vellutino, 1977).

A second notion concerning reading problems, particularly those of older children, is that they reflect not perceptual but verbal difficulties. Hence, Lyle (1968) found that older retarded readers when compared with nonretarded peers showed particular incompetence on tasks calling for verbal skills. The older children with reading problems were particularly likely to be deficient on such tasks as spelling, arithmetic, and the coding task of the WISC. Vellutino and his colleagues have suggested that reading difficulties are the result of the child's failure to *label* perceptual experiences, and reflect faulty cognitive rather than perceptual operations by the child. That is, Vellutino and his colleagues suggest that when such children encounter information to be remembered, they fail to think of words that might describe it or help them remember it.

At this time, it is reasonable to assume that many young retarded readers have problems with visual processing of information, and that for many older retarded readers the problems lie in the labeling of the information they receive. It is not clear, however, that even for the young retarded reader the problems are not also associated with inadequate abilities to label or conceptually code the stimuli. The problem may not be so much visual perception, but rather may reflect either the retarded reader's difficulties in using language to label perceptions or to focus and maintain attention upon the task. We will, within the next few pages, return to the role of language in reading. Right now, however, brief mention should be made of the association between auditory information processing and reading.

Auditory Processing Difficulties

It would seem to make sense that since much reading instruction involves orally presented information, the ability to comprehend or remember information heard might play a critical role in learning to read. Kinsbourne (1973) found that reading scores on a standardized reading test were correlated with the results of auditory tests, such as having the child repeat a pair of speech sounds and indicate whether two words sounded the same or different. He discovered that children's performances on auditory tasks were in fact more predictive of reading achievement than their scores on visual tasks. This general finding was also reported by Rosner (1973). This investigator found the children's performance on tasks that called for repeating a meaningful word with a sound missing was a better predictor of reading achievement scores than a visual task in which the child copied designs. Similar difficulties with auditory rather than visual stimuli by dyslexic children have been reported by Estes and Huizinga (1974) and Zigmond (1966).

On the basis of the evidence, it would seem that the role of visual perceptual dysfunction in producing reading retardation has probably been over-estimated. There is evidence that such dysfunctions may characterize the young child, but even that evidence, as we have seen, is mixed. Language, attention, auditory processes all come to bear upon the acquisition of reading, and many failures may reflect breakdowns in these processes. Indeed, there is evidence that processes are related to reading performance and, no doubt, future work in the area of reading will further delineate this relationship.

Role of Language

We have, on several occasions, alluded to the possible role of language in affecting reading. We now present in some detail the research pertaining to the links between them. There is both direct and indirect evidence to support the view that reading retardation is associated with a deficit in verbal skills. Indirect evidence stems from the studies of information processing in which there frequently are group differences in favor of normal readers when the tasks require the child to respond to verbal instructions. When the task is strictly one of visual recognition demanding no linguistic skills, such differences are rare. The verbal problems of children likely to have reading difficulties are evidenced at the onset of these difficulties. The numbers of children with both early verbal and reading problems led Rabinovitch and Ingram (1962) to propose a subcategory to the classification of dyslexia, primary reading retardation. Owen, Adams, Forrest, Stolz, and Fisher (1971) also found that reading difficulties were associated with early problems in language development. Following a parallel path, DeHirsch, Jansky, and Langford (1966) developed a battery of tests, many of which contained items tapping language skills, in order to predict which child might have reading difficulties. The test, given to kindergarteners, does have some success in prediction, although it yields many false negatives and positives. DeHirsch and coworkers believed that the reading, writing, and spelling difficulties of children failing in school reflect a comprehensive verbal-symbolic disturbance.

The evidence correlating verbal and language problems with reading difficulties is not limited to studies of the young child. The relationship holds for older children as well. Blank, Weider, and Bridger (1968) found that reading retarded and nonretarded first grade children performed differently on tasks that required verbal coding, with retarded readers performing less adequately than the nonretarded. Vellutino (1974) summarizes research conducted on differences in phonic analysis by good and poor readers. Generally, it has been found that normal readers are linguistically more sophisticated, as they have greater verbal fluency and better syntax than poor readers. Vogel (1974) compared good and poor readers, ages 7 and 8, in their achievements on a variety of tests that were administered orally and often required spoken responses from the child. Again, it was found that poor readers were less adequate than good ones in their language skills. To make matters worse, there is evidence to suggest that language handicaps of the poor reader will slow the child's learning of meaningful sentences. Good readers learn syntactically correct spoken sentences faster than poor readers (Weinstein and Rabinowitch, 1971). Hutson, after reviewing the evidence relevant to this issue, has concluded: "Although the ability to read, as a multifaceted phenomenon, is potentially subject to interference from several sources, a principal dimension along which good and poor readers differ is language skill. These differences are not always apparent at the lower levels of difficulty, but become evident in tasks of sufficient complexity to tap differences in the use of language, awareness of language, and in knowledge of more advanced language patterns" (1974, p. 4).

These findings have important implications for efforts at early detection of learning problems. Language undergoes tremendous development during the preschool years and continues to grow during the elementary school period (Palermo and Molfese, 1972). We use language to remember, to organize the lump together material in order to remember it, to develop strategies for attacking problems, and to rehearse what we have learned. We agree with Hutson that while problems of reading are multifaceted, one of their important dimensions is the use of language.

Teaching Reading

In more than 30 years of research and teaching reading, no single approach has been found to overcome or eliminate reading disabilities in children at the first grade level (Lohnes, 1973). Studies of teaching methods find a quagmire of unrelated theories, methods, and poor research designs. Chall (1970) summarizes research from 1910 to 1965, and Diederich (1973) from 1960 to 1970. Chall points out that in many studies the authors have failed to specify the minimum amount of information expected from the research. Thus, they frequently have not discussed on what basis children were assigned to various educational treatment conditions, the length or nature of the instruction given, how the teachers were selected, much less whether the teachers used those teaching methods assigned to them. Diederich points out that there is more research on reading than on any other subject taught in school, more than 1,000 studies each year. In spite of this tremendous effort and cost, Diederich argues that there are *no* important facts about methods of teaching reading that are incontestable.

Moreover, the research on teacher characteristics associated with good reading programs has likewise failed to yield many significant results. The reported findings lead to the conclusions that teacher training may well be unrelated to teacher effectiveness and that bright, friendly people are better at teaching than dull, disagreeable ones (Diederich, 1973).

Holistic and Subskills Techniques

While the data pertaining to the best method of teaching reading has been equivocal, it is obvious that most children do learn to read and they do so under a variety of teaching techniques. The issue is not whether the child can be taught to read—after all, millions of children can—but just what is the best method to do so. For years there has been controversy, in the United States and elsewhere, as to how best to teach reading (Samuels and Schachter, 1978). The dispute has focused on two disparate approaches, the holistic and the subskill techniques. These perspectives yield very different notions as to the nature of learning to read.

The holistic view, characterized by the works of Goodman and Goodman (1976), is based on the idea that reading and speaking are both processes of meaningful communication; that reading is the obtaining of meaning from someone else's written word. The unit of instruction then should be that which carries meaning, whether phrases, sentences, or paragraphs. Those holding this view also believe that the teacher should use the child's own language and experiences to initiate reading instruction, thus increasing the meaningfulness of the printed material. As yet, while the approach of the Goodmans to teaching reading has been well spelled out, studies concerning its efficacy are not yet available.

The subskill perspective, represented by the work of Samuels and coworkers (Samuels and Jeffrey, 1966; Samuels, 1973; Samuels and Schachter, 1978), approaches reading as a complex skill comprised of various subskills (for example, phonics, symbol learning) that must be mastered first before adequate reading is achieved. It is believed that these subskills must be first taught, mastered, and integrated, before concern about meaningfulness of the material is needed. Proponents of the holistic approach accept the notion of subskill mastery but generally believe that these are important only when the child evidences problems.

Factors in Successful Teaching

While the particular method that is best for teaching reading is still unknown, there are some hints as to the factors in successful teaching. Apparently programs that include phonics instruction yield better results than those employing whole-word methods (Diederich, 1973). Samuels and Schachter (1978) have suggested that reading programs with the following features are likely to be more successful than programs lacking them. These features are

1. teachers trained in the instructional method
2. clearly stated and achievable objectives
3. teaching on an individual basis or in small groups
4. highly organized, preplanned lessons
5. much time and effort spent by teachers and children in reading instruction
6. continuous assessments of progress

What about teaching dyslexic children to read? Since we have little in-depth knowledge of what makes for effective reading instruction, it will come as no surprise that our ignorance extends from teaching of normal children to teaching the learning disabled. Strategies for teaching reading have been developed on the basis of tests like the ITPA. Programs have been advanced urging the teacher to match the instructional method to the individual's strengths or weaknesses (Johnson and Myklebust, 1967; Hammill and Bartel, 1975). However, these exhortations are based upon clinical experience and intuition, not systematic and controlled research. While such ideas are valuable resources for hypotheses that should and will be tested, they are not adequate proof of the effectiveness of these instructional strategies. As yet the field of learning disabilities has not developed strategies of teaching reading that have been empirically validated, nor have any teaching strategies been isolated as being more effective for learning disabled than other children.

Mathematics and Arithmetic Disabilities

A second product problem encountered among learning disabled children involves arithmetic and mathematics. Children who have severe difficulty in mastering mathematical concepts and/or computations are referred to as *dyscalculics*, the condition being called **dyscalculia.** Like dyslexia, early notions concerning such problems were generated within the medical model and led to hypotheses about a breakdown in functions of the central nervous system.

In general, it is thought that children who have difficulty learning to read do not have comparable difficulties learning mathematics, and conversely, children struggling to learn mathematics will not necessarily have problems with reading (Johnson and Myklebust, 1967; Kosc, 1974). There thus have been attempts to develop a taxonomy of learning disability syndromes in which dyscalculia is a problem distinct from dyslexia. While these two problems may be somewhat distinct, there may well be an overlap of skills necessary for competence in both reading and mathematics. To the degree that this is so, it is unlikely that these problems will be entirely independent of each other. Chalfant and Scheffelin (1969), in discussing the basic skills needed by the child to succeed in mathematics, do suggest an overlap of necessary abilities between mathematics and reading. One essential characteristic, they say, is intelligence, or those skills tapped by intelligence tests. General intelligence is probably the best known predictor of success in mathematics. A second major factor appears to be spatial ability, the "ability to comprehend the nature of elements within a visual stimulus pattern" (p. 121). A third factor is the child's verbal ability. Mathematics is a form of language and any language deficit may affect the learning of its symbols and operations. A fourth skill is the child's approach to problem solving, the method by which the child compares and organizes data prior to working the problem. Finally, these authors suggest neurophysiological processes that may impede the acquisition of mathematical skills.

Types and Characteristics of Children with Mathematic Product Problems

Children who have severe difficulty learning mathematics have not drawn researchers' attention as much as children with dyslexia. However, while research efforts on these two problems have not been parallel, theorizing about them has. Hence, problems with mathematics are often considered to reflect brain dysfunctions, dysfunctions that differ, however, from those disrupting language and reading development. It has been presumed that dyscalculia reflects disturbances in the nondominant right hemisphere of the brain, while dyslexia is thought to be an outcropping of trauma to the left hemisphere (Johnson and Myklebust, 1967).

Children with dyscalculia have been described as not grasping spatial relationships or mastering number concepts (Kaliski, 1967). Such children are said to exhibit impulsivity and motor disinhibition, both of which are presumed to impair severely their ability to learn arithmetic. Confusion about left-right directions is also thought to be evident, as well as **perseveration,** the inability to shift psychological sets or attention. Finally, Kaliski indicates that dyscalculic children will have language difficulties that prevent adequate mastery of mathematics.

Kosc (1974) has presented an extended taxonomy of dyscalculia in which he suggests the following terms be adopted:

1. *Verbal dyscalculia.* Difficulty in understanding mathematics when presented orally or under conditions in which a verbal response is required.
2. *Practognostic dyscalculia.* Inability to manipulate objects adequately, symbolic or otherwise, for purposes of arithmetic.
3. *Lexical dyscalculia.* Problems in reading mathematical symbols, such as number or operation signs.
4. *Graphical dyscalculia.* Difficulty in writing mathematical symbols.
5. *Ideognostical dyscalculia.* Difficulty in understanding mathematical ideas and relationships, and in doing calculations.
6. *Operational dyscalculia.* Difficulty in carrying out operations. Thus, the child may add when subtraction is called for, divide rather than multiply.

It is distressing to report that the amount of systematically gathered information on childhood dyscalculia is small. The characteristics described in this section are based upon clinical observation and have rarely been demonstrated by more rigorous methods. Indeed, even the data presented by Kosc were such as to suggest that distinct types of dyscalculia were not found. Moreover, the frequency of problems experienced by dyscalculic children have rarely been compared with those of nondisabled children. Aside from clinical observations, we are rather in the dark about the nature of this problem.

While data on how to help children with arithmetic problems are sparse, some are available. Smith and Lovitt (1973, 1976) have conducted several investigations concerning the effect of reinforcements on children's performance in arithmetic. They found that reinforcements are effective in improving mathematics performance, but only when the child already possesses the mathematics skills necessary for the solution. Before this stage, reinforcements do not appear to affect the child's performance. Their results indicate that once children have the prerequisite skills for mathematics, reinforcements for competent performance can increase the likelihood that the child will combine subskills in attacking the mathematical problem.

We have discussed the learning disabled children's difficulties in arithmetic and reading, but have not mentioned their possible problems in other academic areas, such as spelling and writing. We have neglected other possible product problems for a simple reason: Very little is known about them, and hence there is very little to write. Learning disabled children probably do frequently exhibit more than one product problem, and our lack of discussion about them should not be interpreted to mean that they are of no importance or do not exist. It is likely that as the field of learning disabilities expands, so will the research efforts addressed to problems such as writing and spelling. At this point, however, we can only say that such problems are likely to be evidenced by many learning disabled children.

But product and process problems are not the only ones experienced by the learning disabled child. Unfortunately, these children frequently struggle with social problems as well. We now turn to a discussion of the social experiences and interactions of the learning disabled child.

SOCIAL BEHAVIORS OF THE LEARNING DISABLED

In the following section, we present some information about how the social experiences of the learning disabled child may differ from those of the nondisabled one. Before doing so, however, it should be noted that many of the problems in developing adequate social relationships associated with the learning disabled child might well be experienced by many children who are exceptional in other ways.

Parents' Observations

There are now several studies of the social behaviors and personality traits of learning disabled children as viewed by their parents. Wender (1971) has categorized clinical data on children diagnosed as having minimal cerebral dysfunction. This researcher summarizes the parents' view of their preschool learning disabled child as that of an infant "King Kong," a perennial two-year-old who is active and unintentionally destructive.

Support for parts of Wender's results is obtained from a study by Owen et al. (1971). They found that, in general, mothers of learning disabled children described them as having less verbal ability, less ability to control their impulses, and more anxiety than their siblings or other nonhandicapped children. Likewise, Strag (1972) found that parents characterized their learning disabled children as showing less consideration for others, less ability to receive affection, and more clingingness than did the parents of normal children. The ratings of learning disabled children evaluated by their parents were then compared with those of mentally retarded youngsters evaluated by *their* parents. In this aspect of the study, the learning disabled children were seen as less stubborn but more clinging, demonstrating greater jealousy, and being less able to accept affection than the mentally retarded youngster.

While not all learning disabled children can be so characterized, the fact that many can should be clearly recognized. While this has been virtually unexplored, there seems little reason to doubt that living with a learning disabled child may produce considerable stress and strain on the family unit.

Teachers' Observations

Surprisingly few studies have been conducted on teachers' perceptions of the behavior of learning disabled children. Recently, however, some investigations addressed to this issue have been reported. Myklebust, Boshes, Olson, and

Cole (1969) reported that teachers rated learning disabled children lower than their more competent classmates in the following behaviors: cooperativeness, attentiveness, ability to organize themselves, ability to cope with new situations, social acceptability to teachers, acceptance of responsibility, and tact. These results were essentially replicated by Bryan and McGrady (1972). Keogh, Tchir, and Windeguth-Behn (1974) found that 66 percent of teachers associated high aggressiveness with learning disabled children, while over 40 percent felt that these children were withdrawn, had no sense of responsibility or self-discipline, and had poor interpersonal relationships. Learning disabled children are thus seen by many teachers as lacking adequate social skills and internal behavior control.

Peers' Observations

So far we have seen that many learning disabled children tend to be viewed negatively by parents and teachers. How do their peers see them? Bryan has conducted a number of studies concerning this question. To answer the question, Bryan (1974a) employed a sociometric test consisting of items designed to assess both a child's popularity and rejection by others. It was found that the learning disabled child was less popular and significantly more rejected by peers than the nondisabled child. While peers did not view learning disabled children as hyperactive, they did judge them to be more worried and frightened, sadder, less clean and neat, less attractive physically, and more ignored socially than nondisabled children. Peer assessments of the same children were made one year later in order to determine the degree to which the learning disabled child's status with peers remained stable over time (Bryan, 1976). Status did remain stable as, once again, these learning disabled children were more rejected and less accepted by their peers than the competent children.

The data are consistent that many learning disabled children are likely to be rejected by or in conflict with parents, teacher, and peers. Some may well be rejected by virtually all of the significant people with whom they come in contact. As yet we know little about the bases of this rejection, although studies toward this end are now being undertaken.

Factors in Rejection of Learning Disabled

While there are no doubt many factors that might contribute to the social rejection of the learning disabled child, one starting point is the child's ability to understand others. Bryan (1977) completed a study in which an assessment was made of the learning disabled child's ability to discriminate the affective states of another. For this purpose, she employed a test devised by Robert Rosenthal and colleagues that consists of a film and audio tape depicting an adult female expressing either positive or negative feelings combined with dominant or submissive expressions. Taking care to ensure that the child understood the questionnaire by which to indicate his or her understanding of the adult's affect, Bryan found that learning disabled children were less able to describe accurately the scenario than their nondisabled peers. Many disabled children apparently have more difficulty in understanding subtle communications concerning emotions than do other children. Moreover, these children's difficulties in interpreting nonverbal social communications appear to persist into their adolescence. Wiig and Harris (1974) projected for learning disabled and nondisabled adolescents a videotape of a young female's nonverbal expressions of anger, embarrassment, fear, frustration, joy, and love. They report that the handicapped adolescents made more errors than the nonhandicapped subjects; moreover their errors were rather extreme in nature. When nonhandicapped adolescents committed errors, they seem to be age-specific errors, such as substituting the emotion of embarrassment for the display of love. But the errors made by the learning disabled adolescents were more gross, for example, labeling positive emotions negative. Interestingly, the special education teachers rated the children who scored low on this test as also being poor in adaptive social behaviors within the classroom.

To what degree the inability to read nonverbal communications of affect might be tied to the learning disabled child's interpersonal difficulties with parents, teachers, and peers remains to be determined. These findings provide a lead to future possibilities for remediation efforts. The evidence indicates that many of the problems experienced by the learning disabled child involve interpersonal deficiencies. Learning disabled children not only suffer from academic failure; many carry an additional burden of social failure.

Teachers' and Peers' Behavior toward the Learning Disabled

So far we have discussed evidence concerning people's attitudes toward the learning disabled child. The attitudes are such that one would expect teachers, peers, and parents to show their disapproval. While there have been few investigations of parental interactions with the disabled child, some studies are now available concerning teachers' and peers' treatment of such children.

Bryan (1974b) observed teacher and peer interactions of learning disabled and nondisabled children over a period of five days. She reported that these groups of children did not differ in the proportion of time they spent interacting with teachers and peers. There were, however, very significant differences in the patterns of interactions involving a nondisabled child. The teacher was found to respond to the nondisabled child over 75 percent of the time; she responded to the learning disabled youngster less than half of the time. Whatever the reason for the lack of teacher responsiveness, the result may be to foster alienation between the child and instructor. Moreover, when the teacher did interact with children from both groups, the nature of the relationship differed for the two. About 50 percent of the time that the teacher interacted with the learning disabled child was devoted to help with academic work. The communications between them were often formal or tutorial. On the other hand, most interactions between teacher and nondisabled children involved sending them on errands, asking them to help in organizing games or to help other students, and other essentially nonacademic matters. Nor were the differences limited only to these matters. The reinforcements and reproofs given to the two groups by their teachers were different. While the learning disabled children received as many positive reinforcements (that is, praise and other signs of approval) as did the nondisabled ones, they also were scolded and criticized more.

Peer interactions among learning disabled children have also been investigated. Bryan (1974b) has reported that while the learning disabled did not differ from other children in the amount of peer interactions in which they engaged, they were more likely to be ignored by their peers when they initiated contact than were comparison children. Bryan (1978) also reported the findings of several additional studies addressed to this issue. Although social communications apparently depend upon sex, race, and academic status, and are affected in a complex fashion by these factors, it does appear likely that many learning disabled children make and receive more hostile statements than do children who are functioning adequately in school.

Analysis of classroom interactions, then, suggests the social life of many learning disabled children is rather different from that of other children. These girls and boys are more often ignored when attempting to initiate a social interaction, are less likely to be involved with the teacher on nonacademic matters, and get more reproofs from the teacher than their nondisabled classmates.

Most remedial efforts are devoted to correcting the learning disabled child's reading and arithmetic failures. There has been little effort to develop interventions for those children who experience social failure. This is perhaps justified, depending on one's values and resources. However, ignorance of the findings that many learning disabled children are experiencing social difficulties is not justifiable. There is no question that such problems exist; parents, teachers, and psychologists should be aware of them.

SUMMARY

The number of children deemed learning disabled is great, the legislation relevant to them extensive, and the amount of money, time, and effort devoted to aiding them is large. The learning disabled child is not just outside the arena of the handicapped, but has both feet squarely planted in it. The field is young but is growing with considerable rapidity. Its historical traditions have been rooted in the medical profession, while its contemporary emphasis is increasingly on educational models. What are some of the problems and findings that now confront learning disability specialists?

A major problem in this field is the definition of learning disabilities. On the one hand, definitions focusing upon physiological trauma or dysfunctions have been set aside, and in their stead is an emphasis upon the discrepancy between academic achievement and potential. The discrepancy definition, on the other hand, can be criticized on various grounds, including the meaning and measurement of the term potential, and the definition's overinclusiveness, lumping together as it does children with many very different difficulties. A second, related issue is the ever-increasing overlap in functions among several professional groups. To the degree that the medical model is forsaken for the educational one, then just how different are the obligations and competencies of the learning disability specialist from those of the reading expert and other types of academic specialists? A third problem concerns the lack of systematic research pertaining to children defined as learning disabled. This problem is understandable given the newness of the field but that does not lessen its impact. Facts and fashions are likely to wax and wane, and with them will fluctuate the hopes and despairs of learning disabled children and their parents. No doubt time and research will turn some fads into facts and eliminate others as myths. Until a body of knowledge is developed, the learning disability specialist must assume a stance of humility.

What does the research seem to show up to this point? First, the data pertaining to perceptual information processing is rather complex and open to a variety of interpretations. By and large, if poor visual information processing does characterize the learning disabled, it appears to be the case only with relatively young children. Learning disabled children over 10 years of age are unlikely to demonstrate marked inadequacies in the understanding and processing of visually presented material. When nondisabled and disabled children are found to perform differently on tasks presumably assessing visual information processing, such differences might be better explained by other interpretations, such as instructional, attentional, and/or motivational features of the testing situation. The same problem of interpretation arises when discussing auditory information processing. The research is fairly consistent in indicating that many learning disabled children are less competent in dealing with spoken material than are nondisabled youngsters. However, auditory information processing is likely to require and depend upon verbal skills, skills that many learning disabled children lack.

Matters are no more simple when we turn to the question of whether these children have particular problems involving the integration of information presented through two or more sensory modalities. While the hypothesis of cross-modal information processing deficits is a popular one among specialists in this field, empirical support for it is sparse. First, some researchers failed to test whether the children employed in their studies have adequate processing within a particular modality. Hence, findings concerning failure in cross-modality information processing may reflect, in fact, failure to understand and process information within one sensory system. Moreover, adequate performance on tasks of cross-modal integration also depends on language and verbal skills and so findings are subject to this interpretation.

There seems reason to believe that learning disabled children, at least boys, have language deficits. First, their scores on standardized intelligence tests are often lower than those of the nondisabled children with whom they are paired (Bryan and Bryan, 1978). Second, the studies of language skills of these children find them less adept than well-functioning children on a wide variety of measures and do so across various age spans. Measures such as vocabulary, fluency, sentence development, storytelling, and discriminating declarative sentences from questions pinpoint differences between the learning disabled and nondisabled child. Further, such differences are likely to be found not only during the children's early childhood years, but also as late as the adolescent period.

There is evidence gained both in the naturalistic and laboratory setting that many learning disabled children may have attentional problems. Children considered learning disabled spend less time attending to schoolroom tasks (Bryan and Wheeler, 1972; Bryan, 1974b), find it difficult to select the relevant stimuli on which to focus, and are less able to sustain attention on a long, boring task than their more capable peers.

By definition, children with learning disabilities demonstrate severe academic problems. While these problems may consist of arithmetic, reading, writing, and spelling deficits, most researchers have focused primarily upon the study of children with reading problems. As yet, there does not appear to be a highly developed effective technology for teaching of reading. We do not know, as yet, the best method for aiding children with reading problems.

Finally, there is abundant evidence that the learning disabled child lives in a social world markedly different from that of the nondisabled one, that the child with serious learning problems is rejected by others. Whether one assesses the attitudes or the behaviors of teachers and peers, a consistent finding is that the disabled child is one who is often ignored, often the subject of hostile and demeaning exchanges. From parents' reports it would seem that many experience stresses, strains, and negative feelings toward their learning disabled boys and girls.

REFERENCES

Anderson, R. P., Holcomb, C. G., & Doyle, R. B. The measurement of attentional deficits. *Exceptional Children*, 1973, *39*, 534–539.

Barsch, R. H. Achieving perceptual motor efficiency. Seattle, Washington: *Special Child Publication*, 1967.

Beery, K., & Buktencia, N. *Developmental test of visual-motor integration*. Chicago, Ill.: Follett Publishing Co., 1967.

Bender, L. A visual motor gestalt test and its clinical use. *American Orthopsychiatry Association*, Research Monograph, 1938, No. 3.

Birch, H. G., & Belmont, L. Auditory-visual integration, intelligence, and reading ability in school children. *Perceptual and Motor Skills*, 1965, *20*, 295–305.

Blank, M., Weider, S., & Bridger, W. H. Verbal deficiencies in abstract thinking in early reading retardation. *American Journal of Orthopsychiatry*, 1968, *38*, 823–834.

Boder, E. Developmental dyslexia: Prevailing diagnostic concepts and a new diagnostic approach. In H. R. Myklebust (Ed.), *Progress in learning disabilities* (Vol. 2). New York: Grune & Stratton, 1971.

Boyd, J. E. Teaching children with reading problems. In D. Hammill and N. Bartel (Eds.), *Teaching children with learning and behavior problems.* Boston, Mass.: Allyn and Bacon, 1975.

Bruininks, R., Glaman, G., & Clark, C. *Prevalence of learning disabilities: Findings, issues, and recommendations.* Research Report #20, Department of Health, Education, and Welfare, June, 1971.

Bryan, T. Peer popularity of learning disabled children. *Journal of Learning Disabilities,* 1974a, *7,* 304–309.

Bryan, T. An observational analysis of classroom behaviors of children with learning disabilities. *Journal of Learning Disabilities,* 1974b, *7,* 26–34.

Bryan, T. Peer popularity of learning disabled children: A replication. *Journal of Learning Disabilities,* 1976, *9,* 307–311.

Bryan, T. Children's comprehension of nonverbal communication. *Journal of Learning Disabilities,* 1977a, *10,* 501–506.

Bryan, T. Social relationships and verbal interactions of learning disabled children in the classroom. *Journal of Learning Disabilities,* 1978, *22,* 107–115.

Bryan, T. H., & Bryan, J. H. *Understanding learning disabilities.* Sherman Oaks, Calif.: Alfred Publishing Co., 1978.

Bryan, T., & McGrady, H. J. Use of a teacher rating scale. *Journal of Learning Disabilities,* 1972, *5,* 199–206.

Bryan, T., & Pflaum, S. *Linguistic, social and cognitive analyses of children's interactions.* Paper presented at the meeting of the Association for Children with Learning Disabilities, Kansas City, March 1978.

Bryan, T., & Wheeler, R. Perception of children with learning disabilities: The eye of the observer. *Journal of Learning Disabilities,* 1972, *5,* 484–488.

Carroll, J. B. Review of the Illinois test of psycholinguistics. In O. K. Buros, (Ed.), *The seventh mental measurement yearbook.* Highland Park, N.J.: The Gryphon Press, 1972, pp. 819–823.

Chalfant, J., & Scheffelin, M. Central processing dysfunctions in children: A review of research. NINDS Monograph No. 9. Bethesda, Md.: U.S. Department of Health, Education, and Welfare, 1969.

Chall, J. *Learning to read: The great debate.* New York: McGraw-Hill Book Co., 1970.

Chissom, B. S. Review of Frostig DTVP. In Buros, O. K. (Ed.), *The seventh mental measurements yearbook.* Highland Park, N.J.: The Gryphon Press, 1972, pp. 1273–1274.

Christoplos, R., & Renz, P. A critical examination of special education programs. *Journal of Special Education,* 1969, *3,* 317–379.

Clements, S. D. Minimal brain dysfunction in children. (NINDS Monograph No. 3, Public Health Service Bulletin #1415). Washington, D.C.: U.S. Government Printing Office, 1966.

Cratty, B. *Perceptual-motor behavior and educational processes.* Springfield, Ill.: Charles C. Thomas, 1969.

Cruickshank, W. M. The psychoeducational match. In W. M. Cruickshank & D. P. Hallahan (Eds.), *Perceptual and learning disabilities in children.* Syracuse, N.Y.: Syracuse University Press, 1975, 71–112.

DeHirsch, K., Jansky, J., & Langford, Q. *Predicting reading failure*. New York: Harper & Row, 1966.

Dicarlo, L. M. Differential diagnosis of congenital aphasiz. *Volta Review*, 1960, *62*, 361–364.

Diederich, P. B. Research 1960–1970 on methods and materials in reading. *Eric Clearing House on Tests, Measurement & Evaluation*, Princeton, N.J.: Educational Testing Service, 1973.

Division for Children with Learning Disabilities. *Newsletter*, 1973, *3*, No. 1.

Doehring, D. G., & Rabinovitch, M. S. Auditory abilities of children with learning problems. *Journal of Learning Disabilities*, 1969, *2*, 467–475.

Doyle, R. B., Anderson, R. P., & Holcomb, C. G. Attention deficits and the effects of visual distraction. *Journal of Learning Disabilities*, 1976, *9*, 48–54.

Dunn, L. M. *Peabody picture vocabulary test*. Minneapolis, Minn.: American Guidance Service, 1959.

Dykman, R. A., Ackerman, P. T., Clements, S. D., & Peters, J. E. Specific learning disabilities: An attentional deficit syndrome. In H. R. Myklebust (Ed.), *Progress in learning disabilities* (Vol. 2). New York: Grune & Stratton, 1971.

Estes, R. E., & Huizinga, R. J. A comparison of visual and auditory presentations of a paired-associate learning task with learning disabled children. *Journal of Learning Disabilities*, 1974, *7*, 35–42.

Federal Register, 41, No. 230, November 1976.

Freides, D. Human information processing and sensory modality: Cross-modal functions, information complexity, memory and deficit. *Psychological Bulletin*, 1974, *81*, 284–310.

Frostig, M., & Horne, D. *The Frostig program for the development of visual perception*. Chicago, Ill.: Follett Publishing Co., 1964.

Fry, M. A., Johnson, C. A., & Muehl, S. Oral language production in relation to reading achievement among select second grades. In D. V. Bakker and P. Satz (Eds.), *Specific reading disability*. Rotterdam, Netherlands: Rotterdam University Press, 1970.

Goffman, E., *Asylums*. New York: Anchor Books, Doubleday & Company, Inc., 1961.

Goodman, K., & Goodman, Y. *Learning to read is natural*. Paper presented at Conference on Theory and Practice of Beginning Reading Instruction. Pittsburgh, April 1976.

Goyen, J. D., & Lyle, J. G. Effect of incentives and age on the visual recognition of retarded readers. *Journal of Experimental Child Psychology*, 1971a, *11*, 266–273.

Goyen, J. D. & Lyle, J. G. Effect of incentives upon retarded and normal readers on a visual-associate learning task. *Journal of Experimental Child Psychology*, 1971b, *11*, 274–280.

Graham, F. K., Ernhart, C. G., Thurston, D., & Craft, M. Development three years after perinatal anoxia and other potentially damaging newborn experiences. *Psychological Monographs*, 1962, *76* (No. 3).

Hallahan, D. P., & Reeve, R. E. Selective attention and distractibility. In B. K. Keogh (Ed.), *Advances in special education* (Vol. 1). Greenwich, Conn.: J.A.I. Press, in press.

Hammill, D. Learning disabilities: A problem in definition. *Division for Children with Learning Disabilities Newsletter,* 1974, *4,* 28–31.

Hammill, D. D., & Bartel, N. R. (Eds.). *Teaching children with learning and behavior problems.* Boston: Allyn & Bacon, 1975.

Helveston, E. M. *The Role of the Ophthalmologist in Dyslexia.* Dayton, Ohio: Institute for Development of Educational Activities, Inc., 1969.

Hobbs, N. *The futures of children.* San Francisco: Jossey-Bass, 1975.

Hutson, B. A. Language factors in reading disability. Paper presented at the American Educational Research Association, Chicago, Ill., April, 1974.

Jamison, C. B. Review of *The Purdue Perceptual-Motor Survey.* In O. K. Buros, (Ed.), *The seventh mental measurement yearbook.* Highland Park, N.J.: The Gryphon Press, 1972, pp. 874–875.

Johnson, D., & Myklebust, H. R. *Learning disabilities.* New York: Grune & Stratton, 1967.

Jones, R. Labels and stigma in special education. *Exceptional Children,* 1972, *38,* 553–564.

Kagan, J. Reflection-impulsivity and reading ability in primary grade children. *Child Development,* 1965, *36,* 609–628.

Kagan, J., & Kogan, N. Individual variation in cognitive processes. In Paul H. Mussen (Ed.), *Carmichael's manual of child psychology* (Vol. 1). New York: John Wiley & Sons, 1970.

Kagan, J., Rosman, B. L., Day, D., Albert, J., & Philips, W. Information processing in the child: Signficance of analytic and reflective attitudes. *Psychological Monographs,* 1964, *78,* (1, Whds No. 578).

Kaliski, L. Arithmetic and the brain-injured child. In E. C. Frierson & W. B. Barbe (Eds.), *Educating children with learning disabilities.* New York: Appleton-Century-Crofts, 1967.

Keogh, B. K. *Attentional characteristics of children with learning disabilities.* Paper presented at the International Symposium on Learning Disabilities, San Diego, Calif.: November 1973.

Keogh, B. K., & Donlon, G. Field dependence, impulsivity, and learning disabilities. *Journal of Learning Disabilities,* 1972, *5,* 331–336.

Keogh, B. K., & Margolis, J. Learn to labor and to wait: Attentional problems of children with learning disorders. *Journal of Learning Disabilities,* 1976, *9,* 276–286.

Keogh, B. K., Tchir, C., & Windeguth-Behn, A. Teacher's perceptions of educationally high risk children. *Journal of Learning Disabilities,* 1974, *7,* 367–374.

Kephart, N. C. *The brain-injured child in the classroom.* Chicago: National Society for Crippled Children and Adults, 1963.

Kessen, W., Haith, M. M., & Salapatek, P. H. Infancy. In Paul H. Mussen (Ed.), *Carmichael's manual of child psychology* (Vol. 1). New York: John Wiley & Sons, 1970.

Kinsbourne, M. *Perceptual learning determines beginning reading.* Paper presented at the meetings of the Eastern Psychology Association, Philadelphia, Pa.: 1973.

Kirk, S. Introduction to state of the art: Where are we in learning disabilities? *Disabilities and California Association for Neurologically Handicapped Children Publications,* Los Angeles, 1974.

Kirk, S. A., McCarthy, J. J., & Kirk, W. D. *Illinois test of psycholinguistic abilities* (rev. ed.), Urbana, Ill.: University Press, 1968.

Koppitz, E. *The Bender-Gestalt test for young children.* New York: Grune & Stratton, 1964.

Kosc, L. Developmental dyslexia. *Journal of Learning Disabilities,* 1974, *7,* 165–177.

Kukic, S. J. The Washington Scene. *Division for Children with Learning Disabilities Newsletter,* 1976, *4.*

Landis, D. Review of *The Purdue Perceptual-Motor Survey.* In O. K. Buros, (Ed.), *The seventh mental measurement yearbook.* Highland Park, N.J.: The Gryphon Press, 1972, p. 875.

Lawson, L. J. Opthalmological factors in learning disabilities. In H. R. Myklebust (Ed.), *Progress in learning disabilities* (Vol. 1). New York: Grune & Stratton, 1968, 147–181.

Lee, L. L. A screening test for syntax development. *Journal of Speech and Hearing Disorders,* 1970, *35,* 103–112.

Lee, L. L. *Developmental sentence analysis.* Evanston, Ill.: Northwestern University Press, 1974.

Lohnes, P. R. Evaluating the schooling of intelligence. *Educational Researcher,* 1973, *2,* 6–11.

London, P. The end of ideology in behavior modification. *American Psychologist,* 1972, *27,* 913–920.

Lyle, J. G. Performance of retarded readers on the Memory-801-Designs test. *Perceptual and Motor Skills,* 1968, *26,* 851–854.

Lyle, J. G. Reading retardation and reversal tendency: A factorial study. *Child Development,* 1969, *40,* 833–843.

Lyle, J. G., & Goyen, J. D. Visual recognition, developmental lag, and strephosymbolia in reading retardation. *Journal of Abnormal Psychology,* 1968, *73,* 25–29.

Lyle, J. G., & Goyen, J. D. *Effect of speed of exposure and difficulty of discrimination upon visual recognition of retarded readers.* Unpublished manuscript, 1974.

Masland, R. L. Children with minimal brain dysfunction—a national problem. In L. Tarnopol (Ed.), *Learning disabilities.* Springfield, Ill.: Charles C. Thomas, 1969.

McReynolds, L. V. Operant conditioning for investigating speech sound discrimination in aphasic children. *Journal of Speech and Hearing Research,* 1966, *9,* 519–528.

Menyuk, P. Syntactic structures in the language of children. *Child Development,* 1963, *34,* 407–422.

Mercer, J. R. *Sociological perspectives on mild mental retardation.* Paper delivered at Inaugural Peabody—NIMH Conference on Socio-Cultural Aspects of Mental Retardation. Nashville, Tenn., 1968.

Messer, S. B. Reflection-impulsivity: A review. *Psychological Bulletin,* 1976, *83,* 1026–1052.

Myklebust, H. R., Boshes, B., Olson, D., & Cole, C. *Minimal brain damage in children* (Contract 108-65-142), Final Report, U.S. Public Health Service, 1969.

Newcomer, P. L., & Hammill, D. D. ITPA and academic achievement: A survey. *The Reading Teacher*, 1975, *28*, 731–741.

Noland, E. C., & Schuldt, W. J. Sustained attention and reading retardation. *Journal of Experimental Education*, 1971, *40*, 73–76.

Nunnally, J. C. *Popular conceptions of mental health, their development and change.* New York: Holt, Rinehart & Winston, 1961.

Owen, R. W., Adams, P. A., Forrest, T., Stolz, L. M., & Fisher, S. Learning disorders in children: Sibling studies. *Monographs of the Society for Research in Child Development*, 1971, *36*, No. 144.

Palermo, D. S., & Molfese, D. L. Language acquisition from age five onward. *Psychological Bulletin*, 1972, *78*, 409–428.

Rabinovitch, R. D., & Ingram, W. Neuropsychiatric considerations in reading retardation. *The Reading Teacher*, 1962, *15*, 433–438.

Reichstein, J., & Rosenstein, J. Differential diagnosis of auditory defects: A review of the literature. *Exceptional Children*, 1964, *31*, 73.

Roach, E., & Kephart, N. C. *Purdue Perceptual-Motor Survey.* Columbus, O.: Charles E. Merrill, 1966.

Rosner, J. Language arts and arithmetic achievement, and specifically related perceptual skills. *American Educational Research Journal*, 1973, *10*, 59–68.

Ross, D. M., & Ross, S. A. The efficacy of listening training for educable mentally retarded children. *American Journal of Mental Deficiency*, 1972, *77*, 137–142.

Samuels, S. J. Effect of distinctive feature training on paired associate learning. *Journal of Educational Psychology*, 1973, *64*, 164–170.

Samuels, S. J., & Jeffrey, W. F. Initial discriminability of words and its effect on transfer in learning to read. *Journal of Educational Psychology*, 1966, *57*, 337–340.

Samuels, S. J., & Schachter, S. W. Controversial issues in beginning reading instruction: Meaning versus sub-skill emphasis. In S. W. Pflaum (Ed.), *Evolving issues in reading.* National Society for the Study of Education. San Francisco: McCutchan, 1978.

Sartain, H. W. Instruction of disabled learners: A reading perspective. *Journal of Learning Disabilities*, 1976, *9*, 489–497.

Scheff, T. J. *Being mentally ill: A sociological theory.* Chicago: Aldine, 1966.

Seaver, W. B. Effects of naturally induced teacher-expectancies. *Journal of Personality and Social Psychology*, 1973, *28*, 333–342.

Semel, E. M., & Wiig, E. H. Comprehension of syntactic structures and critical verbal elements by children with learning disabilities. *Journal of Learning Disabilities*, 1975, *8*, 46–52.

Senf, G. M., & Freundl, P. C. Memory and attention factors in specific learning disabilities. *Journal of Learning Disabilities*, 1971, *4*, 94–106.

Smith, D. D., & Lovitt, T. C. The use of modeling techniques to influence the acquisition of computational arithmetic skills in learning-disabled children. In E. Ramp & G. Semb (Eds.), *Behavior Analysis*, Englewood Cliffs, N.J. Prentice-Hall, 1973.

Smith, D. D., & Lovitt, T. C. The differential effects of reinforcement contingencies on arithmetic performance. *Journal of Learning Disabilities*, 1976, *9*, 21–29.

Strag, G. A. Comparative behavioral ratings of parents with severe mentally retarded, special learning disability, and normal children. *Journal of Learning Disabilities*, 1972, *5*, 631–635.

Strauss, A., & Lehtinen, L. *Psychopathology and Education of the Brain-Injured Child.* New York: Grune & Stratton, 1947.

Vellutino, F. R. Alternative conceptualizations of dyslexia: Evidence in support of a verbal-deficit hypothesis. *Harvard Educational Review*, 1977, *47*, 334–354.

Vellutino, F. R., Pruzek, R. M., Steger, J. A., & Meshoulam, V. Immediate visual recall in poor and normal readers as a function of orthographic-linguistic familiarity. *Cortex*, 1973, *9*, 368–384.

Vallutino, F. R., Steger, J. A., & Kandel, G. Reading disability: An investigation of the perceptual deficit hypothesis. *Cortex*, 1972, *8*, 106–118.

Vogel, S. A. Syntactic abilities in normal and dyslexic children. *Journal of Learning Disabilities*, 1974, 103–109.

Vogel, S. A. Morphological ability in normal and dyslexic children. *Journal of Learning Disabilities*, 1977, *10*, 35–43.

Weinstein, R., & Rabinovitch, R. O. Sentence structure and retention in good and poor readers. *Journal of Educational Psychology*, 1971, *62*, 25–30.

Wender, H. *Minimal brain dysfunction in children.* New York: Wiley-Interscience, 1971.

Wepman, J. M. *Auditory discrimination test.* Chicago: Language Research Association, 1958.

Werner, E. E., Honzik, M. P., & Smith, R. S. Predictions of intelligence and achievement at 10 years from 20 months pediatric and psychologic examinations. *Child Development*, 1968, *39*, 1063–1075.

Wiig, E. H., & Harris, S. P. Perception and interpretation of nonverbally expressed emotions by adolescents with learning disabilities. *Perceptual and Motor Skills*, 1974, *38*, 239–245.

Wiig, E. H., & Semel, E. M. Productive language abilities in learning-disabled adolescents. *Journal of Learning Disabilities*, 1975, *8*, 578–588.

Wiig, E. H., & Semel, E. M. *Language Disabilities in Children and Adolescents.* Columbus, O.: Merrill, 1976.

Wiig, E. H., Semel, E. M., & Crouse, M. A. B. The use of English morphology by high-risk and learning-disabled children. *Journal of Learning Disabilities*, 1973, *6*, 457–465.

Zigmond, N. *Intrasensory and intersensory processes in normal and dyslexic children.* Unpublished doctoral dissertation, Northwestern University, 1966.

KEY TERMS

cross-modal integration A process involving the incorporation of information presented simultaneously through more than one sensory modality.

reading deficits Learning problems associated with the various processes related to reading. Reflected in low reading achievement scores that are not commensurate with general measures of intelligence.

dichotic listening Relating to the two ears differently in regard to a conscious or physical aspect of sound.

dyscalculia Extreme difficulty or inability in acquiring mathematical concepts and skills.

dyslexia Severe difficulty or inability in acquiring reading concepts and skills.

emotional lability Readily or continually undergoing unexplainable changes in mood or affect.

field dependence Inability to focus on the central features of a task because the learner is distracted by irrelevant aspects of a perceptual array.

hyperactivity Motor behavior that is not demanded by the situation or task and which is disruptive to the group or the expectations of others.

perceptual-motor impairments Problems or difficulty in coordinating a visual or auditory stimulus with a motoric act.

perseveration Inappropriate maintenance of attention or continuation of an activity to an unusual degree or beyond a desired point.

processing A series of actions or operations related to the completion of a task, such as attentional and perception.

product The outcomes of task strategies or processes, such as reading.

reticular activating system A network of neurons that passes through the medulla (hindbrain) and on into sections of the forebrain. Functionally associated with wakefulness, arousal, sleep, and simple learning.

CHAPTER 5

Mental Retardation

There is no question that mental retardation is a major problem in the United States, irrespective of the definition used, the changes in definitions and biases, and the political and funding vagaries of the day. Ignoring for the moment the nuances of various definitions of mental retardation, it is generally recognized that more than six million Americans can be considered intellectually inadequate to meet many of the everyday demands of an increasingly technological society. It has been estimated that a mentally retarded individual is born every four minutes, and that retardation ranks only behind mental illness, cardiac disease, arthritis, and cancer as a major health problem (Robinson and Robinson, 1970; Albee, 1973). Since approximately 3 percent of our population is estimated to be mentally retarded, it behooves teachers, parents, and well-educated laypeople to be aware of the definitions of mental retardation, the developments that affect so many people, and the research that tells us something about their personal characteristics.

DEFINITIONS OF MENTAL RETARDATION

What is meant by the term mental retardation? While there is general agreement that the condition marks millions of people across our land, we shall see that there is no universal agreement as to its definition. Mental retardation is not a disease state like measles and chicken pox, but includes difficulties that may be significantly affected by cultural background, socioeconomic status, and even locale of residence. Some forms of retardation, particularly the more severe conditions, have been tied to genetic and biochemical dysfunction. This has not been the case with most of the less debilitating forms of mental incompetence. As with most forms of aberrant behavior, many factors influence whether one is defined as retarded. Poor schooling, the diagnostician's biases, insufficient motivation or stimulation for the child, may all increase the likelihood of a diagnosis of retardation. The points raised in Chapter 4 concerning the labeling controversy in the field of learning disabilities apply equally well, perhaps more so, to the field of mental retardation. In some cases, the diagnosis of mental retardation, like that of pornography, is closely linked to the social structure and value systems of the local community. However, for political and scientific purposes there have been attempts to develop a consensus concerning the definition of mental retardation. Some of these attempts are now briefly described.

Early History

Early attempts to define mental retardation appear in Roman Law in 1250 (Gearheart, 1972). This may have been the first effort to distinguish legally between "idiots" (that is, the mentally retarded) and "lunatics" (that is, the mentally ill). This was an important distinction, but it was crude and we have since come a long way. Much of the movement to refine our perspectives and treatments of the retarded is attributable to persons like Itard, Howe, and others discussed in Chapter 1. Partly due to their energy and benevolence, public concern for the mentally retarded increased, and more differentiated and precise classification systems developed. Hence the *English Mental Deficiency Act* was passed in 1913. In this act mental retardates were subdivided into four categories: idiots, imbeciles, the feeble-minded, and moral imbeciles. The category system was based on the dimension of self-care that might be expected from or demonstrated by the individual. Idiots were individuals believed incapable of protecting themselves from physical danger. Imbeciles were those persons unable to manage the most rudimentary chores without assistance. Feeble-minded persons needed some care, supervision, and control, while moral imbeciles were moderately intellectually impaired and demonstrated antisocial and illegal "tendencies" (Gearheart, 1972). The stress upon self-care within classification systems of mental retardation, evidenced throughout history, is still with us. While this emphasis is understandable, we shall see that it has produced difficulties within the field of mental retardation. The measurement, assessment, and prediction of self-care are difficult at best and nearly impossible at worst. Nonetheless, the English differentiation among subcategories of retarded persons had a profound effect upon the field of mental retardation within the United States. It is only recently that this classificatory scheme has been replaced (Gearheart, 1972).

Recent History

Currently there are a number of professionals generating definitions and categories that appear better suited to their professional duties, and the particular emphasis in their respective definitions reflects their professional concerns.

Legal experts have tended to stress the degree to which the individual is dependent upon society's aid. Educators, on the other hand, emphasize the individual's deficits in academic subject matter, while medical personnel highlight yet another dimension of retardation, the biological bases that might underlie the disorder. Whatever the professionals' perspectives, in defining mental retardation for daily affairs, the level of intellectual functioning as measured by intelligence tests is the critical factor.

AAMD Definitions

As we discuss the various definitions and perspectives of mental retardation, the central role of intelligence tests will become obvious. To examine the evolution of our current definitions of mental retardation, we turn to those proposed by the prestigious American Association of Mental Deficiency (AAMD). Their definitions have had the most influence in the field (Heber, 1959).

The definition of mental retardation proposed by the AAMD in 1961 was "subaverage general intellectual functioning which originates in the developmental period and is associated with impairment in adaptive behavior" (Heber, 1961, p. 3). The published material expanding on this definition describes some procedures for assessing mental retardation. Subaverage intellectual functioning was to be determined on the basis of the person's scores on individually administered intelligence tests. The individual who obtained a score that was at least one standard deviation below the mean would qualify for consideration as mentally retarded. Practically speaking, this requirement meant that a person who scored below 84 or 85 on the Stanford-Binet (SB) or the *Weschler Intelligence Scale for Children* (WISC) would be considered mentally retarded. Additionally, the definition specified that the problem of adequate intellectual functioning must arise during the person's developmental period.

The developmental period was arbitrarily defined as terminating at the end of the sixteenth year. Presumably a severe intellectual deficit incurred or detected after this period of time would not be called mental retardation. In addition, the definition specified that a person must demonstrate an impairment in **adaptive behavior.** The specific definition of adaptive behavior was left vague, apparently to allow for unexpected events in a person's life (MacMillan, 1977). Nonetheless, some guidelines to the meaning of adaptive behavior were provided. Adaptive behavior might be assessed in the early years by noting the age at which the individual sits, crawls, stands, and walks. During the school years it can be assessed by the individual's learning, while social adjustment is the criterion in later periods (MacMillan, 1977).

There are several features of this definition that warrant comment. First, specifying an intelligence test score of one standard deviation below the average score on a particular test means that about one-sixth of our population could be designated, at least on this dimension, as mentally retarded. This component of the definition was broad enough to allow many children access to available special education services; children of the poor, those who were malnourished, and those belonging to disadvantaged minority groups could be labeled mentally retarded. Given the likely stigma attached to children diagnosed as retarded, such a development could hardly be cheered. Second, the diagnosis of mental retardation lacks any prophecies concerning the individual's ultimate course of development. There is the possibility that a person diagnosed as retarded might leave the category at some future time. Finally, the inclusion of concern about adaptive behavior is important. It represents an attempt to break away from using the IQ score as the only criterion for diagnosing mental retardation. This is partially the result of the recognition that children from racial and ethnic minorities have been incorrectly and excessively labeled mentally retarded. That is, such children often demonstrate competence in dealing with their lives outside the classroom, a capability the IQ test score does not predict with much, if any, accuracy. Unfortunately, however, we do not have good assessment devices for measuring adaptive behavior, a component always believed important in determining mental retardation but implicitly ignored formerly because of the lack of good assessment techniques. The inclusion of adaptive behavior introduces into the measurement procedures all the possible sources of errors, such as the technician's biases, that were to be circumvented by the use of the individual intelligence test. One person's adaptive behavior is another's pathological symptom.

AAMD Definition Revised

In 1973, the AAMD published another definition of mental retardation: ". . . significantly subaverage general intellectual functioning existing concurrently with deficits in adaptive behavior, and manifested during the developmental period" (Grossman, 1973, p. 5). The critical changes in the revision are the words "significantly" and "concurrently." In elaborating upon the definition, the committee indicated that "significantly subaverage" refers to obtaining a score on an individually administered intelligence test which is two standard deviations below the mean, rather than one as in the earlier definition. A mentally retarded person is one who obtains an IQ no higher than 69. The more stringent requirement of two standard deviations below the mean on an intelligence test greatly reduces the number of persons who could be called mentally retarded. Fewer children will now be eligible to receive special education services rendered to the mentally retarded or the stigma they carry. We do not yet know what the impact of the change in definition will be upon children already labeled mentally retarded who no longer qualify, that is, children with IQ scores between 70 and 85. We suspect that many are now being classified as learning disabled, others as slow learners.

The second critical word in the 1973 definition is "concurrently." The individual must show a deficiency in adaptive behavior in addition to significant intellectual impairment. The manual that elaborates on the definition outlines behaviors relevant to the assessment of adaptive behavior at particular periods of growth. During infancy and early childhood adaptive behavior refers to sensorimotor skills, speech and language, self-care (for example, putting on one's shoes), and social or interpersonal skills. During the child's school years, adaptive behavior consists of academic performance, reasoning and judgment in everyday events, and social skills in interpersonal and group relationships. During late adolescence, adaptive behavior is defined on the basis of adequacy in meeting vocational and social responsibilities (MacMillan, 1977).

AAMD Adaptive Behavior Scale

While there are no measures of adaptive behavior comparable to the intelligence test, efforts have been made to develop standardized assessment techniques. There is an AAMD *Adaptive Behavior Scale* (Nihara, Foster, Shellhass, & Leland, 1969, rev. 1974) which divided adaptive behavior into two major categories: (a) maintenance of personal independence and daily living and (b) personality and behavior disorders. The information can be obtained by interviewing the retarded person or someone familiar with the child, such as a parent. The two categories are subdivided as follows:

Maintenance of personal independence and daily living includes

independent functioning—taking care of self
physical development—sensory and motor
economic activity—handling money
language development—receptive, expressive, and social language
number and time concepts
occupational domestic—cleaning house
occupation general—vocation
self-direction
responsibility
socialization

Personality and behavior disorders include

violent and destructive behavior
antisocial behavior
rebelliousness
untrustworthiness
withdrawal
stereotyped and odd mannerisms
inappropriate interpersonal manner
unacceptable vocal habits
unacceptable or eccentric habits
self-abuse
hyperactivity

There are a number of shortcomings associated with this scale. First, little is known about the reliabilities of ratings. Are the terms defined precisely enough so that two independent judges observing the same behaviors will rate the child in the same manner? To obtain reliable ratings of so many behaviors is quite difficult since they vary according to the situation. Behaviors that are maladaptive in one place or at one time are not necessarily maladaptive in another setting or at another time. Moreover, many of the items refer to rather ill-defined concepts, for example, rebelliousness and hyperactivity. We know that the ratings of hyperactivity are greatly affected by who is doing the rating and that agreement is unlikely among raters from different professions, for example, doctors and teachers (Whalen and Henker, 1976). In general, the less explicitly the behavior of concern is spelled out in a test, the lower will be the agreement among judges. Second, we have no information on how normal children might be rated on these items. We suspect that the amount of "pathology" shown by the normal child is typically underrated (LaPouse and Monk, 1964). The margin of error in such observations and the judgments drawn from the *Adaptive Behavior Scale* seems quite wide.

The original definition of mental retardation put forth by the AAMD in 1961 terminated the development period at the end of the sixteenth year. The 1973 revision raised the ceiling to 18 years of age. The impact of this change and the others upon the field is not yet clear. The most significant change in the definition is the lowering of the qualifying IQ score. There will certainly be fewer children labeled mentally retarded. The stress upon adaptive behavior assumes importance because it is viewed as a critical component of the definition. Most workers in the field have always assumed, at least theoretically, that adaptive behavior is important in determining mental retardation. Whether they have translated this assumption into their everyday work is another question. This definition is an attempt to encourage the translation. Remember that the law now demands an assessment, however inadequate, of adaptive behavior (PL 94-142, *Federal Register*, 1976). It will be difficult to meet with any competence the legal and definitional demands for an assessment of adaptive behavior since our measurement techniques are crude and our clinical judgments subject to error (Meehl, 1954). Legal and definitional requirements aside, however, it makes common sense to take account of the adaptive behavior of individuals in the diagnosis of mental retardation. Until more adequate assessment techniques of adaptive behavior become available, we will probably continue to rely heavily upon the intelligence test and stumble along with observational errors and personal biases in the diagnosis of mental retardation.

Alternative Definitions

Harmony rarely prevails in science so it should be no surprise that influential persons, disenchanted with the AAMD definition of mental retardation, have proposed alternative definitions. Clausen (1972) has argued that the diagnosis of mental retardation should be based upon a single criterion, the intelligence test score. He believes this is more straightforward than the inclusion of adaptive behavior as a measure. Since we have not defined adaptive behavior, nor devised a way of measuring it, Clausen suggests it is more realistic, more in accord with what we actually do, simply to use the IQ and stop deluding ourselves about assessing adaptive behavior. This position has merit insofar as the diagnosis of mental retardation would then be tied specifically to a few proven measures. If this definition were accepted, a judgment of mental retardation would be traceable to a set of responses to a set of standardized questions and thus there would be little confusion as to the meaning of the term.

Taking a position quite opposite to Clausen's, Mercer (1968, 1973) attacks definitions of mental retardation that include the use of intelligence tests. To understand Mercer's concerns it is helpful to be familiar with her research. She compared the relative proportion of black and Hispanic children in classes for the mentally retarded with white children enrolled in the same classes. She found that minority group children were overrepresented in these segregated classrooms, and, additionally, that a sizable number of the minority group children in these classes were deficient only while in school. Contrary to what one might expect of a retarded child, many of these minority youngsters were leading apparently normal lives outside school. Since their assignment to segregated classrooms was based primarily upon intelligence test scores, Mercer rejects the usefulness of these tests. She believes that the intelligence test yields too many erroneous diagnoses, particularly when used to classify children from minority groups.

The sociological perspective developed by Mercer views mental retardation as, in part, the result of social expectations and roles. That is, mental retardates have been defined by someone somewhere as defective, with the outcome that the labeled children then adopt the behaviors and characteristics associated with defectives. In addition, once a child is classified as defective, teachers will require or expect less from him or her and thus lower further the downward intellectual spiral in which the child is trapped. The degree to which role playing and teacher expectancies affect a child's intellectual development is open to dispute, but that they do exert some influence is really no longer debatable. There is a growing literature documenting that teachers form judgments about children, treat them in line with these judgments, and that children often respond accordingly, thus fulfilling the teacher's expectations (Bower, 1969; Meichenbaum and Bowers, 1969; Palardy, 1969; Rist, 1970; Brophy and Good, 1974).

Like other assessment devices, intelligence tests are far from perfect. But to stress adaptive behavior and exclude the IQ opens the doors to just those problems that Binet and Simon were assigned to eliminate. While role theory is provocative, its power to explain much of the data concerning mental retardation is far from evident. It seems reasonable that both IQs and assessment of adaptive behavior should be utilized in the diagnosis of mental retardation. The combination of imperfect measures may ultimately result in better categorizing than procedures that employ but a single inadequate device.

CLASSIFICATIONS OF MENTAL RETARDATION

Within the group of children and adults considered retarded, there are many different types of problems and different degrees of severity of retardation. Many attempts have been made to differentiate among retarded children. For purposes of diagnosis, educational and therapeutic planning, and scientific study, various classification systems have been proposed in order to make meaningful distinctions in this area. In this section we will present the different taxonomies used to subcategorize retarded persons. These distinctions have grave implications for the very slow child. A placement in one category rather than another determines the educational program the child will receive and may well affect people's expectations for that child's development and achievement. Categories make a great difference in the life experiences of the mentally retarded.

AAMD Classification System

The AAMD has proposed that the general population of the mentally retarded should be divided into four major groupings. One basis of this group differentiation is the IQ score. Children who obtain between 70 and 55 are called mild retardates. Those who score between 55 and 40 are considered moderately retarded, while those who score between 40 and 25 are labeled severely retarded. Persons who fall below 25 are considered profoundly retarded. It is not clear why these particular IQ points were selected as cutoff points, but it should be noted that each category includes a range of IQs approximately equal to one standard deviation of scores on the *Stanford-Binet* and the WISC. The categories of retardation have thus been linked to the statistical properties of the most frequently used individual intelligence tests.

Remember that the definition of mental retardation developed by the AAMD includes an evaluation of the adaptive behavior of the individual. To be defined as retarded, a person must be significantly deficient in intelligence and adaptive behavior. It is not clear how consideration of adaptive behavior will affect a child's placement within subcategories. If adaptive behavior is weighted heavily in the considerations, then the classification of a child may differ radically from that based solely upon intelligence test scores. The AAMD classification system is likely to be widely used, but it is not the only scheme proposed. A second classificatory system, supported by the educational establishment, has also gained in popularity and visibility.

Educational Classification System

The classification system advanced by the AAMD has not been widely supported by educators. Rather, the educational establishment has urged that greater emphasis be given to classifying the retarded child according to educational achievement, or expected achievement (Peterson, 1974). In addition, educators also stress the importance of the child's adaptive behavior in determining classification, although the intelligence test score remains a critical dimension in affecting decisions.

There are three categories proposed: the educable mentally retarded, the trainable mentally retarded, and the profoundly retarded. Associated with each category is a range of IQ scores and certain expectations concerning current and future achievement. Those children classified as educable mentally retarded will have IQ scores between 50 and 75, and are expected to achieve some measure of success in reading and arithmetic. It is presumed that these children will achieve independence as adults, given the proper educational programs and life experiences. The trainable mentally retarded have IQ scores ranging from 30 to 55, and are expected to achieve little more than rudimentary self-help skills, such as feeding, dressing, and toileting themselves (MacMillan, 1977). It would be premature to foreclose the possibility that the severely and profoundly retarded will achieve mastery of various skills. Within the very recent past there has been a concerted effort to develop educational programs for the gravely handicapped. Until recently these children were treated as medical, not educational, problems.

We have presented the classification system developed by the AAMD and that put forward by those more oriented to education. In addition, a third system has been proposed, one whose classifications are based on the etiology, or the cause of the mental retardation.

Classification Based on Etiology

Two major categories have been proposed for classifying retardation according to the cause of the problem. One category consists of those forms of the disability traceable or presumed traceable to external, or exogeneous, factors. Examples of exogenous causes of mental retardation are infections, brain damage, and injuries to the central nervous system. The second major category covers cases of mental retardation with no known external causes. These types of retardation are referred to variously as *endogenous retardation, garden variety mental deficiency, subcultural mental deficiency,* and *familial mental deficiency* (MacMillan, 1977). Endogenous mental retardation is determined by three standards: (a) the child is mildly retarded, (b) there is evidence of retardation in at least one member of the primary family, and (c) there is no evidence of central nervous system dysfunction or brain damage.

There currently are about 250 known causes of mental retardation, happily not reviewed here. Undoubtedly additional causes of retardation will be identified, some causes will be eliminated, and some will increase in importance as time goes on. For instance, opium and diphtheria were major contributors to retardation in the late 1800s, but are no longer. Furthermore, there has been a great reduction in the number of cases of retardation resulting from birth injury, while thyroid deficiencies have just about been eliminated from the list. But although damage from some conditions has been reduced and/or controlled, other causal factors have arisen. For instance, drug abuse by pregnant women may have increased the incidence of mental retardation (MacMillan, 1977). Causes of mental retardation are apt to change, given varying social conditions and states of knowledge. The American Association of Mental Deficiency has listed several categories of causes of this defect (Grossman, 1973). These include infections and intoxications, trauma and physical agents, metabolism and nutritional difficulties, gross brain damage, unknown prenatal influence, chromosomal abnormality, gestational disorders, psychiatric disorders, environmental conditions.

While many exogenous factors are known to increase the likelihood of mental retardation, the overwhelming number of individuals who are considered retarded have no known demonstrable abnormalities nor a developmental history that suggests such factors (Gearheart, 1972; Albee, 1973). It has been estimated that about 75 percent of retarded persons, of whom three-fourths come from rural or urban poverty areas, have endogenous forms of mental retardation, a fancy way of saying we do not know what has produced the deficiency (Tarjan, 1962; Albee, 1973; The President's Committee, 1973). It is thus inappropriate to conceive of mental retardation as a physical disease or dysfunction insofar as the vast majority of retarded individuals fail to demonstrate physical abnormalities.

Controversies and challenges have accompanied proposed definitions and classification schemes. Dependence upon the highly reliable individual intelligence test has been challenged because such tests measure only a narrow component of human behavior. Adaptiveness, on the other hand, is an elusive criterion. The meaning of the term is vague, the measurement of the concept not yet practically possible. Grouping people according to etiology suffers from the fact that the same forms of mental retardation may have many different causes. But it is important to remember that definitions and classification systems are always arbitrary and must be judged not on the basis of some absolute standard of "truth" but whether the systems best serve the particular goals of society. It is perfectly reasonable that medical personnel might urge classification according to etiology, while the educator prefers groupings according to educational requirements and expectation. After all, these professions serve the retarded in varying ways, however defined, and might well be expected to perceive this heterogenous group differently. It would also be a mistake to assume that the field is enmeshed in so much controversy that little agreement exists. By and large, subtleties in definitions are important for lawyers, fund-givers, and individuals who may be at the borderline of mental retardation. But many retardates are not borderline and they are likely to be considered defective by professionals and nonprofessionals alike.

CHARACTERISTICS OF THE EDUCABLE MENTALLY RETARDED

There are many retarded children who are able to function with some competence. These children are called the educable mentally retarded. Because of their somewhat higher abilities, these children are frequently studied and provide the basis of much of our knowledge concerning the impact of retardation upon intellectual and social skills. We now turn to some of those findings as to how the educable mentally retarded learn, employ speech and language, and conduct their social affairs. The following discussion is generally limited to the educable

FIGURE 5-1 Child taking part in a special program

mentally retarded and so excludes the more severe forms of retardation. Those are the subject of the final section of the chapter.

Learning

Not surprisingly, learning has long been a central concern of professionals in the mental retardation field. Presumably, the IQ score, so critical in determining the mental retardation diagnosis, assesses the individual's intellectual or learning capacity. The central assumption in the field of mental retardation is that the individual is unable to learn or does so inefficiently, and a major thrust in remediation is that of providing the appropriate opportunities to learn. It is believed that the fundamental difference between retarded and nonretarded persons is the speed and efficiency with which they learn (Robinson and Robinson, 1965).

Before turning to the results of learning studies employing mentally retarded subjects, it should be noted that learning is assessed in many different ways using many different tasks. For example, learning may be measured by the speed with which an individual meets a certain standard of mastery over material, or by the length of time the person retains material or behavior. There are many types of experimental procedures for studying learning. Thus, there are no simple conclusions about learning that can be offered in good conscience; the differences between the learning of retardates and nonretardates are complex and often depend upon how learning is measured and how the learning task is presented to the subjects.

This section concerns the learning characteristics of mentally retarded persons when learning is assessed by tasks that do not rely heavily upon verbal skills. Thus, studies of learning ability as assessed by **classical conditioning** and **operant procedures** are reviewed, followed by studies of **discrimination learning**. The reader may recall from other courses that classical conditioning involves the presentation of a conditioned stimulus (such as a bell) with an unconditioned stimulus (for example, food) and the measurement of unconditioned responses (salivation). If the process is successful, the conditioned stimulus will come to evoke the unconditioned response, even in the absence of the unconditioned stimulus. Hence, hearing a bell in the absence of food evokes salivation. In operant conditioning, a particular reinforcement is made contingent upon a response. Eventually, the response will become stronger, and so be made more frequently. In discrimination learning, the task of the subject is to learn which stimuli go together, their union being dictated on the basis of some underlying principle. They might be matched by appearance or by some conceptual similarities (for example animal, mineral, or vegetable).

Generally, it has been found that even moderately retarded subjects will be classically conditioned as rapidly as the nonretarded, although with more severe retardation, this may not be the case (Denny, 1964; Robinson and Robinson, 1970). When the measure of learning is the number of trials a person takes in order to respond in the "correct" fashion, the mildly, or educable, retarded perform as well as the nonretarded. It would seem that the educable retarded have few deficits in learning fairly simple and concrete associations of environmental events. Likewise it appears that differences between retarded and nonretarded subjects' learning in operant conditioning situations are not great. In tasks that require little symbolic or verbal skill, the educable mentally retarded do not differ greatly from nonretarded children in the rate with which they learn a reinforced response. Retarded persons, however, may be less consistent in their responses, show more unusual and erratic pausing in their responses, and have greater difficulty in establishing secondary or learned reinforcers than their nonretarded counterparts (Robinson and Robinson, 1970).

Extinguishing Learning

Although the rapidity with which retarded children might learn behaviors in these learning studies is about the same as for nonretarded children, there are significant differences between the groups in how readily they give up responses once learned. The rates at which retarded and nonretarded children extinguish a learned response are quite different. In classical conditioning and/or operant conditioning procedures, it has been consistently found that retarded subjects extinguish more slowly than normal subjects. In effect, the retarded persons retain their learned responses longer than do their nonretarded counterparts. One could argue that the retarded are "better learners" than the nonretarded insofar as they retain (continue to demonstrate) rudimentary behavior once it is learned. But it could also be construed that the retarded are particularly inflexible since they fail to note or respond to critical change in the environment, in this case the removal of an unconditioned stimulus or the reinforcement.

This is the general theme of the theoretical explanations for this highly reliable finding of group differences on extinction. For instance, Heal and Johnson (1970) suggest that failure on the part of the retarded to extinguish their responses reflects their difficulty in detecting critical features of a situation. When a change is introduced, the retarded fail to note it and respond appropriately. A second idea is that the failure to extinguish, usually measured by some motor response, means that the retarded do not have verbal control over their motor behavior (Denny, 1964). It is assumed that retarded persons are less likely to "talk to themselves," less likely to guide their motor impulses through verbal self-instruction. The hypothesis that retarded persons fail to control their behavior through self-instruction crops up frequently in explanations of other differences between them and normal persons. Irrespective of the explanation, there is little doubt that retarded persons show slower rates of extinction than normals when both are trained through operant or classical conditioning.

Discrimination Learning

While studies concerning the classical and operant conditioning of motor behaviors find comparable learning for retarded and nonretarded subjects, results of discrimination learning analyses yield quite another picture. A major stimulus for studies in this area was the work of Zeaman and House (1963). They employed a task which required the subject to match two stimuli on the basis of their similarity in appearance. They found that retarded children took more trials to reach a standard of learning than did nonretarded, and that moderately and severely retarded subjects actually performed worse on the task than monkeys!

These results were interpreted to mean that retarded persons might have attentional problems. They took longer to fathom the demands of the experiments and thus failed to notice as many dimensions of the learning stimuli as did normal subjects. Moreover, there appeared to be a relationship between the intellectual status of the subject and the number of cues the subject observed. The brighter the retarded, the more likely the attention to useful information. By and large, most studies prior to and following the Zeaman and House research have found that retarded persons show inferior learning in discrimination tasks, which seem to be more difficult for them than for the nonretarded (Robinson and Robinson, 1970). The severity of the retardation is associated with the learning process. The greater the retardation, the less able the person is to master the task.

The retarded's deficits in discrimination learning are explained by an inability to attend to relevant dimensions of a stimulus. Studies have been conducted to determine what manipulations might increase their attention to relevant information. Experimenters have tried using familiar objects rather than pictures, and shortening the time between the subject's giving a correct response and receiving a reinforcement. These techniques have proven effective in improving a retarded's performance on tasks (Robinson and Robinson, 1970). Other tactics have also been suggested, such as attention getting devices, using novel stimuli, sequencing the task so that it progresses from easy to more difficult and structuring it so that the child avoids failure (MacMillan, 1977). It is certainly important to obtain the retarded child's attention for task learning and these are a few methods that might prove helpful.

Memory

The question has been raised as to whether retarded children will retain information as easily as normal children. The answer is complex as there appear to be several kinds of memory. It has been theorized that there is short short-term memory, short-term memory, and long-term, or tertiary, memory. It is an oversimplification to try to talk of one's memory. Distinctions must be made concerning which type of memory is being considered.

The first step in comparing retarded and normal children's memory is to establish whether they differ in registering the material. Do they receive the input to be remembered? This question is investigated through backward masking, a process in which one visual stimulus quickly follows another. If the time interval between the presentation of the visual stimuli is short, the first visual stimulus will not "register"; the person will not retain it for recall. Studies have examined how much of a delay between visual stimuli is necessary for people to register both visual imputs. A number of investigations have found that the delay period necessary for the retarded to register both stimuli is no longer than that required by nonretarded persons (Wilson, 1977). There is no reason to believe that the mentally retarded, if not severely retarded, have more difficulty in receiving simple information than the nonretarded.

Short-term Memory

The second stage of memory is short-term memory: the ability to recall material a short time after receiving it. A technique frequently used to measure short-term memory is digit span tests. On these tests the subject is presented a series of numbers and asked to repeat them after the presentation. The evidence is consistent that the retarded have less short-term memory capacity than normal persons. Spitz (1973) reviewed studies conducted between 1916 and 1973 that employed digit span tests. Using subjects who had had no practice, it was found that normal subjects typically recall five to seven digits, while educable mentally retarded subjects typically recall two to four. Spitz reports that with practice, normal subjects can increase their short-term memory up to 13 or 14 digits while retarded subjects fail to show improvement. Ellis (1970) also reported that normal and retarded persons show differences in measures of short-term memory. Ellis specified that the breakdown in performance occurs during the learning procedure. In short-term memory research it is typically reported that persons of normal ability usually are most likely to remember the first and last items presented, while items that occur in the middle of the sequence are not as easily recalled. Retarded subjects fail to show this characteristic learning pattern. They are more likely to have difficulty remembering the first items.

Ellis reported that normal subjects are more affected by the rate at which information is presented than are retarded participants. This is an important finding because it implies that normal and retarded persons may differ in how they attempt to learn material, that is, in their learning strategies. It is possible that normal subjects benefit from greater time between items because they rehearse the material. Retarded subjects, however, may not benefit from longer time intervals in the presentation of material because they are not rehearsing or they are using the wrong strategy to learn the material. Ellis suggests that retarded persons try to rehearse but do not employ the appropriate strategy for remembering the material. A difference in learning strategies between normal and retarded persons is thought to explain, at least in part, the differences consistently found in their short-term memory.

Long-term Memory

The third question is whether there are differences between the retarded and the nonretarded in remembering material a substantial time after originally learning it. In other words, are there differences in the long-term memory of retarded and normal persons? While there has been little research addressed to this issue, existing studies have failed to find that retarded and normal persons differ in long-term memory (Lott, 1958; Klausmeier, Feldhusen, and Cheek, 1959; Cantor and Ryan, 1962). Once material has been learned, and this is the critical point, the capacity for the retarded to retain the information in long-term memory is comparable to that of normal persons. One would not expect to find such differences when one examines the research on long-term memory among normal subjects. *If the original learning of the material is equal,* there do not appear to be individual differences in long-term memory (Underwood, 1954). People do not have good or bad long-term memories; they differ in the degree to which they learn material in the first place!

The evidence pertaining to memory processes in the retarded, then, indicates that these people have a deficit in short-term memory processing, but do not differ from the nonretarded in short-term memory (receiving or registering simple inputs) or long-term recall. A popular hypothesis to explain the difference found in short-term memory is that retarded differ from normal persons in their rehearsal strategies and their attempts to organize material for the purpose of recall. This hypothesis has received some empirical support (Belmont and Butterfield, 1971; Brown, 1973).

Application to Special Education

Laboratory based experiments on how people learn words may seem far removed from real-life efforts to help retarded children, but there are certain principles that can be translated from this research into aids for helping retarded persons. Baumeister and Kellas (1971) have summarized the factors that influence an individual's performance in laboratory studies of verbal learning. Taking some liberty with these factors, we now summarize them as they might be applicable in home and school contexts.

When faced with the task of learning something, a person evaluates the material along a number of dimensions. One of the most important is the meaningfulness of the material. This dimension determines the strategy an individual is likely to use in attempts to learn it. If the material makes sense, the individual can call on previous learning, either by evoking imagery or words, to facilitate new learning. If the material has little meaning, the person may have to resort to remembering the information through rehearsal, simply repeating it rather than organizing it according to some abstract principles or elaborate conceptual scheme. Rehearsal strategies are also affected by the amount of material to be learned. If the presentation of information exceeds one's short-term memory span, the person may try to reduce the amount of material to be remembered through "chunking," organizing the information into more manageable units. If the material is given too rapidly to permit rehearsal, the individual will not be able to generate a rehearsal strategy.

Finally, the response required affects people's learning and coding strategies. If the task is simply to recognize what one has seen, as in a multiple choice test, one's strategy will be to separate the learned material from irrelevant stimuli. But if a person has to recall information, as in an essay test, coding is more likely to involve attempts to integrate and organize the material. Teachers training retarded children, particularly the educable mentally retarded, should be sensitive to the determinants of coding strategies. Meaningfulness, the rapidity with which the material is presented and learned, the response required of the child, all affect the likelihood that the child will learn and remember the information.

Speech and Language

"If one were to poll those working with mental retardates he undoubtedly would find that the inability to learn verbal materials is widely regarded as their most obvious and critical area of behavioral deficiency" (Baumeister and Kellas, 1971, p. 221).

Nonetheless, in spite of what appears to be consensus that retarded persons demonstrate language problems, there is no large corpus of research that specifies the nature of possible remedies. By and large, this lack of knowledge resulted from the failure of researchers in mental retardation to dovetail their work with the current theoretical and methodological developments in the language sciences (Rosenberg, 1970). However, it would be misleading to suggest that there are no perspectives or evidence concerning the language habits of the retarded. We now examine this evidence.

Two perspectives concerning the retarded child's language problems dominate our thinking. One notion is that such a child's language development is essentially the same as that of the nonretarded, but slower in emerging (Semmel, Barritt, Bennett, and Perfetti, 1968). In this perspective, emphasis is upon the similarities, not the differences, between retarded and nonretarded persons in their language development. The second and quite different notion is that language problems of the retarded reflect a learning deficit, not simply a delayed maturation. It is not that they learn the same things as the nonretarded person, but more slowly; rather, it is argued, they do not learn some things at all. For example, Denny (1966) ties language development to ideas concerning the retarded child's problems in coming to or maintaining attention. He particularly emphasizes the retarded child's problems in *incidental learning,* that is, learning something one is not necessarily directed to master. It is believed that the attentional deficits of the retarded prohibit them from attending to any particular set of events without specific instructions. That such problems may have an important impact upon language learning, Denny suggests, is illustrated by the following. The learning of relational terms, such as "behind," "through," and "over," requires some sustained attention since it might take a while to experience going behind or through or over something. Presumably the lack of attention prevents the experiencing of such actions, which in turn prevents learning the language reflecting them.

Apparently the bulk of studies concerning the language characteristics of the retarded have focused more on speech than language. Most have been concerned with speech problems such as stuttering, voice use, mutism, and difficulties in pronouncing sounds, rather than, for example, problems with syntax and semantics (Spradlin, 1963). In general it has been found that speech problems are prevalent among the retarded populations. Among the most severely retarded, it is estimated that from 57 to 82 percent have problems in pronouncing sounds, stuttering, voice projection, and mutism. Of the less severely retarded, those who are in public school special classes, it is estimated that between 8 and 26 percent have speech defects, as compared with about 3 percent of nonretarded schoolchildren (Spradlin, 1963). However, it is also clear that speech problems are associated with personal characteristics like intelligence and sex. Not surprisingly, articulation of speech sounds has been found to be correlated with intelligence test scores (Spradlin, 1963). Retarded girls are less likely to show speech problems than retarded boys, a difference often found in studies of nonretarded children.

While most studies have focused upon the speech problems of the retarded, several have analyzed the language skills of this group. Semmel et al.

(1968) have studied word associations of the mentally retarded and the nonretarded child. Previous studies have indicated that certain responses, called **syntagmatic responses,** are likely to occur relatively early in language development. Syntagmatic responses are those in which the person, when presented a word, responds by giving a sequential answer. For example, a response of "work" to the word "school" would be considered a syntagmatic response. A later development in language is the **paradigmatic response,** answering a word with one that is of the same grammatical class. An example is the response "run" to the word "walk." Semmel et al. (1968) have found that retarded children are less likely to respond with paradigmatic responses than nonretarded children, and older children are less likely than younger ones to respond with syntagmatic association. These investigators have determined that older retarded children respond much like very young nonretarded youngsters. In another study, Semmel and Bennett (1970) uncovered evidence that retarded children were less able to organize and retrieve verbally presented information. They reported that these children had greater difficulty than nonretarded ones in supplying a missing word from a meaningful sentence. Indeed, Semmel and Bennett (1970) learned that meaningfulness of verbally presented material is less likely to affect the recall of retarded children than of the nonretarded. Finally, Rosenberg (1970) cites a study conducted by Lovell and Dixon which found that mentally retarded children performed very much like younger nonretarded ones when asked to imitate words, point to pictures representing spoken words, and describe pictures to the examiner.

In light of the recognition of the speech and language problems of the retarded, it is not surprising that a number of remediation studies have been conducted. The popularization of behavior modification techniques has triggered several studies of language training for the retarded. Barnett, Pryer, and Ellis (1959) had success in increasing the number of "I" and "we" statements by giving retarded children verbal approval contingent upon their using these words. Guess, Sailor, Rutherford, and Baer (1968; cited by Sitko and Semmel, 1973) were able to get a mute, severely retarded girl to use plurals. They accomplished this by first getting her to imitate them, then to use words when she saw the object the words represented, and then to use the plural when two of the objects were shown to her. Finally, Wheeler and Salzer (1970) used reinforcements to train children who spoke in telegraphic speech (that is, speech in which the main words of a sentence are not connected by words such as "the" or "and") to use syntactically correct sentences. These and other studies have demonstrated that retarded children benefit from speech and language training.

A number of investigators have recommended various procedures and concepts for language training. According to Rosenberg (1970), there should be a complete assessment of the child's language disabilities. Second, the language program should make use of our knowledge of the impact of behavior modification and learning (that is, the influence of reinforcements, timing, and practice) upon language performance. Third, an effective language program will emphasize learning the meaning of words. It is not so much that the educable retarded cannot properly string words together as it is that they do not understand the meaning of the communication. Fourth, we need to recognize that language training is affected by both the child's and the teacher's use of speech. For example, we know that language from a sender to a receiver is frequently adjusted according to the sender's estimate of the receiver's competence. Oftentimes, such judgments are based on the receiver's age and size. Given the discrepancy between the retarded's abilities to process verbal information and his or her age and size, the sender's messages may be too complex for adequate learning. Finally, Rosenberg suggests that since normal children appear to acquire language through activity, language training programs should attempt to reproduce this process by having the retarded child actively participate in the lessons.

Social Perceptions

A part of the concern for the personality and social characteristics of the retarded person stems from the eugenics movement, which attributed all manner of evil deeds to mental retardation. Prior to 1930, estimates of the incidence of criminality in the retarded population ranged from 22 to 90 percent. Indeed, one leader in the field of mental retardation is quoted as saying that retarded women are "almost invariably immoral" (sic) and that mental retardation is the "mother of crime, pauperism, and degeneracy" (MacMillan, 1977, p. 414). Retardation then was not simply associated with lack of intellectual skills, but also tied directly to a variety of personal and social ills. While the leaders of the eugenics movement of the early 1900s overstated their case, there is nonetheless a consensus that retarded persons are particularly likely to suffer from emotional and behavior disorders. Such problems may reflect the impact of confinement to an institution or the frustrations of trying to "make it" in the community. Perhaps they are generated by failure to learn the subtleties of social intercourse, the inhibition of socially unacceptable behaviors, or parental and community disappointment with the retarded's development. Unfortunately, adequate studies have not been conducted to determine the incidence of such problems in the retarded, much less the causal relationships between emotional and intellectual problems. There does, however, appear to be a general belief that the retarded child will suffer more than the nonretarded "the slings and arrows" of emotional traumas. In the following pages, we discuss findings on how the retarded perceive themselves and their abilities, and how they are viewed by their peers and teachers.

Self-concept

Many psychologists and laypeople believe that one's perception of self is critical in determining behavior. They think that the more positive one's feelings about oneself, if those feelings are based upon realistic assessments, the better the person's mental health and adaptiveness. Since the mentally retarded have difficulty in problem solving and managing their everyday affairs, research has been generated to test whether the views such children have of themselves are commensurate with their abilities. If so, negative feelings about themselves will be developed as a consequence of poor adjustment.

Theories

Theorizing concerning the source of negative self-evaluations has taken several forms. First, it has been hypothesized that notions about ourselves are formed by measuring ourselves against others. Self-concepts may be affected by a social comparison process (Festinger, 1954). Robinson and Robinson (1965) have suggested that retarded children are likely to develop an acute sense of incompetence, particularly when entering school, since they will compare their own performance with those of more able classmates. Second, a poor self-concept might follow from the many instances of social rejection these children are likely to experience (Johnson, 1950; Johnson and Kirk, 1950). Finally, there is concern that a poor self-concept might be generated not from school comparisons or from rejection based upon incompetent performance, but simply from being called a retarded child. That is, the label carries stigma, the stigma is communicated to the child, and the child's self-esteem and estimates of his or her abilities are adversely affected. There certainly is good reason to suspect that the retarded child's self-concept will carry a less positive affective state than will that of the nonretarded child.

Studies of Self-concept

Not surprisingly, conclusions reached about self-appraisals of the mentally retarded depend a good deal upon how such appraisals are derived. If one infers self-concept from the verbal responses of the retarded, the inferences drawn will be very different from those gained through observations of the child's behaviors. Let us look briefly at some studies concerning the verbal pictures the retarded draw of themselves.

There is evidence that retarded children's verbal descriptions of themselves and their expectancies for success imply a positive self-concept. For example, Guthrie, Butler, and Gorlow (1962) found that institutionalized girls were less likely to describe themselves in negative terms than were noninstitutionalized girls. Ringelheim (1960) found that all of his retarded subjects stated that they expected to do well on a task. Moreover, Ringelheim (1960) as well as Starkman and Cromwell (1958) found that these positive expectancies about future performance were not affected by subsequent failures. It would appear then that the verbal statements made by the retarded about their future successes and perhaps their own attributes are not strongly affected by experiencing failure.

These verbal reports, however, are open to several interpretations. First, they may indeed reflect the self-appraisal of the retarded concerning their competence. An alternative and more popular interpretation, however, is that their verbal presentations reflect efforts to appear normal, to "pass" as just another nonstigmatized person. According to Edgerton (1967), the retarded will often assume a "cloak of competence" so as to avoid the stigma associated with the defect. That this may well be the case is suggested by studies assessing the individual's expectancies for success by the person's motor rather than verbal behavior.

Inferences about the retarded's expectancies concerning competencies can be made by seeking answers to several questions. First, how does the retarded behave when confronted with failure? Does the person act as if success is expected, or failure? Secondly, inferences can be drawn about self-concepts by weighing the goals individuals impose upon themselves. Do they set high goals, suggesting faith in their ability, or do they set noticeably low goals, implying a lack of confidence? Finally, inferences can be made about self-concept on the basis of relative independence from others. Do they appear to seek guidance and cues on how to behave more frequently than nonretarded children, or do they have enough confidence to be relatively autonomous from others? Inferences about the retarded's self-concept based upon these various approaches yield a single answer: They have very little confidence in themselves.

While the evidence is not entirely consistent (Zigler, 1968), several investigators have found that retarded children frequently withdraw from a task in which they are failing. Unlike the nonretarded child, who, when faced with failure, will often try harder to master the task, the retarded child is more likely to avoid the difficult challenge (Gardner, 1958; Ringelheim, 1958; Zeaman and House, 1963). Additionally, these children apparently set lower goals for themselves than their abilities might dictate. For example, Zeaman and House (1963) found that after repeated failures, their subjects were unwilling to tackle problems that they had formerly been able to solve. More dramatically, Zigler and Harter (1969) report a study by Osler in which retarded children were unable to solve a problem after 150 to 200 trials that monkeys solved in 35 to 40 trials. When the experimenter told the children that they would have to return some earned candies after each failure, the subjects learned to solve the problem correctly in only two or three attempts. The retarded child's efforts to avoid failure by setting goals lower than his or her capabilities would imply may well be an important source of frustration and irritation to the child's teachers and parents (Zigler and Harter, 1969).

Finally, the work of Zigler and his colleagues (Green and Zigler, 1962; Turnure and Zigler, 1964; Balla, Styfco, and Zigler, 1971; Yando and Zigler, 1971) demonstrates that the retarded lack faith in their abilities. These investigators have repeatedly found evidence to suggest that retarded children are particularly "outer-directed," that is, they are often likely to look to others for clues as to appropriate actions. These youngsters are more sensitive to verbal cues, more likely to imitate the behavior of peers and adults, and more apt to scan the environment visually than are nonretarded children. Presumably, their lack of faith in their own ability dictates a strategy of basing their conduct on cues given by others.

In summary, while there is little question that some retarded children may have very positive views of their capacities, it does appear that most have, relative to normals, rather grave doubts. These doubts apparently can lead the retarded to give up in the face of failure, set low goals for their performance, and to be particularly concerned with the behaviors of others. But how do others respond to them? We now turn to studies of this significant issue.

Peers and Teachers

The interpersonal relationships of retarded children have been given great importance in attempts to understand their behavior. Zigler (1968), a prominent leader in the field of mental retardation, has stressed the retarded child's outer-directiveness and need for benevolent and supportive relationships with others. Zigler has argued that the typically high level of anxiety these youngsters experience stems from concern about, and relative deprivation of, supportive interpersonal relationships. Additionally, peer relationships become a central issue when practical matters like schoolroom placement (that is, segregated versus integrated classes) and the effects of labeling are considered.

It is clear that normal children do not like retarded ones. For example, Johnson (1950) found that retarded children located in regular classrooms received four times the number of rejections from peers than did nonretarded children. Goodman, Gottlieb, and Harrison (1972) also found the retarded are rejected by their peers. It appears that wherever peer popularity of the retarded is assessed, and by whatever method, they are rejected relative to nonretarded children (Johnson and Kirk, 1950; Miller, 1956; Baldwin, 1958; Gottlieb and Budoff, 1973; Gottlieb and Davis, 1973; Gottlieb, 1974). Of perhaps greater interest is whether the retarded child within the regular classroom receives more rejection than one who is placed in a segregated schoolroom. The answers to this question, at this time, suggest that difference in the rejection rates of these two groups of retarded children is quite small. As far as we can tell, the retarded are rejected equally as often whether the child is in a special or a regular classroom (Goodman, Gottlieb, and Harrison, 1972; Gottlieb and Budoff, 1973; Gottlieb and Davis, 1973). These findings should not be taken to indicate that there are no benefits to the retarded child from integration into the regular classroom. For example, Gottlieb, Gampel, and Budoff (1973) have found that integrated retardates were less aggressive verbally and physically and performed more socially desirable acts than children who were segregated. However, it appears that the retarded child's popularity with classmates is not affected by class placements and that wherever the child is placed there is likelihood of peer rejection.

Although there is no question that retarded children are more likely to be rejected by their peers, the specific reasons for this are still not clear. While a relationship between social acceptance and academic competence is frequently found, the relationship is not one that would account for such rejection (Gottlieb, 1974). What other factors may account for it?

In spite of the observation that it is social incompetence rather than intellectual performance that frequently brings on the rejection of retarded persons, there are few studies concerning their social skills and social development. Gottlieb

and Budoff (1973) did find that social rejection of the retarded was related to verbally aggressive behavior on their part, and the absence of rejection was related to
the absence of such aggression. This finding corresponds to those of studies involving normal nursery school children (Hartup, Glazer, and Charlesworth, 1967) and
those centered on learning disabled children (Bryan, 1978). Other possible determinants of peer rejection of the retarded remain to be discovered.

While there are considerable data pertaining to peers' views of retarded children, the evidence is much less abundant when it comes to studies of
teachers' attitudes. The current emphasis upon educating the handicapped child in
the regular classroom (called mainstreaming) will, it is hoped, stimulate research
into this important area. In one of the few studies examining this question, Shotel,
Iano, and McGettigan (1972) compared teacher attitudes toward children with
various types of disabilities. Of the various groups, teachers were most positive and
optimistic about the learning disabled child, while least positive about the educable
mentally retarded. Informal discussions with the teachers revealed that their lack of
enthusiasm for the retarded student stemmed from these children's low classroom
achievement, their failure to participate in classroom activities, and the fact that
they were often the object of ridicule. By and large, few regular classroom teachers
were in favor of integrating disabled children into the regular classroom. One would
expect then that classroom teachers would not be eager to accept the educable
mentally retarded within the regular classroom. Indeed, they apparently reject the
learning disabled child, a child who performs and acts more appropriately than
would be expected from the retarded child (Bryan and Bryan, 1978). As yet, however,
the lack of research on this topic prevents any definite statements concerning
teacher attitudes toward the educable mentally retarded.

SEVERE FORMS OF MENTAL RETARDATION:
THE TRAINABLE AND THE
SEVERELY/PROFOUNDLY RETARDED

So far this chapter has dealt primarily with the educable mentally
retarded. The heavy emphasis upon this group was dictated by several considerations. There are more educable retarded than there are children with severe
handicaps. In addition, teachers and parents are more likely to interact with educable than with trainable or severely/profoundly retarded children. Nonetheless,
children who have very limited intellectual capacities also require care and educational programs. We turn now to children who are quite handicapped, who typically
have intelligence test scores below 55, and who frequently have other handicapping
conditions in addition to low intellectual capacity. While people can have multiple
handicaps and not be mentally retarded, it is very likely that with increasing
degrees of retardation, the person will have other disabilities.

In the following sections we discuss the severely and profoundly
mentally retarded. First we examine events and factors that are known causes of

retardation and then present some of the characteristics of and educational placements for the severely and profoundly retarded. A few words of introduction are in
order. First, severe and profound retardations are low incidence handicaps that
strike across socioeconomic, racial, and cultural groups, although not equally so
(Berkson and Landesman-Dwyer, 1977). Second, while 90 percent of those defined as
retarded are physiologically no different from nonretarded persons, in severe and
profound retardation there are a greater number of cases in which physiological or
genetic causes are known (Tarjan, 1962; Stein and Susser, 1975). The lower the
person's IQ, the greater the likelihood that the specific cause of retardation can be
identified. Third, great changes are currently underway in attitudes toward and
treatments of the severely and profoundly retarded. It is with some hesitation that
we discuss characteristics of this population because by and large the data are
based on institutional groups who have not benefited from more recent educational
efforts.

Incidence and Physiological Causes of Mental Retardation

Spradlin and Girardeau (1966) estimated that the incidence of severe
and profoundly retarded is 0.36 percent to 0.50 percent of the world's population.
This translates to about 10 to 15 million persons in the world, and about 800,000 in
the United States. Not all, but perhaps most, instances of severe mental retardation
are the result of a biologic insult which occurred "(a) to genetic material prior to
conception, (b) to the early embryo, (c) to the developing fetus, (d) to the fetus during
labor and delivery, (e) to the newborn infant during the hours and days he was
adapting to extrauterine existence" (Graves, Freeman, and Thompson, 1970, p. 697).
Genetically related defects associated with mental retardation can
result from a number of events. These defects might be the result of mutations that
are a "radical transformation of a gene resulting in the formation of a new characteristic" (London, 1975, p. 599). Additional things may go wrong in the division of the
cells during early fetal growth or during the matching of recessive genes in parents;
or a mishap may occur because of the presence of defective genes on sex chromosomes. The chance matching of unfortunate recessive genes and accidents during the
chromosomal divisions are the two most frequent reasons for genetically linked birth
defects associated with mental retardation (MacMillan, 1977).

Down's Syndrome

A high incidence genetic defect, and probably the most familiar, is
Down's Syndrome, or **mongoloidism,** which is responsible for approximately 10 percent of the cases of moderate to severe mental retardation. The child with Down's
Syndrome is characterized by low intelligence; a small, low-bridged nose; upward
slanting eyes with colored spots and folds of skin at the inner corners; unusually
small ears; and a tongue that protrudes from too small a mouth. Other body parts

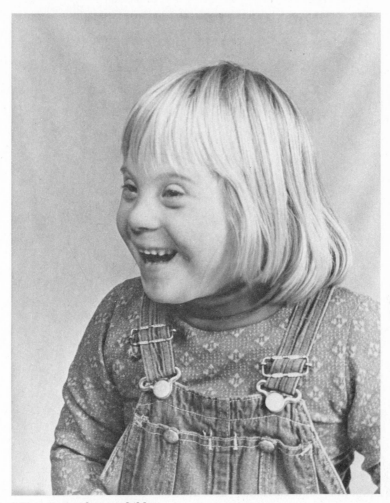

FIGURE 5-2 A Down's Syndrome child

may also be affected as these children often have abnormally small hands; fine, sandy-colored hair; and a short, broad neck. Dental and skin problems are also common. The Down's Syndrome child thus has rather distinctive features and appearance, as shown in Figure 5-2.

   In addition to an unusual appearance and low intellectual capacities, these children may suffer from other congenital physical problems such as heart and respiratory malfunctions and biochemical abnormalities (MacMillan, 1977).

   Down's syndrome is an example of a genetic defect resulting when the chromosomes fail to distribute themselves properly. Children thus affected are known to have a problem involving chromosome 21, known as "trisomy 21." This means that chromosome 21 was formed by the matching not of two, but of three chromosomes. This problem has long been associated with the age of the mother at the time of conception. Women over the age of 35 are more likely than younger women to give birth to such children. It is now possible to determine before delivery whether the child will have Down's Syndrome. This is accomplished by *amniocentesis,* a process in which fluid from the sac in which the fetus develops is removed and analyzed. High risk mothers, those who are older or who have had a retarded child, can determine in advance whether their offspring will suffer from Down's Syndrome.

Phenylketonuria

A second genetically linked form of mental retardation involves **phenylketonuria** (PKU). PKU is an enzyme deficiency in which the liver fails to produce the substance necessary to metabolize certain amino acids. When the acids are not metabolized, they enter the blood and are poisonous. The end result is brain damage. This occurs when both parents carry recessive genes that happen to match up during fetal development. Typically, this chemical disaster is not evidenced immediately at birth, but its ill effects soon appear. This form of retardation also results when the mother has PKU. In this case, the infant is born with a condition that will, if untreated, eventuate in severe mental retardation. Whatever the origin, if PKU is not treated, mental retardation will be severe and will be accompanied by an array of physical and psychological problems.

Approximately 1 in 13,000 to 1 in 20,000 births involve PKU. The condition can be treated, if intervention is prompt. One of the difficulties in rendering treatment, however, is detection of the condition. As noted, the defect may be evidenced upon birth. On the other hand, it may take months for it to appear. Tests for this problem should be administered more than once (MacMillan, 1977). Treatment of PKU involves manipulating the infant's diet, omitting the substance the child does not metabolize, phenylaline. While this may sound easy, it is not, since some of this material is necessary for the child's growth. Hence, too much produces brain damage, while too little stunts growth. With successful management of the diet, however, the condition can be controlled and remarkable changes in the child may be observed after a treatment period as short as 48 to 72 hours (Woolf, 1964).

Maternal Illness

There are many illnesses and accidents that can occur to the mother that may produce retardation in her offspring. While different events have different effects depending on the stage of fetal development, by and large the fetus is most vulnerable during the first three months of pregnancy. The list of possible sources of damage is extensive. Temporary conditions like infections and diseases contracted by the mother may have severe negative effects upon the embryo. Too little food or vitamins, or too much alcohol, drugs, or tobacco may also produce untoward results. In addition, some chronic health problems of the mother may harm the unborn. We now look at these effects in more detail, particularly those that are rather frequent or of popular concern.

While any one of a host of chronic maternal illnesses might injure the infant during the prenatal period, an important one is diabetes. Formerly, women with diabetes found it difficult to conceive or, if pregnant, to avoid a miscarriage. Through advances in medical technology, more diabetic women now succeed in becoming mothers. Their infants, however, are at considerable risk, since diabetic mothers have greater difficulty in avoiding or controlling infections, and are more likely to develop hypertension and/or toxemia. In addition, the infant is often quite large and thus birth may occur several weeks prematurely, making the child vulnerable to difficulties associated with birth injury and prematurity.

Kernicterus

Another problem associated with retardation is **kernicterus,** a blood disease in which the red blood cells are destroyed and the infant's liver is incapable of eliminating the residual. The resulting oxygen deficiency destroys the infant's brain cells. The best known cause of kernicterus is Rh incompatibility between the mother and child. The problem arises when the mother's blood type is Rh negative and her baby's is Rh positive. Fortunately, there is a treatment available for Rh incompatibility. It consists of administering gamma globulin to the mother within 72 hours before the birth of an Rh positive baby.

Rubella

As mentioned above, viral infections in pregnant women during the first three months of pregnancy can have serious consequences for the fetus. One of the most dangerous is *rubella,* which has devastating effects on about 50 percent of the fetuses of mothers who contract it. The rubella virus is most often associated with hearing impairments in newborns, but the child may also show evidence of mental retardation, cerebral palsy, blindness, seizures, orthopedic difficulties, cardiac disturbances, or various combinations of all of these problems (MacMillan, 1977).

Syphilis

A second infection, *syphilis,* can also gravely impair fetal development. While the detection and treatment of syphilis have decreased the number of damaged newborns, in recent years there has also been a dramatic rise in the number of people suffering from it. The danger is that women do not necessarily have overt symptoms of the disease and, even if they do, these symptoms may recede even though the virus lives on. Given that the fetus survives, it is likely to show one or more of the following: mental retardation, deafness, cardiac abnormalities, kidney disease, liver and spleen enlargements, bone deformities, and skin problems (MacMillan, 1977).

Social or Environmental Factors

Other causes of birth defects and mental retardation have their roots in social or environmental factors. One such problem is malnutrition. Deficiencies in iodine, protein, Vitamins A, B6, and B12 have all been implicated as causes of severe retardation (MacMillan, 1977). In addition, there are problems associated with drug usage. Hence alcoholism, LSD, antithyroid drugs, nicotine, phenobarbital, insulin, and even excessive use of aspirin are known to be, or suspected of being contributors to mental retardation (National Foundation, March of Dimes, 1971). Also, exposure to radiation and lead poisoning have been implicated in some forms of mental retardation (Wood, Johnson, and Omori, 1967; Wilson, 1974; MacMillan, 1977).

Some of the hazards to fetal development during gestation have been described, but the fetus who escapes intrauterine harm is not yet home safe as mishaps are possible during the birth process. Among the most common is anoxia, in which the infant's brain is so severely deprived of oxygen that brain cells are destroyed. A second source of difficulty is premature birth. Prematurity is defined as a "live-born infant delivered before 37 weeks from the first day of the last menstrual period" (Grossman, 1973, p. 66). There are a variety of causes for premature births but whatever the cause, the immature infant is apparently more susceptible to the ill-winds that blow from his or her immediate environment.

While we have not discussed the more than 250 causes of mental retardation, we have reviewed some of the most common conditions and their causes. There is a great deal yet to be learned, but being conscious of the negative effects of seemingly harmless drugs like aspirin, for instance, should make one aware of the multitude of factors that can lead to mental retardation. After cataloging these truly horrendous symptoms, we need to remember that most women do in fact produce nonretarded and healthy offspring. While things can go seriously amiss, they do not do so with great frequency.

Characteristics of Individuals with IQs below 50

Individuals with very low IQ scores have been called by a variety of labels and grouped in a number of ways, depending upon the theoretical predilections of the investigators. For example, Farber (1968) defines these people as severely mentally retarded whereas Spradlin and Girardeau (1966) divide them into two groups: those with IQs between 25 and 50 and those with IQs below 25. The terminology and the IQ cutoff points used are somewhat arbitrary, but the current practice is to divide this population into two groups. Those with IQs between 25 and 50 are generally referred to as severely retarded while those with IQs below 25 are considered profoundly mentally retarded. The distinction, that is, the diagnosis, can be complicated by the presence of multiple handicaps. The retarded child with cerebral palsy, for instance, may have so much difficulty responding to assessment procedures due to physical limitations that it may be risky, at best, to class the child with either the severely or the profoundly retarded. Indeed, the current trend is to postpone classification until after the child has been exposed to educational, medical, and psychological interventions.

Persons with IQs of 25 to 50 are described by Spradlin and Girardeau as follows:

> Able to dress themselves partially, to take care of most of their own toilet needs, and to feed themselves without assistance. The social reactions of moderately retarded children to adults are somewhat more varied than those of the severely retarded, and they usually exhibit a more extensive verbal repertoire. They are frequently able to imitate rather wide ranges of adult or peer activities . . . engage somewhat less frequently in stereotyped activities . . . they have a wider range of appropriate behavior (socially defined) which is under the control of both physical and social stimuli. Nevertheless, they fail to meet community norms. They usually do not read, and they speak with poor syntax and articulation. Arithmetic and writing skills are quite limited (1966, p. 258).

Hewett and Forness (1977) further describe the severely retarded as usually requiring continuous supervision in all aspects of daily living: in self-help, economic, and social skills. While these children usually learn to talk, many are handicapped by other physical and sensory disorders. There is every reason to believe, though, that severely retarded children can be taught behaviors through either classical or operant conditioning, discussed earlier in this chapter. Indeed, work involving the reinforcement and punishment of the behaviors of the severely retarded has frequently produced predictable and beneficial effects (Weisberg, 1971). Some learn to count; some even learn to read. Many are able to achieve skills that allow them to earn money, but this is typically in a sheltered workshop, a setting in which a group of retarded work under close supervision, and in which the work to be done is arranged for and set up by the supervisory staff.

Educational programs for the severely retarded emphasize self-help skills, language development, social adjustment, and occupational skills. Self-help skills include training in dressing, feeding, toileting, grooming, taking care of one's belongings, and safety. School activities are likely to include reading lessons that emphasize learning to read functional items like street signs. Telling time, counting, listening, and following directions also are viewed as important preparation for a structured but satisfactory life in the community.

With structured programs, the severely retarded should be able to live at home or in a small residential setting in the community. They may also be expected to work in a sheltered workshop or other facility that provides the necessary supervision. The success of community placement rests, in part, with the adequacy of the school program to train the retarded child to be sufficiently independent to cope with the stresses and strains of daily living.

Spradlin and Girardeau (1966) describe the profoundly retarded, those with IQ scores of less than 25, as likely not to be toilet trained or capable of dressing themselves. Many fail to exhibit speech and language and when they do, it consists of a few words or phrases. Spradlin and Girardeau write: "Their communication with other persons is more often than not limited to crying, screaming, crude gesturing, and tugging at the person as a small child would do" (1966, p. 258). The severely retarded are also likely to engage in repetitive behaviors such as rocking, flicking their fingers, rolling their heads from side to side, and thumb-sucking.

It is important to remember that the lower the IQ the more likely the individual is to have additional handicapping conditions. One should also keep in mind that presently only about 5 percent of all mentally retarded persons in the United States are in residential institutions. This means that communities are developing programs for the profoundly and multihandicapped child and adult. Such programs require educational curricula, medical prevention and care, and family support services.

To parents of the profoundly and multihandicapped, it may sound cavalier to say that the most important step we can take is prevention. These families need a wide range of services for their children. While it is our responsibility to provide these services, we can hope, through public education as to the causes of profound retardation and multiple handicapping conditions, we might come to greatly reduce the number of affected children. For the profoundly and multihandicapped already with us, the concern now is to provide the most humane living conditions. This can be in community based facilities or in large institutions. The quality of the program, the degree to which it meets the needs of the individual, should be the chief criteria for judgment and decision making. The second major issue is that we not give up on education for these persons, and that we bring to bear the most updated educational, medical, and psychological technologies. It is too soon to limit the goals we set for ourselves, for the profoundly and the multihandicapped are just beginning to get their share of the resources due them.

SUMMARY

Mental retardation is a problem affecting about 3 percent of Americans, a problem sometimes, but not often, caused by genetic or physiological dysfunctions. Most often, in about 90 percent of the instances, the cause of mental retardation is not known. While the most important clue to diagnosing mental retardation is a person's score on an individually administered intelligence test, there have been consistent and steady efforts to expand the definition to include measures of a person's adaptive behavior. The emphasis on adaptive behavior measures is, in part, the result of findings that individuals from economically disadvantaged groups were being diagnosed as retarded and placed in segregated classrooms, even though these children were functioning quite well outside of school. The results of an intelligence test predict school achievement, but do not predict the ability to acquire the whole range of human skills and abilities needed in daily living.

The emphasis on measures of adaptive behavior is important for a second reason. Whereas mentally retarded individuals were previously viewed as medical problems and provided custodial care in residential institutions, today the majority of them are being housed and educated in community based programs. The shift is toward educational programs, whose goals, therefore, must be redefined. Concern for daily living skills replaces the former emphasis on mastery of academic subjects. Assessment of adaptive behavior, analysis of the skills needed to maintain a person in a community, and the provision of educational programs from early childhood through adulthood to ensure learning these skills become the focus of education. While measurement techniques to assess adaptive behavior are currently less sophisticated technically than tests of intelligence, it is likely that the measurement of daily living skills will improve as a result of the redefinition of education goals for the retarded.

In reviewing characteristics of the mentally retarded, we find that studies of learning ability indicate that many retarded individuals appear to have difficulty in learning discrimination and changing (or extinguishing) a response once it is acquired. It is also important to note that in tasks requiring little verbal skill, the retarded are not greatly different from nonretarded, and that even severely retarded persons can learn a wide variety of behaviors through operant conditioning methods. Teaching programs in which reinforcement and punishment have been used have been quite effective in helping retarded persons learn many skills. Many researchers feel that differences between the retarded and nonretarded are traceable to differences in learning strategies. Retarded persons exposed to a learning task are less likely to "talk to themselves," less likely to guide themselves through the task with verbal self-instruction.

A number of tactics have been found to be effective in helping retarded children improve their learning. These include the systematic use of reinforcements, attention getting devices, careful sequencing of a task so that it progresses from easy to more difficult, diligent attention to motivational factors. It is necessary to catch the child's attention for task learning, help the child develop rehearsal strategies, and to structure success and failure in tasks in such a way that the retarded child maintains faith in his or her ability to learn.

The characteristic most often associated with retardation is difficulty in learning language. While we do not have a great deal of data concerning the development of language skills in the retarded, problems of this nature appear to be prevalent. The degree to which speech and language deficits present a problem is related to the severity of the retardation. Among the severely retarded, the estimate is that 57 percent to 82 percent have speech defects, while 8 percent to 26 percent of nonretarded children in public school programs have speech defects. Studies of language skills of retarded children suggest that these children perform like younger nonretarded children; their language development is slower than that of nonretarded children, but the process of learning language follows the same maturational sequences found in nonretarded children.

There have been several programs developed to help retarded children acquire speech and language skills. To be effective, the program should include a complete assessment of the child's use of language and make full use of our knowledge of behavior modification and learning. Training should emphasize the meanings of words, and the program should be action based to reproduce the method by which the nonretarded child naturally acquires language.

The evidence concerning the motivational and social attributes of mentally retarded children reveals that many retarded children are more likely than the nonretarded to be rejected by others, and to have grave doubts about their abilities. They are more apt to give up in the face of failure, to set inappropriately low goals for their performance, and to be particularly sensitive to others' judgments of it. In light of current practice to integrate educable mentally retarded children into regular school programs, it is believed important to provide them with training in social skills, and with supportive mechanisms that allow them to find satisfaction with achievement.

In the last section we discussed, rather briefly, severe mental retardation and multiple handicaps. Since severe and profound mental retardation is more likely to be organically caused, it is also more likely that multiple physical handicaps will be presented in this population. There is great diversity in the form that multiple handicaps can take. Persons with severe and profound mental retardation require many kinds of professional services; nonetheless, we emphasize the need for appropriate educational programming as a major goal for these individuals. The role of the family, their problems in coping, and their assistance in training are very important considerations in the provision of services for these children. Finally, it is important to keep in mind that multihandicapped persons may not be mentally retarded.

REFERENCES

Albee, G. W. A revolution in treatment of the retarded. In Anthony Davids (Ed.), *Issues in abnormal child psychology.* Monterey, Calif.: Brooks/Cole Publishing Co., 1973.

Baldwin, W. D. The social position of the educable mentally retarded in the regular grades in the public schools. *Exceptional Children,* 1958, *25,* 106–108.

Balla, D., Styfco, S. J., & Zigler, E. Use of the opposition concept and outer-directedness in intellectually average, familial retarded, and organically retarded children. *American Journal of Mental Deficiency,* 1971, *75,* 663–680.

Barnett, C. D., Pryer, M., & Ellis, N. R. Experimental manipulation of verbal behavior in defectives. *Psychological Reports,* 1959, *5,* 393–396.

Baumeister, A. A., & Kellas, G. Process variables in the paired-associate learning of retardates. In N. R. Ellis (Ed.), *International review of research in mental retardation*. New York: Academic Press, 1971, 226–270.

Belmont, J. M., & Butterfield, E. C. Learning strategies as determinants of memory deficiencies. *Cognitive Psychology*, 1971, *12*, 411–420.

Berkson, G., & Landesman-Dwyer, S. Behavioral research on severe and profound mental retardation (1955–1974). *American Journal of Mental Deficiency*, 1977, *81*, 428–454.

Bower, E. M. Early identification of emotionally handicapped children in school (2nd ed.). Springfield, Ill.: Charles C. Thomas, 1969.

Brophy, J. E., & Good, T. L. *Teacher-student relationships*. New York: Holt, Rinehart & Winston, 1974.

Brown, A. L. Judgment of recency for long sequences of pictures: The absence of a developmental trend. *Journal of Experimental Child Psychology*, 1973, *15*, 473–480.

Brown, A. L. The role of strategic behavior in retardate memory. In N. R. Ellis (Ed.), *International review of mental retardation*. New York: Academic Press, 1974.

Bryan, T. Social relationships and verbal interactions of learning disabled children in the classroom. *Journal of Learning Disabilities*, 1978, *11*, 107–115.

Bryan, T., & Bryan, J. H. *Understanding learning disabilities*. Sherman Oaks, Calif.: Alfred Publishing Co., 1978.

Cantor, G. N., & Ryan, T. J. Retention of verbal paired-associates in normals and retardates. *American Journal of Mental Deficiency*, 1962, *66*, 861–865.

Clausen, J. A. Quo vadis, AAMD? *Journal of Special Education*, 1972, *6*, 51–60.

Denny, M. R. Research in learning and performance. In H. A. Stevens & R. Heber (Eds.), *Mental retardation*. Chicago: University of Chicago Press, 1964.

Edgerton, R. B. *The cloak of competence: Stigma in the lives of the mentally retarded*. Berkeley, Calif.: University of California Press, 1967.

Ellis, N. R. Memory processes in retardates and normals. In N. R. Ellis (Ed.), *International review of research in mental retardation*. New York: Academic Press, 1970.

Farber, B. *Mental retardation*. Boston: Houghton Mifflin, 1968. *Federal Register, 41*, November 1976, No. 230.

Festinger, L. A theory of social comparison processes. *Human Relations*, 1954, *7*, 117–140.

Gardner, W. I. Reactions of intellectually normal and retarded boys after experimentally induced failure—A social learning theory interpretation. Ann Arbor, Mich.: University Microfilms, 1958.

Gearheart, B. R. *Education of the exceptional child*. Scranton, Pa.: Intext, 1972.

Goodman, H., Gottlieb, J., & Harrison, R. H. Social acceptance of EMRs integrated into a nongraded elementary school. *American Journal of Mental Deficiency*, 1972, *76*, 412–417.

Gottlieb, J. *Public, peer and professional attitudes toward mentally retarded.*

Paper presented at conference: The Mentally Retarded and Society: A Social Science Perspective. Niles, Mich., April 1974.

Gottlieb, J., & Budoff, M. Social acceptability of retarded children in non-graded schools differing in architecture. *American Journal of Mental Deficiency,* 1973, *78,* 15–19.

Gottlieb, J., & Davis, J. E. Social acceptance of EMRs during overt behavioral interaction. *American Journal of Mental Deficiency,* 1973, *78,* 141–143.

Gottlieb, J., Gampel, D. H., & Budoff, M. Classroom behavior of retarded children before and after reintegration into regular classes. *Studies in Learning Potential,* 1973, *3,* No. 49.

Graves, W. L., Freeman, M. G., & Thompson, J. D. Culturally related reproductive factors in mental retardation. In H. C. Haywood (Ed.), *Social-cultural aspects of mental retardation.* New York: Appleton-Century-Crofts, 1970, 695–736.

Green, C., & Zigler, E. Social deprivation and the performance of retarded and normal children on a satiation task. *Child Development,* 1962, *33,* 499–508.

Grossman, H. J. (Ed.). *Manual on terminology and classification in mental retardation.* Washington, D.C.: American Association on Mental Deficiency, 1973.

Guthrie, G. M., Butler, A., & Gorlow, L. Patterns of self-attitudes of retardates. *American Journal of Mental Deficiency,* 1962, *66,* 222–229.

Hartup, W. W., Glazer, J. A., & Charlesworth, R. Peer reinforcement and sociometric status. *Child Development,* 1967, *38,* 1017–1024.

Heal, L. W., & Johnson, J. T. Inhibition deficits in retardate learning and attention. In N. R. Ellis (Ed.), *International review of mental retardation.* New York: Academic Press, 1970, 107–149.

Heber, R. F. The relation of intelligence and physical maturity to social status of children. *Journal of Educational Psychology,* 1956, *47,* 158–162.

Heber, R. F. A manual on terminology and classification in mental retardation. *American Journal of Mental Deficiency Monograph,* 1959 (Supp. 64).

Heber, R. F. A manual on terminology and classification in mental retardation (Rev. ed.). *American Journal of Mental Deficiency Monograph,* 1961, (Supp. 64).

Hewett, F. M., & Forness, S. R. *Education of exceptional learners.* Boston: Allyn & Bacon, 1977.

Johnson, G. O. A study of the social position of mentally handicapped children in the regular grades. *American Journal of Mental Deficiency,* 1950, *55,* 60–89.

Johnson, G. O., & Kirk, S. A. Are mentally handicapped children segregated in the regular grades? *Exceptional Children,* 1950, *17,* 65–68, 87–88.

Klausmeier, H., Feldhusen, J., & Cheek, J. Cited by J. Belmont. Long term memory in mental retardation. In N. R. Ellis (Ed.), *International Review of research in mental retardation.* New York: Academic Press, 1966.

LaPouse, R., & Monk, M. A. Behavior deviations in a representative sample of children: Variation by sex, age, race, social class and family size. *American Journal of Orthopsychiatry,* 1964, *34,* 436–446.

London, P. *Beginning psychology.* Homewood, Ill.: The Dorsey Press, 1975.

Lott, B. E. Paired-associate learning, generalization and retention as a function of intelligence. *American Journal of Mental Deficiency*, 1958, 63, 481–498.

MacMillan, D. L. *Mental retardation in school and society*. Boston: Little, Brown & Co., 1977.

Meehl, P. E. *Clinical versus statistical prediction: A theoretical analysis and a review of the evidence*. Minneapolis: University of Minnesota Press, 1954.

Meichenbaum, D. H., & Bowers, K. S. A behavioral analysis of teacher expectancy effect. *Journal of Personality and Social Psychology*, 1969, 13, 306–316.

Mercer, J. R. *Sociological perspectives on mild mental retardation*. Paper delivered at Inaugural Peabody—NIMH Conference on Socio-Cultural Aspects of Mental Retardation. Nashville, Tenn., 1968.

Mercer, J. R. *Labeling the mentally retarded*. Berkeley, Calif.: University of California Press, 1973.

Miller, R. V. Social status of mentally superior, mentally typical and mentally retarded children. *Exceptional Children*, 1956, 23, 114–119.

National Foundation, March of Dimes. *Drugs causing fetal malformations in humans*. White Plains, N.Y., 1971.

Nihira, K., Foster, R., Shelhaas, M., & Leland, H. *AAMD adaptive behavior scale*. Washington, D.C.: American Association on Mental Deficiency, 1969.

Palardy, J. What teachers believe—what children achieve. *Elementary School Journal*, 1969, 69, 370–374.

Peterson, D. Educable mentally retarded. In N. G. Haring (Ed.), *Behavior of exceptional children*. Columbus, O.: Charles E. Merrill, 1974, 295–374.

President's Committee on Mental Retardation. *MR-72: Islands of excellence*. Washington, D.C.: U.S. Government Printing Office, 1973.

Ringelheim, D. The effect of failure on verbal expectancies in male defectives. *Abstracts of Peabody Studies in Mental Retardation*, 1960, 1, No. 14.

Rist, R. Student social class and teacher expectations: The self-fulfilling prophecy in ghetto education. *Harvard Educational Review*, 1970, 40, 411–451.

Robinson, H. B., & Robinson, N. M. *The mentally retarded child: A psychological approach*. New York: McGraw-Hill Book Co., 1965.

Robinson, H. B., & Robinson, N. Mental retardation. In Paul H. Mussen (Ed.), *Carmichael's manual of child psychology* (Vol. 2). New York: John Wiley & Sons, 1970.

Rosenberg, S. Problems of language development in the retarded. In H. C. Haywood (Ed.), *Social-cultural aspects of mental retardation*. New York: Appleton-Century-Crofts, 1970.

Semmel, M. I., Barritt, L. S., Bennett, S. W., & Perfetti, C. A. Grammatical analysis of word association of educable mentally retarded and normal children. *American Journal of Mental Deficiency*, 1968, 72, 567–576.

Semmel, M. I., & Bennett, S. W. Effects of linguistic structure and delay on memory span of EMR children. *American Journal of Mental Deficiency*, 1970, 74, 674–680.

Shotel, J. R., Iano, R. P., & McGettigan, J. F. Teacher attitudes associated with the integration of handicapped children. *Exceptional Children,* 1972, *38,* 677–684.

Sitko, M. C., & Semmel, M. I. Language and language behavior of the mentally retarded. In L. Mann and D. A. Sabatino (Eds.), *The first review of special education* (Vol. 1). Philadelphia: Journal of Special Education Press, 1973, 203–259.

Spitz, H. H. Consolidating facts into the schematized learning and memory system of educable retardates. In N. R. Ellis (Ed.), *International review of mental retardation.* New York: Academic Press, 1973, 149–168.

Spradlin, J. E. Language and communication of mental defectives. In N. R. Ellis (Ed.), *Handbook of mental deficiency.* New York: McGraw-Hill Book Co., 1963.

Spradlin, J. E., & Girardeau, F. L. The behavior of moderately and severely retarded persons. In N. R. Ellis (Ed.), *International review of research in mental retardation.* New York: Academic Press, 1966, *1,* 257–296.

Starkman, S. S., & Cromwell, R. L. Self-evaluation of performance and subsequent practice effects in mental defectives. *Psychological Reports,* 1958, *4,* 414.

Stein, Z., & Susser, M. Public health and mental retardation: New power and new problems. In M. J. Begab and S. A. Richardson (Eds.), *The mentally retarded and society: A social science perspective.* Baltimore: University Park Press, 1975.

Tarjan, G. Research and clinical advances in mental retardation. *Journal of the American Medical Association,* 1962, *182,* 617–621.

Turnure, J. E., & Zigler, E. Outerdirectedness in the problem-solving of normal and retarded children. *Journal of Abnormal and Social Psychology,* 1964, *69,* 427–436.

Underwood, B. J. Speed of learning and amount retained: A consideration of methodology. *Psychological Bulletin,* 1954, *51,* 276–282.

Weisberg, P. Operant procedures with the retardate: An overview of laboratory research. In N. R. Ellis (Ed.), *International review of research in mental retardation* (Vol. 5). New York: Academic Press, 1971.

Whalen, C. K., & Henker, B. Psycho-stimulants and children: A review and analysis. *Psychological Bulletin,* 1976, *83,* 1113–1130.

Wheeler, A. J., & Salzer, B. Operant training and generalization of a verbal response form in a speech-deficient child. *Journal of Applied Behavior Analysis,* 1970, *3,* 139–147.

Wilson, J. G. Teralogic causation in man and its evaluation in nonhuman primates. In B. V. Beidel (Ed.), *Proceedings of the Fourth International Conference,* Dordrecht, The Netherlands: Excerpta Medica, 1974, 191–203.

Wilson, K. *Mental retardation and memory.* Unpublished manuscript, Northwestern University, 1977.

Wood, J. W., Johnson, K. G., & Omori, Y. In utero exposure to the Hiroshima atomic bomb: An evaluation of head size and mental retardation 20 years later. *Pediatrics,* 1967, *39,* 385–392.

Woolf, L. I. Phenylketonuria and phenyldlanimemia. In J. Wortis (Ed.), *Mental retardation* (Vol. 2). New York: Grune & Stratton, 1970, 29–42.

Yando, R. M., & Zigler, G. Outerdirectedness in the problem-solving of institutionalized normal and retarded children. *Developmental Psychology*, 1971, 4, 277–288.

Zeaman, D., & House, B. J. The role of attention in retardate discrimination learning. In N. R. Ellis (Ed.), *Handbook of mental deficiency*. New York: McGraw-Hill Book Co., 1963.

Zigler, E. Mental retardation. In P. London & D. Rosenhan (Eds.), *Foundations of abnormal psychology*. New York: Holt, Rinehart & Winston, 1968.

Zigler, E. F., & Harter, S. The socialization of the mentally retarded. In D. A. Goslin (Ed.), *Handbook of socialization theory and research*. Chicago: Rand McNally Book & Co., 1969.

KEY TERMS

adaptive behavior The degree to which individuals meet the standards of personal independence and social responsibility deemed appropriate for their age and cultural group.

classical conditioning A type of learning in which a response to a stimulus becomes elicited because of that stimulus's repeated association with an unconditioned stimulus.

discrimination learning The production of a differential response when presented with more than one stimulus as a result of previous experiences.

Down's Syndrome (mongoloidism) A genetic abnormality associated with the presence of an extra chromosome in the twenty-first chromosome pair. Causes moderate to severe mental retardation and distinctive physical features.

kernicterus A disorder of the liver often associated with Rh incompatibility that results in excess amounts of bilirubin in the blood and oxygen deprivation. If untreated within a few days after birth, it can cause mental retardation, cerebral palsy, seizures, speech difficulties, or deafness.

operant conditioning The increase in frequency of an operant response after it has been followed by a favorable or reinforcing outcome.

paradigmatic response Verbal response to a stimulus word that is a member of the same grammatical class.

phenylketonuria A metabolic disorder of the liver resulting in toxic levels of phenylalinine. If not controlled by early dietary intervention, it may result in severe mental retardation.

syntagmatic response Verbal response to a stimulus word that is sequential in nature.

CHAPTER 6

Emotional and
Behavioral Disorders

There is probably no area of exceptionality more difficult to define and assess than emotional and behavioral disorders. While learning disabilities are frequently defined on the basis of reading tests, and mental retardation on the basis of intelligence tests, there are no parallel measures for behaviors and attitudes deemed different, undesirable, or inappropriate.

Because of the problem in defining emotional and behavioral disturbances, it is difficult to estimate the incidence of such problems, and estimates vary greatly. Kirk (1972) reported estimates of prevalence ranging from 8 percent to 22 percent, while Schultz, Hirshoren, Manton, and Henderson (1971) found estimates varied from .05 percent to 15 percent across the United States. The United States Office of Education (1975) indicated that approximately 2 percent of children suffer some form of emotional problem, while Bower (1969) suggested that as many as 10 percent experience emotional and behavioral difficulties. Clearly, there are thousands of children labeled emotionally and behaviorally disturbed who receive both the bounty and stigma associated with the diagnosis. We now examine attempts to define and clarify the concept of emotional and behavioral disorders to gain some understanding of what people mean when they use these terms.

DEFINITION AND CLASSIFICATION

It should be recognized that many of the behaviors associated with emotional disorders are observed in nonlabeled children. Lapouse and Monk (1958) found that about half of a group of children from randomly selected homes who were between 6 and 12 years of age showed many fears and had frequent temper tantrums. About one-third of these children had nightmares and chewed on their fingernails, while approximately 15 percent wet their beds and sucked their thumbs. If single or occasional demonstrations of these behaviors were considered sufficient to define emotional or behavioral disorders, it is likely that most children would fall into this classification. But unusual or maladaptive behavior exhibited for a brief period does not define the presence of a behavioral or emotional disorder. The child must commit rather ordinary actions either too intensely, too frequently, or too frequently in the wrong places to be diagnosed as a problem child. In addition, some emotional problems are not limited to acts of commission; they are associated with failure to do certain actions. Emotional and behavioral disturbances may be reflected in behavioral deficiencies as well as behavioral acts. Behavioral problems must be judged, therefore, in the social context in which they are found, the frequency with which they occur, and their intensity (Kauffman, 1977). Bower (1969) has indicated characteristics of children that should be frequently manifested across time before the child is labeled emotionally disturbed. These include:

1. An inability to learn which cannot be explained by intellectual, sensory, or health factors . . .
2. An inability to build or maintain satisfactory interpersonal relationships with peers and teachers . . .
3. Inappropriate types of behavior or feelings under normal conditions . . .
4. A general, pervasive mood of unhappiness or depression . . .
5. A tendency to develop physical symptoms, pains, or fears associated with personal or school problems . . ." [p. 22–23].

Grumbard states: "Behavioral disabilities are defined as a variety of excessive, chronic, deviant behaviors ranging from impulsive and aggressive to depressive and withdrawal acts (1) which violate the perceiver's expectations of appropriateness, (2) and which the perceiver wishes to see stopped" (1973, p. 246).

Kauffman (1977) has suggested that there are five features that comprise the defining process. Definitions should include a recognition of the role of the perceiver, of social norms and situational influences, and of the fact that the behavior must be chronic. Moods and attitudes about the self, as well as motor acts, should also be considered, while symptoms produced by known physical agents should be excluded from lists of emotional problems.

Classification of Emotional Disturbance

Part of the task confronting diagnosticians in their work with emotionally disturbed children is that of classifying the disturbance in the particular category that is most descriptive of the child's condition. After defining a child as emotionally disturbed, it is often necessary to specify just what type of disturbance is being demonstrated. A major classification scheme is that proposed by the American Psychiatric Association in the publication *Diagnostic and Statistical Manual of*

Mental Disorders. According to Kauffman (1977), children can be classified using the categories devised to describe disturbed adults. In addition, there are a number of categories specific to children. For instance, the major category Behavior Disorder of Childhood and Adolescence includes: hyperkinetic reaction (that is, hyperactivity), withdrawal reaction, overanxious reaction, runaway reaction, unsocialized and group delinquent reaction, and the catchall "other reactions." Children may also be classified as schizophrenic or suffering from transient situational adjustment disturbances. (That is, temporary problems resulting from situational stresses.) This particular diagnostic classification system has been quite popular in psychiatric circles for some time.

Deficiencies in APA Classifications

Unfortunately, it is clear that judgments concerning the categories into which particular people should be placed are very unreliable (Kauffman, 1977; Zigler and Phillips, 1961). Two independent judges who see the same person are likely to use very different classification categories. If diagnoses are unreliable, the predictions that stem from the diagnoses will frequently be in error. It appears that the particular diagnostic classification and treatment given adults is dependent upon their social class, areas of residence, and other presumably irrelevant factors (Redlich and Hollingshead, 1958). In addition, there is a great reluctance on the part of psychiatrists to retract a diagnosis or pronounce a "cure," at least of adults who have been diagnosed as disturbed. Even if you get well following a diagnosis of schizophrenia, you are likely to end up with the diagnosis schizophrenia *in remission.* This means you are not crazy at this moment, but you may well be in the next (Rosenhan, 1973).

We are unaware of studies concerning the vagaries of defining children as emotionally disturbed. It may be that diagnoses and treatments of children are not affected by variables like social class and geography and are less durable once applied. On the other hand, the diagnoses and treatments of children may correspond to practices for adults, and if this is the case, individuals working with emotionally disturbed youngsters should be alert to classification problems.

The classification system provided by the American Psychiatric Association is not founded upon systematically gathered information. The various subcategories are based on clinical experiences of the group's membership rather than upon data as to which behaviors do and do not vary. A different category system was developed by a well-known psychologist, Herbert Quay. Quay and colleagues methodically gathered information about children's behaviors and used factor analysis to determine which behaviors do and do not occur together.

Other Classifications

Quay (1972, 1975) suggested that there are three dimensions, or classifications, of behavior that characterize the majority of nondelinquent children who have emotional disturbances. One dimension is *conduct problems.* This refers to behaviors like disobedience, fighting, temper tantrums, destructiveness, and undue attention seeking. Children who have conduct problems are likely to show these behaviors but not those specified in the remaining two dimensions. The second dimension is *personality problems* or *neuroticism*. Children who score high on this dimension usually feel inferior and are self-conscious, socially withdrawn, shy, and hypersensitive. The third dimension is *inadequacy* or *immaturity*. Children in this group are apt to demonstrate short attention spans, passivity, sluggishness, and clumsiness.

Other investigators report results that parallel those of Quay (Anthony, 1970). In essence, children can be categorized into three rather distinct groups. The primary groups include youngsters with conduct problems such as aggressiveness and destructive behavior and personality problems such as shyness, fear, and withdrawal. The third problem, immaturity, is less frequently found or studied.

In the remaining sections of this chapter, theories of emotional disturbance are discussed, along with studies concerning the correlates of specific emotional problems. Since we believe there is a continuum of behaviors that range from "normal" to "abnormal," we will present various views of aggression, fear, and immaturity as studied in the normal and exceptional child. Theories and studies of the development and role of aggression and fear in normal children are seen as applicable to discussions of emotionally disturbed youngsters.

CONDUCT PROBLEMS

Many of the children in special education classes for the emotionally disturbed have conduct problems (Quay, Morse, and Cutler, 1966; McCarthy and Paraskevopoulos, 1969), making this a logical starting point for our scrutiny of emotionally disturbed children. The central characteristic of children with conduct problems is their difficulty in controlling their aggression. These girls and boys are destructive, engage in many fights, and are disruptive to ongoing activities, to name a few examples. There are theories concerning the nature of aggression, factors that lead to aggressive acts, and possible treatments of antisocial actions.

Definitions of Aggression

Based on the work of Albert Bandura, Kauffman suggests that the following factors determine whether a particular act will be defined as aggressive:

1. Characteristics of the behavior itself (for example, physical assaults, humiliation, property destruction) regardless of the effects on the recipient
2. Intensity of the behavior; high intensity responses (such as talking very loudly to a person) being labeled *aggressive* and low intensity responses (talking softly) being labeled *nonaggressive*

3. Expression of pain or injury or escape behavior by the recipient of the action
4. Apparent intentions of the performer of the deed
5. Characteristics of the observer (such as sex, socioeconomic status, ethnic background, child's own history of nonaggressive or aggressive behavior)
6. Characteristics of the aggressor (many of the same items could be listed here as for characteristics of the observer) [1977, p. 174].

As Kauffman indicates: "Labeling an act aggressive, then, depends for some people on criteria inherent in the behavior itself, while for other people the criteria for labeling aggression are subjective and apart from the act per se" (1977, p. 174).

Bandura (1973) has suggested that aggression is defined by behavior intended to cause injury to others, be it psychological or physical, but not done for socially sanctioned ends. As he indicated, pain induced by the dentist does not make the dentist's act an assault, nor is a person peaceable who shoots at someone and misses the target.

Feshbach (1970) also stresses that while aggression often includes injury to people or property, it is important to separate intentional or motivated aggression from other pain producing or destructive acts. This same author also indicates that intentional or motivated aggression does not necessarily mean the individual is aware of the attack or its motives, but that the aggression may serve some important function or bring some benefit to its perpetrator.

Most people agree that aggression means an attempt to injure or destroy somebody or something for reasons that are not socially sanctioned and that somehow fill the needs or goals of the individual committing such acts. Obviously, the range of aggressive acts encompassed within this definition is great. Such actions range from murder to nasty comments, from breaking a nose to breaking a balloon. In spite of the inclusion of very diverse behaviors, there are theories that attempt to outline the principles governing the commission of all aggressive acts. We now consider several of the more prominent notions.

Psychoanalytic Theory

Freud (1927) viewed aggressive behavior as the result of an aggressive drive or instinct. He thought that while all people possess aggressive drives or instincts, their ultimate expression in human conduct can take many forms. Thus, aggressive drives might be channeled into either socially acceptable or socially destructive actions, depending upon the particular life experiences of the individual.

Several features of Freud's ideas need to be stressed. First, Freud considered human beings to be hostile to each other. Second, the aggressive drive is rooted largely in people's biological nature; it is as much a part of human nature as the propensity to love and propagate. Third, aggressive drives could be reduced through their behavioral expression. Following an attack, one's aggressive drive or instinct is reduced, at least temporarily. This drive reduction can be accomplished through direct aggression or by nonaggressive behaviors; however, it does not diminish as much in the latter instance as in the former. The mechanisms that channel aggressive drives into socially acceptable behaviors include the adoption of values making aggressive expressions of the drive unacceptable. But if the values block too much of the aggressive drive, the individual suffers from some psychological disturbance. Thus, Freud argues a rather middle-of-the-road position. People have to be somewhat constrained but too much constraint will increase their miseries.

Finally, Freud hypothesized that aggression can be reduced through *vicarious* experiences. This hypothesis has caused no end of controversy. It was, and still is, often assumed that observing the aggressive actions of others will weaken an individual's own aggressive instincts. While Freud's theories have been somewhat modified by more contemporary analysts, the basic assumptions remain: Aggressive drives are rooted in instincts that are largely unconscious and that direct the behavior of the individual (Kauffman, 1977).

This particular perspective about aggression is still rather popular, at least among laypersons. Unfortunately, however, its application in the everyday affairs of parents, teachers, and children has not always been wise. The translation of this perspective by laypeople and some mental health workers seems to yield the following ideas:

1. Aggressive behavior should not be frequently inhibited since children need to express such drives.
2. Exposure to other forms of violence, such as is seen on television, will help control children's aggressions since such drives are then satisfied vicariously.
3. Since awareness of one's motives is the route to a better life, children should be made aware of their aggressive instincts.
4. Awareness of one's aggression is facilitated by expressing aggression.

While these notions have been rather popular, there is little evidence to support them, and much that contradicts them (Berkowitz, 1962; Bandura, 1969; Feshbach, 1970). Indeed, witnessing the assaultive behavior of others, being able to express aggression without negative consequences to oneself, and being made "aware" of one's aggressive instinct might all be reasonably expected to increase, not decrease, aggressive behavior. "Letting it all hang out" is quite likely to produce more aggression.

The Frustration-Aggression Hypothesis

A major alternative theory of aggression was proposed by Dollard, Doob, Miller, Mower, and Sears in 1939. While acknowledging the influence of Freud in their work, these psychologists proposed to explain aggression on the basis of experimental work in learning. They departed from Freud's theorizing on several important grounds. First, they rejected the notion of aggression as an instinct and argued instead that it is a result of frustration. Combativeness is greater, they suggested, if frustrating experiences are frequent, or if the strength of the drive that is frustrated is great. While the most likely response to frustration is aggression, alternate responses can be taught by means of reinforcing appropriate or desired actions.

These theorists provided a major stimulus to the study and understanding of aggression. In part, their impact was due to the way they worded their ideas. They made their theory testable. In part, their impact was the result of the fact that they were partially right; frustration often does produce aggression. Finally, these authors made the important suggestion that assaultive behavior can be predictably altered through the application of learning principles. Like Freud, they stimulated a great deal of research and thus increased our knowledge concerning aggression. Like Freud's, their theory also came under attack. First, the frustration-aggression hypothesis did not take into consideration qualitative differences in frustrating experiences. Some forms of frustration may kindle greater and/or different aggressive responses than other forms. Hence, frustration produced by practical necessity or the fates may well arouse less protest than that brought on by the arbitrary actions of a parent or teacher. Likewise, attacking the child's self-esteem may trigger more belligerence than the denial of candy, gum, or ice cream. Aggression is modified by such factors as the individual's expectations for the future, his or her trust in the frustrator, the moral justification for aggression, and a host of situational factors (Berkowitz, 1973). Finally, it is clear that aggressive actions can spring from experiences other than frustration.

Reinforcement and Modeling

Most theorists believe that aggressive behaviors are very much influenced by learning processes. This does not mean to say that aggression does not have a genetic or hormonal link; it clearly does, as numerous animal breeders have demonstrated (Fuller and Thompson, 1960). Rather, it is argued that the situational and learning experiences of the individual will play a paramount role in affecting the commission of an aggressive act.

It has been well documented that aggressive responses, like other types of behavior, are learned or sustained through reinforcement processes (for instance, Davitz, 1952; Buss and Durkee, 1958). A child who gets what he or she wants through aggressive behaviors is more likely to aggress in the future than one who has not had the initial rewarding experience. This reinforcement may stem from various sources, ranging from pleasure at the attention of disapproving adults to that generated by the victim's pain or distress. Moreover it is likely that a child's aggression can be elicited through vicarious reinforcements; to wit, the child's observations of other people's gains through overassertiveness. If Johnny sees Billy aggress and win some undeserved bounty, then Johnny is more likely to follow suit than if Billy had been unsuccessful. Thus either *direct* or *vicarious* reinforcements may serve to maintain or increase aggressive activities.

Yet another important source of instilling aggressiveness in children is that of behavioral examples. It has been repeatedly demonstrated that children learn methods of aggression from observing the acts of others. Given the right circumstances, children will imitate aggression. While learning and performance of aggressive acts will vary according to the power or status of the model and the constraints of the situation that affect the child, there is simply no room for doubt that aggressive models teach children how to be aggressive.

We have presented, in brief sketch, some popular perspectives concerning aggression. However, this kind of behavior is a much-studied phenomenon and some of the important "facts" about it should be presented. We now turn to some of the correlates of aggression, which will be followed by a description of techniques that have been employed to control it.

Sex, Social Class, and Aggression

Perhaps the most consistent finding in this area is that boys are more aggressive than girls, at least when the aggression involves physical assaults (Feshbach, 1970). Several possible explanations have been offered to account for this finding. First, there are constitutional differences between the sexes, differences involving hormones, as well as skin and pain sensitivity differences (Feshbach, 1970). For example, there is considerable evidence that hormones will affect aggressive actions of lower animals. The injection of the male hormone testosterone is likely to increase the aggressive behaviors of female lower animals (Feshbach, 1970). A second notion, more popular than scientifically demonstrated, is that boys learn to be aggressive and girls to be nonaggressive because of society's expectations concerning sex-appropriate behaviors. It is argued that on the basis of sex roles, males should be more aggressive than females. The evidence indicating a differential reinforcement for physical aggression by males, either by direct approval or through the lack of efforts to control such behavior, is quite limited and by and large negative (Maccoby and Jacklin, 1974; Parke, 1977). Whatever the possible causal factors in physical aggression by boys, sex differences are quite apparent. It should not be surprising then that boys are more frequently labeled behavior or conduct problems than are girls (Anthony, 1970; Kauffman, 1977).

While boys may throw "sticks and stones," both girls and boys are likely to call "names." (Girls are as likely as boys, perhaps more likely, to employ indirect forms of aggression.) Indeed, Feshbach (1970) has argued that the sexes are probably alike in their aggressive urges and that differences between male and female pugnacity are largely the result of differences in muscularity. The forms of aggression girls use appear to be more socially acceptable than those of boys and, consequently, reduce their chances of being called conduct disordered.

A second variable often assumed to be related to children's aggression is parental social class. Early studies addressed to this correlation repeatedly demonstrated that middle- and upper-class parents were more suppressive of their children's aggression than lower-class parents. Their children consequently were less likely than their lower-class counterparts to be aggressive. Lately, however, these early beliefs have been challenged. Recent studies have suggested that middle class parents are less likely to punish their child's aggression severely than are lower-class parents. It appears that both groups of parents attempt to suppress aggression, but tend to use somewhat different procedures. The middle-class parent is more likely than the lower-class one to be warmer to the child in general and less constraining of the child's activities, and to employ guilt or induction methods of disciplining. Feshbach nicely summarizes the current state of knowledge concerning social class and aggression when he writes: "The data bearing on the relationship between the social class background of the child and his aggressiveness are contradictory and not easily reconcilable" (1970, p. 197).

Catharsis

For many years people generally accepted the psychoanalytic hypothesis that the suppression of aggressiveness might ill serve the mental health of the individual being curbed. Many people have believed that it is beneficial for the child to express anger, "let off steam," and "get it off his chest." Moreover, the notion that some "steam letting" was possible through the observations of another's aggression has served the movie and television industry in their attempts to justify violence in their productions. Finally, it has been long thought possible to help the emotionally disturbed child through eliciting and rewarding expressions of aggression. As the reader might suspect, these views have been challenged by recent studies concerning reinforcement and modeling. By and large, the notion of catharsis has been discredited. There is ample evidence that rewarded aggression leads to more of the same, that "letting off steam" might well stoke the boiler, and that seeing others aggress is likely to elicit aggression by the observing child. Much like other forms of behavior, aggressive behavior is affected by rewards, punishments, and models (Bandura, 1969; Feshbach, 1970; Berkowitz, 1973). While it would be correct to argue that some children, sometimes, do benefit from successful expressions of aggression, it is probably also correct to argue that encouraging such expressions leads to more aggression in most children at most times. Aggression training might be suitable for children who have difficulties in asserting themselves in everyday social intercourse, but it is likely to be detrimental to the child already too assertive and uncontrolled.

We have discussed some of the notions and determinants of aggression. It is now time to turn to what is known about the child who is considered to have a conduct problem.

The Aggressive Child

While boys may be more aggressive than girls, and situational factors such as television, aggressive models, and reinforcements may affect aggression in virtually all children, there are children whose antisocial behaviors are particularly extreme in either their frequency or illegality. This section of the chapter will describe some results of studies pertaining to this group of youngsters.

Conduct problems range from difficulties primarily with school authorities and/or parents to those antisocial behaviors that result in incarceration. While most problems that occur during a child's development tend to disappear, given nonanxious parents, such is not the case with problems of aggression. Children who are viewed as conduct problems apparently mature to be adult conduct problems (Pritchard and Graham, 1966; Robins, 1966; Feldhusen, Roeser, and Thurston, 1977). Relative to shyness, irritability, insomnia, and speech defects, the worst prognosis is associated with conduct difficulties.

Most studies concerning the life and trials of children with conduct problems focus upon their parents. Early studies involving parents have investigated their attitudes and affects about their offspring, and their methods of disciplining them. More recently, our notions concerning reinforcements and punishments have directed our attention to the interactions between parent and child. There is now considerable information concerning the parents of aggressive children.

Lack of Parental Warmth

It is clear that these parents do not view their children with much warmth or benevolence. Parents of hostile and/or delinquent children are likely to have deprived them of love and to have treated their needs cavalierly (Hewitt and Jenkins, 1946; Glueck and Glueck, 1950; Bandura and Walters, 1959). Whether the parents' lack of warmth and their anger toward the child are the causes or the results of the child's conduct problems, however, remains a moot point. One thing is certain and that is that there is not much affection between child and parents. This is particularly important to note since the effects of specific forms of discipline and child-rearing are likely to be influenced by the general warmth or coldness with which the parents impose their views upon the child. Punishment from a loving parent is likely to have effects quite different from the same sort of punishment administered by an indifferent one.

Restrictiveness versus Permissiveness

A second variable of child-raising that has concerned researchers is that of the parents' restrictiveness or permissiveness in governing the behavior of the child. The question is asked whether the degree of parental control over the child's behavior is associated with the inhibition or the venting of aggression. There is really no simple statement that can summarize the facts. Sometimes permissiveness, at other times restrictiveness, have been found to be factors in children's aggression. The effects of permissiveness appear to depend upon whether it is the father or mother who is the tolerant one, whether it is a daughter or son who is given relative freedom, and at what age such child-rearing practices are put into effect (Feshbach, 1970). What might clarify the relationship between permissiveness-restrictiveness and aggression is whether such policies are carried out within the context of parental hostility or warmth. Feshbach (1970) suggested that strictness in combination with parental hostility is likely to be the breeding ground for subsequent aggressive behaviors. Such conditions both provide a model of interpersonal rejection and cause considerable frustration in the child. However, it has been observed that many parents of aggressive children make few demands upon their offspring to behave in socially acceptable ways. There is relatively little emphasis on training the child to behave in a prosocial manner. It is likely that many highly aggressive children come from homes that model interpersonal rejection, severely frustrate the child, and fail to help the child to conform to the customary standards of good conduct.

Control of Aggression

A third consideration prominent in studies of parental correlates of conduct problems involves the parents' attempts to control and inhibit their child's aggressiveness. There is considerable evidence that physical punishment of aggression will probably increase the child's belligerence. Boys with conduct problems are likely to have parents who attempt to control behavior through frequent use of physical assaults (Becker, 1964; Baumrind, 1966). The reasons underlying this relationship between assaults and subsequent aggressiveness are open to dispute. The relationship may be a fairly direct one, as might be expected according to social learning or modeling theory. Victims of aggression might imitate the behavior to which they have been exposed (Parke, 1977). The relationship, however, could be considerably less direct. Becker (1964) noted that parents who resort to physical punishments for disciplining are less inclined than other parents to control behavior with reasoning or rewards. Finally, as indicated in Chapter 3, while punishment can be an effective device for behavior control, its effectiveness depends on the variety of factors, such as its intensity, timing, and consistency.

It should be noted that not all parents are brutal toward their aggressive offspring. Patterson, Cobb, and Ray (1972), after observing families of aggressive boys, identified three parental patterns of handling children's aggressive actions. In one the parents were insensitive to actions that ultimately led to the aggressive behaviors. These parents failed to spot the sequence of behaviors building to an aggressive outcome and thus did not intervene to break the undesirable chain. These parents did not notice what was happening until the aggression erupted; then they responded with scolding and nagging, but not intense punishment. Interestingly, these parents spent little time or effort attempting to train their children in prosocial, or socially desirable, behaviors.

The second type of parenting involves very different dynamics. These parents do pay attention to the child's behaviors and do attempt to develop prosocial habits. However, they do not attempt to stop the aggressive actions, and perhaps may even subtly reward children for such behavior. Finally, in the third type of parental pattern suggested by Patterson et al., the father is unusually harsh in his disciplining and the mother is particularly indulgent toward the child. Thus, the punishments and reinforcements to the child are inconsistent between parents.

In summary, it appears that aggressive behavior problems are among the most frequent and the most stubborn of a broad group of emotional disturbances. These children apparently often have parents who are either unloving, brutal, inconsistent, or grossly incompetent in their attempts to manage their children's aggressive conduct. Such children are thus likely to be presented with models of rejection and aggression, to be exposed to contradictory messages concerning the appropriateness of their aggression, and to receive relatively little training in socially desirable conduct. It would be misleading, however, to suggest that such children cannot be helped, that their condition cannot be corrected. That such help can be rendered should be apparent from the earlier chapter on socialization and from the subsequent chapters on remediation.

Hyperactivity

While hyperactivity is not necessarily a symptom characterizing conduct disorders, we include it within this section because it is frequently associated with antisocial behaviors. In addition, hyperactive children appear to resemble more closely children who are called conduct problems than those with personality or immaturity difficulties.

Approximately 3 to 20 percent of our school age population are defined as hyperactive, and approximately 50 percent of all referrals for childhood behavior disorders are for this problem (Langhorne and Loney, 1976; Whalen and Henker, 1976). But what does hyperactivity mean? Typically, people view hyperactivity as excessive and/or inappropriate motor activity, and perceive the hyperactive child as one who repeatedly demonstrates such behavior. Judgments about excessive activity, either formalized in rating scales or expressed during interviews by parents, teachers, or physicians, usually serve as the evidence upon which the diagnosis is made. The typical remediation for this "condition" is the administration of stimulant drugs. Indeed, the diagnosis and the drug treatment have become so popular that Offir (1974) has estimated that between 500,000 and two million children are taking drugs like Ritalin (methylphenidate) or Dexedrine (dextroamphetamine) to control their hyperactivity. What are the characteristics of children labeled hyperactive?

Characteristics of the Hyperactive

First and foremost, it is apparent that, as a group, these children are no more active than nonhyperactive children. This is to say, hyperactive children do not appear to demonstrate greater motor activity than other children. At least this is true when activity is measured within "unstructured situations," situations that do not demand that the child concentrate on tasks imposed by others. Whalen and Henker, who have provided an excellent review of the findings pertaining to hyperactivity, write: "It should be noted that the failure to find consistent differences in general activity level holds whether global ratings, behavioral observations, or electromechanical recordings are used to assess motoric response" (1976, p. 1115). The hyperactive child is not a motoric machine run amok. Since hyperactive children are generally not more active than their nonlabeled counterparts, is there any evidence that they differ from other children on any type of motoric expression? Apparently there is. Whalen and Henker suggest that "the issue is one of quality rather than quantity of movement, and the data indicate that hyperactive children may show atypically high levels of motor restlessness when an external agent (e.g., teacher or examiner) requires performance on a structured task. In other words, the difficulty may not be one of inordinately high activity levels, but rather an inability to modulate motor behavior in accordance with situation (and particularly social) demands" (1976, p. 1115). Whalen and Henker also argue that the hyperactive child does not wiggle or jiggle excessively, even within a structured task situation, but rather seems less able to keep his or her mind on the task.

While the general level of activity has been thought to be a primary indicator of hyperactivity, associated characteristics of this "condition" have also been postulated (Stewart, Pitts, Craig, and Dieruf, 1966). Hence, hyperactive children are thought to be not only overly active, but also to show distractibility, short attention span, clumsiness, emotional lability, poor academic performance, antisocial behavior, poor peer relationships, low self-esteem, and irritability (Langhorne and Loney, 1976; Whalen and Henker, 1976). It is believed that such characteristics should be associated with the diagnosis of hyperactivity and with each other. Most of the investigations concerned with how these behaviors are linked have employed rating scales as the means of measurement. The results of these analyses have generally failed to find that the listed behaviors are connected with the diagnosis of hyperactivity or even with each other. The results of studies both reviewed and conducted by Langhorne and Loney (1976) suggest that correlations, if any, found between these characteristics reflect the source of the judgment rather than the behavior being judged. This means that the correlations among ratings of behaviors that should not theoretically be correlated are likely to be higher when they are made by the same judge than the correlations found in ratings of the same behavior measured by two different judges. Given that judges, such as physicians, teachers, and parents, view the children in very different situations, and given that the differences between hyperactive and nonhyperactive children are manifested only in "structured" situations, then it is perhaps not surprising that these judges would not agree when evaluating the same child on the same behavior but in varying situations. They may see different actions because of the differences in the situations in which they view the child. The doctor's office is different from the classroom and both are different from the home. In addition, there are difficulties associated with many of the rating scales currently employed. While rating scales do generally differentiate children previously diagnosed as hyperactive from youngsters not so diagnosed, the scores obtained are rather unstable across time, and the ratings obtained are frequently found to be uncorrelated with behavior actually observed (Whalen and Henker, 1976).

Although there is little evidence that various behaviors are associated with the category of hyperactivity or with each other, it is true that many children so diagnosed have problems in school performance and interpersonal relationships (Achenbach, 1977; Bryan and Bryan, 1978; Kauffman, 1977). Indeed, it is quite possible that the combination of poor academic performance and social obnoxiousness becomes critical in determining a child as hyperactive. Thus if a child cannot maintain attention in structured situations, and, in addition, suffers from poor interpersonal relationships and academic performance, that child is likely to be diagnosed as hyperactive.

While we do not know much about hyperactive children there are some reasonable statements that can be made about them. Whatever differentiates these children from others (aside from taking pills) is likely to be situationally specific. Behavior differences between hyperactive and normally active children are not evidenced in all situations, but may be pronounced in a few. Second, behavioral differences are more likely to be based on attentional rather than gross motor problems. Third, it is also clear that children labeled hyperactive have a rather bleak future, with or without pills. Weiss, Minde, Werry, Douglass, and Nemeth (1971) conducted a five-year follow-up of girls and boys previously diagnosed as hyperactive and found them to show no improvement in academic grades and to have few friends. Even more discouraging, as many as 15 percent had been referred to the courts for significant antisocial behaviors. In another follow-up investigation of hyperactive children, parents reported to Mendelson, Johnson, and Stewart (1971) that more than 50 percent of the children had stolen, had been in serious fights, or were habitual liars. Over 33 percent had threatened to kill one or both of their parents. Indeed, 59 percent of the children in this sample had had some contact with the police. These authors report further that over 50 percent of the sample indicated low self-confidence and rejection by others. Fifteen percent had either talked about or attempted suicide. Finally, as Whalen and Henker point out, previous administration of drugs does not seem to affect most of these behaviors.

Drugs and Hyperactivity

While we have avoided discussing remediation techniques for the various problems suffered by children, it is appropriate to discuss briefly the use of drugs for controlling hyperactivity. The reason for this departure is that while reinforcements, models, and other forms of therapy have applicability to any number of problems experienced by the exceptional child, drug therapy has been generally confined to the hyperactive child.

The literature concerning drugs and hyperactivity is vast. The following section relies heavily upon the report by Whalen and Henker (1976), and interested readers are referred to their article for references to original sources. These researchers concluded that Ritalin appears to help from 60 to 90 percent of the children who receive it. The success rate of Dexedrine is somewhat lower than that of Ritalin, but still substantial numbers of children seem to improve with its administration. There is a catch, however, and Whalen and Henker explicate it when they write: "We know that the drugs can and often do have powerful, positive effects; we do not know when, why, how or with whom. It is also becoming apparent that many of the children who show marked improvement while taking medication fail to maintain these gains once medication is discontinued . . ." (1976, p. 1114). Some of the conclusions that can be drawn from this review are:

Motor Activity   Drugs are not likely to reduce motor activity of the hyperactive child when that child is in an unstructured situation as, for example, on the playground. In such contexts, medication might even increase activity. However, drugs do appear to reduce motor activity of children when they are confronted with structured tasks.

Impulsivity   Stimulants like Ritalin and Dexedrine appear to reduce children's impulsivity when they attempt to solve difficult problems. When the answer to a question is uncertain, the stimulants seem to help the child refrain from answering and subsequently to perform more competently on the task. When the responses are easy, that is, when the correct answer is obvious, the drugs seem to increase response speeds. Evidently the drugs allow the child to integrate and control his or her motor responses better so as to cope more competently with the task. Sometimes the responses the tasks require are fast, at other times, slow. Apparently drugs help many children under both conditions.

Attention Span   Stimulants appear to aid the hyperactive child to maintain attention. They increase vigilance to the task. On the other hand, reasoning, complex problem solving, reading achievement, and intelligence test scores do not show improvement after administration of the drug.

Social-Emotional Behavior   Drugs affect some forms of social-emotional behavior, at least when behavior is assessed by means of rating scales. Using such measures, stimulants have been found to reduce aggressive conduct and hyperactivity (that is, *perceptions* of the child's activity, concentration, impulsiveness, irritability, temper outbursts, and schoolwork). However, the meaning of these changes is not clear since scores on the rating scales are found to be correlated only infrequently with the child's observed behavior.

Drugs versus No Drugs   Children who had previously received medication but no longer do so do not fare any better in social or academic pursuits than those who had never received medication. Moreover, the effects of medication do not appear to persist in its absence.

Response to Drugs   While a number of attempts have been made to determine which child is likely to benefit from drugs, it is not possible to predict responses to medication.

In many instances drugging children is apt to be a stressful and controversial procedure. This has been the case in prescribing drugs for hyperactive children. Emotions aside, there have been warnings voiced concerning the undesirable side effects that such procedures may entail. Offir (1974) suggested that the use of drugs like Ritalin may well be associated with the suppression of normal growth along with increased irritability, depression, nausea, and insomnia. Greenberg (1976) voiced the same concerns, plus uneasiness over possible addiction and the use of drugs as a "cop-out" for inept teachers and poor teaching techniques. Whalen and Henker place their warning within the context of attributional therapy. They suggest that the prescribing drugs allows children to attribute their difficulties to physiological problems, problems beyond their control. Such attributions severely curtail the child's belief that it is possible to remediate the condition through his or her own efforts. Thus, while drugs apparently help many children to attend better and perhaps to be less aggressive, they may also be associated with undesirable side effects in exchange for only short-term benefits.

WITHDRAWAL

A second major problem experienced by children consists of their withdrawal from humans or objects. Of course, most children do pull back from something sometimes so withdrawal does not become problematic until it is shown so frequently or with so much emotion that it debilitates the child. There are many forms and degrees that a child's withdrawal may take, ranging from excessive fears concerning a particular object or person to such complete withdrawal that virtually no social intercourse is possible. In the first case, the child is said to have a **phobia;** in the second case **autism** or **schizophrenia.** Besides these particular forms of withdrawal, children may display a degree of social withdrawal that, while not extreme, substantially reduces the child's opportunities for obtaining gratifications from others. Such children are seen as shy, reclusive, sensitive about the opinions of others, and typically sad or depressed. Given that these children's actions tend to make them wallflowers, producing a kind of social invisibility, such children are only infrequently placed in special education classrooms (Kauffman, 1977). Nonetheless, these children do appear to live lives of quiet misery.

In the following sections, we describe some of the thinking and research concerning children's withdrawal behaviors, beginning with phobias.

Phobias

Most children have fears. This is to be expected. However, most such fears are temporary (Jersild and Holmes, 1935). While phobias are essentially extreme fears, they are often not so temporary, and are frequently quite incapacitating. "Phobic reactions are specialized anxiety states in which the patient experiences intense fear when confronted with a particular object or situation. Unlike 'free-floating' or general anxiety, the source of fear is specific and can be identified. The patient, along with most other people, sees it as unreasonable, however, and cannot account for his overwhelming fear" (DeNike and Tiber, 1968, p. 346). A person's extreme fear of something or some situation that is inexplicable by the fearful person constitutes a phobic response. Intense and irrational fears may be directed toward almost anything: heights, the outdoors, closed spaces, dirt, bugs, school, animals, vehicles, to name but a few possibilities. Virtually any object or place or circumstance can elicit a phobic response.

Another significant feature of phobias is that they often show generalization. In other words, if the child has a phobia about one object or situation, that individual may develop other fearful responses to objects or situations that are somehow similar to that triggering the first phobia. Phobias can be crippling for several reasons. First, they may be focused on an object that if avoided can seriously disrupt one's life, for example, the fear of water. Secondly, phobias might generalize to such an extent that they incapacitate the child. For instance, imagine how destructive would be the generalization of a phobia about water to all liquids. Phobias can be serious matters. While they can take many forms, it is likely that the most frequent phobia exhibited by children is *school phobia*. The child is terrified of attending school. Although many children are frightened on their first day of school, and a good number remain genuinely reluctant to attend thereafter, a number of children will develop an absolute terror of the classroom, usually after having attended school for some time.

How Phobias Develop: Psychoanalytic View

There are several ideas about how children may acquire a phobic response. Psychoanalytic theory suggests that such fears are the result of unconscious conflicts and the desire to avoid recognition of the conflict between values and biological drives. According to this line of reasoning, the fear object may give rise to the conflict and/or recognition of it, and thus the individual seeks to avoid it. Frequently, the feared object does not directly mirror the conflict, but rather is thought to symbolize it. Thus a phobia concerning a horse may reflect fear of castration, while school phobia may reflect a conflict about separation from the mother (Freud, 1955a; Kauffman, 1977). While psychoanalytically oriented interpretations of phobic responses may still retain some popularity among the psychiatric community, by and large they have lost stature with educators and psychologists. A more popular view with these latter groups seeks to understand phobias through principles of learning.

Conditioning

An interpretation of phobias using principles of learning is that children learn fears and phobies by means of traumatic experiences. Proponents of this idea stress principles of conditioning. A classic experiment conducted by Watson and Rayner (1920) demonstrated how fears and phobias might be learned. In this experiment a child was simultaneously exposed to a rabbit (a conditioned stimulus) and a loud noise (an unconditioned stimulus). The loud noise was used to frighten the child. Eventually the rabbit acquired the capacity to frighten the child in the absence of the noise and became as aversive as the noise itself. Thus a previously benevolent rabbit became an object of considerable fear through the simple procedure of pairing it with a frightening event. Moreover, the child also demonstrated a generalization of his fear, becoming eventually frightened of some objects that looked "furry," such as a Santa Claus costume. The power of repeated pairings of an emotionally neutral stimulus with an emotionally provoking one to elicit fear and avoidance responses has been well documented since 1920.

Vicarious Experiences

It has been shown that phobias may be learned through vicarious experiences. Bandura writes: "Many phobic behaviors, for example, arise not from actual injurious experiences with the phobic objects, but rather from witnessing others either respond fearfully toward, or be hurt by, certain things . . ." (1969, p. 167). A variety of studies have determined that people can be emotionally aroused by witnessing the experiences of others. Apparently most people are sensitive to the emotional states of others and are likely to experience empathic reactions to the emotions they see others display. However, is it possible that such instances of empathic responses can be transformed into a habit so that a phobic response might occur? Is it possible that a child witnessing another person's fear will become terrified of the object that frightened the observed person?

There is evidence that such conditioning does occur. For example, Berger (1962) was able to elicit fear responses from observers who had not been directly threatened by an emotionally neutral stimulus by having them believe that another person was receiving shocks. Similar evidence of such conditioning has been reported by Craig and Weinstein (1965) and Bandura and Rosenthal (1966).

Direct Tutoring

Besides simple conditioning and observational learning, there is yet another way to teach a child a phobic response: by direct tutoring. As children can be taught to eat with knives and forks, go to the toilet, and to read, they also can be directly taught to be afraid of the world about them. A number of investigators have found that many parents, particularly mothers, of school phobic children are overprotective of their offspring, tending to produce in the child both fear of the world and an overdependence upon the parents for security. These parents apparently teach the child to be fearful and train him or her to reduce this fear through physical closeness with the parent (Hetherington and Martin, 1972). This particular combination of events does not bode well for the child since it has been repeatedly demonstrated that fears can be overcome by exposing the child to small doses of the fearful object or event. Gradually introducing the child to the feared object in a manner that allows him or her to experience some anxiety but not overwhelming panic will help the youngster extinguish the fear (Jersild and Holmes, 1935). The behavior of the parent of the school phobic child may often prevent such therapeutic experiences.

While childhood fears are common, and phobic reactions rather frequent, the elimination of fears is possible. Of all the emotional disturbances that might afflict youngsters, phobias are perhaps the easiest to treat. Treatment programs based upon conditioning and upon modeling have proven to be effective in eliminating many types of strong fears and, in addition, can be implemented very cheaply. These will be discussed in subsequent chapters on remediation.

Social Withdrawal and Depression

Among the patterns of behavioral disturbances found by Quay and associates is that called personality disorder. Children who are so diagnosed are likely to exhibit feelings of distress, fear, anxiety, physical complaints, and considerable unhappiness (Quay, 1972). These children show a pattern of withdrawal rather than assertiveness, and are more likely to exhibit phobias than truancy. In this section we discuss how investigators assess social withdrawal and some of the characteristics of children with personality disorders. The most extreme form of social withdrawal, childhood schizophrenia or autism, is discussed in the following section. We do not extensively discuss the predominant theorizing concerning the origins of such behavior. These stress principles of conditioning, reinforcement, and modeling and would be redundant to material already presented. Finally, we conclude this section with a brief discussion of childhood depression.

While teachers, and perhaps parents as well, are not likely to be aroused to action by the conduct of a withdrawn child as opposed to an aggressive one, it is also clear that social withdrawal can be, and often is, a serious behavior disorder (Greenwood, Walker, and Hops, 1977). It is generally assumed that individuals do have rather strong motives to affiliate and interact with others (London, 1964, 1975) and thus the failure to do so suggests a serious problem. While the evidence is far from convincing, many believe that social withdrawal by a child is a precursor of the later development of a psychotic condition known as schizophrenia. It does seem to be the case that social withdrawal in childhood is associated with later indices of mental health (Greenwood et al., 1977).

Isolation

Social withdrawal can stem from a variety of causes. First, the child may simply not wish to initiate many social interactions because his or her interests lie elsewhere. Second, the child may initiate social interactions but either receive no positive reinforcements or be rebuffed. In the former case, the affiliative behaviors

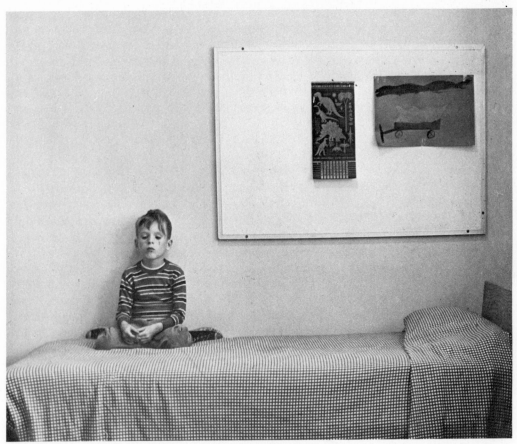

FIGURE 6-1 A socially withdrawn, depressed child

may be extinguished; in the latter case, they may become associated with fear. There are three methods by which social withdrawal can be measured. The first is asking the classroom teacher to judge the child's popularity and/or the frequency with which the child interacts with peers. The second method involves asking classmates about the child. This procedure often includes sociometric assessments, a task wherein children indicate their friends and foes. The child may be asked whom he or she would like to invite to a birthday party, have as a friend, or sit next to in the classroom. If a child is frequently named by classmates, he or she is considered popular. Children are also asked to name their foes by indicating whom they would not like to have as a friend, invite to a birthday party, or sit next to. Children who receive such nominations are considered rejected. Finally, those children who are not named as either friend or foe are considered social isolates. A third method of assessment is through observational procedures wherein a person enters the classroom and tallies the frequency and/or duration of children's social intercourse.

While sociometric measures assess a child's popularity, they are not a direct measure of social withdrawal. A child may be outgoing and yet be socially ignored. In fact, however, evidence does suggest that social isolation is correlated with both teacher ratings and the observed behavior of the child. Children who do not initiate much interaction are ignored by their peers and perceived as socially withdrawn by their teachers (Greenwood et al., 1977). Thus, a child's social withdrawal may be accompanied by peers' social indifference.

Low Self-Esteem

A second characteristic associated with social withdrawal, or in Quay's terminology, personality disturbances, is that of low self-esteem and high self-criticism. These qualities might be acquired in a variety of ways. For example, Aronfreed (1968) has argued that self-critical responses are learned through reinforcements. In this case, by displaying self-criticism, children may frequently terminate a punishment and the anxiety it begets. Self-criticism and low self-esteem might also be generated from observing the behaviors of others. Coopersmith (1967) found that mothers of boys who had high self-esteem also had high self-esteem. Insofar as personality problems in childhood are frequently linked to personality problems of the parents, it is quite possible that low self-esteem is directly induced through observational learning (Hetherington and Martin, 1972). However, it should be noted that Coopersmith also found that boys with high self-esteem had higher IQ scores, better physical coordination, and better physical development than those with low self-esteem. Reality factors may play an important role in determining low self-esteem.

Parental Role

Evidence pertaining to parent-child interactions of socially withdrawn and inhibited children have generally found that the parents of such children are more constraining, more repressive, more overcontrolling than parents of non-inhibited children (Hewitt and Jenkins, 1946; Lewis, 1954; Jenkins, 1968). Moreover, studies employing normal children have found that children who were self-punishing, lacked dominance, and showed more dependence and conformity behaviors were more likely to have overprotective and restricting parents than children lacking these characteristics (Kagan and Moss, 1962; Sears, 1961). While these results have not always been found (compare Becker, Peterson, Hellmer, Shoemaker, and Quay, 1959; Baumrind, 1967) and some studies have been criticized on methodological grounds (Hetherington and Martin, 1972), the evidence does seem to indicate that children's social isolation and accompanying personality difficulties are correlated with parental overprotectiveness and restrictiveness. Other factors have been implicated in affecting the child's social withdrawal. Oftentimes children who are social isolates receive a considerable amount of attention from available adults as the latter attempt to manipulate the child into social activity. The social isolation of the child may actually be reinforced by adults acting as social facilitators or therapists (Allen, Hart, Buell, Harris, and Wolf, 1964).

Depression

Finally, a word about depression. One result of social withdrawal can be extreme unhappiness. The ultimate response to such misery is suicide. While suicide is rarely reported in young children, it is the fourth leading cause of death for high school students and the second leading cause for college students (London, 1975; Kauffman, 1977). Automobiles kill the greatest number of adolescents and young adults, but suicide is certainly not a rarity within these age groups. Severe depressions, whether in the young or the old, must be treated as a grave matter. Depressions are generally associated with low self-esteem, social withdrawal, high self-blame, negative expectations about the future, and an inability to make a decision (Abramson and Sackeim, 1977).

Depressions are frequently precipitated by the loss or the impending loss of something important to the individual. The loss of a loved one or of money, the failure to graduate from high school or to gain entrance into college, or any number of other significant deprivations, may elicit this state of personal misery. The probability of suicide attempts are increased if the individual has no one with whom he or she is close during the period immediately preceding the experience of deprivation (such as in the spring for high school students, when academic failures will have their most serious repercussions), on the anniversary of the deprivation, or during a holiday period. The wise parent or teacher will treat childhood and adolescent depression as a very serious matter and will initiate referrals to professionals who have competence and experience in dealing with depressions. Not to do so may seriously jeopardize the individual's life.

Functional Childhood Psychosis

Psychosis represents the most extreme form of children's behavioral disturbances; the symptoms are often frightening to those who observe them and are always greatly debilitating to those who experience them. Psychosis, whether suffered by an adult or child, can be produced by a variety of events. These include toxic agents, brain damage, metabolic events, tumors, infections, and unspecifiable environmental conditions. The condition is called a **functional psychosis** when viruses, physical traumas, tumors, or faulty metabolism that might cause the condition are not found or suspected. In this section we look at functional psychosis in children, its appearance, correlates, and possible causes.

Before discussing functional psychosis, it should be recognized that definitions and classification systems vary greatly among professionals. One professional may call a child autistic, another schizophrenic, yet another may term the symptoms an atypical child syndrome. Of particular popularity are two diagnostic labels, childhood schizophrenia and autism, or infantile autism. While the distinctions between these two groups are controversial, it is generally believed that the autistic child shows a severe disturbance in functioning at an early age, while the schizophrenic child does not; that the autistic child will not develop delusions and hallucinations in later life, while the schizophrenic child might; and that the personality problems of the parents of autistic children are presumed different from those of the parents of the schizophrenic child (Werry, 1972). Although these distinctions are gaining in popularity, they are not universally applied. The lack of uniformity of diagnosis and classification makes generalizations concerning incidence, treatments, and characteristics difficult, since one is not entirely sure which children are being called which names. Given this ambiguity of definition, we will not differentiate between the autistic child and schizophrenic child in our discussion of this psychosis. By the use of the term schizophrenia, we mean to include those children whom some theorists might consider autistic.

A Rare Condition

As mentioned, statistics concerning the frequency of childhood schizophrenia are very difficult to evaluate. One statement that does seem true is that such disorders in children are extremely rare (Goldfarb, 1970). Estimates of incidence have ranged from .008 percent of the population to .06 percent (Werry, 1972), but almost all investigators have concluded that this condition is a relatively unusual event. Another area of agreement concerning these children is that boys are considerably more likely than girls to exhibit such a disorder. The ratio of boys to girls has been estimated to range between 1.7 to 1 and 9.5 to 1 (Andrews and Cappon, 1957; Hinton, 1963).

Characteristics

Nine diagnostic signs have been proposed to characterize psychotic children and they appear to have some support. These are:

1. Gross and sustained *impairment of emotional relationships* with people.
2. *Apparent unawareness of his own personal identity*. This may be seen in abnormal behavior towards himself, such as posturing or exploration and scrutiny of parts of his body. Repeated self-directed aggression. . . .
3. *Pathological preoccupation with particular objects* . . . without regard to their accepted functions.
4. *Sustained resistance to change in the environment*. . . .
5. *Abnormal perceptual experiences* . . . implied by excessive, diminished, or unpredictable response to sensory stimuli. . . .
6. Acute, excessive, and seemingly illogical *anxiety* is a frequent phenomenon.

7. *Speech* may have been lost or never acquired, or may have failed to develop beyond a level appropriate to an earlier stage.
8. *Distortion in motility patterns*—for example, . . . ritualistic mannerisms, such as rocking and spinning (themselves or objects).
9. *A background of serious retardation* in which islets of normal, near-normal, or exceptional intellectual function or skill may appear [Goldfarb, 1970, p. 780].

It should be made clear, however, that no one particular symptom is indicative of childhood schizophrenia, and children who are so diagnosed may show great individual differences in their particular combinations of symptoms. Let us now look at some of the research findings on schizophrenic children.

Perhaps the most frequent characteristic of such children is their social withdrawal. First, they often cannot or will not speak, or if they do, they do so in such a manner as to make social communication impossible. Second, they avoid physical or sensory contact with others. That is, they usually will not touch nor even look at other people (Kauffman, 1977). For example, their eye contact with others is almost nonexistent; when they do look at others, they do so furtively and through the corners of their eyes. Because their withdrawal is so complete, one frequent question is: Do they not have some profound deficiency in their sensory receptors? Are they in fact deaf or blind or otherwise sensorily impaired? The answer is no. These children do have intact sensory processes, at least to the extent that they visually avoid dangerous objects and do respond to sounds, but they do so selectively. Thus, they are more likely to respond to tones than to voices; more likely to "see" objects, than people. They are very adept at "tuning out" social stimuli. Sensory reception is among the few functions in the schizophrenic child that do appear normal.

One dimension of concern is the intellectual functioning of these children. A number of investigations have indicated that such children are likely to have rather low intelligence test scores. Indeed, psychotic conditions are frequently associated with mental retardation. Pollack (1967), after reviewing related studies, found that two-thirds of the children tested had IQ scores below 80. Goldfarb (1961) also found intellectual impairment in psychotic children, as have many others (compare Werry, 1972). But IQ test scores are not the only evidence that the thinking or conceptual capacities of these children are amiss. Several investigations have revealed that psychotic children conceptualize the world in a more concrete fashion than do nonpsychotic children (Friedman, 1961; Schulman, 1953). Hence, such children are more likely to be struck by the surface features of an object, for example, its color or texture, than by the functions it may serve; more apt to categorize objects according to the number of legs they possess (elephant with chair) than by some abstract concept (animate versus inanimate).

It is apparent that many psychotic children show deficiencies in cognitive processes. It also should be remembered, however, that all such children are not concrete in their thinking nor do all obtain low scores on intelligence tests; some show abstract reasoning ability and obtain very high scores on intelligence tests.

Not surprisingly, psychotic children have speech and language problems. Indeed, it is these problems that are one of the salient features of the psychotic child. Speech problems are reflected in mutism (about 50 percent do not speak at all), echolalia, a condition in which the child repeats what he or she has heard, reversal of pronouns (for example, "he" or "she"), and literalness (Kanner, 1946; Kauffman, 1977). In addition, others have found that psychotic children who do speak do so in unusual ways. Thus, such children are likely to show an absence of inflection, or a poor integration of speaking with breathing. Individuals working with schizophrenic children often believe that language might be used to gauge the severity of the problem and its prognosis. The worse the speech, the greater the severity and the poorer the chances for benefit from treatment (Goldfarb, 1970).

A number of hypotheses have been developed to explain the causes of childhood schizophrenia. These emphasize either organic or psychological agents. Theories focusing on organic causes cite the influence of genes or brain damage during the pre- and perinatal periods. Specific sites of brain damage have been suggested such as the midbrain and cortical speech areas, as well as general brain damage. The genetic hypothesis has not received much support, but ideas concerning brain damage and childhood schizophrenia are being investigated with vigor and improved medical technology.

Studies of possible psychological causes of childhood schizophrenia have focused primarily upon the parents. Kanner (1943) and Eisenberg and Kanner (1956) have stressed that children they term autistic are likely to have parents who are detached emotionally, and who are intellectually far above average. While this notion has gained popularity, the evidence supporting it has not been convincing (Goldfarb, 1970). Others have suggested that anxiety and conflict within the mother, perhaps in combination with overprotectiveness, produce the psychotic child. Finally, some have proposed that the parents have produced such an offspring by failure to reinforce the child's adult-directed social behaviors (Ferster, 1961). There appears to be little solid evidence supporting the idea that childhood psychosis is related to particular parent practices or traits.

Finally, a word about the treatment of psychotic children. While the phobic child may be the easiest of the emotionally disturbed to treat, the young schizophrenic is probably the most difficult to help. Typical treatment techniques are rather drastic, such as electric shocks, in order to break into the world of these children. While many show some improvement with or without treatment, rather few make any great progress (Werry, 1972).

INADEQUACY AND IMMATURITY

A third major pattern of disturbance found by Quay and others is that of immaturity or inadequacy (Quay, 1972). Children who somehow do not fit the expectations of teachers or parents in their everyday conduct, but who are not obviously aggressive, mentally retarded, extremely fearful, or withdrawn, are likely to be seen as immature or inadequate. The pattern of behaviors found by Quay and others that defines this problem includes excessive preoccupation, short attention span, clumsiness, passivity, sluggishness, daydreaming, and a preference for younger playmates. None of these behaviors by itself would seem deviant, but too many of them too frequently exhibited become a cause for concern.

Kauffman (1977) included under the term immaturity-inadequacy additional behavior problems: negativism, excessive crying and temper tantrums, **psychophysiological disorders, obsessions, compulsions,** and **regression.** *Negativism* is rather common in two- and three-year-olds and is no doubt the bane of many a mother's existence. The child says no to most requests and commands, even when the requests might enhance the child's immediate pleasures. Teacher and parent firmness is necessary in handling negativism, which is likely to be exacerbated by permissiveness.

Probably all of us have had crying and temper tantrums, behaviors not unusual in small children. Parents and teachers should, and probably do, realize that crying behaviors may reflect either the child's need to be soothed and succored or a need to dominate or manipulate others. When the aim is to dominate, and the parent or teacher provides sympathy, support, and indulgence, the ultimate result is that the child is reinforced for unreasonable and obnoxious behaviors. By and large, withdrawal of reinforcements, coupled with punishments and firmness in dealing with such manipulations, is likely to result in their extinction within a relatively short time (Williams, 1959). On the other hand, rendering sympathy and support to a child who is really miserable does not appear to reinforce crying behaviors (Maccoby and Masters, 1972).

Regression

Regression occurs when a child with a repertoire of more advanced behaviors starts to behave like a much younger child. The condition might be indicated when the child resumes thumbsucking after an extended period of abstinence, prefers baby talk to age-appropriate communication, or when his table manners become even more barbaric. When regression is extensive, the problem must be treated with great seriousness. Such behaviors might be the result of grave physical problems, for example, brain tumors, or be a sign of a deep psychological disturbance. When, however, the regression is not extensive, when it is not too frightening to observe or too disruptive to life, it is probably best treated by careful attention to the reinforcing events possibly sustaining it. Behavior modification techniques are likely to be beneficial in the treatment of such behaviors (Kauffman, 1977).

There are two psychophysiological disorders that are relatively common and often distressing to both parent and child. These are *enuresis*, inadequate urine control, and *encopresis*, inappropriate defecation. The first occurs frequently; about 13 to 20 percent of first graders manifest enuresis, as do about 2 to 3 percent of all 14-year-olds (Kauffman, 1977). This is a problem experienced primarily in boys rather than girls. Since almost everyone in our culture over the age of two realizes that uncontrolled toileting is a major social faux pas, children who suffer from enuresis or encopresis are truly in misery. Again, however, these problems can be treated very successfully through conditioning and reinforcement procedures.

Obsessions and Compulsions

Obsessions and *compulsions* are repetitive behaviors that seriously interfere with the child's capacity to carry out daily affairs. Obsessions refer to repetitive thoughts (somewhat like when you are unable to get a tune out of your mind), while compulsions refer to behaviors that are committed repeatedly. Individuals suffering from such repetitive actions almost always feel that they have no control over them. The child may well recognize that the thoughts or behaviors are "silly," "irrational," and/or a waste of time, but he will also feel that such actions or thoughts are well beyond his control. There is some evidence to suggest that these difficulties are associated with phobias and that treatment with behavior modification techniques may be effective in helping such children (Kauffman, 1977).

SUMMARY

This chapter provides definitions, classification schemes, descriptions, and explanations of emotional and behavior disorders. A major problem in understanding emotional and behavior disorders is the paucity of methods for measuring children's social problems. While standardized assessment techniques are far from perfect, as discussed in the chapters on mental retardation and learning disabilities, the absence of techniques analagous even to these exposes the diagnosis of emotional and behavior disorders to subjective and unreliable judgments (Quay, 1972). Prevalence rates indicate that about .05 percent to 22 percent of children in the United States may manifest emotional and behavioral problems, but these estimates vary greatly due to difficulties in defining such problems.

Many of the behaviors attributed to children who are diagnosed as emotionally and behaviorally disordered are present in youngsters who are never seen by a mental helper nor considered to be experiencing other than the normal vagaries of development. Thus, for a child to be considered as emotionally or behaviorally disordered requires that maladaptive behaviors be judged in light of their frequency, intensity, and social context.

Classification schemes to categorize children's emotional and behavioral disorders, developed by the American Psychiatric Association, include disturbances experiences by adults as well as some specific to children. In addition, the subcategories range from mild or transient emotional problems (such as phobias) to severe, chronic problems (such as schizophrenia). The categories developed by the American Psychiatric Association have been popular but since they have not been validated empirically, more recent efforts to define such disorders have been initiated. Much of this later work has been based on systematically based data. Within this context, three major categories of emotional and behavioral disorders in children have been described. These include conduct problems, personality problems, and problems of inadequacy and immaturity.

Conduct problems have probably captured the greatest amount of professional attention, and for good reasons. First, such problems are among the most frequent. Second, they involve uncontrolled aggression and thus are among the most disruptive of the behavior problems. We have therefore examined a number of theories that attempt to explain the development and persistence of aggressive behavior, hence the discussions of Freudian theory, the frustration-aggression theory, and principles of modeling and reinforcement. It has been well documented that aggression is caused by frustration, can be learned by observing others, and is affected by the outcomes of aggression either for the self or for observed others. It is also clear that males are more likely than females to engage in physical aggression, but that females do not want for aggressive urges. Finally, it was shown that the relationship of parents' rearing practices are related, albeit in complex ways, to their offsprings' aggressiveness. Parents who are unloving, brutal, inconsistent, or incompetent in child-rearing are more likely to produce aggressive children.

Hyperactivity, variously estimated as affecting from 3 to 20 percent of our children, is behavior that is qualitatively rather than quantitatively different from that of nonhyperactive children and reflects a child's inability to modulate motor behavior in accordance with the demands of a situation. These children frequently have problems in academic achievement and social relationships. The most frequently used treatment for hyperactivity is stimulant drugs, a therapy that helps many children some of the time but carries with it potentially destructive influences. Follow-up data on hyperactive children indicate a rather bleak future as many of them continue to have behavior problems and an inordinate number become unhappily involved with the courts. The administration of drugs does not seem to make a difference in long-term outcomes for hyperactivity.

A number of childhood behavior disorders involve various types of withdrawal, among which are withdrawal from people, fear and avoidance of objects and situations, and depression. While adults are not as aroused by withdrawal problems as by aggression, social withdrawal can be a serious disorder. Significant persons in the child's life should be aware of the problem's seriousness, and the suicide rates, of depressed adolescents and young adults.

Finally, we discussed the most severe forms of emotional disorders, the functional psychosis of schizophrenia/autism. While little is really known of the causes for severe emotional disturbance, current theorizing and efforts tend to focus more on physiological reasoning that includes concerns for genetic influences and damage to various parts of the brain. The symptoms exhibited by children with functional psychosis are severe and affect all areas of their behavior: intelligence and cognitions, speech and language, relationships with people. Functional psychosis does not occur often, but its impact upon children and parents is devastating. While some children do show improvement, with or without treatment, the prognosis for most of them is very guarded.

REFERENCES

Abraham, W. *Common sense about gifted children.* New York: Harper & Row, 1958.

Abramson, L. Y., & Sackeim, H. A. A paradox in depressions: Uncontrollability and self-blame. *Psychological Bulletin,* 1977, *84,* 838–851.

Achenbach, T. M. Behavior disorders in preschool children. In H. L. Hom, Jr., & P. A. Robinson (Eds.), *Psychological processes in early education.* New York: Academic Press, 1977.

Allen, K. G., Hart, B. M., Buell, J. S., Harris, R. F., & Wolf, M. M. Effects of social reinforcement on isolate behavior of a nursery school child. *Child Development,* 1964, *35,* 511–518.

Andrews, E., & Cappon, D. Autism and schizophrenia in a child guidance clinic. *Canadian Psychiatric Association Journal,* 1957, *2,* 1–25.

Anthony, E. J. The behavior disorders of childhood. In P. H. Mussen (Ed.), *Carmichael's manual of child psychology* (Vol. 2). New York: John Wiley & Sons, 1970.

Aronfreed, J. *Conduct and conscience: The socialization of internalized control over behavior.* New York: Academic Press, 1968.

Bandura, A. Social-learning theory of identificatory processes. In D. A. Goslin (Ed.), *Handbook of socialization theory and research.* Chicago: Rand McNally and Co., 1969.

Bandura, A. *Aggression: A social learning analysis.* Englewood Cliffs, N.J.: Prentice-Hall, 1973.

Bandura, A., & Rosenthal, T. L. Vicarious classical conditioning as a function of arousal level. *Journal of Personality and Social Psychology,* 1966, *3,* 54–62.

Bandura, A., & Walters, R. H. *Adolescent aggression.* New York: Ronald Press, 1959.

Baumrind, D. Child care practices anteceding three patterns of pre-school behavior. *Genetic Psychology Monographs,* 1966, *75,* 43–88.

Becker, W. C. Consequences of different kinds of parental discipline. In M. L. Hoffman and L. W. Hoffman (Eds.), *Review of child development research* (Vol. 1). New York: Russell Sage, 1964.

Becker, W. C., Peterson, D. R., Helmer, L. A., Shoemaker, D. J., & Quay, H. C. Factors in parental behavior and personality as related to problem behaviors in children. *Journal of Consulting Psychology,* 1959, *23,* 107–118.

Berger, S. M. Conditioning through vicarious instigation. *Psychological Review,* 1962, *69,* 450–466.

Berkowitz, L. *Aggression: A social psychological analysis.* New York: McGraw-Hill Book Co., 1962.

Berkowitz, L. Control of aggression. In B. M. Caldwell & H. N. Ricciuti (Eds.), *Review of child development research* (Vol. 3). Chicago: University of Chicago Press, 1973.

Bower, E. M. *Early identification of emotionally handicapped children in school* (2nd ed.). Springfield, Ill.: Charles C. Thomas, 1969.

Bryan, T., & Bryan, J. J. *Understanding learning disabilities* (2nd ed.). Sherman Oaks, Calif.: Alfred Publishing Co., 1978.

Buss, A. H., & Durkee, A. Conditioning of hostile verbalizations in a situation resembling a clinical interview. *Journal of Consulting Psychology*, 1958, *22*, 415–418.

Coopersmith, S. *The antecedents of self-esteem*. San Francisco: W. H. Freeman, 1967.

Craig, K. D., & Weinstein, M. S. Conditioning vicarious affective arousal. *Psychological Reports*, 1965, *17*, 955–963.

Davitz, J. The effect of previous training on postfrustration behaviors. *Journal of Abnormal and Social Psychology*, 1952, *47*, 309–315.

DeNike, L. D., & Tiber, N. Neurotic behavior. In P. London & D. Rosenhan (Eds.), *Abnormal psychology*. New York: Holt, Rinehart & Winston, 1968.

Dollard, J., Doob, L. W., Miller, N. E., Mowrer, D. H., & Sears, R. R. *Frustration and aggression*. New Haven, Conn.: Yale University Press, 1939.

Eisenberg, L., & Kanner, L. Childhood schizophrenia. *American Journal of Orthopsychiatry*, 1956, *26*, 556–564.

Feldhusen, J. F., Roeser, T. D., & Thurston, J. R. Prediction of social adjustment over a period of six or nine years. *The Journal of Special Education*, 1977, *11*, 29–36.

Ferster, C. Positive reinforcement and behavioral deficits of autistic children. *Child Development*, 1961, *32*, 437–456.

Feshbach, S. Aggression. In P. H. Mussen (Ed.), *Carmichael's manual of child psychology* (Vol. 2). New York: John Wiley & Sons, 1970.

Freud, S. *Beyond the pleasure principle*. New York: Boni & Liveright, 1927.

Freud, S. *Collected papers* (Vols. 1–5). New York: Basic Books, 1959.

Friedman, G. Conceptual thinking in schizophrenic children. *Genetic Psychology Monographs*, 1961, *63*, 149–196.

Fuller, J. L., & Thompson, W. R. *Behavior genetics*. New York: John Wiley & Sons, 1960.

Glueck, S., & Glueck, E. *Unraveling juvenile delinquency*. Cambridge, Mass.: Harvard University Press, 1950.

Goldfarb, W. *Childhood schizophrenia*. Cambridge, Mass.: Harvard University Press, 1961.

Goldfarb, W. Childhood psychosis. In P. H. Mussen (Ed.), *Carmichael's manual of child psychology* (Vol. 2). New York: John Wiley & Sons, 1970.

Grumbard, P. S. Children with behavioral disabilities. In L. M. Dunn (Ed.), *Exceptional children in the schools* (2nd ed.). New York: Holt, Rinehart & Winston, 1973.

Greenberg, J. S. Hyperkinesis and the schools. *Journal of School Health*, 1976, *46*, 91–97.

Greenwood, C. R., Walker, H. M., & Hops, H. Issues in social interaction/withdrawal assessments. *Exceptional Children*, 1977, *43*, 490–550.

Hetherington, E. M., & Martin, B. Family interaction and psychopathology in children. In H. C. Quay & J. S. Luerry (Eds.), *Psychopathological disorders in childhood*. New York: John Wiley & Sons, 1972.

Hewett, L. E., & Jenkins, R. L. *Fundamental patterns of maladjustment: The dynamics of their origin*. Chicago: State of Illinois, 1946.

Hinton, G. Childhood psychosis or mental retardation: A diagnostic dilemma. Paediatric and neurological aspects. *Canadian Medical Association Journal,* 1963, *89,* 1020–1024.

Jenkins, R. L. The variates of children's behavioral problems and family dynamics. *American Journal of Psychiatry,* 1968, *124,* 1440–1445.

Jersild, A. T., & Holmes, F. B. Children's fears. *Child development monograph,* 1935, No. 20.

Kagan, J., & Moss, H. A. *Birth to Maturity: A Study in Psychological Development.* New York: John Wiley & Sons, 1962.

Kanner, L. Autistic disturbance of affective contact. *Nervous Child,* 1943, *2.* 217–250.

Kauffman, J. M. *Characteristics of children's behavior disorders.* Columbus, O.: Charles E. Merrill, 1977.

Kirk, S. A. *Educating exceptional children.* Boston: Houghton Mifflin, 1972.

Langhorne, J. E., & Loney, J. Childhood hyperkinseses: A return to the source: *Journal of Abnormal Psychology,* 1976, *85,* 201–209.

Lapouse, R., & Monk, M. A. Behavior deviations in a representative sample of children: Variation by sex, age, race, social class and family size. *American Journal of Orthopsychiatry,* 1964, *34,* 436–446.

Lazarus, R. S., Speisman, J. C., Mordkoff, A. M., & Davison, L. A. A laboratory study of psychological stress produced by a motion picture film. *Psychological Monographs,* 1962, *76* (Whole No. 553).

Lewis, H. *Deprived children.* London: Oxford University Press, 1954.

London, P. *Modes and morals of psychotherapy.* New York: Holt, Rinehart & Winston, 1964.

London, P. *Beginning psychology.* Homewood, Ill.: The Dorsey Press, 1975.

Maccoby, E. E., & Jacklin, C. N. *The psychology of sex differences.* Stanford, Calif.: Stanford University Press, 1974.

Maccoby, E., & Masters, J. C. Attachment and dependency. In P. H. Mussen (Ed.), *Carmichael's manual of child psychology* (Vol. 2). New York: John Wiley & Sons, 1970.

McCarthy, J. M., & Paraskevopoulos, J. Behavior patterns of learning disabled, emotionally disturbed and average children. *Exceptional Children,* 1969, *36,* 69–74.

Mendelson, W., Johnson, N., & Stewart, M. A. Hyperactive children as teenagers: A follow-up study. *The Journal of Nervous and Mental Disease,* 1971, *153,* 273–279.

Offir, C. W. Are we pushers for our own children. *Psychology Today,* December 1974, 49.

Parke, R. D. Punishment in children: Effects, side effects, and alternative strategies. In H. L. Hom & P. A. Robinson (Eds.), *Psychological processes in early education.* New York: Academic Press, 1977.

Patterson, G. R., Cobb, J. A., & Ray, R. S. Direct intervention in the classroom: A set of procedures for the aggressive child. In F. W. Clark, P. R. Evans, & L. A. Hammerlynek (Eds.), *Implementing behavioral programs in schools and clinics.* Champaign, Ill.: Research Press, 1972.

Pollack, M. Mental subnormality and "childhood schizophrenia." In J. Zubin (Ed.), *Psychopathology of mental development.* New York: Grune & Stratton, 1967.

Pritchard, M., & Graham, P. An investigation of a group of patients who have attended both the child and adult departments of the same psychiatric hospital. *British Journal of Psychiatry*, 1966, *112*, 487–603.

Quay, H. C. Patterns of aggression, withdrawal and immaturity. In H. C. Quay & J. S. Merry (Eds.), *Psychopathological disorders in childhood*. New York: John Wiley & Sons, 1972.

Quay, H. C. Classification in the treatment of delinquency and anti-social behavior. In H. Hobbs (Ed.), *Issues in the classification of children* (Vol. 1). San Francisco: Jossey-Bass, 1975.

Quay, H. C., Morse, W. C., & Cutler, R. L. Personality patterns of pupils in special classes for the emotionally disturbed. *Exceptional Children*, 1966, *32*, 297–301.

Redlich, F., & Hollingshead, A. B. *Social class and mental illness*. New York: John Wiley & Sons, 1958.

Robins, L. N. *Deviant children grown up*. London: E. & S. Livingston, 1966.

Rosenhan, D. L. On being sane in insane places. *Science*, 1973, *179*, 250–258.

Schulman, I. Concept formation in the schizophrenic child: A study of ego development. *Journal of Clinical Psychology*, 1953, *9*, 11–15.

Schultz, E. W., Hirshoren, A., Manton, A. B., & Henderson, R. A. Special education for the emotionally disturbed. *Exceptional Children*, 1971, *38*, 313–319.

Sears, R. R. Relation of early socialization to aggression in middle childhood. *Journal of Abnormal and Social Psychology*, 1961, *63*, 466–492.

Stewart, M. A., Pitts, F. N., Craig, A. G., & Dieruf, W. The hyperactive child syndrome. *American Journal of Orthopsychiatry*, 1966, *36*, 861–867.

U.S. Office of Education. *Estimated number of handicapped children in the United States, 1974–75*. Washington, D.C.: U.S. Office of Education, 1975.

Watson, J. B., & Rayner, R. Conditioned emotional reactions. *Journal of Experimental Psychology*, 1920, *3*, 1–14.

Weiss, G., Minde, K., Werry, J. S., Douglass, V., & Nemeth, E. Studies in the hyperactive child: A five year follow-up. *Archives of General Psychiatry*, 1971, *24*, 409–414.

Werry, J. S. Childhood Psychosis. In H. S. Quay & J. S. Werry (Eds.), *Psychopathological disorders of childhood*. New York: John Wiley & Sons, 1972.

Whalen, C. K., & Henker, B. Psychostimulants and children: A review and analysis. *Psychological Bulletin*, 1976, *83*, 1113–1130.

Williams, C. D. The elimination of tantrum behavior by extinction procedures. *Journal of Abnormal and Social Psychology*, 1959, *59*, 269.

Zigler, E., & Phillips, L. Psychiatric diagnosis and symptomatology. *Journal of Abnormal and Social Psychology*, 1961, *63*, 69–75.

KEY TERMS

autism A severe psychological disorder of childhood characterized by extreme self-isolation, lack of interest in the environment, little meaningful language, and insistence by the child on the preservation of sameness.

compulsions A behavior or set of behaviors that are repeated continuously and inappropriately.

echolalia The continuous repetition of what is said by other persons.

functional psychosis The inability to meet the usual demands of life due to psychological problems. Characterized by severe behavior deficits and may be accompanied by inappropriate thought, mood, or action without known organic causes.

obsessions Disruptive, persistent thoughts that are beyond the control of the person.

phobia Intense and excessive fear of specific objects, persons, or situations.

psychophysiological disorders Psychological problems that are specifically associated with damage to physical structures—typically injury to some part of the central nervous system.

regression A defense mechanism that is characterized by an individual resorting to earlier modes of functioning.

schizophrenia A form of psychosis with no known organic cause having symptoms including thought disorders, bizarre emotions, hallucinations, and delusions.

CHAPTER 7

The Hearing Impaired Child

Hearing impairments are relatively rare among children. Kirk (1972) indicated that about 3 to 5 percent of school-aged children suffer from hearing problems that are sufficiently acute to require special education services, while about 1 in 1000 children can be considered deaf. Meadow (1975) reported that only 0.1 percent of all schoolaged children were enrolled in special schools and classes for hearing problems during 1971. However, while there may be a relatively small percentage of children who have hearing problems, Meadow did find that about 46,000 children in the United States require special services for hearing defects. That is a lot of children!

Although part of a relatively small group, the individual child with a hearing loss suffers considerably. For centuries people with hearing impairments were socially and physically isolated, ridiculed, considered not only deaf but "dumb," and generally prevented from leading a normal life. After all, many did not speak and if they did their speech was apt to be unintelligible. During the past one hundred years or so their lot has tended to improve, primarily because of the efforts of Alexander Graham Bell and Thomas Hopkins Gallaudet, among others, whose work stimulated the development of technical and educational assistance. Residential schools for the deaf, hearing aids, and even the telephone were the direct result of the efforts of these pioneers. Thanks to recent advances in our ability to detect hearing problems, improvements in hearing aids, and shifts in national policy, the hearing impaired child is being integrated into school and community programs (Glasscock, 1975). It is no longer the rule that the deaf child is placed in residential schools isolated from parents, peers, and community.

We begin our study of hearing impaired children with a description of the auditory mechanism, the structure and process by which we hear. We then review definitions and classifications of hearing loss, the methods used to assess hearing, the types of hearing problems, characteristics of hearing impaired children, and available special education programs. The reader might pay particular attention to this chapter because if lucky to live long enough, he or she is likely to suffer a hearing loss.

THE HEARING MECHANISM

To understand the different types of hearing losses and their impact upon children, it helps to know a bit about how we hear. Hearing is the result of the passage of sound energy through a number of bone, nerve, and related structures that eventually carry the message to the brain. The auditory mechanism consists of an outer, middle, and inner ear, and the nerves that carry the transmissions to areas in the brain where they are interpreted and remembered. The outer ear serves to scoop up sound waves from the external environment. These waves are then transmitted through an inch-long canal to the eardrum. The canal amplifies the sound, increasing by twofold the pressure of the sound waves upon the eardrum, a membrane separating the outer from the middle ear. In the middle ear there are three very small bones: the **hammer,** the **anvil,** and the **stirrup.** The pressures exerted upon the eardrum set up vibrations in these bones, the hammer triggering the anvil, the anvil triggering the stirrup. The transmitted energy is further amplified with each stimulation. The stirrup then strikes the oval window, a membrane that separates it from the inner ear. In the inner ear is the **cochlea,** a fluid-filled structure resembling a snail's shell and containing some 25,000 neatly arranged hair cells on which there are nerve endings. The stimulation from the stirrup causes the fluid in the cochlea to ripple and thus stimulate the hairs in the cochlea. The hair cells are arranged in a way that makes them sensitive to various patterns of ripples. These stimulations are sent through the auditory nerve to various parts of the brain. In effect, the ear turns sound waves or air pressure first into vibrations that displace bones, then into waves in the form of changes in the fluids in the inner ear. Finally, the waves and the changes in the fluid stimulate nerve endings, transmitting the message through the auditory nerve, an impressive bundle of fibers, to various brain centers (Frisina, 1967; London, 1975).

Types of hearing loss are often discussed according to the site where this process breaks down. When the defect impairing a person's ability to hear is in the outer or middle ear, the problem is called a **conduction problem.** In **sensorineural problem** the point of breakdown occurs in the inner ear or in the auditory nerve that transmits the information to the brain.

To summarize, the ability to detect sound is associated with the outer and middle ear; the ability to detect and interpret sound is associated with the inner ear (the cochlea), the auditory nerve, and parts of the brain including the midbrain and auditory cortex.

DETECTING HEARING IMPAIRMENTS

In this section, we review some of the procedures used to detect children's hearing problems and some of the current ways of classifying hearing losses. As you learn about the assessment techniques, it is important to bear in mind that a single test is usually insufficient for making a definitive diagnosis. Most typically, a battery of tests will be required before one can determine the presence, degree, type, and site of a hearing problem.

A major problem in rendering services to hearing impaired children is locating the children who need them. It is generally agreed that the earlier a hearing loss is detected, the greater the likelihood that the child might benefit from intervention. Thus, there are hopes that some methods can be devised to allow detection of hearing problems during infancy.

The High Risk Registry

One proposal is that a *high risk registry* be established in which infants who appear to be particularly susceptible to hearing impairments are listed at local hospitals and a central agency so that frequent hearing assessments can be conducted as the child develops. It has been proposed that since it is currently impossible to screen all newborns for hearing difficulties, precious resources should be allotted to locate infants who are particularly likely to have or to develop hearing impairments and to make their potential vulnerability known to the appropriate agencies. Gerber (1977) suggests that interviews with responsible and knowledgeable adults might yield the necessary information so that suitable decisions concerning the child at risk can be made. The questions that he recommends include: Does the family have a history of hearing loss, particularly genetic hearing loss? Did the mother experience intrauterine infections that are known to affect the developing fetus, such as rubella or syphilis? Was the infant's birth weight low (under 1500 grams)? Was the infant born with anomalies of the skull or face? Gerber cites evidence that through such an interview, 60 to 70 percent of congenitally deaf children would be detected, and this rate would increase to 80 percent if both a physical examination of the child and a family interview were conducted. This proposal is very recent and has not yet been widely adopted.

The Crib-O-Gram

The assessment of hearing in infants takes quite a bit of ingenuity; the infant does not talk, is impervious to instructions, and by and large, is a most uncooperative subject for study. But ingenious devices have been contrived, and one such is the **Crib-O-Gram**. This device consists of a motion-sensitive transducer that is attached to the infant's crib, a strip of paper that records the infant's motions, automatic timing equipment, and a loudspeaker (Simmons, 1977). As you no doubt have figured out, the hearing test consists of recording the baby's movements in response to sounds sent over the loudspeaker. The test is administered as follows: First, a record of the baby's spontaneous movements is obtained for about 10 seconds. This is followed by the presentation of sound and a further recording of the child's movements. These assessments of movement, with and without sound presentations, are repeated every hour or so. The estimate of the infant's ability to hear is based upon the change of the child's activity level at the onset of sound. Simmons indicates that the test is most accurate when administered to a sleeping infant, and if the infant responds to the test sound within two seconds of its presentation, the odds are better than 99 to 1 that the baby hears.

Clinical Screening of Infants

The Crib-O-Gram is not the only procedure employed to determine hearing impairments in infants and very young children. Sweitzer (1977) has described procedures for the audiological assessment of young infants. He too suggests that one make observations of young infants' movements in response to sounds. However, this is a much less systematic method than the Crib-O-Gram. Between ages 5 months and 18 months, infants with adequate hearing can be expected to orient themselves to the source of sound. Between ages 18 months and 39 months, Sweitzer suggests that it is possible to obtain a more stringent assessment of hearing through the use of conditioning techniques. For example, the youngster might be presented with a light paired with an auditory signal presented through earphones. After exposure to several of these pairings, the auditory stimulus is presented without the light. The child is observed to see if he orients himself toward the light source. If the child turns, he or she has learned to associate the sound with the light, and is able to hear. If the child fails to turn toward the light source, there is the possibility of hearing loss.

From age 30 months children's hearing is generally assessed through one of two types of speech tests. In one method, the child's ability to identify spoken words is assessed. In this case a **speech reception threshold** is obtained. This refers to the lowest sound intensity at which the child can identify spoken words 50 percent of the time. The second method of assessment is the **speech detection level**, which is the lowest intensity at which the child detects a word 50 percent of the time. This method differs from the first as the individual does not have to interpret or understand the word; one simply has to respond to the presence of the sound.

The Audiometer

Once a child reaches an age at which he or she can sit relatively still, follow instructions, and talk with the tester, hearing assessments rely primarily upon **audiometer** tests. The audiometer is a calibrated machine that presents pure tones at different frequencies and intensities. When pure tones are presented directly through the individual's ear, it is referred to as *air conduction.* Presenting the tones through the bones behind the ear is referred to as *bone conduction.* If a person has difficulty responding to pure tones, responses to air and bone conduction are compared to determine if the source of the problem is in the middle ear. Bone conduction allows testing by bypassing the middle ear, so if a person fails to respond to pure tones presented through air conduction, but does respond to those presented through bone conduction, this is a clue that the source of the problem is in the middle ear.

The sound frequencies commonly presented in audiometric tests are 125, 250, 1000, 4000, and 8000 Hz (hertz). Sound frequencies refer to the rate of a cycle of a sound wave and the psychological experience is the pitch of the sound. The higher or more shrill the pitch, the faster the frequencies of the sound waves. In terms of loudness, the tones are presented at the lowest intensity to which the person is able to respond. Loudness is indexed by reference to **decibels** (dB); the greater the number of decibels, the louder the sound.

It should be noted that a hearing loss may be specific to particular sound frequencies. An inability to hear sounds between the frequencies of 500 and 2000 will have a particularly heavy impact on the individual's ability to understand speech as these frequencies are often used in speech. This does not mean to say, however, that an inability to detect sounds at other frequencies will have no effect. A child who has difficulty in hearing higher frequency sounds may well develop speech and language problems (Frisina, 1967). Nonetheless, deficits at one level of sound frequencies are likely to have very different effects upon the child's development than deficits at other frequency levels.

The subject's task during an audiometric examination is to indicate when a sound is heard. The person administering the test, an audiologist, records the subject's response to the sound on an **audiogram,** a chart that allows responses to be recorded as a function of both the intensity and frequency of the sound. The points marked on the audiogram are the intensity (loudness) at which the individual responds to each sound frequency (pitch). The intensity of sound (decibels, or dB) is charted on the ordinate; the sound frequencies, pitch, are shown on the abscissa of the graph. An example of an audiogram recording is provided in Figure 7-1.

The method of recording the responses to the audiometric test have been standardized. There is a system of symbols to record responses so that anyone familiar with the system can "read" the results. For instance, responses to sounds presented to the left ear (or bone) are recorded in blue while responses from the right ear are marked in red. The standardized symbols are also seen in the figure.

Tympanometry

The most common cause of hearing loss in children is related to diseases and disorders of the middle ear. More than 50 percent of children with hearing impairments have malfunctions in the middle ear (Feldman, 1977). One good

AUDIOLOGICAL RECORD

Date_____

Birthdate_____

Name_____   Age_____
     (last)   (first)   (middle)   (years)   (months)

Address_____   Ped. Inst. #_____

Phone_____   Sex_____

Parent(s)_____   Referred by_____

Audiometer: P/T_____Speech_____

Test Reliability_____

KEY TO AUDIOGRAM

EAR	A/C	B/C	COLOR
Right	0	[	Red
Left	X	]	Blue
Both/Either	▨	⌐	Green*

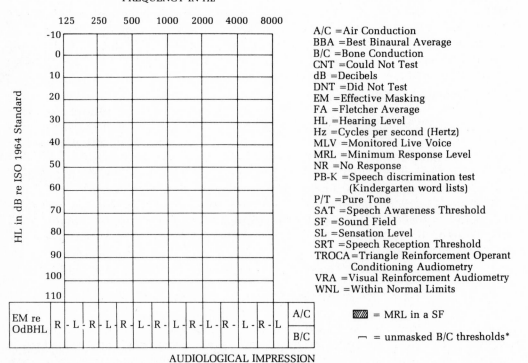

A/C = Air Conduction
BBA = Best Binaural Average
B/C = Bone Conduction
CNT = Could Not Test
dB = Decibels
DNT = Did Not Test
EM = Effective Masking
FA = Fletcher Average
HL = Hearing Level
Hz = Cycles per second (Hertz)
MLV = Monitored Live Voice
MRL = Minimum Response Level
NR = No Response
PB-K = Speech discrimination test
          (Kindergarten word lists)
P/T = Pure Tone
SAT = Speech Awareness Threshold
SF = Sound Field
SL = Sensation Level
SRT = Speech Reception Threshold
TROCA = Triangle Reinforcement Operant
              Conditioning Audiometry
VRA = Visual Reinforcement Audiometry
WNL = Within Normal Limits

▨ = MRL in a SF

⌐ = unmasked B/C thresholds*

AUDIOLOGICAL IMPRESSION

FIGURE 7-1 An audiogram chart

test for assessing problems in the middle ear is **tympanometry.** This test requires cooperation but not participation from the subject and thus has been used quite successfully with very young children. An electroacoustic device is inserted into the ear canal, allowing one to measure how much sound energy passes through the middle ear and how much is reflected back toward the source of the sound. This provides a way to measure how much sound passes through the middle ear to the inner ear. The use of tympanometry yields very accurate information concerning the middle ear's processing of sound transmissions.

We have reviewed some of the methods used to assess hearing in infants and children. We now consider the classification of hearing loss.

CLASSIFICATION OF HEARING PROBLEMS

Classification systems have been developed to serve both the medical and educational problems manifested by children with hearing impairments. Physicians are understandably interested in the cause of the hearing difficulty, the site of pathology, and the specifics of the hearing loss (for instance, the extent and type of hearing loss). The physician's concern is for medical treatment as it may be possible to alleviate the problem through medication, surgery, and/or the use of a hearing aid. Those concerned with the child's education are primarily interested in the impact of the hearing impairment upon the child's development, particularly of speech and language and social relations. Classification systems thus incorporate both a description of the hearing problem and the expected impact of the hearing loss upon the child's development.

ISO and the ASA

The best-known classification systems in use in the United States are the International Standard Organizations (ISO) standard and the American Standard Association (ASA) standard. The various categories proposed by each system are defined on the basis of a person's ability to hear pure tones within the frequency range (125 to 8000 Hz) at various levels of loudness (dB). These two classification systems categorize the degree of hearing loss somewhat differently and these differences are shown in Table 7-1.

Conductive and Sensorineural Hearing Losses

Hearing losses are commonly categorized as one of two types: conductive loss or sensorineural loss. In a conductive hearing impairment something is amiss in either the outer or middle ear that prevents the sound from being adequately transmitted to the inner ear. The individual with a conductive hearing

TABLE 7-1 Classification of Hearing Impairments by ASA and ISO Standards

Degree of Handicap	Effect of Hearing Loss on the Understanding of Language and Speech	Educational Needs and Programs
Slight 16 to 29 dB (ASA) or 27 to 40 dB (IS0)	May have difficulty hearing faint or distant speech. Will not usually experience difficulty in school situations.	May benefit from a hearing aid as loss approaches 30 dB (ASA) or 40 dB (ISO). Attention to vocabulary development. Needs favorable seating and lighting. May need lip-reading instruction. May need speech correction.
Mild 30 to 44 dB (ASA) or 41 to 55 dB (ISO)	Understands conversational speech at a distance of 3 to 5 feet (face to face). May miss as much as 50% of class discussions if voices are faint or not in line of vision. May exhibit limited vocabulary and speech anomalies.	Child should be referred to special education for educational follow-up if such service is available. Individual hearing aid by evaluation and training in its use. Favorable seating and possible special class placement, especially for primary children. Attention to vocabulary and reading. May need lip-reading instruction. Speech conservation and correction, if indicated.
Marked 45 to 59 dB (ASA) or 56 to 70 dB (ISO)	Conversation must be loud to be understood. Will have increasing difficulty with school situations requiring participation in group discussions. Is likely to have defective speech. Is likely to be deficient in language usage and comprehension. Will have limited vocabulary.	Will need resource teacher or special class. Special help in language skills, vocabulary development, usage, reading, writing, grammar, etc. Individual hearing aid by evaluation and auditory training. Lip-reading instruction. Speech conservation and speech correction.
Severe 60 to 79 dB (ASA) or 71 to 90 dB (ISO)	May hear loud voices about one foot from the ear. May be able to identify environmental sounds. May be able to discriminate vowels but not all consonants. Speech and language defective and likely to deteriorate. Speech and language will not develop spontaneously if loss is present before one year of age.	Will need full-time special program for deaf children, with emphasis on all language skills, concept development, lip-reading, and speech. Program needs specialized supervision and comprehensive supporting services. Individual hearing aid by evaluation. Auditory training on individual and group aids. Part-time in regular classes only as profitable.

TABLE 7-1, *cont.*

Degree of Handicap	Effect of Hearing Loss on the Understanding of Language and Speech	Educational Needs and Programs
Extreme 80 dB or more (ASA) or 91 dB or more (ISO)	May hear some loud sounds but is aware of vibrations more than tonal pattern. Relies on vision rather than hearing as primary avenue for communication. Speech and language defective and likely to deteriorate. Speech and language will not develop spontaneously if loss is present before one year of age.	Will need full-time special program for deaf children, with emphasis on all language skills, concept development, lip reading and speech. Program needs specialized supervision and comprehensive supporting services. Continuous appraisal of needs in regard to oral or manual communication. Auditory training in group and individual aid. Part-time in regular classes only for carefully selected children.

impairment will have difficulty in hearing sounds that are not very loud, primarily those with a decibel intensity between 0 and 70. The reason that people with this type of loss can hear louder sounds is that these sounds are intense enough to be detected and transmitted by cranial bones. These more intense sounds then are transmitted to the inner ear through the cranial bones. Conductive losses may be the result of infections in the middle ear, a very common childhood problem, from blockage or abnormal constriction in the outer or middle ear, or from dysfunctioning of the bones in the middle ear (Northern and Downs, 1974). Sometimes conductive hearing losses correct themselves; however, they leave a long-lasting residual effect. Depending upon the degree of impairment, conductive hearing problems can seriously impede the child's educational progress. The child's language development, as well as the acquisition of reading and other academic skills, may be retarded. Happily, many of these problems can be corrected if they are detected and treated. If they are not, there is the possibility of a permanent hearing deficit (Frisina, 1967; Glasscock, 1975).

Sensorineural hearing losses refer to problems generated by damage to either the cochlea (that is, the inner ear) or to the auditory nerve. Since it is technically difficult to determine whether the damage is to the inner ear or to the auditory nerve, the two types of damage are classified under one term, sensorineural problems. Often these hearing losses originate in the destruction of the hair cells in the inner ear. When this occurs, the effect is to limit the person's ability to hear the sounds to which these cells are sensitive. Hence, the person will be able to hear certain sound frequencies while being deaf to others. Sensorineural hearing losses are most often medically irreversible.

It is also possible that an individual may have both types of hearing problems, a condition referred to as **mixed loss.** When the site of the damage is not in the ears or the auditory nerve, but in the cortex of the brain, the problem is called **central auditory dysfunction** and is associated with delay in, or lack of, speech and language development (Kemker, 1975). Individuals with this kind of damage may hear the sounds, but they cannot interpret their meaning.

Classification by Severity of Impairment

There are common terms to describe the severity of children's hearing losses. The term "deaf" refers to grave hearing loss that occurs before the child develops language and is sufficiently severe to preclude the child's spontaneously developing speech and language. The term "hard of hearing" means that while the child's hearing is not normal, the hearing loss is not so severe that the child will fail to develop some spoken language (Kemker, 1975). A hearing loss is considered to be mild when the child cannot detect a sound presented in the range of 15 to 30 dB; moderate when a sound between 30 and 50 dB is not detected; severe when a stimulus in the 51 to 80 dB range does not register; and profound when the stimulus is undetected at the 81 to 100 dB range (Northern and Downs, 1974).

Kemker (1975) has pointed out some of the educational implications of the various severities of hearing loss. The following material is based on his classification scheme. Children who cannot hear sounds below 25 dB in intensity may well pass the usual school hearing screening test. Nonetheless, these girls and boys can be expected to have difficulty hearing within noisy contexts and may well benefit from preferential classroom seating.

When the child is mildly hearing impaired, i.e., able to detect sounds presented between 26 to 40 dB, the impairment is likely to affect the child's ability to understand speech and his or her language development will probably be delayed. These children usually need help in developing vocabulary and in lip-reading. The more severe the loss of hearing within this range of sounds, the greater the likelihood that the child could benefit from a hearing aid.

Kemker considers a moderate hearing loss to be one in which the child first begins to detect sounds presented in the range of 41 to 55 dB. Children with such losses are more likely than the mildly impaired to have delayed and difficult language development and are less likely to develop language spontaneously. The child who suffers the loss before developing a good command of language will in all likelihood need special education services for assistance in developing speech and language. The youngster will likely need practice to retain whatever language has been developed along with training in lip-reading; he or she probably will benefit from a hearing aid. Hearing losses more profound than those listed require extensive educational services, and the child's language defects will be more severe.

ETIOLOGY OF HEARING LOSSES

As with mental retardation, hearing losses may have causes that are either exogenous, endogenous, or both. Exogenous causes of hearing deficits are those brought about by nongenetic influences. Endogenous causes refer to those factors traceable to genetic influences.

Hereditary Factors in Deafness

About half of the cases of hearing impairment are the result of a genetic problem. There are more than 60 types of genetically transmitted hearing problems, and many of these involve other types of handicaps as well (Meadow, 1975). Deafness may frequently be accompanied by other inherited defects.

About 80 percent of hearing problems caused by genetic influences are the result of the matching of recessive genes, and most often will affect the inner ear or the auditory nerve (Nance and Sweeney, 1975). It is less frequent, although possible, to have middle-ear damage as a result of genetic influences. At this time, about the only genetically determined hearing losses that are amenable to treatment are those stemming from the middle ear.

Acquired Hearing Losses

As discussed in the chapter on mental retardation, viral diseases and other infections suffered by the mother can injure the developing fetus. The harm suffered by the fetus may include damage to auditory mechanisms. Rubella, measles, mumps, influenza, chickenpox, and other forms of virus can all impair the fetus's or newborn's hearing, often by damaging sensorineural processes (Altenau, 1975). Aside from viral diseases, other mishaps, such as ingestion of various drugs, Rh incompatibility, middle-ear infections, and trauma, can also produce hearing losses. For example, the antibiotic, quinine, when taken by the mother, may disrupt the development of the fetus's hearing apparatus. Rh incompatibility between mother and offspring, if not treated properly, may damage the inner ear as well as parts of the brain (Vernon, 1967). A trauma like a blow to the head can result in a fracture, hemorrhage, or constriction of the blood supply to the inner ear and thus produce a hearing impairment (Altenau, 1975). An infection in the middle ear, *otitis media*, can result in a serious hearing loss. This type of infection is particularly common during the first six years of life and often has no effect on a child's hearing. Moreover, the use of antibiotics renders hearing losses unlikely. However, if the child has repeated middle-ear infections that are not treated appropriately, profound hearing losses can result.

CHARACTERISTICS OF THE HEARING IMPAIRED AND THE DEAF

The inability to receive and send social messages has profound consequences on a person's development and manner of living. In this section we present information concerning some of the personal characteristics apparently associated with hearing impairments. We will look at the speech and language, the intellectual and cognitive abilities, and the social development of the hearing impaired child.

Speech and Language of the Hearing Impaired

The most basic problem confronting children with a hearing problem is that of learning their native language. Children vary as to how they cope with this challenge. The degree to which the hearing impaired child can acquire speech (the motor act of producing sounds) and language (the understanding of communication symbols) depends on a host of factors, such as the degree and type of hearing loss, the child's age when the loss occurred, intellectual abilities, willingness and capacity to use a hearing aid, and the attitudes of the family toward the child and the problem.

For purposes of education, children with hearing problems have been generally divided into two major categories, the hard of hearing and the deaf. The primary difference between children placed in the two categories is the degree of their hearing loss. Roughly speaking, the hard of hearing child can detect sounds that are 80 or 90 dB. The deaf child is one who requires an even louder sound, one at a higher level of intensity. First, let us look at the speech and language charac- teristics of the hard of hearing child.

The Hard of Hearing Child

The hard of hearing child is likely to develop speech spontaneously but will show difficulty in learning high frequency sounds, such as *s, sh, z, the, t, k, ch,* and *f.* Generally, the child will show difficulty with high frequency sounds by either omitting them in speech or by substituting other sounds for them. In addition to problems with high frequency sounds, the child's speech may have a strange quality; it may be quite nasal and too loud or too soft. Generally, the child's voice will be appropriate in voice inflection and pitch and the rate at which he or she speaks (Frisina, 1967). Not surprisingly, these children often have difficulty in understand- ing directions, frequently ask for repetition of spoken sentences, misunderstand others, and have difficulty in conversations involving more than one person.

The Deaf Child

The speech and language development of deaf children is even more disrupted than that of hard of hearing children. Deaf children, by definition, do not spontaneously develop speech. The child must be taught both how to "hear" and how to "speak"; that is, the child must be educated in both receptive and expressive communication. As an example of why the development of speech and language is so deficient in deaf children, imagine the following conversation:

Mother: "Let's go camping in a state park next August."

The child will *see* only certain sounds by the speaker's lip move- ment: "Let's o ampi in a state par ne t Au ust," and may *hear* only: "Le o amp n a ar ne Au u."

Frisina (1967) summarizes the speech characteristics of the deaf child. They are likely to show the following difficulties:

1. slow, labored speech
2. breathy speech (expending too much air when talking)
3. Inappropriate rhythm in speech
4. voice pitch too high or low
5. frequent substitutions, omissions, and additions of inaccurate sounds
6. confusions of consonants, such as p for b, t for d
7. poor phrasing of words
8. poor articulation (about 21 percent of the consonants and 12 percent of the vowels are misarticulated)

Most of the evidence concerning speech and language development of the deaf child indicates that even when training is initiated early in the child's life, many problems in this area remain (Frisina, 1967; Furth, 1971). And those that remain can be very severe indeed. For example, Templin (1966) compared the language of deaf and hearing children and found that in some language skills, the deaf child failed to show development in skills beyond 11 years of age, while the hearing child continued to increase his skills until about 14. Furth (1971) underscores the problems of language development by the deaf by pointing out that even though the majority of congenitally deaf children attend, for periods up to 15 years, schools in which the primary educational emphasis is upon the development of language, these deaf children do not obtain language competence. Moreover, they are not likely to establish high level skills in speech or lip reading. Furth writes, "Apart from a few notable exceptions, the difference in linguistic skill between persons born profoundly deaf and hearing persons is not merely statistically significant, but it is as great as the difference in level of hearing. At one extreme, there are hearing youngsters steeped from earliest childhood in the conventional language; at the other extreme, there are deaf youngsters who during the early formative years of their lives have no ready-made symbol system available" (Furth, 1971, p. 69).

Finally, mention should be made of deaf children's written language. For some time, it has been recognized that the writing skills of the deaf child are clearly inferior to those of the hearing child. Heider and Heider (1941) reported that in comparison with hearing children, the written sentences of the deaf child are shorter, employ simpler and fewer grammatical forms, and generally resemble the sentences of younger, hearing children. Myklebust (1960) has also reported that the compositions of deaf children are less sophisticated than those of hearing youngsters.

The writing styles of the deaf are simple, relatively sparse in vocabulary and styles of presentation, and consist of unrelated language units that follow each other (Moores, 1970). Deaf children do not have a command of language that will allow them to function at a high level in their written expression (Meadow, 1975).

Visual Information Processing: Acuity, Perception, and Memory

According to folklore, people who suffer a sensory loss compensate for it by having or developing high skills in some other sense. Thus the blind are often thought to have exceptional hearing, the deaf exceptional sight. Whether this belief is correct or not, it is true that hard of hearing and deaf children are more reliant on visual information processing than children not so disabled. Educational decisions for such children, therefore, should be based upon a consideration of these skills and the realization that their ability to process visual information will be critical to their development and well-being.

In this section, we will examine some of the findings about three aspects of visual information processing by the deaf child: the ability to see (visual acuity), the ability to interpret what is seen (visual perception), and the ability to remember what is seen (visual memory).

First, what is the visual acuity of the deaf child? The folklore about compensatory development appears to be quite incorrect when applied to the visual acuity of the deaf child. Indeed, it appears that the hearing impaired child is more likely to suffer from poor sight than the hearing child (Frisina, 1967). This really should not be very surprising since hearing loss is often associated with other abnormalities resulting from trauma or genetic mishaps. The probability of the deaf child's having any abnormality is likely to be greater than that of the hearing child.

What about the visual perception of the deaf or hearing impaired child? The evidence is rather mixed. For example, Gilbert and Levee (1967) found that deaf children make more errors in copying design than do hearing youngsters. On the other hand, Frisina (1967) reports that deaf children were much more competent than their hearing peers in imitating an observed sequence of actions. Schwartz and Bryan (1971) observed that deaf children were quite able to imitate a person whom they observed on television. It may well be that deaf children are particularly likely to imitate the gross motor behaviors of those around them. Additionally, it seemed to the investigators that they not only imitated the critical, important acts of the performer but the trivial ones as well.

The studies concerning the deaf child's visual memory have also yielded mixed results. For instance, the deaf child appears to perform as adequately as the hearing child when asked to remember visual forms but does significantly worse when trying to recall digits (Furth, 1966). It is likely that deaf children, like everyone else, can recall familiar words better than unfamiliar ones. Thus words represented in sign language are better recalled than those that are not (Odom, Blanton, and McIntyre, 1970). Finally, deaf children seem to have less difficulty remembering words that look alike and more difficulty in remembering words that sound alike than do hearing children (Blanton, Nunnally, and Odom, 1967).

In summary, it appears that deaf children may be more likely to have visual acuity problems than hearing children, and that categorical statements concerning their perceptual processes cannot be made. Their memory for visually presented material is apparently based upon their familiarity with the words, and they employ somewhat different strategies or cues in their attempts to remember material.

Intellectual and Cognitive Development

It has long been thought that there is an intimate link between intellectual or cognitive skills and language development. Since this notion is widespread, it is not surprising that investigators have been particularly interested in the development of the intellectual abilities of the hearing impaired, a population suffering from profound language problems. While interest is great, so are the problems inherent in trying to assess the cognitive skills of this group. The major problem facing any investigator is ensuring that the subject's performance is an accurate reflection of skills rather than the result of deafness. The question must always be asked whether the level of achievement of the hearing impaired on any test or task reflects intellectual skills or the inability to understand the instructions or test items due to the hearing impairment (Blank, 1974). It is not surprising then that most investigators have employed measures of intellectual or cognitive abilities that do not require verbal responses from the subject and that can be administered without much verbal instruction.

By and large it is generally found that deaf children achieve within the normal range on most performance or nonverbal measures of intelligence, although their scores tend to be somewhat lower than those of hearing children of comparable age. This is surprising given the fact that many hearing deficient children also have other significant weaknesses, such as central nervous system dysfunctions (Meadow, 1975). The same general finding of some delay in intellectual development of the deaf child is found when studies are conducted on their acquisitions of concepts. Two frequently used measures of concept acquisition are the concept of classification and the concept of conservation. Measuring the concept of classification involves determining whether the child can take a group of items and categorize them according to a common dimension such as size, color, or function. We assess the concept of conservation by determining whether the child understands that the amount of something, its weight or volume, remains constant even though its visual form may change. A common test of conservation is to pour water from a short, wide glass into a tall, narrow one and ask the child if the amount of water is the same or different. It appears that hearing impaired children are slower in obtaining the concepts of classification and conservation, although the degree of delay is a matter of some debate (Best, 1970; Furth, 1964, 1966, 1971; Templin, 1950).

In summary, it seems that many deaf children are less intellectually able than hearing youngsters, but do not show marked intellectual deficits.

Educational Achievement

Educational achievement is associated with success in life, and the attainment of academic skills is a prerequisite for many occupations. Academic deficiencies are likely to close off many of life's opportunities for an individual. The most important academic skill is reading; thus, the reading achievements of hearing impaired youngsters have been a matter of concern to investigators. The general findings about reading skills of the hearing impaired is that these children are grossly deficient relative to hearing children. This finding has been repeatedly shown since 1916 (Pintner and Paterson, 1916a,b). In our own time, Wrightstone, Aronow, and Moskowitz (1963) have examined the reading scores of about 5000 deaf children between the ages of 10½ and 16½ years, and found that barely 10 percent of these children had a reading level above grade four.

More recently, the Office of Demographic Studies of Gallaudet College (1971, 1972, 1973) tested the reading and arithmetic achievement of about 17,000 hearing impaired children. Children 12½ years were found to have an average reading achievement level of grade 3. The average arithmetic computation scores were at grade 4.

There really is no doubt that the hearing impaired child is likely to be quite retarded in academic achievement. It has been found that these children perform rather adequately in reading until about the third grade, after which they make little progress (Wrightstone, Aronow, and Moskowitz, 1963. Office of Demographic Studies at Gallaudet College, 1971, 1972, 1973; Meadow, 1975.)

The occupational choices made by the hearing impaired reflect their educational problem. Schwab (1977) reports that only 3 to 9 percent of deaf children in high schools aspire for a college degree or advanced technical education, and this is in spite of the fact that some 70 to 80 percent of these children probably have the intellectual abilities, if not the academic skills, to continue their education. Hearing impaired high school graduates are very likely to be employed in manual labor jobs, as some 80 percent of the sample studied by Schwab were found in such occupational positions. This is distressing since hearing impaired individuals can perform competently and happily in positions that do not require extensive communication skills, and many are doing so (Kirk, 1972).

Social Relations

We gain most of our ideas about the world around us, avoid loneliness, and get to know the people with whom we interact through verbal communication, so it is not surprising to find that the social relations of the deaf child may differ considerably from those of the hearing youngster. In this section, we examine briefly some of the major differences between these two groups of children in their relationships with parents and peers.

What is the nature of the communications between parent and child? First, parents frequently feel that the major blockage in communicating with their deaf offspring is their inability to express their thoughts to the child. Understanding the child's communications is apparently less difficult for the parents than the parents' attempts to get their ideas across to the child (Meadow, 1975). Moreover, the nature of communications to the deaf is likely to be quite different from that to the hearing child. Schlesinger and Meadow (1972) report that almost all the communications between the deaf child and parent are limited to subjects that are immediately present. Things that are in sight are discussed, those that are out of sight are not. This limitation in the substance of communications can have important results. Heider and Heider (1941) compared the play of hearing impaired and hearing preschool age children and found that the hearing child spends considerably more time than the deaf organizing and coordinating play activities. According to Heider and Heider, hearing children have the distinct advantage of being able to refer to their expectations concerning the possible future outcomes of various play styles. Given the important role of imagery, fantasy, and role-playing in young children's social interactions, it would be likely that the deaf child, so bound to the here and now, would be at a distinct disadvantage in play and social development.

There is a second feature of the deaf child's relationship with his or her parents that should be noted. Parents of these children are likely to be rather controlling and overprotective. Chess, Korn, and Fernandez (1971) studied rubella children, 70 percent of whom had a hearing loss, and found that their parents viewed them as very fragile. It was reported that although about 50 percent of these children were capable of carrying out many tasks, such as dressing themselves, they rarely did so. The parents were described as being unsure of just how independent their child could or should be, and reluctant to allow the child much opportunity to develop an independent life style. Moreover, hearing mothers of deaf children appear to be more intrusive and commanding in their interactions with their deaf children than are mothers of hearing children, a quality that may retard the children's social development and independence (Meadow, 1975).

A final area of concern is the relationship of hearing impaired children to their hearing peers. In light of the emphasis on mainstreaming handicapped children into regular classrooms, studies of peer relationships take on importance. In general, it has been found that hearing impaired children are not as well liked as hearing youngsters of comparable age, and apparently familiarity does not change the deaf child's social status (Justman and Maskowitz, 1957; Elser, 1959). However, there is some evidence suggesting that if hearing impaired children are integrated into preschool programs where they probably receive a good deal of language training, they will not be socially rejected (Kennedy and Bruininks, 1974). By and large, however, hearing children are more likely than not to reject their hearing impaired peers.

Personality

There have been a number of studies attempting to determine whether the hearing impaired child or adult has a particular set of personality traits or problems. When evaluating these studies, keep in mind that the analysis of personality often requires the use of instruments that demand verbal responses from the subject. Moreover, there are many personality tests on the market that have not been validated. Given these limitations, what is the consensus concerning the personality characteristics of the deaf? It is not surprising to find that deaf children have feelings of social isolation and difficulty in establishing interpersonal relationships (Meadow, 1975). In fact, it would be rather surprising if they did not experience difficulties, given the nature of their hearing and language deficiencies.

Hearing impaired adults appear to have a number of problems in their everyday living. Ranier, Altshuler, and Kallman (1969) found, for example, that deaf individuals have a higher incidence of arrests and marital, sexual, and vocational problems than hearing persons. On the other hand, there is no evidence that deaf individuals are more likely to have serious emotional and behavioral disorders. Indeed, when investigators have combed the ranks of persons who have been institutionalized for such difficulties, they have not found that a disproportionate number of deaf individuals were in these institutions (Meadow, 1975). In effect, deaf individuals are likely to have feelings about themselves that seem appropriate given their condition, have some problems in conducting their everyday lives, but are not particularly likely to have severe emotional or behavioral difficulties.

Educating the Deaf and Hard of Hearing

For almost 200 years professionals in the field have been heatedly arguing over whether training in language should be focused upon teaching the child to communicate through speech or sign language (Meadow, 1975). The debate centers upon the virtues and limitations of each of these methods. The manual method of training focuses upon teaching the hearing impaired child to communicate through hand movements. The virtue of this system is that it is relatively easy to learn and allows the child, at an early age, to communicate with others who understand signs. The system's limitation is that not many people understand manual sign language, and that it limits the child to conversing with those who do. The manual method sets rather narrow bounds to the deaf individual's social world. The oral training method attempts to teach the child to talk like hearing persons and to understand others by watching their facial movements. The advantage of this method is that it may allow the child to converse with hearing as well as nonhearing individuals. However, because the oral method is very difficult to learn, the child may end up unable to communicate with anybody.

Ideally, the best educational approach would be to match the child's strengths to the educational approach and thus maximize learning. This is a shopworn phrase in educational circles and, as is often the case, refers to a matching procedure often impossible to follow. In fact, we do not know what strengths are necessary to learn speech-reading, aside from perhaps adequate vision, residual hearing, and a moderate amount of intelligence. Unfortunately, we do not have the knowledge necessary for matching person and plan. The current status of deaf education has elicited considerable criticism. According to Northern and Downs: "Since the initial contributions of early deaf educators such as Abbé de l'Epée, Thomas Hopkins Gallaudet and Alexander Graham Bell, education of the deaf is almost exactly where it was 150 years ago. Except for innovations in medical technology and sophistications in psychology and linguistics, the educational establishment is still graduating the deaf from high school with a fourth to sixth grade reading level, and a very crude command of the English language" (1974, p. 247).

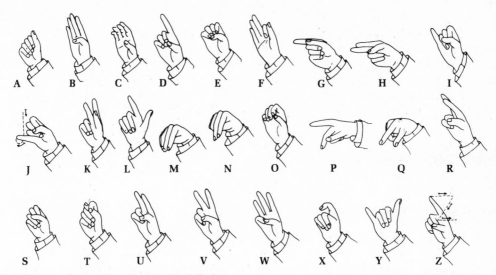

FIGURE 7-2 The one hand manual alphabet

Source: One Hand Manual Alphabet, National Center for Deaf-Blind Youths and Adults, New Hyde Park, New York

The teaching method one employs depends upon several factors. For example, Kirk (1972) suggests that oral methods of education should be tried on children whose hearing loss is not severe or profound. Others believe that all children should be initially trained in the oral method and only those who fail to progress should be taught by manual techniques (Northern and Downs, 1974). Finally, some urge that only the oral method be used, believing that exposure to manual methods will hinder the child's education (Northern and Downs, 1974).

Whatever one's preference, it behooves the student to be familiar with both methods. We now turn our attention to these methods of instruction.

Sign Systems

When sign language is employed, most workers and most parents of the deaf employ the *American Sign Language, Ameslan.* Ameslan is a combination of symbolic gestures in which the shape of the hand, its location in relation to the body of the sender, and movement of one or both hands provide the meaning of the communication. Figures 7-2 and 7-3 illustrate the meanings of various common signs.

While the Ameslan method is the most frequently employed signal system, others have also been proposed. There are Cued Speech, Seeing Essential English, Signing Exact English, and Linguistics of Visual English. The interested reader is referred to the book by Northern and Downs (1974) that describes these sign systems.

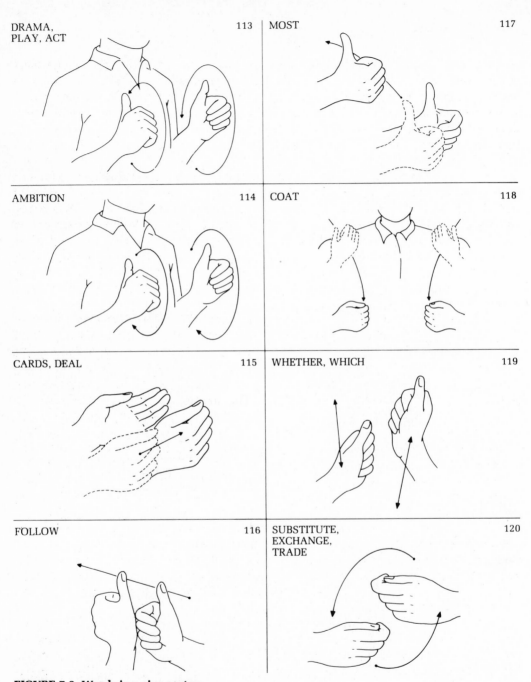

DRAMA,   113
PLAY, ACT

MOST   117

AMBITION   114

COAT   118

CARDS, DEAL   115

WHETHER, WHICH   119

FOLLOW   116

SUBSTITUTE,   120
EXCHANGE,
TRADE

FIGURE 7-3 Words in a sign system

Source: A Basic Course in Manual Communication, The National Association of the Deaf, 1970, p. 20.

Oral Methods

Oral methods of training are based on the notion that since most hearing impaired children detect some sound, it is possible to use their hearing to teach language. The goals of oral method programs are to teach the child to understand the speech of others by using residual hearing and lip reading, and to teach the child how to communicate with others through oral rather than manual methods. Using a hearing aid, the child is trained, it is hoped, to recognize and discriminate among sounds.

There are several kinds of auditory training systems designed for use in classes for hearing impaired children. One type is referred to as a hard-wire trainer. This training method employs an audio power amplifier into which many hearing aids may be connected. The amplifier is located on the teacher's desk and is under his or her control. There is an electrical connection from each child's desk to the teacher's desk. This system allows the instructor to have direct contact with students individually or in groups. One problem with this system is that communication between teachers and students can take place only when both are at their desks.

Various other systems are employed as well. For example, there is the portable desk trainer, a system that is essentially the same as that described above but that is portable and allows both the teacher and students greater freedom to move about and still communicate. In yet another technique, the audio loop induction system, a wire is looped around the room so that an audio signal from an electronic amplifier passes into the loop. The arrangement allows the child to switch on his or her own hearing aid to pick up the signals from the loop, which are converted to sound. Finally, a fourth method is the FM-radio frequency system. This consists of a wireless FM-radio frequency system in which communications are broadcast by FM waves to receiving units, the children's hearing aids. There have been complaints that mechanical problems often plague the use of these electronic devices, but before long their reliability will probably be improved and their prices perhaps lowered.

A major limitation of the auditory method of training resides in the dependency upon the hearing aid. First, a hearing aid can amplify sounds only so much. Second, these appliances require proper fitting and prescriptions, and like other mechanical units, they do break down (Porter, 1973). Moreover, many children will simply not wear their aids (Schein, 1968). To the degree that any of these factors are present, oral instruction will be difficult.

While training hearing impaired children to understand and distinguish the sounds they hear helps them utilize their residual hearing, it is also necessary that they learn to observe carefully the facial movements in others' speech. This process is called speech-reading or lip reading. Training the child in speech-reading calls for directing his or her attention to the speaker's facial and lip movements so that the child can learn to recognize what various sounds look like when spoken. The problem is that there are few sounds that are actually visible, while many that are visible look alike on the lips (for example, *p/b*, *t/d*). Only about 20 percent of the spoken message can actually be seen. Moreover, we often slur words in conversational speech. In any case, speech-reading is taught through analytic and synthetic methods. In analytic methods the child learns to recognize sounds presented one at a time; in synthetic training the child learns to respond to whole messages, filling in missing segments through contextual cues. It is most likely that teachers use both methods to foster speech-reading skills.

Given the importance of speech-reading for oral communication, there have been many attempts to discover what skills or traits are associated with the ability to read speech. Speech-reading ability has been found to be correlated with reading and writing skills, although the data are contradictory (Meadow, 1975). There have been attempts to relate speech-reading skills to intelligence, but the findings usually do not show a strong relationship between the two. Some investigators have examined a variety of visual perceptual skills, again with rather mixed but generally negative results. There are low but positive relationships found between age and speech-reading, thus suggesting that this is not an ability that evolves naturally with age. Evidently the one factor that does relate to speech-reading ability is residual hearing (Meadow, 1975). The more hearing a person has, the more able to read speech.

When you cannot hear yourself speak, it is difficult to monitor the loudness and quality of your voice. Hearing impaired persons have problems in modulating their speech production. Parenthetically, they often have difficulty monitoring other kinds of sounds as well, such as their footsteps or placing objects on a table. To help them monitor their spoken language, the children are taught to notice kinesthetic feedback from their speech organs. By feeling the nose and throat of the speaker, the child can be taught to match his or her muscle movements with the speaker's and to control the flow of air for sounds.

A number of mechanical feedback devices have been developed for the hearing impaired. The basic idea is to translate the spoken word into a visual presentation. For instance, Pronovost (1970) has developed the Instantaneous Pitch Period Indicator. This device translates speech into a wavelike pattern shown on an oscilloscope (which transforms sound waves into electrical waves seen on a screen). Using this technique the teacher talks, the child tries to imitate, and the child can see the degree to which he or she has matched the teacher's output.

Efficiency of Methods

Much of the research into the impact of these various training methods has focused on the speech learning of the hearing impaired child. But before noting these results, you should be aware that the method of teaching the hearing impaired to communicate depends a great deal upon the hearing status of the child's parents. If they are deaf, the child is very likely to learn sign language. If they can hear, the child is quite likely to be exposed to training in oral communication, given the presence of residual hearing and some progress in speaking.

What are the effects of these two forms of training? The answers to this must be tentative insofar as the number of research projects examining the question is small, and the number of subjects they test are few. What seems to be the case, however, is the following:

1. Children who learn sign language seem to learn it in much the same sequence as hearing children learn spoken language. Sign language appears really to be a language, showing regularity in what is learned at various stages of the child's development (Bellugi, 1967; Bellugi and Klima, 1972).
2. Vocabulary acquisition may increase as rapidly in learning sign language as it does for hearing children exposed to spoken words (Meadow, 1975).
3. Language development of children taught *only* by oral methods is quite retarded. Thus, by the age of 4 or 5 the deaf child may have a vocabulary of only 200 words, while that of a hearing child is expected to be about 2,000 words (Meadow, 1975).

It is, of course, possible to combine both oral and sign language training, although such a combination has until recently been rather rare. The combination of oral and manual training methods is referred to by the title **Total Communication Method.**

Total Communication Method

To get around the limitations of both the oral and manual methods, some experts are recommending that a total communication system be used to help hearing impaired children acquire a language system (Lowenbraun and Scroggs, 1974; Northern and Downs, 1974). Such a method combines several techniques to help children develop communication. Auditory training, speech-reading, finger-spelling, sign language, reading, and writing all might well be used. What defines these systems is that they will muster both oral and visual techniques to help the child. Whatever methods will facilitate acquiring language will be employed, and concerns about whether manual or visual training will detract from the effects of oral language training are suspended. In effect, these systems incorporate whatever support systems seem appropriate.

Proponents of the oral method feel somewhat uneasy about the Total Communication Method because they reasonably fear that children will use primarily manual forms of communication, avoiding the more difficult learning demanded by oral training. Persons supporting the Total Communication Method, however, argue that by and large the oral method has not been very successful in developing speech and language and that the combination of both manual and oral training may well increase the child's ability to speak and lip-read (Northern and Downs, 1974).

An interesting example of this integrated method has been developed by Horton (1975). Horton's program is designed for hearing impaired children 6 years of age or under. The regimen is initiated as soon as the child's hearing problem is detected, it is hoped before the child reaches 24 months of age, and frequently before 12 months of age. The child is immediately fitted with a hearing aid. Horton assumes that the residual hearing of the child can be used early to facilitate the development of oral language. In addition, training begins very early, preferably prior to 12 months if the hearing loss is detected that early. Finally, much of the training of these very young children is to be accomplished by the child's parents. These parents undergo intensive training in methods for stimulating their child's oral language. For example, parents are trained to reinforce verbal behavior; relate language to the immediate situation, interest, and experiences of the child; and to give the child feedback as to the adequacy of his or her oral efforts. Horton reports that children exposed to this particular Total Communication Method were similar to hearing subjects in the sentences they produced, and the words and grammatical structures they employed. The language of both the hearing and hearing impaired children exposed to this method was far superior to that of a group of hearing impaired youngsters who were given a regular course of instruction within a special education classroom. The results of this study, plus others weighing the combined techniques of training versus the oral-only method, do suggest that the combined method is more likely to yield beneficial results than the oral-only techniques (Moores, McIntyre, and Weiss, 1972; Quigly, 1968). The early evaluations of the combined method approaches suggest that important techniques for aiding the hearing impaired child, a youngster often deprived of adequate diagnostic, educational, and therapeutic services, may be on the horizon.

SUMMARY

In this chapter, we reviewed information concerning hearing impaired children: the mechanism of hearing and the two forms of hearing problems, *conduction* and *sensorineural* hearing deficits. Methods of detecting hearing impairments in very young infants, the high risk registry, the Crib-O-Gram, and clinical screening, were described. Tests commonly employed for older children include audiometry, while tympanometry is appropriate for young and older children. Several systems of classifying hearing impaired children were discussed, including those proposed by the International Standard Organization and the American Standard Association. The causes of hearing loss are many and include factors both genetic and nongenetic. Drugs, disease, genetic mishaps, and traumas are among the major factors that can produce serious hearing impairments. We also reviewed the characteristics associated with hearing impairments, the most frequently studied being intelligence and language and speech development. When intellectual abilities of the hearing impaired youngster are assessed by nonverbal measures, their test scores will fall within the normal range. As a group, however, they obtain somewhat lower scores than hearing children do. Many hearing impaired children, however, do show marked deficiencies in their speech and language development as well as in their academic achievements. Additionally, many of these children are not very popular with their peers, are somewhat overprotected by their parents, and may feel socially isolated.

While deaf children are not any more likely than most to develop severe emotional and behavioral disorders, they seem to have some difficulty in their social development. Finally, information was presented as to the techniques of aiding the hearing impaired child to communicate. These methods include the oral, the manual, and the combined methods. Of the various methods available it appears that the combined method of training the hearing impaired child may yield the highest academic achievement and the fullest language acquisition.

REFERENCES

Altenau, M. M. Histopathology of sensorineural hearing loss in children. In Glasscock, M. E. (Ed.), *The otolaryngologic clinics of North America* (Vol. 8). Philadelphia: W. B. Saunders, 1975.

Bellugi, U. *The acquisition of negation.* Unpublished doctoral dissertation, Harvard University, 1967. Cited by K. P. Meadow. The development of deaf children. In E. M. Hetherington (Ed.), *Review of research in child development* (Vol. 5) Chicago, Ill.: University of Chicago Press, 1975, 441–508.

Bellugi, U., & Klima, E. S. The roots of language in the sign talk of the deaf. *Psychology Today,* 1972, 6, 631–640, 1976.

Best, B. Development of classification skills in deaf children with and without early manual communication. Unpublished doctoral dissertation, University of California, Berkeley, 1970. Cited by K. P. Meadow. The development of deaf children. In E. M. Hetherington (Ed.), *Review of research in child development* (Vol. 5). Chicago, Ill.: University of Chicago Press, 1975.

Blank, M. Cognitive functions of language in the preschool years. *Developmental Psychology,* 1974, *10,* 229–245.

Blanton, R. L., Nunnally, J. C., & Odom, P. B. Graphemic, phonetic, and associative factors in the verbal behavior of deaf and hearing subjects. *Journal of Speech and Hearing Research,* 1967, *10,* 225–231.

Chess, S., Korn, S. J., & Fernandez, P. B. *Psychiatric disorders of children with congenital rubella.* New York: Brunner/Mazel, 1971.

Elser, R. The social position of hearing handicapped children in the regular grades. *Exceptional Children,* 1959, *25,* 305–309.

Feldman, A. S. Tympanometry. In B. F. Jaffe (Ed.), *Hearing loss in children.* Baltimore: University Park Press, 1977.

Frisina, D. R. Hearing disorders. In N. G. Haring & R. L. Schiefelbusch (Eds.), *Methods in special education.* New York: McGraw-Hill Book Co., 1967, 302–350.

Furth, H. G. Research with the deaf: Implications for language and cognition. *Psychological Bulletin,* 1964, *62,* 145–164.

Furth, H. G. *Thinking without language: Psychological implication of deafness.* New York: Free Press, 1966.

Furth, H. G. Linguistic deficiency and thinking: Research with deaf subjects 1964–1969. *Psychological Bulletin,* 1971, *76,* 58–72.

Gerber, S. E. High risk registry for congenital deafness. In B. F. Jaffe (Ed.), *Hearing loss in children.* Baltimore: University Park Press, 1977.

Gilbert, J., & Levee, R. F. Performances of deaf and normally-hearing children on the Bender Gestalt and the Archimedes spiral tests. *Perceptual and Motor Skills,* 1967, *24,* 1059–1066.

Glasscock, M. E. (Ed.), *The otolaryngologic clinics of North America* (Vol. 8, No. 1). Philadelphia: W. B. Saunders, 1975.

Heider, F., & Heider, G. M. Studies in psychology of the deaf. *Psychological Monographs,* 1941, *53,* No. 242.

Horton, K. B. Early intervention through parent training. In M. E. Glasscock (Ed.), *Otolaryngologic clinics of North America* (Vol. 8, No. 1). Philadelphia: W. B. Saunders, 1975.

Justman, J., & Maskowitz, L. *The integration of deaf children in a hearing class.* Publication No. 4, New York: Bureau of Education Research, Board of Education, 1957.

Kemker, F. J. Classifications of auditory impairment. In M. E. Glasscock (Ed.), *The otolaryngologic clinics of North America* (Vol. 8). Philadelphia: W. B. Saunders, 1975.

Kennedy, P., & Bruininks, R. H. Social status of hearing impaired children in regular classrooms. *Exceptional Children,* 1974, *40,* 336–344.

Kirk, S. A. *Educating exceptional children.* Boston: Houghton Mifflin, 1972.

London, P. *Beginning psychology.* Homewood, Ill.: The Dorsey Press, 1975.

Lowenbraun, S., & Scroggs, C. Hearing impaired. In N. G. Haring (Ed.), *Behavior of exceptional children.* Columbus, O.: Charles E. Merrill, 1974, 495–528.

Meadow, K. P. The development of deaf children. In E. M. Hetherington (Ed.), *Review of child development research* (Vol. 5). Chicago: University of Chicago Press, 1975.

Moores, D. F. An investigation of the psycholinguistic functioning of deaf adolescents. *Exceptional Children,* 1970, *36,* 645–654.

Moores, D. F., McIntyre, C. K., & Weiss, K. L. Evaluation of programs for hearing impaired children report of 1971–72. Research Report No. 39, Research, Development, and Demonstration Center in Education of Handicapped Children. University of Minnesota, September 1972. Cited by K. P. Meadow, The development of deaf children, in E. M. Hetherington (Ed.), *Review of child research development* (Vol. 5). Chicago: University of Chicago Press, 1975.

Myklebust, H. R. *The psychology of deafness.* New York: Grune & Stratton, 1960.

Nance, W. E., & Sweeney, A. Genetic factors in deafness of early life. In M. E. Glasscock (Ed.), *Otolaryngologic clinics of North America* (Vol. 8, No. 1). Philadelphia: W. B. Saunders, 1975, 19–48.

Northern, J. L., & Downs, M. P. *Hearing in children.* Baltimore: Williams & Wilkins, 1974.

Odom, P. B., Blanton, R. L., & McIntyre, C. K. Coding medium and word recall by deaf and hearing subjects. *Journal of Speech and Hearing Research,* 1970, *13,* 54–58.

Odom, P. B., Blanton, R. L., & Nunnally, J. C. Some "Cloze" technique studies of language capability in the deaf. *Journal of Speech and Hearing Research,* 1967, *10,* 480–484.

Office of Demographic Studies. *Academic achievement test results of a national testing program for hearing impaired students: United States, 1971.* Data from the annual survey of hearing impaired children and youth. Series D, No. 9. Washington, D.C.: Gallaudet College, 1972.

Office of Demographic Studies. *Further studies in achievement testing, hearing impaired students: United States, Spring 1971.* Data from the annual survey of hearing impaired children and youth. Series D, No. 13, Washington, D.C.: Gallaudet College, 1973.

Pintner, R., & Paterson, D. G. Learning tests with deaf children. *Psychological Review Monographs,* 1916a, *20.*

Pinter, R., & Paterson, D. G. The ability of deaf and hearing children to follow printed direction. *Pediatric Seminary,* 1916b, *23,* 477–497.

Pronovost, W. The Instantaneous Pitch-Period Indicator. *Education of the Hearing-Impaired.* 1970, *1,* 37–39.

Quigley, S. P. *The influence of fingerspelling on the development of language, communication, and educational achievement in deaf children.* Urbana/Champaign: University of Illinois, Institute for Research on Exceptional Children, 1968.

Ranier, J. D., Altshuler, K. Z., & Kallmann, F. J. (Eds.), *Family and mental health problems in a deaf population* (2nd ed.). Springfield, Ill.: Charles C. Thomas, 1969.

Schein, J. D. *The deaf community: Studies in the social psychology of deafness.* Washington, D.C.: Gallaudet College Press, 1968.

Schlesinger, H. S., & Meadow, K. P. *Sound and sign: Childhood deafness and mental health.* Berkeley, Calif.: University of California Press, 1972.

Schwab, W. A. Effects of hearing loss on education. In B. F. Jaffe (Ed.), *Hearing loss in children.* Baltimore: University Park Press, 1977, 650–654.

Schwartz, T., & Bryan, J. H. Imitation and judgments of children with language deficits. *Exceptional Children,* 1971, *38,* 151–158.

Simmons, F. B. Automated screening test for newborns: The Crib-O-Gram. In B. F. Jaffe (Ed.), *Hearing loss in children.* Baltimore: University Park Press, 1977.

Sweitzer, R. S. Audiological evaluation of the young infant and young child. In B. F. Jaffe (Ed.), *Hearing loss in children.* Baltimore: University Park Press, 1977.

Templin, M. The development of reasoning in children with normal and defective hearing. Minneapolis: University of Minnesota Press, 1950.

Templin, M. Vocabulary problems of the deaf child. *International Audiology,* 1966, *5,* 349.

Vernon, R. Rh factor and deafness: The problem, its psychological, physical and educational manifestations. *Exceptional Children*, 1967, *34*, 5–12.

Wrightstone, J. W., Aronow, M. S., & Moskowitz, S. Developing reading test norms for deaf children. *American Annals of the Deaf*, 1963, *108*, 311–316.

KEY TERMS

air conduction The process in which air-borne sounds are detected and passed through all parts of the ear on to the auditory nerve.

anvil, hammer, stirrup Three small bones located in the middle ear, which function in an interactive way to amplify and transmit sound vibrations from the outer ear to the inner ear.

audiogram A graphic record of hearing acuity at various intensities throughout the normal hearing range recorded from an audiometer.

audiometer An instrument used in the measurement of the acuity of hearing.

bone conduction The process in which sounds are conducted from the bones behind the ear through the inner ear on to the auditory nerve.

central auditory dysfunction Auditory processing problems occurring somewhere in the cerebral cortex.

cochlea Small coiled structure located in the inner ear, which transmits vibrations from the middle ear to the auditory nerve.

conduction problem Condition in which sound vibrations fail to reach the inner ear and auditory nerve because of defects in the outer or middle ear.

Crib-O-Gram Instrument used to detect and graph changes of infant activity as a response to sounds.

decibels A unit for expressing the relative intensity of sounds. The scale ranges from 0 (least perceptible sound) to about 130 for the average pain level.

mixed loss Hearing loss involving both conductive (outer and middle ears) and sensorineural (inner ear or auditory nerve) structural damage.

sensorineural problem Defective condition of the inner ear or auditory nerve, causing faulty transmission of sound impulses to the brain.

speech detection level Minimum sound level at which a child detects a word at least half of the time.

speech reception threshold The lowest sound intensity at which a child can identify spoken words.

total communication method Approach to deaf education that employs simultaneous use of oral communication, fingerspelling, and sign language.

tympanometry Assessment procedure using an electroacoustic device inserted into the ear canal to detect the amount of sound energy that passes through the middle ear to the inner ear.

CHAPTER 8

Speech and
Language Disorders

Most of us take language for granted. Talking is about as automatic as breathing and walking. Although countless numbers of people can neither read nor write adequately, relatively few cannot speak properly. We communicate by the spoken word more than by any other method. Thus, when an individual meets a person who has speech or language problems, the primary method of social communication is affected. Speech problems are not a new phenomenon; indeed they have been recognized for centuries. Among Egyptian hieroglyphics there are references to stuttering and cleft palates, and even Moses is thought to have been a stutterer (Lundeen, 1972). Early explanations for speech and language problems were many and varied, ranging from possession by the devil to weak, cold, or stiff tongues.

Given the importance of speech, it is little wonder that speech problems have been of concern to cultures throughout the ages and that they currently receive considerable attention and remedial efforts. In this chapter, we discuss problems interfering with the motor movements necessary to produce words (speech) and those affecting one's ability to communicate a message (language).

Definitions and Incidence

Before addressing the nature of language and speech disorders, let us consider some basic definitions. What is language? Language has been defined as "the system of communication among human beings of a certain group or community which comprehends and uses symbols possessing arbitrary conventional meanings according to the rules current in that community" (Scheifelbusch, 1967, p. 50). It is an agreed-upon method to employ sounds, gestures, and other signals with accepted meanings to communicate ideas to one another. This definition is very broad, and for study purposes language has been delineated into categories that represent sub-systems of the communication process. **Phonology** is the subsystem by which we study the production of single sounds and the rules governing the combining of sounds. Phonologists study the production of sounds like r and sh and the process by which we produce words like "rush." Syntax is a second subsystem and represents the study of how we combine words to express ideas. Syntax refers to grammar. **Semantics** is the study of the use of words to convey meaning.

It is common to distinguish between speech and language disorders. When reference is made to speech disorders, the phonology system is usually involved. In speech disorders people have difficulty producing single sounds or in combining them fluently. Articulation problems and stuttering fall into this category. When reference is made to language disorders, syntax and semantics difficulties are involved.

Speech problems exist under two circumstances: when a person's speech produces negative reactions from those listening and/or when the individual speaker experiences great distress as a result of his or her difficulty in communicating (Van Riper, 1952). There are many kinds of speech problems. Sometimes speakers sound peculiar because they mispronounce individual sounds. For instance, the person may say "wed" for "red." Sometimes so many sounds are mispronounced that the person cannot be understood. In other cases the style of speaking disrupts the flow of social interactions. This is seen when people stutter. Stuttering disrupts the flow of social interaction, producing stress in both the speaker and audience. Sometimes speakers falter because they forget the words they wish to use.

While speech disorders are not crippling or life threatening, they may have serious consequences for the individual. For the school-aged child, the ability to acquire academic skills and socialize with others may be affected, as classroom life is very language oriented and language dependent (Blank, 1977). For the adult with speech defects, there may be economic as well as psychological costs. Johnson et al. (1952) indicated that a person with speech problems may earn 25 percent less than one who speaks normally. It has been found that some speech problems are so severe the person cannot work at all. The academic retardation caused by difficulty in speaking may keep a student in school longer. In other cases an otherwise able individual may fail to go to college because of a low perception of his or her own abilities.

How many individuals are affected by speech problems? As usual, estimates vary according to definition. However, Johnson (1959) has estimated that about 4 percent of children have speech problems significant enough to require specialized attention. The American Speech and Hearing Association and Bureau of Education for the Handicapped estimated that the incidence rate is 5 percent of school-aged children. As speech problems take many forms, the incidence of particular problems will vary. Table 8-1 presents estimates of the approximate percentages of children who have various types of speech problems.

In this chapter, we first describe the physical mechanism involved in speech, and then picture in some detail the normal developmental sequence of

TABLE 8-1 Approximate Percentages of School-aged Children with Speech Problems

Problem	Percentage of Children with Serious Problem
Articulation	3.0
Stuttering	0.8
Voice	0.2
Cleft palate speech	0.1
Cerebral palsy speech	0.1
Retarded speech development	0.3
Speech problem related to hearing loss	0.5

Source: Adapted from the American Speech and Hearing Association and Bureau of Education for the Handicapped data, 1972 estimate. (Lundeen, 1972, p. 158).

acquiring communication skills. We then turn to the various types of disrupting events possible in speech and language development and how they affect the child.

At the outset it is important to note that not all speech and language problems occur alone. Virtually all types of handicapping conditions may have associated communication problems. For example, physical conditions, such as cerebral palsy and cleft palate are likely to carry with them speech and language problems. Difficulties in the development and use of language have been noted in mentally retarded, learning disabled, as well as autistic and schizophrenic children. Thus, problems of communication are embedded in many handicapping conditions.

PRODUCTION OF SPEECH SOUNDS: PHONOLOGY

People are uniquely equipped to use mechanisms for speech and language that are also used for breathing and digestion. Because humans have control over various body parts used in breathing and digestion, they are able to use these parts to produce the many sounds in the various languages. By using the larynx, we can protect our lungs from the intrusion of food particles. Conversely, air from the lungs can be pushed through the vocal cords in the larynx and produce sound. The sound is pushed through cavities in the mouth and nose to make distinct differences in the type of sound produced. This sound is then further shaped by the placement of the tongue and the shape of the mouth. The place where the sound is pushed and the movements of the mouth, tongue, and lips serve as the mechanism by which we produce speech.

Sounds

It is interesting that each language has only a small set of sounds that its speakers emit (McLean, 1974). English, for instance, has 45 to 50 speech sounds (Compton, 1976). But because of the manipulations possible with our tongue, teeth, lips, and oral cavities, we make hundreds of variations on these sounds when speaking. For instance, the sound *k* is different in the beginning of the word "kick" than it is at the end of this word, and the *k* sounds in "keep," "cup," and "coupe" are not identical (Compton, 1976).

The production of sounds is investigated by studying how vowels and consonants are made alone and in combination. There are four basic kinds of speech production: vowels, **glides,** consonants, and **resonant consonants.** *Vowels* are made by producing a sound at the larynx ("voice box") and then shaping it as it moves upward through the oral cavities. A vowel is shaped by altering the placement of the tongue without disrupting the air flow. This is the way we utter the sounds *a, e, i, o* and *u.* Certain sounds, (for example, *y* in the word "young") require that we go from one vowel to another. This type of sound is a *glide,* and is produced by a noninterrupted air flow in which the tongue shifts from one vowel position to another. The sounding of *consonants* requires disruption of the air flow. The way in which the air flow is disrupted serves as the basis of the classification of different kinds of consonants. When the air flow is completely stopped followed by a short burst of air, we produce the sounds *p, b, t, k, b, d* and *g.* When we partially stop the air flow and force it through small apertures formed by various tongue movements, we produce **fricatives,** *f, th, s, sh, v, z* and *zh.* To utter the sounds *ch* (as in "church") and *dz* (as in "judge"), we use air stoppage followed by a fricative. *Resonant consonants,* which are *r* and *l,* resemble vowels because they too are made by an uninterrupted air flow and the shaping of the oral cavity through positioning of the tongue.

This overview of the taxonomy of speech sound production is provided because so many speech disturbances can be understood better if one knows how vowels, consonants, glides, and resonant consonants are produced. Let us now consider the developmental sequence in which children require the use of these speech sounds.

Development of Speech Production in Children

Phonology refers to the study of the emergence and production of single sounds and the principles by which sounds are combined in sequences. There are considerable data concerning the development in children of the use of speech sounds, but interest in studies of the development of sound itself is only recent. The stages and ages at which children emit various sounds are fairly well known, but much less is known about the manner in which sounds are combined and the principles governing these combinations (McNeill, 1970; Ingram, 1976).

When infants babble they emit sounds appropriate to virtually all languages. As they get older, their babbling becomes specific to the language of their immediate culture. Sounds not represented in the language to which the child is exposed disappear from the child's repertoire (Berry, 1969). The child's acquisition of the sounds of his or her native language progresses rapidly. By the age of 3, approximately 90 percent of the normal youngster's speech can be correctly interpreted by an adult listener (Templin, 1957). Table 8-2 summarizes the stages of development in children's use of sounds and intelligibility of speech.

SPEECH DISORDERS: PHONOLOGY/ARTICULATION

There are many factors that produce problems in children's speech production. Very young children, immature and inexperienced, are often plagued by mispronunciations of sounds and words. This common occurrence was captured in the song "All I Want for Crithmath Ith My Two Front Teeth." Articulation errors are expected as young children acquire the sounds of their language. Remember that children differ in the rate at which they learn to utter sounds just as they vary in the ages at which they sit, crawl, and walk. Assuming that the failure to articulate sounds within the expected developmental time frame is not due to a temporary lag, the presence of speech production errors may reflect several conditions. Articulation mistakes might be the result of difficulties in motor muscle movements, referred to as **dysarthria.** In such a case the child's articulation problems may be caused by an inability to generate air flow, move the tongue properly, or shape the oral cavities for articulation. Articulation problems can also result from structural defects. One such defect is cleft palate, a condition in which the parts of the palate, the roof of the mouth, fail to grow together during the fetal period. The resulting split in the palate varies in severity from child to child. Cleft palates make speaking difficult because the opening prohibits the child from building up the air flow and directing it through the oral cavities. Fortunately, surgery can usually correct structural problems and the child can develop normal speech production. Finally, there are *functional* speech disorders, disorders whose origins are a mystery. The term functional means that the cause of the problem is not known, that there are no known physical explanations for it. Thus, articulation problems may be the result of developmental immaturity, motor deficits, structural defects, or a host of other factors we do not understand.

Errors in Articulation

Phonological disorders are typically categorized into errors of *substitution, omission, distortion,* and *addition* of inappropriate sounds (Kirk, 1972). The most common articulation error is the substitution of one sound for another. Some-

TABLE 8-2 Pattern of Normal Language Development in Articulation and General Intelligibility

Age (yrs.)	Articulation	General Intelligibility
1–2	Uses all vowels and consonents *m, b, p, k, g, w, h, m, t,* and *d*; omits most final consonants, some initial; substitutes consonants above for more difficult; much unintelligible jargon around 18 mos.; good inflection and rate	Words used may be no more than 25% intelligible to unfamiliar listener; jargon near 18 mos. almost 100% unintelligible; improvement noticeable between 21 and 24 mos.
2–3	Continues all sounds above with vowels but use is inconsistent; tries many new sounds, but poor mastery; much substitution; omission of final consonants; articulation lags behind vocabulary	Words about 65% intelligible by 2 yrs.; 70% to 80% intelligible in context by 3 yrs.; many individual sounds faulty but total context generally understood; some incomprehensibility because of faulty sentence structure
3–4	Masters *b, t, d, k,* and *g* and tries many others, including *f, v, th, s,* and *z* and consonant combinations *tr, bl, pr, gr,* and *dr,* but *r* and *l* may be faulty so substitutes *w* or omits; speech almost intelligible; uses *th* inconsistently	Speech usually 90% to 100% intelligible in context; individual sounds still faulty and some trouble with sentence structure
4–5	Masters *f* and *v* and many consonant combinations; should be little omission of initial and final consonants; fewer substitutes but may be some; may distort *r, l, s, z, sh, ch, j* and *th;* no trouble with multisyllabic words	Speech is intelligible in context, even though some sounds are still faulty
5–6	Masters *r, l* and *th,* and such blends as *tl, gr, bl, br, pr,* etc.; may still have some trouble with blends such as *thr, sk, st* and *shr;* may still distort *s, a, sh, ch* and *j;* may not master these sounds until 7½ years	Good

Note: "Inflection" refers to (a) modulation of the voice in speaking; and (b) variations of nouns, verbs to express differences in gender, person, number, case, and time.

Source: DeWeese, D. D., and W. H. Saunders. *Textbook of Otolaryngology.* St. Louis: Mosby, 1973, p. 402. Originally appeared in *Journal of American Medical Association,* 1958, *167,* 850. Copyright 1958, American Medical Association.

times children substitute sounds that are similar in the way they are emitted. One plosive (a sound made with a sharp expulsion of air) may be used in place of another as in saying *k* for *t* (McLean, 1974). Children sometimes err in substituting sounds produced in adjacent tongue positions, for instance, using the sound *t* for *s.*

Children also distort sounds by using an inappropriate tongue movement or positioning to produce them. Lisps are familiar distortions. The child who lisps has difficulty pronouncing sibilant fricatives. In this case the child has a particularly hard time pronouncing s, sh, z and ch. When the sound is difficult for the child to produce, it may be omitted entirely. In addition, children sometimes add inappropriate sounds to words. The reason for children's phonological errors are often not understood, but it does appear that there is order and consistency in children's articulation errors (Compton, 1976).

Recent research on children's speech articulation has taken a new and rather radical course. Whereas it was once assumed that children's speech errors were the result of failure to produce adultlike sounds, there are those who currently believe that the child's speech errors reflect a deviant but complicated phonological system. It is suggested that the child who regularly produces deviant sounds employs a highly integrated system of substitutions, omissions, or other aberrant speech patterns that are as complex as the phonological patterns of normal speech. Compton (1976) hypothesizes that as a matter of course, the child makes errors in the normal developmental sequence of acquiring speech sounds. These errors typically disappear with the more advanced stages of development. The child who fails to advance sequentially in the acquisition of sounds appears to retain and accumulate the aberrant patterns and to develop idiosyncratic but nonetheless complex forms of speech production. The child with deviant speech production may then be making errors of substitutions as well as distortions, omissions, and additions.

Disorders of Stuttering

It has been estimated that about 1 percent of the people in this country stutter and that about 75 percent of them are male. Stuttering is one of the most puzzling speech problems, one for which there exists a good deal more theorizing than successful therapeutics. The impediment is age related, sex related, and very difficult to eliminate. It is notable that most of the symptoms associated with this disorder are not speech related, but rather consist of facial and body contortions.

Stuttering is described as consisting of two age-related states. The first stage is considered **primary stuttering** and affects children 3 to 5 years old. During this period, language skills are expanding rapidly and, as a normal part of this development, the youngster will make many speaking errors. He or she may not be able to find the right word, coordinate speech articulators as quickly as necessary, or effectively catch and hold a listener's attention. Learning to speak is in part a motor task; as in learning any motor skill, errors are to be expected and practice makes perfect. The disfluencies we find in children's speech at this time are thus considered normal steps in the acquisition of the motor act of speaking. In these early years the disfluencies are usually limited to repetitions of sounds and syllables and are common even in adult speech.

For a variety of reasons these normal disfluences sometimes evolve into **secondary stuttering.** Now the speech pattern is not limited to repetitions of sounds and syllables as in the past, but rather the individual develops various idio-syncratic facial and body symptoms. Eye blinks, gasps, facial contortions, struggle for breath are some of the symptoms of secondary stuttering (McLean, 1974). At this point the stuttering pattern is no longer considered a manifestation of normal development, but a problem likely to be enduring, disruptive, and difficult to eliminate.

Many notions have been put forth about why people become stutterers. One is that the problem is the result of an organic dysfunction, such as brain damage and neurological disorders. Organic breakdowns are thought to result from a delay in the development of cerebral nerve tracts responsible for speech muscles; from epilepsy in which small seizures affect the flow of speech; and/or from poor speech muscle coordination, which affects the individual during times of stress (Van Riper, 1952). Since there is no conclusive evidence to indicate that stutterers are different in their physiological or neurological status from those who speak fluently, organic hypotheses are in doubt (McLean, 1974).

Because of the lack of evidence concerning the organic basis of stuttering, most experts believe that the problem reflects psychological rather than physiological difficulties. Psychological theorizing concerning problems of stuttering takes several forms. Some psychoanalysts perceive the impediment as a reflection of early childhood frustrations. Others, in the mental health and speech fields, view it as a result of particular parent-child interactions in which the parents set inappropriately high standards for the child's speech and general conduct. This produces considerable pressure on the child, which affects his or her speech (Hewett and Forness, 1977). Another variation on the interaction hypothesis stresses the child's fear of losing the attention of the listener. This then produces anxiety, which increases stuttering, and a vicious cycle is then created.

Stuttering has also been interpreted within the framework of reinforcement theory. According to Goldiamond (1968), stuttering is a behavior that is maintained by differential reinforcement in ways that are complex but systematic and related to the child's environment. Goldiamond describes how this works. Imagine the child yells "Daddy! D-D-D-Daddy!" and gets no response. Becoming increasingly vehement, the child may yell "D-D-D-Daddy! D-D-D-Daddy!" and then get a response. It may be that the child is shaped to nonfluency by adult responses. If the family has other members who stutter, Goldiamond suggests they may give differential attention to the child's speech errors. The family perceives the child's normal stages of disfluency as abnormal, responds differentially, and then actually produces the problem. Goldiamond points out that speech is responsive to different audiences and refers to the evidence that stutterers do not falter in their speech under all circumstances. They may be fluent when singing, speaking on stage, speaking in a foreign language, or when talking to a pet.

Voice Disorders

Voice disorders may take a variety of forms. A child may speak too loudly or softly, or with a voice pitched too high or too low. While voice disorders are rare, occurring in about 0.1 percent of the school population, they must not be ignored as they may be associated with some physical problem. For example, a child who speaks in a noticeably hoarse, harsh, or breathy voice may have an ulcer or nodule on his vocal cords (McLean, 1974). The individual who speaks too softly or loudly could possibly be suffering from hearing loss. In cleft palate speech, sounds are usually excessively nasal as the air is improperly channeled through the nasal cavity. The human voice may thus reflect a variety of serious problems that may well signal the need for medical attention. Some voice disorders can be medically treated, for example a nodule on the vocal cords; or alleviated through prosthetic devices, as in some cases a cleft palate. Others, such as removal of an individual's vocal cords, may be treated by speech therapists following surgery (McLean, 1974).

Treatment of Articulation Disorders

Intervention for articulation problems begins with identification procedures. In public school programs, it is customary for speech therapists to screen for speech problems among kindergarteners and first graders and to respond to referrals from teachers and parents of older children. The speech therapist will typically speak informally with the child as a means of identifying any speech disturbances. The child may be asked to count to 10, to talk about a series of pictures selected because they "pull" a variety of sounds, and to perform other tasks enabling the therapist to determine whether the child has a problem in producing sounds and/or in discriminating among sounds. In addition to these informal methods of assessment, the speech therapist may administer standardized tests such as the *Wepman Auditory Discrimination Test* (Wepman, 1958) or the *Northwestern Syntax Screening Test* (Lee, 1970). Since speech problems are often associated with other handicapping conditions, it is important for the speech therapist to check into the possibility of such conditions. For example, the child's speech patterns may be the most obvious signal that a child has a mild or moderate hearing loss. The speech therapist thus has an important role in signalling appropriate treatments for handicaps other than speech problems.

Before discussing intervention techniques, you should know that strategies applied to the stutterer are quite distinct from those employed with other speech problems. We will first describe the intervention strategies for dealing with articulation problems, then those used in helping the stuttering child and adult.

Articulation Disorders

Intervention techniques for children with articulation disorders usually consist of several components. First the child is trained to discriminate appropriate production of sounds from those he or she produces. This is referred to as "ear training." Second, the child is given practice in the correct production of words, sentences, and then conversational speech. The methods employed are typically gamelike as any method of producing sounds can serve as the springboard for speech training. Stories, pictures, or any technique that leads to speech can be

FIGURE 8-1 Speech therapist working with child to improve production of appropriate sounds by imitation

used. The learning procedures may rely heavily upon the child's ability and willingness to imitate. If imitative learning is not possible, then training may involve the physical positioning of the tongue. Toothpicks, tongue depressors, and even peanut butter on the roof of the mouth may all be important therapeutic instruments. Treatments may take about 40 minutes a week during the school year and the duration of the training program may exceed one year.

Stuttering

Interventions with stutterers take quite another form insofar as the psychological, rather than the physical, components of speech are stressed. Psychoanalysts and therapists not oriented to learning theory are likely to provide treatment in which the goal is to resolve the presumed psychological conflicts and fears producing the stuttering. Insights into the causes of the problem, it is thought, will facilitate the symptom's disappearance. By and large, the effectiveness of these methods has not been impressive. Some temporary improvement in stuttering may occur but it is likely to be short-lived. Relapses are common to such "cures."

The most successful form of intervention has been based upon principles of reinforcement. Irrespective of how stuttering starts, it is clear that just like other kinds of behavior, it is susceptible to reinforcement effects (Martin, 1968). The therapeutic approaches to treating children in the primary stage of stuttering focus upon the parent rather than the child. Specifically, parents are encouraged to avoid giving reinforcements during the periods of the child's nonfluency. Thus, parents are urged to avoid increasing their attention and conversation with the child during periods of disrupted speech. In addition, parents are often advised to reassure the child about disfluencies and reduce their demands for speech by the child (Van Riper, 1952).

The treatment of secondary stuttering is addressed directly to the stuttering child or adult and often uses the methodologies associated with operant conditioning. The treatment location is typically the clinic and the initial evaluation of the stutterer involves the collection of data pertaining to the frequency of the impediment and symptoms associated with it. Treatment consists of administering aversive stimulation when the individual stutters. For example, Flanagan, Goldiamond, and Azrin (1958) played a loud noise whenever their patient stuttered, and Goldiamond (1968) has used noise and electric shock feedback during the blockage episodes. Interestingly, Goldiamond (1968) has also employed as punishment an auditory feedback of the stutterer's own impediment. Martin (1968) has indicated that most of the research in the control of stuttering with adults whose problem is chronic has employed punishment as a treatment device, a procedure that does reduce the disfluencies.

While punishment has been demonstrated to be effective in decreasing the occurrence of speech blockages, the effects may be rather short-lived once the punishment is stopped. Thus, additional training of speech production is often required. The stutterer may be taught to use a different speech pattern. The individual may be trained to prolong sounds, lower the pitch of sounds, or use a different rhythmic pattern (Goldiamond, 1968). These alterations are produced through the use of positive reinforcements and shaping. That is, reinforcements are used and become increasingly contingent upon the matching of the subject's speech to the desired standard. It is important also to train the stutterer in other settings than the clinic or laboratory. The reason for this is that behaviors that are instilled by means of positive reinforcements and punishments will often only be demonstrated in the setting in which the training occurs. Recognizing this problem, Goldiamond takes stutterers into the "field," where they have further training to help them engage in normal conversation.

Interactions with a stutterer are often distressing to the listener. Many are tempted to advise the child to relax, take a deep breath, think about what is to be said, or follow some other folksy and presumably helpful course of conduct. In fact, however, it is clear that such attention and concern may well serve as a positive reinforcement for the stuttering and thus do more harm than good. Essentially, one must be patient with the very young child. If the child is a secondary stutterer, help is needed from a professional speech pathologist, preferably one with a background in operant conditioning.

SYNTACTIC AND SEMANTIC DEVELOPMENT

When children start to speak, they do not spout isolated words; their utterances from the start reflect meaningful concepts and intention to communicate with others. In an effort to understand how children acquire language, investigators study syntactic development in children, how they come to use the correct grammar of the language; and children's semantic development, the acquisition of meaning. Lately there has been growing interest as well in children's acquisition of the use of language: that is, pragmatics, their knowledge of when to say what to whom. As a result of the growing interest in syntactic and semantic development, and the burgeoning of data concerning how children acquire syntax and semantics, there has been a shift in the definitions and treatments of speech disorders in handicapped children. For many years, speech therapists were primarily concerned with children's disorders of articulation, stuttering, and voice. As a result of the current work in linguistics, speech therapists are focusing more on assessment and intervention of language disorders. We do not know whether children with speech disorders have language disorders or whether these represent two distinct sets of problems. Experts suspect that there are children who have one problem or the other, and children who have both speech and language problems. In any case it is important to recognize that many handicapping conditions do involve language as well as speech disorders, and that careful attention to both speech and language should be part of a language assessment and intervention program.

Following is a brief overview of the stages and ages at which children acquire the syntactic and semantic systems of their language. The emphasis in this section is upon normal development rather than language disorders. The reason is that relatively little is known about language disorders, mainly because the interest in syntax and semantics is really quite recent. There has not been enough time to apply the newest developments in linguistic research to the study of handicapped populations. This gap is expected to be narrowed in the near future, but until more information is gathered, parents and teachers will probably have to use knowledge concerning normal development as a crude measuring stick for inferring the presence of a language disorder.

What is striking about the child's acquisition of systems of syntax and semantics is that there is an orderly progression that each child goes through in the learning of increasingly complex forms. While the ages when children acquire particular parts of language vary a good deal, there is considerable consistency in the order in which these developments take place. It is also remarkable to find that children at various stages of language development seem to be using their own rule systems. These systems appear to be similar among children at the same linguistic developmental stage, but are different from the rule systems followed by adult speakers.

Development of Syntax

The first development in language is **holophrastic speech,** that is, single-word utterances of young children, typically around the age of 12 to 18 months (McNeill, 1970; Dale, 1972). These single-word utterances, however, are not random vocalizations or object identifications, but are believed to represent some complex idea. An example of holophrastic speech is the instance where the child says "Walk" and then proceeds to do so. It is often linked to some forms of action, either expressing the child's intent to act, or attempts to get others to act on his or her behalf.

When children start to combine words at about 18 to 20 months, they employ **telegraphic speech.** This refers to the first usage of combinations of words to imply an idea but without using all the words necessary for it. For example, by saying "Me milk," the child is communicating a desire for milk.

During the child's second and third years, the number of words that he or she can combine increases. At the same time the average child will learn to apply a rule system to language productions. Pflaum (1978) indicates that children show an early use of subject and object in their sentences ("It doggie"), will combine verbs and objects ("See train"), and unite subjects and verbs ("I see"). Children combine words to reflect sentence structures of modification ("more hot"), conjunction ("and hot"), genitive (ownership meanings such as "Daddy mitten"), and location ("banana table"). Children's initial language systems are imperfect in the sense of adult grammar, but focus on the critical elements they wish to communicate.

The rapid expansion of children's syntactic development can be seen in an examination of the acquisition of verb forms. Pflaum (1978) indicates that there are two early major events in the development of verb forms. One is the acquired use of auxiliary verb forms, such as in the use of "ing" and "ed." Adults use auxiliary verb forms to express tense, indicate questions, make negative statements, and to show passive voice. During this period of language expansion, children will begin to use auxiliary verb forms, often in past tense ("He feeled it"). The second major factor in developing verb forms at this time is the acquisition of the verb "to be." Once children begin to use these verb forms, they have the mechanics to produce complete sentences.

The ability to form negative sentences is another important step in the child's syntactic development. Klima (1964) indicates that children acquire negative forms by first attaching a negative ("no") to a holophrase. The child then learns to position negative words within the sentence. For instance, a little girl initially may say "No cookie," while later she will say "Me no cookie." This development is followed by the use of auxiliary verbs with transformational rules as in the example "Me don't want no cookie." Transformations are rules that permit us to change words around and put sentences together. The child can construct very complex sentences by the age of 36 months.

The child's ability to ask questions also appears during this time period. Children initially ask questions by raising the pitch of their voice. The intonation is the tag that signals a question (for example, "Ball go?"). Children then ask questions beginning their sentences with "who," "where," "why." The most advanced stage occurs when children ask questions by inverting the order of words in the sentences. This inversion appears to be one of the first transformations, or transformational rules acquired by children. In a few months children change from using "Who that?" to "See my doggie" to "Does lions walk?" While not having learned all the rules of adult language, by 3½ years of age children are nearly as competent as adults in their ability to ask questions.

Another major change that takes place during this same time frame is the acquisition of inflections, word parts which make nouns plural and which then result in noun-verb agreement. The order of acquisition appears to go from noun plurals to the possessives and finally to verb inflections. By 3½ years children's sentence structure is amazingly adultlike as children's uses of verb forms are quite sophisticated. The acquisition of transformational rules is well under way.

From 3½ to 6 years of age children's language continues to grow even more complex. Menyuk (1963) studied the language production of nursery school and first grade children. There were syntactic similarities between these two groups in the frequency with which they used various linguistic structures. Both groups emitted contractions ("didn't"), possessives ("Mary's hat"), pronouns ("He can"), adjectives ("brown hat"), infinitive complements ("I wanted to do it"), main clause conjunctions ("He sang and Mary danced"), and conjunctions with deletions ("Mary sang and danced"). With other kinds of transformations there is a shift in the frequency of occurrence, with first graders using these transformations more frequently than nursery school children. First graders thus use relative clauses more frequently than nursery school aged children: ("The man who sang is old"); *because* clause embedded (". . . because he said so"); participle separation ("Put down the box"); reflexives ("I did it myself"); imperatives ("Shut the door"); passives ("The boy was hit by the girl"); participial complement ("I saw her washing"); *if* clause embedded (". . . if you want to"); *so* clause embedded (". . . so he will be happy"); compound of nominals ("baby chair"), iteration ("You have to clean clothes to make them clean").

According to Pflaum (1978) children learn subject and predicate, then sentence parts that make their simple sentences more like those of adults: then rules that allow them to form compound and complex sentences. In all, their speech follows a progression of development thought by linguists to mirror the evolution of human language.

Semantic Development

During the 1960s researchers in language were concentrating heavily on studying children's syntactic development. Since the late 1960s it has been recognized that we need to extend the study of syntax to include semantics if we are to gain a better understanding of the development of language. Thus, there has been more interest recently in how children acquire the meanings of words and sentences, what types of meanings they try to express as they acquire language, and the relationship between the acquisition of semantics and children's cognitive development. The study of semantics is intimately linked to both the study of syntax and the study of cognition.

Linguists disagree as to how children acquire the meanings of words, how they learn to combine words into sentences and the relationship of all this to cognitive development. Such disagreements might well be expected, given the difficulties in studying semantic development. First, children vary greatly in the age at which they acquire different word meanings, their manner of expressing the import of a word, and the different meanings they choose to communicate. In addition, the units investigators study are large and cumbersome. They do not focus upon the production of a particular sound, but rather must investigate large chunks of children's language in their attempts to understand semantic development. Given that this emphasis is relatively new, conclusions about semantic development must be tentative. There is a lot we do not know.

In any case, comparisons of how children acquire different languages reveal that initial vocabulary and initial word combinations across languages are highly similar. Irrespective of the tongue the child is mastering, the first words and sentences likely involve naming ("See mommy"); recurrence ("More milk"); disappearance ("Cookie all gone"); denial ("No baby"); location ("Where daddy?"); possession ("My doggie"); and relationships among agents, actions and objects ("Mommy push," "Man dance," "Bite finger," "Drive car," "Spank me") (Bowerman, 1976, p. 139).

Categorization

To acquire the semantic system the child has first to be able to generate in a new situation words that had been learned in a familiar context. The application of known words to novel circumstances is one way the child extends semantic skills. Thus the child extends "doggie" from his or her pet to all four-legged creatures and "open" the door of the house to "open" the refrigerator. When the child broadens the use of a word like "open," he or she is underway in learning to categorize. Learning to categorize experiences, objects, and people is a major step in the acquisition of meaningful word usage.

There is some disagreement as to the basis for children's initial categorization of words. According to Clark (1973) children initially categorize words according to their perceptual properties, such as their shape, size, sound, texture, or movement. On the other hand, Nelson (1974) suggests that children acquire their first words and categories on the basis of function, that is, how the object is used. In the Clark perspective the child discriminates the word "ball" because it is round; in the Nelson approach "ball" is categorized as something to bounce. It does appear, however, that for children in their first six years the perceptual features of objects are important in categorizing words (Wepman, 1976). It also appears that children are more likely to use words, and categories, for objects that move or that can be acted upon rather than immovable objects. This does not mean to say that children do not have ideas about immovable objects before they begin to use the words. A little girl may be able to point to her father's chair well before she can say "daddy's chair."

Preciseness

The child begins to learn the exact meanings of words gradually. Initially, young children overextend the meanings of words, using them in contexts that are inappropriate. For example, the very young child may call all four-legged creatures "doggie," while the older child discriminates dogs from cats. However, just because the child calls all four-legged beings "dogs," does not necessarily mean that he or she does not perceive differences between dogs and cats. It may simply mean that the youngster does not yet have the right word to describe or label the object. Evidently children also contract a term, using it in very restricted circumstances, as for example, using the word "car" to refer to a moving, but not a parked, vehicle (Bowerman, 1976). The young child also may associate a word with characteristics of objects in seemingly idiosyncratic fashion, as when one word is used to describe all round objects.

Recent studies indicate that children differ in the classes of words they first acquire. Some seem to learn words that are general names for objects while others concentrate on proper names for people or on personal-social words like "no" and "please" (Nelson, 1974). Rosenblatt (1975) has indicated that children who learn words related to playing with toys differ from others by having short latency to touch toys, paying visual attention to toys, being persistent on tasks, and not being geared toward social interaction. But, according to this researcher, children who tend to learn personal and social vocabulary first are those who are more responsive to adults and spend comparatively less time playing. The interests of the young child thus are important in early semantic development.

For children to learn the meanings of words, they must learn a rule that indicates the necessary preconditions for using the word correctly. Sometimes words refer to specific concrete objects, events, or property, but sometimes they have no referents (for instance, "Good night"). The child does not appear to be taught the rules directly for using words, but rather develops inferences about word usage, primarily from intercombinations of words by hearing the words "in relation to each other, in relation to the events in which they occur, and using such words successively in the same kinds of situations" (Bloom, 1973, p. 120).

Not stressed but nevertheless obvious is the important effect that the parents' labeling of events and situations to the child will also have upon the child's semantic development. For example, parents directly link objects to words in their interactions with the child. In addition, parents provide discrimination training, as when they correct the child for calling a dog a cat, or the strange male "Daddy."

Getting the word connected to exactly the right object and employed in the right context is no mean feat. Learning the meaning and use of a word is dependent upon a number of factors. Parental labeling and discrimination training are clearly important, as are the perceptual and functional attributes of the object. The overlap of novel situations with familiar ones may affect the degree to which

**TABLE 8-3 Pattern of Normal Language Development
in Expressive Speech and Comprehension of Speech**

Age (yrs.)	Expressive speech	Comprehension of speech
1–2	Uses 1 to 3 words at 12 mos., 10 to 15 at 15 mos., 15 to 20 at 18 mos., about 100 to 200 by 2 yrs.; knows names of most objects he uses; names few people, uses verbs but not correctly with subjects; jargon and echoalia; names 1 to 3 pictures.	Begins to relate symbol and object meaning; adjusts to comments; inhibits on command; responds correctly to "Give me that," "Sit down," "Stand up," with gestures; puts watch to ear on command; understands simple questions; recognizes 120 to 275 words.
2–3	Vocabulary increases to 300 to 500 words; says "Where kitty?" "Ball all gone," "Want cookie," and "Go bye-bye car"; jargon mostly gone; vocalizing increases, has fluency trouble; speech not adequate for communication needs.	Rapid increase in comprehension vocabulary to 400 at 2½ yrs., 800 at 3 yrs.; responds to commands using "on," "under," "up," "down," "over there," "by," "run," "walk," "jump up," "throw," "run fast," "be quiet," and commands containing two related actions.
3–4	Uses 600 to 1000 words, becomes conscious of speech; 3 to 4 words per speech response; personal pronouns, some adjectives, adverbs, and prepositions appear; mostly simple sentences, but some complex; speech more useful.	Understands up to 1500 words by 4 yrs., recognizes plurals, sex difference, pronouns, adjectives; comprehends complex and compound sentences; answers simple questions.
4–5	Increase in vocabulary to 1100 to 1600 words; more 3- and 4-syllable words; more adjectives, adverbs, prepositions and conjunctions; articles appear; 4-, 5-, and 6-word sentences, syntax quite good; uses plurals; fluency improves; proper nouns decrease, pronouns increase.	Comprehends from 1500 to 2000 words; carries out more complex commands, with 2 to 3 actions; understands dependent clause, "if," "because," "when," "why."
5–6	Increase in vocabulary to 1500 to 2100 words; complete 5- and 6-word sentences, compound, complex, with some dependent clauses; syntax near normal; quite fluent; more multisyllabic words.	Understands vocabulary of 2500 to 2800 words; responds correctly to more complicated sentences, but is still confused at times by involved sentences.

Source: DeWeese, D. D. and W. H. Saunders. *Textbook of Otolaryngology.* St. Louis: Mosby, 1973, p. 403. Originally appeared in *Journal of American Medical Association,* 1958, *167,* 850. Copyright 1958, American Medical Association.

the child will learn to apply words appropriately to new events. As mentioned earlier, even the interests of the child will play an important role in learning and using new words. These many sources of influence continually, and for a long time, nourish the child's learning of meaning and use of words.

Table 8-3 presents information about the ages at which children learn to understand others and to express themselves. It should be remembered that there is great variation among children in the ages at which they develop these skills.

There is a question as to whether the child's language reflects his or her thinking or conceptual abilities. That is, is the child's thinking constrained by and reflected only through language? By and large, most people believe that this is not the case, that children do conceptualize and think about objects or events in the absence of appropriate language (Bowerman, 1976). Lenneberg writes, for example: "The modes of conceptualization that happen to be tagged by a given natural language need not, and apparently do not, exert restrictions upon an individual's freedom of conceptualizing" (1967, p. 334). The evidence suggests that children do develop concepts without having words to express them. Sometimes they make up their own words to express ideas for which they have not yet acquired the proper vocabulary. Clearly, when a child says "Boom! Boom!" and points to a phonograph record, some concept has been acquired in advance of the proper words. At the same time it makes sense that children's concept learning is strengthened by their development of vocabulary, categories, and abstract terms. While concepts can be formed in the absence of vocabulary, there is no doubt that language development will facilitate the child's acquisition of concepts.

LANGUAGE DISORDERS

In our discussion of phonology, we reviewed children's development of the phonological system. This was followed by a description of the ways in which the acquisition and use of this system can break down into speech disorders. When we turn our attention from the child's development of syntax and semantics, we do not have the same transition to language disorders. There has not been the same paralleling of research on language development and language disorders as there has been on phonology and speech problems. However, language problems have not been entirely ignored. There have been studies and hypotheses advanced that are relevant to such difficulties, and they will now be presented.

Brain Trauma and Language

While the individual is progressing through stages of language development, the impact of any damage that interferes with brain processes and language will depend upon its severity and locale and the child's physical maturity and physiological status. According to Lenneberg (1967), if the child experiences traumas before reaching 20 months of age, that child's language development will be delayed but will still progress in the same fashion, if not at the same speed, as that of nondamaged children. It is believed that during this period in the child's development, nondamaged areas of the brain can assume the functions previously served by the traumatized areas. If the child is over 21 months of age, traumas are likely to have a more debilitating effect. The period between 21 and 36 months of age is particularly important insofar as the child is acquiring a great deal of language and most of this learning is new and unpracticed. Thus, for children within this age range, traumas to the left side of the brain might well prove seriously weakening. While this age child may show spontaneous recuperation of language, it is also possible that he or she will have to repeat much previous language learning.

When children suffer brain damage between the ages of 3 and 10 years, they exhibit symptoms of **aphasia.** Aphasia refers to the loss of language, a condition most often seen in adults who suffer from a stroke that affects the left side of the cerebral cortex. It is a serious condition in which the ability to understand others as well as to express oneself may be severely limited. Children who suffer aphasic symptoms due to trauma during this period may spontaneously recover their language, but even if they do, they are likely to have problems with reading and writing. The child who suffers a trauma during the ages from 11 to 14 years or older will manifest the symptoms of aphasia, which are likely to persist. Such a child may have grave difficulties in speaking and understanding others.

Delayed Speech

Many children for no apparent reason fail to develop their language skills at the expected ages. There is now a respectable amount of information about delayed language development, particularly with respect to the child's acquisition of syntax.

Morehead and Ingram (1976) summarize the differences between children who do and do not develop language at the expected ages. In general, linguistically deviant children do not develop idiosyncratic or "abnormal" speech; they do not generate a new language. Rather, such children acquire the same rules of language as normally developing children, but do so more slowly.

It should be noted that the degree of language delay can be substantial. For example, Johnston and Schery (1976) discovered that children without language delays were using two to three words per utterance by age 28 months, while language delayed children were not using this many until 81 months. In addition, Menyuk, (1969) found that linguistically delayed children between the ages of 3 to 5 used very similar syntactic forms in their expressions, a finding hardly expected given the enormous advances typical of children in this age range. Additionally, once linguistically deviant children begin to use morphemes (the smallest meaningful units of language), it takes them much longer to employ them correctly and with ease than the normally developing child (Johnston and Schery, 1976).

Let us note some of the specific language errors made by language delayed children. They are likely to omit articles (such as "the"); fail to expand a phrase ("Boy likes doggies" versus "Boys like big, soft doggies who run after sticks"); employ words incorrectly and violate grammatical rules ("My like cookie"). Additionally, these children use simple transformational structures, as for example, using two short simple sentences rather than one somewhat more complex sentence

("I want popcorn" and "I want candy," versus "I want popcorn and candy"). Finally, Menyuk reports that the language delayed child is likely to use incorrect forms of negatives and questions ("No go to store" versus "Don't go to store," and "Daddy go work?" versus "Will daddy go to work?). Menyuk suggests that these children's inability to remember morphemes produces the serious errors and delays in language development.

Lee (1974) has also studied children's language acquisition extensively and has reported important differences in language development between the linguistically deviant and nondeviant child. She suggests that whereas children who speak normally learn to use complicated linguistic structures by the age of 4, language delayed children do not. For instance, most children learn to use pronouns very early, but language delayed children have an inordinately difficult time doing so. The use of negatives (like "no," "neither," "nobody") is apparently easily achieved by normal speaking children, but not by linguistically delayed ones. Additionally, the normal child learns to pose questions and use infinitives, gerunds, and participles at a much earlier age than language delayed children.

When language delayed and nondelayed children are compared, there is evidence that the former group are deficient in the acquisition of syntactic structures. In virtually all aspects of the use of structural forms, the language delayed child demonstrates shortcomings in relation to normally developing peers. What we do not yet know is how delays and/or deficits in the acquisition of syntax are related to the acquisition of semantics. Does the absence of various syntactic structures limit the child's vocabulary, sentence, or conceptual growth? As we cannot specify the relationship of speech disorders to language disorders, we cannot yet specify the relationship of one type of language disorder—delays in the acquisition of syntactic structures—to other types of language learning, such as vocabulary growth or the use of language in context. Finally, there is controversy as to whether language deficits represent developmental delays in which the child acquires language at a slower rate than others or a problem in which the child develops deviant language patterns. While we do not yet have answers to these questions, the reader who works with handicapped children should be aware of them. In assessment and intervention programming, a thorough analysis of the child's language status should reveal the various components of language the child still needs to learn.

The Relationship of Language to Other Cognitive Processes

We know very little about the relationship of cognitive development and processes to linguistic development. The data on linguistically deviant children cited here were based on youngsters who did demonstrate intelligence within the normal range. Nonetheless, it is legitimate to ask what impact linguistic delays have upon information processing and cognition. The data are more than sparse; at best we can only suggest possible areas of information processing and cognition that might be negatively affected by delayed and deviant language systems.

First, language has the primary task of communication with others. What is the effect on social communications when the child fails to acquire adequate language, or at least fails to acquire it at the expected age? Research is needed to determine what happens to such children during their social communications with others. Are they treated with contempt, with overprotectiveness, with assumptions of competence or incompetence? It is likely that many of our inferences about the personality of the child will be based not only on what the child says, but on how it is said.

Second, the individual uses language to process information for storage, understanding, and application of information to other situations and concepts. For example, verbal rehearsal of newly learned material has been shown to facilitate the individual's ability to remember bits of information (Bandura, 1969), and individuals develop their own verbal strategies for coding and rehearsing information. Just what impact linguistic deficits may have on coding and rehearsal operations has not yet been determined. It is entirely possible, however, that such difficulties will handicap language delayed children in their learning.

Language is ubiquitous in school settings and critically important in academic achievement. As we mentioned in chapter 4, it has been discovered that a significant number of children who fail to acquire reading skills also have language problems (Vellutino, 1977). This relationship between reading and language has been found under quite diverse methods of assessment. Whether the facet of language tested is vocabulary, story telling, or the ability to learn to match symbols in paired-associate learning tasks, the evidence consistently shows a relationship between language and reading skills. What is striking about these data is that there has not been similar evidence of a connection between perceptual skills and reading. Rather, it appears that there is a complex relationship between language and learning. As a result language delays or deficits may play havoc with the child's academic and social development.

ASSESSMENT AND INTERVENTION GUIDELINES

It is beyond the scope of this chapter to provide an extensive review of the many assessment devices or intervention strategies used in helping children with speech and language problems. Rather, we provide some guidelines that might be of use to parents and teachers in detecting signs that indicate that professional help for the child is required, and some ideas of how language intervention is programmed.

Warning Signals

The following conditions have been suggested by DeWeese and Lillywhite (1973) as significant indicators that the child's speech is sufficiently aberrant to warrant a medical and educational assessment:

1. fails to speak by age 2 years
2. speech is unintelligible after the age of 3
3. is more than a year retarded in producing sounds, given the developmental sequence in which most children produce sounds
4. continues to omit initial consonants (for instance, the *b* in "book") after reaching 3 years
5. makes substitutions on sounds after 5 years of age
6. uses vowels excessively
7. has not produced sentences by age 3 years
8. continues to drop word endings after age 5
9. sentences are still agrammatical after 5 years
10. appears to be embarrassed by his or her speech at any age
11. is notably disfluent after 5 years of age
12. continues to distort, omit, or substitute any sounds after age 7
13. voice a monotone, very loud or very soft, or has a strange quality
14. pitch not appropriate for child's age or sex

These various signals may be clues to different conditions requiring differential treatment. As noted earlier, voice or articulation problems may indicate that the child has a hearing loss, and severe delays in language acquisition may seriously delay a number of developmental milestones for the child.

Guidelines for Language Intervention

There are many programs available that offer guidelines and activities for helping language deficient children. But in this section we rely on those provided by Bowerman (1976) since they are research based, and are focused on semantic development. We offer these suggestions because we believe that a focus on the development of concepts through language training is the type of programming many language deficient children need. However, many types of handicapping conditions are accompanied by language problems and specific disabilities may require different remediation processes. For example, programs for the severely mentally handicapped are likely to include a heavy emphasis upon behavior modification techniques, while programs for the multihandicapped will focus initially upon developing physical capacities. The following, then, are suggestions for remediation processes for children with language delays who do not display multiple or severe handicaps.

There are several categories of words that are often the target of the initial stages of interventions. These categories are vocabulary words for common objects and actions which the child does frequently. Teaching strategies vary somewhat, depending upon which category of words is selected for training. First let us look at the training of action words. Bowerman suggests that to begin to develop a language program, one must recognize that language is categorical, that learning is helped by the child's recognition that certain words and concepts go together.

Concept learning facilitates language development. Second, the child's acquisition of concepts is related to experiences. The child must "see" the similarities of events and their descriptions of them. Language development is facilitated when the child is able to grasp that there are connections between such events as a boy running, a baby eating, and a dog barking. Initially, then, a language intervention program might be directed toward helping the child acquire concepts or ideas that unite similar but somethat different events or situations. Following this, an effort might be made to teach the child combinations of words, particularly those indicating an action and those suggesting that a person is doing the action. Earlier we indicated that some children initially have vocabularies that are more oriented to people or social interaction while others have vocabularies geared more to action and toys. Bowerman suggests that initial attempts to help the language deficient child might be more effective if the youngster is taught words related to his or her personal style of classifying experiences.

When teaching vocabulary relevant to common objects, Bowerman recommends that since children initially classify objects on the basis of perceptual similarities, especially by shape, initial word training should incorporate the description of the perceptual characteristics of the object designated by the word. Thus, to teach the word "ball," it is advisable to link it with the word "round." In addition, language development might be facilitated if the words selected for early training refer to objects with which the child is actively involved in everyday experiences. Teaching the words "shoe," "ball," and "cookie" would be preferable to teaching the words "couch," "window," or "cupboard," since children are more likely to be actively engaged with the first group of items than the second.

Words that refer not to an object but to relations (such as "under" or "over"), or to events ("leaving," "arriving," "disappearing") should be taught in conjunction with actions or happenings. For example, suppose you wish to teach the word "under," the adult should relate that word to a situation that is currently going on. The adult might point out that the pencil is under the table or the dog is under the table. But one such training experience will not necessarily help the child to understand the concept of "under"; hence, the adult should link the word to many instances that illustrate it. In this manner, children may learn the concept of under. What is notable about Bowerman's suggestions is that they are focused upon helping the child develop the semantic or meaning aspects of language.

As in other instances of inadequate functioning, behavior modification patterns have been successful in helping the language deficit child (Fygetakis and Ingram, 1973; Gray and Fygetakis, 1968). Gottsleben, Wright, Foster, Giddan, and Stark (1968) describe the necessary steps for developing a behavior modification approach in helping children with severe language deficiencies. They suggest that the desired behavioral goal be specified, that one language concept at a time be presented to the child and repeated frequently, and the sequence of instruction be arranged so that it leads to the acquisition of specific language structures. They also advise that changes in the units of instruction be very gradual, and that the program provide cues that prompt the child to make correct responses. Reinforcement is recommended following each correct response.

SUMMARY

This chapter has covered many topics relevant to speech and communication. First the ubiquitous nature of language was mentioned, a point reiterated in the final sections of the chapter. We stressed that language skills are essential for a host of human activities, from communicating with others to communicating with oneself. The child or adult who experiences problems in the acquisition or use of speech and language is at a disadvantage in school, at work, and in interpersonal relationships. Language was defined and discussed in terms of its subcomponents. These components—phonology, syntax, and semantics—were defined, the normal course of their development described, and children's difficulties in mastering them outlined. Disruptions in the development of the phonological system, the production of sounds in isolation and combined, result in articulation, voice, and stuttering disorders. Articulation disorders are difficulties in the production and combination of individual sounds. Voice problems refer to incorrect production of sound either at the level of the larynx, or by misdirection of the air flow during speech. Stuttering has two stages: a primary stage, when it is viewed as a part of normally developing speech patterns; and a secondary stage, when disfluencies in speech are accompanied by facial grimaces and body contortions. Disorders of the phonological system have recently been found to be logical, in the sense that the person who has such disorders develops some kind of rule system, albeit an aberrant one, to generate speech. Disorders of the phonological system are most frequently treated by speech therapists, although voice problems may also require medical attention. It is important to note that articulation problems are very common in many types of handicapping conditions.

While syntactic development has been studied more extensively than semantic development, there is great interest in how children acquire meaningful units of language as well as how they acquire grammar. When development of language is affected by traumas to the brain, the young child is likely to be able to compensate for such effects. The older the child when traumatized, the more difficult the recovery of language. When, in the absence of brain trauma, children fail to develop language, we see that many aspects of syntactic language development are affected. Children with delayed speech will not develop an aberrant language, but will be markedly slower in virtually all phases of syntactic development. It is not yet clear what the impact of a language delay is upon the semantic development of the child. There is concern, however, that a problem in the syntactic development will have parallel delays in semantic development. Since the use of language is so fundamental in social relationships, school adjustment, and academic achievement, children with deviant speech are at considerable disadvantage, particularly once they reach school age. Such children may well experience severe problems in other areas.

Finally, we offered some guidelines for the recognition of speech and language problems and some suggestions for a productive language intervention program. It is hoped the reader has gained awareness of the complexity and importance of language, and some feeling for the devastating impact a deficient linguistic system can have on a child's development.

REFERENCES

Bandura, A. *Principles of behavior modification.* New York: Holt, Rinehart & Winston, 1969.

Berry, M. F. *Language disorders of children: The bases and diagnoses.* New York: Appleton-Century-Crofts, 1969.

Blank, M. Language, the child, and the teacher: A proposed assessment model. In H. L. Hom & P. A. Robinson (Eds.), *Psychological processes in early education.* New York: Academic Press, 1977, 203–232.

Bloom, L. *One word at a time: The use of single-word utterances before syntax.* The Hague, Netherlands: Mouton, 1973.

Bowerman, M. Semantic factors in the acquisition of rules for word use and sentence construction. In P. M. Morehead & A. E. Morehead (Eds.), *Normal and deficient child language.* Baltimore: University Park Press, 1976, 99–179.

Clark, E. What's in a word? On the child's acquisition of semantics in his first language. In T. M. Moore (Ed.), *Cognitive development and the acquisition of language.* New York: Academic Press, 1973, 65–110.

Compton, A. J. Generative studies of children's phonological disorders: Clinical ramifications. In D. M. Morehead & A. E. Morehead (Eds.), *Normal and deficient child language.* Baltimore: University Park Press, 1976.

Dale, P. S. *Language development.* Hinsdale, Ill.: Dryden Press, 1972.

DeWeese, D. D., & Lillywhite, H. Speech disorders in children. In D. D. DeWeese & W. H. Saunders (Eds.), *Textbook of otolaryngology,* St. Louis, Mo.: C. V. Mosby, 1973, 400–410.

Flanagan, B., Goldiamond, I., & Azrin, N. Operant stuttering: The control of stuttering behavior through response contingent consequences. *Journal of Experimental Analysis of Behavior,* 1958, *1,* 73–77.

Fygetakis, L. J., & Ingram, D. Language rehabilitation and programmed conditioning: A case study. *Journal of Learning Disabilities,* 1973, *6,* 60–64.

Goldiamond, I. Stuttering and fluency as manipulative operant response class. In H. N. Ivan & B. D. Macauley (Eds.), *Operant procedures in remedial speech and language.* Boston: Houghton Mifflin, 1968.

Gottsleben, R. H., Wright, T. S., Foster, C., Giddan, J. J., & Stark, J. Developmental language programs for aphasic children. *Academic Therapy Quarterly,* 1968, *3,* 278–282.

Gray, B. B., & Fygetakis, L. Mediated language acquisition for dysphasic children. *Behavior Research & Therapy,* 1968, *6,* 263–280.

Hewett, F. M., & Forness, S. R. *Education of exceptional learners.* Boston: Allyn & Bacon, 1977.

Ingram, D. Current issues in child phonology. In D. M. Morehead & A. E. Morehead (Eds.), *Normal and deviant child language*. Baltimore: University Park Press, 1976, 3–27.

Johnson, W. *Children with speech and hearing impairment: Preparing to work with them in the public schools*. Bulletin No. 5, Washington, D.C.: Office of Educatoin, U.S. Department of Health, Education and Welfare, 1959.

Johnson, W., Anderson, V., Kopp, G., Mose, D., Schuell, H., Shover, J., & Wolfe, W. ASHA committee on the midcentury White House conference, speech disorders and speech correction. *Journal of Speech and Hearing Disorders*, 1952, *17*, 129–137.

Johnston, J. R., & Schery, T. K. The use of grammatical morphemes by children with communication disorders. In D. M. Morehead & A. E. Morehead (Eds.), *Normal and deficient child language*. Baltimore: University Park Press, 1976, 239–258.

Kirk, S. A. *Educating exceptional children*. Boston: Houghton Mifflin, 1972.

Klima, E. S. Negation in English. In J. J. Fodor & J. A. Katz (Eds.), *The structure of language*. Englewood Cliffs, N.J.: Prentice-Hall, 1964, 246–323.

Lee, L. L. A screening test for syntax development. *Journal of Speech and Hearing Disorders*, 1970, *35*, 103–112.

Lee, L. L. *Developmental sentence analysis*. Evanston, Ill.: Northwestern University Press, 1974.

Lenneberg, E. *Biological foundations of language*. New York: John Wiley & Sons, 1967.

Lundeen, D. J. Speech disorders. In B. R. Gearheart (Ed.), *Education of the exceptional child* (Vol. 19). Scranton, Pa.: Intext, 1972, 152–184.

Martin, R. The experimental manipulation of stuttering behaviors. In H. N. Sloane & B. D. MacAuley (Eds.), *Operant procedures in remedial speech and language training*. Boston: Houghton-Mifflin, 1968, 325–347.

McLean, J. Language development and communication disorders. In N. G. Haring (Ed.), *Behavior of exceptional children*. Columbus, O.: Charles E. Merrill, 1974.

McNeill, D. The development of language. In P. H. Mussen (Ed.), *Carmichael's manual of child psychology* (Vol. 1). New York: John Wiley & Sons, 1970.

Menyuk, P. Syntactic Structures in the language of children. *Child Development*, 1963, *34*, 407–422.

Menyuk, P. *Sentences children use*. Cambridge, Mass.: MIT Press, 1969.

Morehead, D. M., & Ingram, D. The development of base syntax in normal and linguistically deviant children. In D. M. Morehead & A. E. Morehead (Eds.), *Normal and deficient child language*. Baltimore: University Park Press, 1976, 209–238.

Nelson, K. Structure and strategy in learning to talk. *Monographs of the Society of Research in Child Development*, 1973, *38*, No. 1–2.

Nelson, K. Concept, word and sentence: Interrelationships in acquisition and development. *Psychological Review*, 1974, *7*, 461–479.

Pflaum, S. W. *The development of language and reading in the young child*. Columbus, O.: Charles E. Merrill, 1978.

Rosenblatt, D. *Learning how to mean: The development of representation in play and language*. Paper presented at the Conference on the Biology of Play, Farnham, England, June 1975.

Schiefelbusch, R. L. Language development and language modification. In N. G. Haring & R. L. Schiefelbusch (Eds.), *Methods in special education.* New York: McGraw-Hill, 1967, 49–75.

Templin, M. C. Certain language skills in children. *Child Welfare Monograph No. 26.* Minneapolis: University of Minnesota Press, 1957.

Van Riper, C. *Speech correction: Principles and methods.* Englewood Cliffs, N.J.: Prentice-Hall, 1952.

Vellutino, F. R. Alternative conceptualizations of dyslexia: Evidence in support of a verbal-deficit hypothesis. *Harvard Educational Review,* 1977, *47,* 334–354.

Wepman, J. M. *Auditory discrimination test.* Chicago: Language Research Association, 1958.

KEY TERMS

aphasia The inability to produce speech sounds, specifically associated with brain damage.

dysarthria Problems in the articulation of words associated with cerebral dysfunction.

fricative Speech sound that involves forcing air through small openings, created by a variety of tongue movements.

glide Speech sound that involves a smooth tongue shift from one vowel position to another.

holophrastic speech Single word utterances that convey the meaning of a complete sentence, often related to action.

morpheme The smallest meaningful linguistic unit.

phonology The branch of linguistics concerned with the production of speech sounds.

pragmatics The branch of linguistics concerned with the social, communicative aspects of language.

primary stuttering Disfluencies of speech sounds that are considered a part of normal language development, in which the young child attempts to master the motor aspects of speech production.

resonance The amplification of sounds through various cavities by changing the direction of the airstream.

resonant consonants The speech sounds ('r' and 'l') that are produced like vowel sounds by an uninterrupted air flow through the oral cavity modified by tongue position.

secondary stuttering Disruptions or disfluencies in speech production and facial and body movements that are not considered aspects of normal development or normal speech patterns.

semantics The branch of linguistics concerned with the study of meaning.

telegraphic speech Language characteristic of young children in which their utterances are composed mainly of nouns and verbs, deleting pronouns, articles, and so on, thus appearing like adult telegrams.

CHAPTER 9

Low Incidence Handicaps: Visual Impairments and Physical Handicaps

There are certain conditions of exceptionality that occur quite infrequently but nevertheless require the services of educators, psychologists, physicians, and other professionals. These conditions include severe mental retardation, severe visual impairments, and certain physical handicaps. Although few persons have these deficiencies, this minority has the right to educational and psychological services. In fact, the results of recent litigation (for example, *Wolf v. Utah,* 1969; *Mills v. The Board of Education and The District of Columbia,* 1972) make it clear that local educational agencies are responsible for providing appropriate education programs for handicapped persons irrespective of how frequently the condition occurs. In this chapter we will consider some of these low incidence forms of exceptionality.

Before doing so, however, we need to discuss briefly the notion of severe and profound handicaps. The reader will recall that the distinctions between severe and profound conditions is mostly used in reference to mental retardation. Indeed, the terms severe and profound are associated with specific intelligence test scores, as indicated in Chapter 5. There are, however, efforts to establish severe and profound handicaps as a distinct category of exceptionality. Essentially it is argued that children should be categorized by the severity of their handicapping condition rather than by the particular difficulty the child experiences. Insofar as severe and profound handicapping conditions are relatively rare, a discussion of these terms is now presented.

THE SEVERELY AND PROFOUNDLY HANDICAPPED

Children with some type of handicapping condition may have a minimal or an extreme form of it. A child might be mildly or severely physically handicapped or slightly or severely retarded. What are the conditions for using the term severely handicapped? The Bureau of Education for the Handicapped defined the severely handicapped as:

> Those who because of the intensity of their physical, mental, or emotional problems, or a combination of such problems, need education, social, psychological, and medical services beyond those which are traditionally offered by regular and special education programs, in order to maximize their full potential for useful and meaningful participation in society for self-fulfillment.
> A. The term includes those children who are classified as seriously emotionally disturbed (including children who are schizophrenic or autistic), profoundly and severely mentally retarded, and those with two or more serious handicapping conditions, such as the mentally retarded blind, and the cerebral palsied deaf.
> B. "Severely handicapped children" 1. May possess severe language and/or perceptual-cognitive deprivations and, evidence of abnormal behaviors such as: I. Failure to respond to pronounced social stimuli, II. Self-mutilation, III. Self-stimulation, IV. Manifestation of intense and prolonged temper tantrums, and V. The absence of rudimentary forms of verbal control, and 2. May also have extremely fragile psychological conditions.
> (*Federal Register*, Vol. 40, No. 35, Feb. 20, 1975, p. 7412)

It has been estimated that about 0.2 percent of the general population meet the requirements of this definition (Haring, 1975). In addition, it is also clear that children who are severely or profoundly handicapped have a wide variety of difficulties.

There appears to be some movement to employ the term severely/profoundly handicapped as a distinct and separate category of handicapping conditions. That is, rather than indicating that a child has an extreme form of cerebral palsy, some professionals suggest that we categorize the child as severely handicapped. In some ways such a category makes sense. For example, children with grave defects frequently have many different types of difficulties. The severely retarded child may also have hearing, vision, and/or heart problems. If services are rendered to a child on the basis of a single handicapping condition, say mental retardation, it may make it more difficult to coordinate additional services for the same child for another equally serious problem. It has been reported that various state and local agencies responsible for treating children with a particular disorder have refused services because the child had other disabilities. Thus, agencies serving blind children might refuse to help a particular blind boy because of his mental retardation, while those helping the mentally retarded might refuse their services because the boy is blind. Perhaps the reorganization of present categories to include the category severely/profoundly handicapped might overcome the bureaucratic logjam. On the other hand, it may create more problems than it solves.

Sontag, Smith, and Sailor (1977) have expressed considerable concern that a separate category might be quite detrimental and have offered several objections. First, there is the possibility that labeling children as severely or profoundly handicapped will result in their isolation from the educational and social mainstream, an isolation that might not be warranted. Additionally, these authors believe that such labeling might well lead to unnecessarily low and unrealistic expectations for these children's development. They see the specter of the self-fulfilling prophecy. Finally, they fear that such a category will place under one definitional umbrella children of varying skills and difficulties, perhaps adding even more to confusion over their assessment and treatment. Children with different types of severely or profoundly handicapping conditions often require very different assessment techniques and education programming.

That controversies exist over the extent and nature of appropriate categories is really not surprising since such taxonomies serve a multitude of functions. Scientists are interested in studying homogeneous groups of children to determine what regularities in their existence are significant in a particular handicap. Local, state, and federal agencies want a reasonable basis for the distribution of money so that services can be provided. Therapists need categories that enable them to offer appropriate remediation programs. Sometimes these various aims clash.

VISUAL IMPAIRMENTS

With the exception of those suffering from a multitude of handicaps, youngsters with visual handicaps represent the smallest number of exceptional children (Hewett and Forness, 1977). The United States Office of Education has estimated the incidence of visual defects, that is, **legal blindness,** to be about 0.10 percent of the population. But half of those persons who are defined as legally blind are more than 65 years old. Among children under 7 years old, it has been estimated that 12.9 per 100,000 have serious visual problems; among school-aged children the estimates range from 34 to 71 per 100,000 (Hatfield, 1972). The reason that estimates vary, and may be lower than the true number of visually impaired children, is that the figures are usually based on those persons defined as legally blind. These are individuals with more severe visual impairments who are eligible for various kinds of benefits and assistance. Those with partial visual impairments are thus not necessarily counted in estimates of the frequency of blindness. Bateman (1967) indicated that 1 child in 500 may have some visual impairment, but the majority probably do not need special education services as corrective lenses may give them normal or near-normal vision. While the number of children with significant visual defects appears to be small, blindness has historically received more attention, money, and public concern than any other physical impairment (L'Abate and Curtis, 1975). Their numbers are few, but their plight is serious. In this section we review the functions of the eye, the development of vision in young children, the ways in which visual processing breaks down, definitions of visual impairment, and the signs that a child may be having some visual problems. In addition, we discuss some unique problems associated with educating visually impaired children.

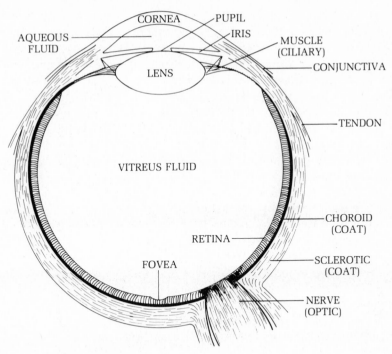

FIGURE 9-1 Section of the human eye

Source: PRINCIPLES OF MODERN BIOLOGY, Fourth Edition, Douglas Marsland. Copyright © 1957, 1964 by Holt, Rinehart and Winston, Inc. Reprinted by permission of Holt, Rinehart and Winston.

The Function of the Eye

The eye is a complex organ that transports and bends (refracts) light rays so that they reach nerve endings, which then transmit the visual information to the occipital lobe in the cortex of the brain. The light rays enter the cornea, pass through a watery substance (aqueous humor), through the pupil (colored part of the eye), and through the lens, which focuses them on the retina. There they are transferred to nerve endings connected to the optic nerve, which carries the information to the brain. The eye's function is to focus incoming light on light sensitive receptors. The receptors convert the light into electrical impulses that are sent to the brain. The eye is responsible for: (1) **central vision** (perception and discrimination of objects); (2) **accommodation** (making adjustments for distant and near vision when focusing); (3) **binocular vision** (coordinating the two eyes so that the person perceives one object in focus); (4) **peripheral** vision (ability to see small amounts of light at the sides of the visual field; and (5) color vision (ability to detect different colors) (DeMott, 1974).

The development of vision begins as soon after birth as the newborn can see, albeit not very well. The new baby demonstrates a number of eye movements, suggesting that visual inputs are being received. For example, children under five days of age will show a preference for one visual array over another; will track a horizontally moving object, though not very well; and will show changes in pupil dilation that indicate adaptations to light intensity. While the eyesight of the newborn is far from perfect, the child is receiving visual inputs. The visual acuity of the newborn has been estimated between 20/150 and 20/400. As might be expected, the visual system changes as the child matures. By 1 month, the infant apparently can perceive complex stimuli, that is, shows a preference for a visual display of stripes, checks, or patterns over displays that are homogeneous or have little variety in colors and shading. Until about 4 months of age, the infant has difficulty in adjusting his or her eyes so as to perceive distant objects. It appears as if the child has a fixed focus point about eight inches from the body until roughly 4 months old. At that age, however, the child is able to adjust his or her eyes to receive information about more distant objects. By this time the child should be able to recognize familiar objects and people. Initially the infant and young child tend to be farsighted, but as the eyes mature the child is apt to become nearsighted. Ordinarily, these states are self-correcting but occasionally they are not. There is some debate as to the age where the self-corrections are completed, some placing the attainment of 20/20 visual acuity at age 6, others at age 10 (Lawson, 1968; Pick and Pick, 1970).

Assessment of Vision

The most frequently used method of assessing visual acuity is to have people read the **Snellen Chart.** This chart is used by ophthalmologists (physicians who specialize in diseases of the eye), optometrists, and school nurses in vision screening programs. The Snellen Chart has eight rows that present letters of the alphabet in graduated sizes; for young children, the letter E is used in different orientations and sizes. In both charts the sizes correspond to the estimate of distance at which the typical person can see the figure. These distances are 15, 20, 30, 40, 50, 70, 100 and 200 feet. The chart is constructed so that when, from a distance of 20 feet, a person can read the figures on the chart corresponding to what the normal eye sees at 20 feet, the person is said to have 20/20 vision. A person who has 20/20 vision, with or without corrective lenses, and good stereopsis (that is, both eyes working in coordinated fashion) has normal vision. The person who does not have 20/20 vision is categorized in terms of that size print (that is, distance) he or she can see. Thus, someone who sees from 20 feet the figures comparable to what a person with normal sight can see at 70 feet or 200 feet is described as having 20/70 or 20/200 vision. The individual's responses to the Snellen Chart test will determine the category of visual impairment in which the individual is placed. A person is considered *legally blind* if his or her vision is 20/200 or worse. The **partially sighted** person is one whose vision is between 20/70 and 20/200 (Kirk, 1972).

There are shortcomings in using the Snellen Chart to determine visual impairments. While the chart assesses an individual's ability to see objects at various distances, it does not indicate how well the person sees near objects. Measuring distance vision by means of the Snellen Chart is not a very good predictor of competence in visual processing of objects and tasks that are close at hand. Screening of school-age children for visual competence by means of the Snellen Chart may well fail to detect those children who are having some forms of acuity difficulties other than distance vision.

Another limitation to the Snellen Chart procedure is that it tells the diagnostician very little about how the child uses his or her vision. For example, how well does the child discriminate the lightness or darkness of an object, estimate its size or determine its correct spatial location? Finally, the results yielded by assessments employing the Snellen Chart are not readily translatable into educational programs. Children with the same visual acuity for distance may differ in their responses to an educational program.

The direction currently being followed in visual assessment is to analyze how the individual functions in close tasks and in distance viewing (Hallahan and Kauffman, 1978). For example, Scholl (1975) developed the following classification system of visual handicaps:

1. The person cannot read or write through the use of vision, even with special aids, cannot identify familiar objects in the surroundings, and is unable to get around without the assistance of another person or a dog.
2. The person who cannot see objects at close range but can from a distance is, is unable to read through the use of vision but is able to get around unfamiliar territory without the assistance of others.
3. Individuals who can use their vision for close objects but cannot make out distant ones. Can read with or without special aids, can visually identify objects, but need assistance when in unfamiliar environments.
4. The person is visually impaired but nonetheless can read and write with or without special aids and also manages to function well in unfamiliar territories.

Obviously this last category of visual impairment is the least severe. Whether there are such clearcut and distinct types of impairment remains to be seen. What is important about this category system is the attempt to categorize people along several dimensions of visual functioning rather than on a single dimension such as distance acuity.

It should be noted that the definition of blindness that seems to appeal to educators is based upon the techniques required to educate the child. The child who learns to read through the use of vision, even if the materials presented must be adapted, should be considered, according to this view, as partially sighted. The child who has to learn by means of braille should be considered blind (Bateman, 1967).

Types of Visual Impairments

Visual impairments can be congenital, that is, present at birth, or adventitious, becoming apparent some time after birth. They can be the result of genetic influences, prenatal, perinatal, or postnatal events, or environmental accidents. By and large, severe blindness is easily detected and is usually identified before the child is 1 year of age. Less severe forms of visual impairments are not so readily detected and may not be discovered until the child is well into an educational program. Difficulty in detecting moderate visual impairments may be one reason that the estimates of the incidence of visual handicaps are relatively low (Bateman, 1967).

Less Serious Defects

There are two common types of visual defects, refractive errors and poor binocular vision. A refractive error is the result of a defect in the eye lens (Lerner, 1971). There are three types of such errors. One is called **myopia** (nearsightedness). While this problem can develop any time, it is likely to show an increase in incidence around age 11 and 12 years for girls and 13 to 14 years for boys (Tanner, 1970). Myopia is characterized by images coming to a focus in front of, rather than on, the retina. This causes the child difficulty in seeing distant objects. A second refractive error is called **hyperopia** (farsightedness). Here the images are brought to a focus behind the retina, with the result that the child has difficulty in seeing objects which are nearby. In the third type of problem, **astigmatism,** the lens fails to transmit the light or image correctly to the retina, causing the child to see distorted images.

Binocular vision is the coordination of the two eyes in bringing together two visual inputs to produce one image. There are three principal processes involved: the coordination of extraocular and intraocular muscles (muscles outside and inside the eye), the fusion of the two monocular images into a single perception, and the individual's personal response to the visual stimulus (Park, 1969). The binocular defects that occur in children are *strabismus, inadequate fusion,* and *aniseikonia.* Strabismus occurs when one of the eyes strays from the proper direction so that both eyes do not look at the same thing at the same time. This, believe it or not, is called a squint. Inadequate fusion is a defect in which the eyes do not accommodate to get a monocular effect. Simply put, one eye is adjusted to see at a different distance than the other. In aniseikonia the images of an observed object are unequal in size or shape in the two eyes (Lerner, 1971). Unless detected early, strabismus can have serious outcomes. What happens to some children is that one eye represses the image and eventually the eye stops functioning. This condition is *amblyopia,* and can be corrected, but only if detected early. *Nystagmus* is another condition related to poorly functioning eye muscles, and refers to rapid involuntary movements of the eyes that may cause dizziness and nausea.

More Serious Defects

There are a number of conditions that cause visual impairments more handicapping than the aforementioned. These are more serious in that they may not be correctable. *Cataracts, glaucoma, diabetic blindness, coloboma, albinism,* and *retrolental fibroplasia* are among the more serious visual defects. When a person develops cataracts, there is a clouding of the lens of the eye that causes blurred vision (DeMott, 1974). Children who suffer congenital cataracts have seriously impaired distance vision and color vision (Barraga, 1973). In glaucoma there is a buildup of fluid behind the eye. The increased pressure caused by the excess fluid damages the retina and interferes with the blood supply to the optic nerve. Diabetes can cause blindness if the person develops *diabetic retinopathy.* This means that there is an interference in the blood supply to the retina. Since diabetics are living longer now due to advances in medical treatment, the incidence of diabetic retinopathy may be increasing (Telford & Sawrey, 1977).

Several serious visual handicaps are related to hereditary or congenital factors. Coloboma is a degenerative disease in which parts of the retina are not completely formed (Hallahan and Kauffman, 1978). Likewise, albinism, a deficiency of skin pigmentation, is also associated with visual defects such as less acuity, nystagmus, and an excessive sensitivity to light, called photophobia (Kirk, 1972).

No presentation of vision defects would be complete without a discussion of retrolental fibroplasia, a "man-made" disease. Retrolental fibroplasia literally means "fibrous tissue behind the lens," but in fact refers to a condition in which the retina detaches itself and eventually ends up floating behind the lens of the eye (Kirk, 1972). Evidently this disease did not exist prior to 1938 and it is virtually nonexistent now. The reason it occurred was that premature babies were placed in incubators and given oxygen. It took ten years of research to determine that the occurrence of retrolental fibrophasia was attributable to these infants' exposure to excessive amounts of oxygen. While retrolental fibroplasia is no longer a major threat since this causal relationship was established, there were large numbers of children blinded during the 1940s from incubator treatments. Moreover, according to Hallahan and Kauffman (1978), there has recently been an increase in retrolental fibroplasia. These authors speculate that this may be related to medical advances in saving more premature babies with the necessity of providing high concentrations of oxygen in the incubators in order to save their lives.

Causes of Visual Impairments

Visual impairments may result from genetic mishaps, injury, disease, malfunctioning, and malformations. The impairment may affect any or all of the eye's five functions. That is, an individual's central vision, accommodation, binocular vision, peripheral vision, and color vision may all be defective. Hewett and Forness (1977) indicate that about 47 percent of serious visual problems stem from prenatal causes, most often unknown. About 33 percent are the result of poisoning, as in retrolental fibroplasia, while approximately 7 to 8 percent are caused by infectious disease. Only about 2 percent of visual impairments are the aftermath of injury.

Myopia and hyperopia are the most common visual impairments (National Medical Foundation for Eye Care, 1959), while strabismus accounts for about 2 percent of the vision problems in the total population (DeMott, 1974). Thus, refractive errors make up 49 percent of visual defects; cataracts and albinism, 22 percent; muscle malfunctions, 17 percent; and infection and injury account for 11 percent.

Signals of Impairment

While children often get eye examinations during their early school years, it is important for both parents and teachers to be sensitive to the more casual but often revealing signs of visual impairment. The National Society for the Prevention of Blindness has listed characteristics that signal that the child is experiencing visual problems. According to the society, the following behavioral signs, physical appearances, and verbal complaints should alert the parent and teacher to possible difficulties:

Behavioral Signs:
rubs eyes excessively
shuts or covers one eye; tilts head forward
tries to avoid, or has difficulty in, close use of the eyes
tries to avoid, or is unable to see, objects in the distance
blinks more than expected
holds books or objects too close to the eyes
squints eyes or frowns

Appearance:
the eyes are crossed
red-rimmed, encrusted, or swollen eyes
watery or inflamed eyes
recurring styes

Complaints:
child complains that his eyes are bothersome, that he cannot see
says eyes itch, burn, feel scratchy
complains of blurred or double vision
suffers dizziness, headaches, or nausea when performing tasks that
    require close vision

Given such complaints or behaviors, it is important to have the child's vision examined by an ophthalmologist, a physician who specializes in the treatment of eyes.

Characteristics of Legally Blind Children

A good deal of thought has been given to the impact of blindness upon the person's intellectual and emotional functioning. By and large, studies consistently indicate that there is no special "psychology of blindness," that the major problems faced by the blind are directly related to their visual problems (Bateman, 1967; Hewett and Forness, 1977; Lowenfeld, 1963).

There have been a number of studies concerning the intellectual and conceptual abilities of the blind. These suggest that if the blind are given tasks that are not related to their visual problems, they perform intellectually and conceptually at a level comparable to that of sighted persons (Bateman, 1967; Friedman and Pasnak, 1973). There is no doubt, however, that the visually impaired child will show the effects of the deficit on tasks that require eyesight. For example, visual discrimination tasks are often used in tests of conceptual abilities, and the amount that the blind child can learn will be limited to the sense of touch. Tactual learning places limits on the amount of information about the environment that can be learned and integrated (Hallahan and Kauffman, 1978).

There is an old wives' tale that blind persons, like the deaf, develop particular sensitivity to other sense modalities in order to compensate for their handicap. While it is not true that blind persons' hearing becomes more acute, blind children probably do learn good attentional skills (Hallahan and Kauffman, 1978).

The language development of the blind child has also drawn a good deal of attention. Brieland (1950) had individuals rate the speech of blind and seeing speakers from audio recordings. From what they heard, the judges were not able to differentiate the speakers. Cutsforth (1951), however, has argued that the blind learn verbal expressions for attributes they cannot experience. For example, these children have vocabulary words for colors. Cutsforth refers to the use of such terms as *verbalisms*. That blind children develop verbalisms is not surprising given these children's dependence upon language for relating to others and learning about the world. It should be remembered, however, that their verbalisms may have a meaning quite different from the words used by the sighted person (Suppes, 1974).

There does not appear to be much information on the academic performance of blind children. It is most striking that most visually impaired persons can see something; there are few totally blind persons. Additionally, visually handicapped persons prefer to employ any vision that they can rather than other modes of sensory information such as their fingers. Jones (1961) found that 82 percent of a group of legally blind persons used their vision to read, even if the written material was in braille. It is undoubtedly true, however, that whether using vision or fingers, braille or large printed matter, the legally blind child finds visual tasks more difficult and more time consuming to master than the sighted child. While blind children probably will show some academic retardation relative to the sighted, they appear to be accelerated academically when compared with hearing impaired youngsters. Given their adequate performance on intelligence tests, one might presume that their academic deficits are more related to the method by which the information is communicated to them than to some inherent properties of defective vision.

Blindness impedes the process of socialization as people react adversely to the sightless. This is not to infer that the blind are more numerous among populations of the emotionally disturbed and behaviorally disordered. Rather, the socialization of blind children and their acceptance by the public are not run-of-the-mill processes. First, sighted people have been reacting negatively to the blind for centuries. The blind, perceived as dependent and helpless, are devalued as people. "To be able to blow your own nose without assistance and to refrain from showing suicidal tendencies in public" seems to characterize the seeing person's expectations of the behavior of a well-adjusted blind individual (Greenwood, 1948; cited by Bateman, 1967, p. 277). Let us consider some possible reasons why sighted people are uncomfortable with the blind.

First, much of our social intercourse depends not only on spoken words but also on our body behavior such as gazing, mutual eye contact, and shifts in facial and body expressions. From these visual cues, we make inferences about other people's emotions, sincerity, and affection; they even tell us when shifts in conversation should occur (Dittman and Llewellyn, 1969; Mehrabian and Williams, 1969; Dittman, 1972; Hall, Rosenthal, Archer, Dimatteo and Rogers, in press). All of these visual cues, so important in determining the flow and harmony of social intercourse, are lost to the blind child. These children are unable to "read" many nonverbal cues to another's emotions or attitudes, nor will they be very competent in sending their own nonverbal messages.

A second factor possibly contributing to stress relates to our fear of blindness. Blindness is second only to cancer as a source of national anxiety (Hallahan and Kauffman, 1978). It is not clear whether the sighed avoid the blind because of unrealistic fears of contagion or simply for fear of being reminded of fears. But our our dread of blindness may contribute to the stigmatization and social isolation of the blind.

There is evidence that some of these negative attitudes toward the blind can be altered, at least when they are held by children. Bateman (1964, 1967) has studied the attitudes of children and adults toward the blind. When she compared the attitudes of children who had known and attended school with blind children with attitudes held by youngsters who had had no contact with the blind, she found that the former group had more positive feelings about the blind than did the latter group. This suggests that children could become more accepting of the blind, given some familiarity with visually impaired children. Batemen found adult attitudes less flexible. When sighted adults encounter skillfulness and competence in blind persons, they tend to perceive these persons as rare exceptions rather than typical cases.

While blind children do not appear to have particularly severe emotional or personality problems, they probably do encounter negative reactions from others. Social rejection, however subtle, might well be ubiquitious in these children's lives.

Partially Seeing Children

Although partially sighted children outnumber the legally blind, there is far less information available concerning them. The general status of educational consideration for these children was summed up as "put him in the front row or in the blind school" (Bateman, 1967, p. 286). Children with partial vision appear to have educational handicaps that are more debilitating than the visual impairment itself; and the emotional and social problems of the partially seeing may be more severe than those of either the sighted or the legally blind. For example, Underberg (1958) when comparing one partially sighted adolescent with with totally blind, legally blind, and seeing peers, found that the partially sighted adolescent was more likely to feel that others pitied him and that his parents were less understanding than those of adolescents who had more severe visual defects. Moreover, Bateman (1964) found that when comparing teachers' ratings of adjustment of children with mild visual impairments (visual acuity greater than 20/70), moderate visual problems (visual acuity between 20/70 and 20/200) and legal blindness, that the moderately impaired were judged as the least adjusted.

There appears to be little information concerning the intellectual and social status of the visually impaired child, in spite of the current emphasis on mainstreaming. Bateman (1964) did report that teachers generally feel that most of these children are average or above average in their school achievement and classroom demeanor. However, she also reports that sighted children are likely to hold negative attitudes toward their partially sighted classmate. It is possible then that the partially sighted child will be more likely to suffer from social isolation and/or rejection than the sighted one.

Educational Strategies for Blind and Partially Sighted Children

The first schools to open for visually handicapped children were residential schools in Massachusetts, New York, and Pennsylvania, while the first public school program for these children did not open until 1900 in Chicago (Hewett and Forness, 1977). For many years it was believed that children should "save" their remaining vision, that using their vision would somehow damage or exhaust residual vision; thus, classes for visually impaired youngsters were called "sight-saving" classes. Things have changed dramatically since then; today children are being trained to use whatever visual abilities they possess. They are likely to be in a regular public school program, and are encouraged to participate as much as possible in academic tasks and even sports. While special education personnel, such as specialists in vision training, and special materials, such as books printed in braille, are provided to the child, current educational strategies emphasize the integration of children with visual impairments into the regular school setting.

Learning by Touch

In planning educational strategies for the visually handicapped, it is important to recognize that touch is their substitute for vision. Touch is the primary method by which the blind child learns about the world. However, it has serious limitations. Touch can never replace vision since tactile learning does not reveal the spatiality of objects or information about their relationships to one another. Second, the blind person and the sighted person, having experienced objects differently, may have different meanings when they use the same word. For instance, the sighted and the blind person's mental images of a tree are likely to be quite different. Moreover, it is difficult for blind persons to distinguish between objects in the same class. So the visually impaired child may learn about trees by building models from clay in the classroom, but to that child all trees are likely to be the same, whereas the sighted child learns to see the differences among them. The blind child is further limited because it is not always possible to explore every object by touching it. Boiling water is not easy for the blind child to understand, nor is it likely that he or she will be free to explore many people tactually. The teacher of blind children should then bear in mind that the sensory impressions upon which language and cognition are built differ between sighted and blind persons (Scott, 1969). An example sums up this point. Scott reports that a teacher was conducting a unit on animals with a class of blind children. A stuffed squirrel that had been mounted on a tree branch was passed around for the children to feel. Later the teacher removed the squirrel, passed the branch around the class, and asked the children what they had in hand. They replied, "A squirrel."

For blind children to explore, they must have the environment brought to them. They must be able to experience the environment directly by physically engaging it. While the teacher can and should use language to help the children make discriminations among objects, classify experience, and develop abstractions, that teacher must also keep in mind the critical importance to children of providing them opportunities to explore the environment tactually. Through taction and talk, the teacher can greatly assist many blind children.

Mobility Training

A major task in educating visually impaired children is that of mobility training. The child must learn to move around in order to be independent in the community, school, home, and strange places. A mobility program has a number of components: attention to physical fitness, motor coordination, posture, freedom of movement, as well as training to use whatever senses the child has intact. For the visually impaired child, training in olfaction (using the sense of smell), tactile-kinesthesia (accurate perception through touch), directionality, body image, and obstacle perception are critical. It is important to recognize that training the mobility skills of the visually impaired child is possible. It has even been demonstrated that blind children's visual discrimination can be significantly improved through training without increasing their visual acuity (Barraga, 1973). Parents of the visually impaired have an understandable tendency to overprotect their child and fear for the child's physical safety, but it is important for special educators and other professionals to institute such training.

While some blind persons develop very good representations of the environment and can move about in remarkable freedom, others do not. There are a number of means for helping blind persons maneuver through space. The most well known are human guides and guide dogs, though both have several disadvantages. The human guide is terribly burdened by the task, and guide dogs are appropriate for only about 5 percent of the blind population. As Hallahan and Kauffman (1978) point out, dogs are too large for little children, often walk too fast for anyone, require special care, and, most important, cannot lead the person where the person wishes to go. They help avoid objects and obstacles, but they cannot lead. The blind person still must know how to reach his or her destination. A third well-known aid is the Hoover cane, a long cane blind people sweep in front of them as they walk.

In addition, some interesting electronic techniques are now being developed and tested. One is the *Pathsounder,* a device worn around the neck that makes a sound when an object is being approached. Another invention is sonar glasses, modeled on the notion that humans can learn to locate objects through echoes like bats. A third device, worn on the hand, emits ultrasound and then converts the reflections from objects into audible sound (Hallahan and Kauffman, 1978). Using the pitch, loudness, and clarity of the sound, the child can learn to detect the directions of the objects.

Developing Intellect

Blind children, however, need more than mobility training. They need to acquire academic skills and to be exposed to the intellectual, as well as the physical, world about them. Since they can hear, much of the information they receive is delivered through spoken language. One problem in the auditory presentation of information is that it must be presented relatively slowly. It takes much longer to hear a story told on a record, usually provided by the *American Printing House for the Blind* or the *Library of Congress,* than it does to read the same story in print. There are a number of techniques to reduce the time it takes to present information orally. These include playing the auditory information at a faster speed, having the speaker talk more rapidly, and employing compressed speech. Compressed speech is a kind of telegraphic language in which small units of the sentence, such as "of" or "the," are eliminated. Compressed speech does seem to be an effective teaching strategy as children's comprehension of material presented this way is greater than that obtained through braille or large type (Hallahan and Kauffman, 1978). It would seem that auditory presentation of material is an efficient and appropriate educational tool.

Braille

A popular method of teaching academic subject matters and reading is through the use of material presented in braille. This is a method of embossing paper so that raised imprints can be felt. Different patterns have different meanings. The braille system consists of six dots that can be arranged in 63 different characters. Alphabet letters are represented through 26 combinations of the dots, while punctuation signs and word contractions are represented through the other 37 dot patterns. There are several versions of braille. The variations among the different systems are, in part, determined by their use of contractions. Typically, braille systems do not spell words completely, but use a shortened form for the word's representation. There are a number of methods for writing in braille. One method is the use of a *Perkins brailler,* a kind of typewriter by means of which embossed dot patterns are produced on paper by pressing keys in different combinations. It is also possible to write in braille by using a slate and stylus. The stylus is pressed through an opening in the slate which contains the paper. The result is raised indentations on paper.

There are serious disadvantages to the use of braille. First, it is difficult to learn. Second, blind children are likely to have spelling problems because the system does not expose them to the correct spelling of words. Third, braille print is very bulky, expensive, and takes a long time to produce. Worse yet, it takes significantly longer to read braille than regular print. In addition, Scholl (1975) found that children with residual vision actually read the braille with their eyes rather than with their fingertips. Finally, the small number of blind children makes maintaining large braille libraries quite costly. The moral seems to be that the visually impaired child, unless totally blind, should be given every opportunity to learn to read print visually.

Large Type

For visually impaired children taught to read regular type, the materials may be presented in large print. The large-type reading material is about 1/8-inch high which prohibits the child from reading at the same speed as seeing children. Hewett and Forness (1977) report that many visually impaired children prefer to read regular size print using some type of magnification or even by holding the book very close to their eyes. These children can read as quickly and comprehend as well using regular print under appropriate conditions as they can reading large print (Hewett and Forness, 1977; Sykes, 1972).

Although blind individuals are intellectually capable and do not suffer any greater emotional or behavioral problems than the sighted, the traditional attitudes of seeing people appear to have prohibited the blind from being as independent and self-sufficient as they might be. Advancing technology, however, may help blind persons achieve greater status and independence. One successful new advance allows blind persons to work as telephone operators. Using computers that "read and talk," blind persons are able to work as long-distance operators in Mountain View, California. The computer scans a console that has 12 tiny television type cameras, translates the numbers from the console, and reads them to the operator. The computer also tells how much the call cost, who made the call, and who received it. The operators communicate with the computer through one ear and to the customer through the other. Future technological advances for the blind are likely to increase their mobility and improve their everyday work opportunities.

PHYSICAL HANDICAPS

In this section we will discuss conditions and diseases that affect the child's physical mobility and health and interfere with the child's participation in regular school programs.

The conditions defining the category of exceptional children with physical handicaps vary along a number of dimensions. Some of these handicapping conditions, such as cerebral palsy, are present at birth, while others, like muscular dystrophy, may be acquired. Some are the result of a single defect, such as many heart conditions, others reflect a multitude of physical dysfunctions, as in cerebral palsy. Additionally, a number of these conditions are progressive in nature, while others neither worsen nor improve. Moreover, some may be corrected, others cannot; the debilitating effects of some may be very severe, of others relatively mild. Some are primarily a medical problem. For some, treatment is enormously expensive; for others, less costly.

Incidence

Unlike other forms of exceptionality it is not difficult to reach agreement on the diagnosis of a physical handicap or disease. If a child has cerebral palsy or rheumatoid arthritis, professionals usually agree on its presence. While we know relatively little about the etiology of many of these disorders, their diagnoses are probably reliable.

The United States Office of Education estimated that about 0.5 percent of school aged children were physically handicapped in 1975. This means that about 328,000 children in our country have serious physical problems. About half of them have cerebral palsy and other crippling conditions, while the rest suffer chronic health problems (Hallahan and Kauffman, 1978). Wilson (1973) has suggested that the incidence rate of physical handicaps has changed during a relatively short period of time, the number of crippled children being provided programs increasing 87 percent between 1950 and 1963. In addition, in 1964 there was an additional 5.7 percent jump. Whether this trend continues to this day is difficult to say. It may be that the increase in frequency of physically handicapping conditions was the result of new federal and state programs for children. When programs are created, parents are more likely to register children who may have previously escaped notice by the authorities. In other words the increased incidence may be an artifact resulting from the greater availability of special programs. On the other hand, there may be a real increase in physical handicaps among children. Advances in medical technology may be resulting in more high-risk newborns surviving, but only with severe and multiple disabilities. Infant mortality rates may be down, but with the decline, the frequency of physical defects may be up.

Conditions Related to Central Nervous System Damage and Dysfunction: Cerebral Palsy

Cerebral palsy is the most common of those disorders that affect physical mobility as a result of brain damage. This is a condition that interferes with a person's ability to move in a coordinated, continuous fashion; it is a motor disability that affects 1 to 3 per 1000 children (Smith and Neisworth, 1975). While the major symptom of this condition is movement problems, the damage to the brain may also affect other important functions.

Categories of Cerebral Palsy

There are different classification systems to describe cerebral palsy. One is based on the parts of the motor system affected; the other, on the types of motor movement displayed (Wilson, 1973). There are five types of motor movement associated with this condition. About 50 percent of cerebral palsied individuals have *spasticity*, involuntary contractions of muscles when they are stretched. This results in tenseness along with difficult and inaccurate voluntary movements. A second type of palsy is termed *athetosis*, a condition in which there are involuntary contractions of successive muscles in the hand, legs, and mouth. The contraction of one muscle is associated with the contraction of other nearby muscles. Athetosis characterizes about 25 percent of cerebral palsy cases. *Ataxia*, a third type, refers to a lack of balance and defective spatial orientation. Almost all cases of cerebral palsy can be placed in one of these three categories. An infrequent cerebral palsy condition is one marked by excessive rigidity or tremor. The rigidity is produced by a continuous muscle tension, while the tremors are uncontrollable motions of specific groups of muscles. Many people will demonstrate a mixture of these three types of motor problems.

Cerebral palsy can also be classified according to the body parts affected. If brain damage prevents both the arm and leg of one side of the body from functioning, this is referred to as *hemiplegia*. The term *biplegia* is used when both sides of the upper part of the body are affected, while the same condition in the lower part of the body is termed *paraplegia*. When all four limbs are affected by brain damage, we term it *quadriplegia*.

Cerebral palsy is often associated with other kinds of handicaps. It carries a high frequency of hearing impairments, cognitive problems, visual impairments, speech defects, and epilepsy. While some cerebral palsied children are gifted (Cruickshank, Hallahan, and Bice, 1976), about one-half of them have intelligence quotients below 70 (Wilson, 1973).

Education of the Cerebral Palsied

Cerebral palsy is both a medical and an educational problem. While the condition is not progressive, appropriate medical treatment is necessary to prevent a degeneration of muscles through lack of use. Training is also essential to maximize the child's ability to function. The child may be trained to use intact limbs, braces, or prosthetic aids. Physiotherapists can provide training in muscle reeducation and in various self-help skills, such as feeding and dressing. Orthopedic surgery to lengthen contracted tendons, transplant muscles, and to alleviate extreme muscle tension may also be required.

As for education, some cerebral palsied children may attend a regular school but many are taught at home or in the hospital. Other children may be enrolled in private or special public school programs for the physically handicapped and/or mentally retarded. With slight modifications of school facilities, more children might be able to attend regular public schools, and the current trend is in this direction. Wherever these children are taught, it is of utmost importance that the educator resist the temptation to infer the child's intellectual or language comprehension abilities from his or her motor capacities.

Epilepsy

Epilepsy is a condition in which a person is subject to convulsions, an event marked by rapid contractions of many muscles resulting from an abnormal discharge of electrical energy from the brain. Accompanying the convulsion is a sudden loss of consciousness.

Epilepsy is found in about 1 percent of the total population (Wilson, 1973) but is seen primarily in young children and older people. Persons who have seizures before they reach 2 years or after they are 25 usually have some kind of organic brain damage; and an early onset of convulsions is often related to impaired mental abilities in the adult (Dikmen, Matthews, and Harley, 1975). As might be expected, individuals who are suffering from other forms of brain damage are more likely to have epilepsy than those not suffering from such damage (Robinson and Robinson, 1965).

Seizures may take a variety of forms. There are generalized convulsions in which the entire cortex is affected, partial seizures involving a focalized part of the brain, unilateral seizures affecting only one side of the brain, and finally, seizures we cannot classify that are called simply unclassified seizures (Hallahan and Kauffman, 1978). The most frequent classification of epilepsy uses a three-category system referred to by the French terms *grand mal, petit mal,* and *psychomotor* epilepsy.

There are great differences among these forms of epilepsy. With a *grand mal,* the typical convulsion is marked by a cry, a loss of consciousness, falling, muscle rigidity followed by involuntary muscle contractions of the extremities, trunk, and head (Hallahan and Kauffman, 1978; Wilson, 1973). Following the seizures the person may fall into a temporary coma or sleep. Upon awakening, the individual is likely to show confusion, disorientation, nausea, soreness, headaches, and exhaustion. Also, the person will probably not remember the convulsion. Occasionally, the individual about to have an attack has a consistent signal, typically some strange sensory experience. This signal is called an *aura.* The aura can be used as a preparatory signal, so that the person may be able to find a place where the dangers of a fall can be minimized. *Petit mal* seizures do not involve motor activities but do bring a loss of consciousness (Wilson, 1973). While these seizures are less debilitating, they may occur more frequently than those of *grand mal* epilepsy. During a *petit mal* seizure the person stops what he or she is doing, stares, blinks, may twitch, and then continues with the activity at hand. Unless one is watching closely, *petit mal* seizures may go undetected. These seizures are more often seen in children and may be expected to cease as the child gets older. Wilson states that some temper tantrums, bad behavior, or "not paying attention" may reflect *petit mal* seizures, thus suggesting that strange, persistent behavior by a child is grounds for a complete physical examination.

The predominant symptom in psychomotor epilepsy is amnesia. The individual who experiences this type of epilepsy will lose consciousness but will continue with his motor activity. The seizures are longer than those experienced in *petit mal,* possibly lasting for hours. More men than women have this type of epilepsy, which is more common among adults than children.

The treatment of epilepsy is primarily medical in nature. There are very effective anticonvulsant drugs, such as *dilantin,* which greatly reduce, and even eliminate, seizures. If anticonvulsant drugs are ineffective and the episodes are extremely debilitating, brain surgery may be employed. Such surgery may involve implanting a pacemaker to regulate the electrical activity of the brain, or, less commonly, removing parts of the brain. The main problem faced by the educator is that of managing the situation when the child experiences a seizure. During the episode, it is important to make sure the individual is comfortable, and, if possible, to place a soft object, like a folded handkerchief, between the child's back teeth to keep the tongue from being bitten. This object should not be your finger since it may be injured during the seizure when the child's teeth clamp.

While nearly all epileptics can lead almost normal lives, they are likely to be concerned about the implications of the condition for their personality, their offspring, and their social lives. Epilepsy that is not associated with other developmental disabilities will not be passed to offspring, has few implications for one's personality other than what the sufferer attributes to it, and no doubt does carry unfortunate social stigma. Additionally, it sets some limitations to everyday activities. Epileptics may be prohibited by law from engaging in tasks that can be dangerous, for example, operating an auto or airplane.

Spina Bifida

Spina bifida is the failure of the spinal column to close during the fetus's growth. There are a number of reasons for this failure, as well as several points along the column where it is manifested. Sometimes a number of nerve fibers, rather than running down the spinal column, protrude from it. Other times, a sack containing nerve fibers may form outside of the spinal column, paralyzing the body functions below the point of the sack. Thus, the bladder and kidneys, as well as the lower limbs, cannot function as the appropriate nerve endings are isolated in the sack. Persons with this problem often have other congenital anomalies. They may suffer from defects of the heart, intestines, or brain, as well as skeletal defects including clubfoot and dislocated hips.

At one time these children did not survive infancy. Now, very early surgery can correct the defect and the child may be helped sufficiently through orthopedic and prosthetic devices to attend regular school programs. When spina bifida is the only problem suffered, the child's intelligence should lie within the normal range. This means that the major problems such children face in school will be bowel and bladder control. According to Hallahan and Kauffman (1978), behavior modification techniques have been successfully used to help toilet train a young boy who had spina bifida. It is possible then that behavior modification techniques may provide a technology that could prove of considerable benefit to the child with this malformation.

Muscular Dystrophy and Rheumatoid Arthritis

Muscular dystrophy, some forms of which are hereditary, is a condition in which there is a degeneration of muscle fibers, with progressively increasing muscle weakness. This is a serious disease that results in early total disability or death. The cause and the cure are unknown; the treatment is to keep the person active as long as possible.

Another problem affecting children is rheumatoid arthritis, a condition that cripples muscles and joints. In young children there is a high percentage of remission. As with other handicaps, the arthritis may be severe or mild; it ranges from debilitating atrophy and deformity to mild swelling and stiffness. This is primarily a medical problem. The educational problem is to help the child not suffer from missing school and to recognize that the child may sometimes be unable to engage in all of the usual school activities. Again, the causes and cures are not known.

Congenital Malformations and Teratogens

In addition to the conditions already described, children may have other kinds of problems that are present at birth. There may be malformations of skeletal systems or body organs. Some children are born with malformations of the heart and/or blood vessels leading to the heart; others are born with dislocations of the hip, or malformations of the hands or feet such as webbing of the fingers. Some children are born with missing or too many parts, and some have deformities of the head or face. Advances in heart surgery and plastic surgery have provided great relief for many of these children.

Teratogenic refers to producing fetal malformations. We now know that many diseases, drugs, and poisons subject the fetus to teratogenic effects. One example of a drug that was teratogenic is thalidomide, a sedative taken by many pregnant women throughout the world during the late 1950s and early 1960s. The children of these women were gravely handicapped, showing a wide variety of developmental difficulties including, among other things, missing or deformed limbs, and severe and profound mental retardation. It has become ever more apparent that pregnant women must be very careful about taking potentially harmful drugs.

Miscellaneous Physical Handicaps

Children may be victims of other types of illnesses and accidents. *Rheumatic fever* is an infectious disease that may seriously damage the connective tissues of the body, the joints, and the heart and blood vessels. *Hemophilia* is a condition in which the person lacks the elements needed for the blood to coagulate. This is a particularly cruel disease as the child, either from internal or external bleeding, can literally bleed to death, or suffer severe and permanent crippling. *Diabetes,* mentioned earlier as a hazard to the unborn, is also found among children. It is the result of the body's inability to produce insulin, essential to the adequate processing of glucose or sugar. Diabetes is treated with insulin, administered through shots or pills, but diabetics still face serious health problems. *Nephritis,* another serious condition, causes damage to the child's kidneys, giving rise to a variety of symptoms such as anemia, headaches, and puffiness about parts of the body. *Infectious hepatitis* and *infectious mononucleosis* (which, no doubt, some of you have already experienced) are both thought to be caused by a virus. Hepatitis is a liver disorder. Both produce similar symptoms; fever, loss of appetite, constant fatigue, abdominal pain, headache, and occasional jaundice.

The Effect of a Physical Disability upon the Child and Family

Given the wide range of types of physical disabilities, it is not possible to describe these children in terms of their intellectual abilities, personality characteristics, or academic achievement. The severity of the problem, its progressiveness, its specific nature, its chronicity, all influence in complex ways the child's functioning. We should not leave this topic of physical disabilities, however, without some discussion of the social impact of a physical disability upon the child and family. When a child is disfigured and this disfigurement colors the parents' and others' reactions to him or her, that child can suffer serious social and psychological damage.

What happens when a child is born with visible deformities? Strasser and Sievert (1969) studied 100 German families with such children and found that almost all could be described as grieving, depressed, and guilt-ridden. Apparently these families felt some personal responsibility for the defects. Richardson (1969) has also analyzed the effects of such births upon the family. He points out that when a baby is born, there are many social rituals that involve the family. These rituals are not only disrupted by the birth of a disabled child, but the family must undertake some unexpected activities, such as obtaining correct diagnosis and treatment for the afflicted infant. Moreover, as the normal child grows, the child is expected to attain a variety of benchmarks of growth, like turning over, sitting up, smiling, and responding to family members. The disabled child not only fails to demonstrate some or many of these benchmarks but, as an unwitting side effect, deprives the family of the joys such signs of well-being customarily bring. As the child fails to develop normally, the parents' expectations for performance may drop while their anxiety over the child's disability increases, perhaps at the expense of their other children. The disabled child then is often treated as if sick, and thus given little responsibility. It is also important to realize that many of these handicapping conditions place an enormous economic burden upon the family. Medical costs, babysitters, special training, prosthetic devices, and other illness related costs may well drain the family financially.

For numerous reasons, the physically disabled child may develop without having the same number, quality, or opportunities for social relationship as the nondisabled child. First, there is no doubt that disabled children and their parents are likely to be objects of rejection, pity, even revulsion, by peers and adults, strangers and friends. For understandable reasons, if not necessarily justifiable ones, parents may wish to shield themselves and their offspring from social stigma. This protection may deprive the child of the opportunity to learn coping responses to social reactions. But parental overprotectiveness aside, it is still true that physically disabled children are more likely to be kept from their peers and the everyday experiences of the normal child by their often extended hospital stays, their participation in special education programs, and the difficulties in removing them from the convenient environment of the home. In addition, the disability itself may limit the child. He or she may be unable to dance, participate in active games, or even talk by words or "body language" with others. All of these factors would contribute to preventing the disabled child from learning social skills that might help offset the stigma attached to the disability. Thus a vicious cycle may well be established where the disability produces social isolation that produces a deficit in learning social skills that leads to further isolation. Whether this isolation is caused by these or other factors, the physically handicapped child among nonhandicapped peers will probably be, in effect, alone. Richardson, Hastorf, and Dornbusch (1964), for example, studied the social status of handicapped and nonhandicapped children, ages 8 to 14, attending a three-week camp. They reported several interesting findings. First, nonhandicapped children preferred nonhandicapped children as friends. Secondly, it was found that the boy who is most likely to befriend a handicapped boy is one socially isolated from his peers. This was interpreted as indicating that the nonhandicapped child interacting socially with a handicapped child is more isolated, has less social experience, and has not learned the peer value system as well as others (Richardson, 1969). Thirdly, while familiarity does not breed contempt, it was found that it does not produce affection either. Other children's knowing the handicapped child over a period of time did not soften the negative effect of the handicap upon social status.

The relationships that disabled children have with others are particularly important given the current emphasis upon educating exceptional children in regular classroom settings. There is evidence that the nature of these relationships differs from that usually encountered. Kleck, Ono, and Hastorf (1966) found that high school students who interacted with handicapped persons were more likely to refrain from disagreeing with them and to give short verbal responses to questions than when dealing with nonhandicapped peers. In a review of physical disabilities, Richardson (1969) suggests that people feel ambivalent toward handicapped others and may well keep the interaction more formal, inhibited, and overcontrolled than they would when interacting with nonhandicapped persons. This suggests that in addition to having less opportunity for interaction, the interactions the handicapped person does have with others is apt to be less informative and contain less feedback than interactions among nonhandicapped persons.

We have already mentioned that placing handicapped children in segregated classrooms might deprive them of appropriate social interactions. On the other hand, segregated placements also allow them to meet others like themselves who may hold more benevolent attitudes toward physical disabilities than children encountered in the regular classroom setting. Indeed, if the physically disabled child is surrounded by persons, whether peers or teachers, who view handicaps negatively, he or she may develop similar attitudes. Moreover, being in the ordinary classroom, the child may be deprived of learning from other handicapped children those coping skills that could make life more fulfilling. Mainstreaming these children is probably a mixed blessing.

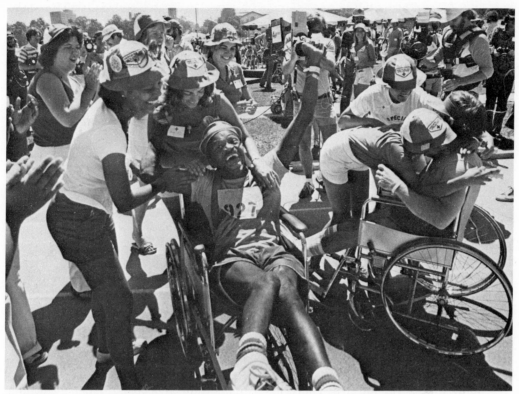

FIGURE 9-2 Ernie Breedlove winning Special Olympics wheelchair race

SUMMARY

In this chapter we reviewed the definitions, classifications, and characteristics of children with low incidence handicaps. We saw that low incidence does not mean little impact because among such defects are some of the most gravely debilitating conditions, diseases, and damage that children suffer. In the first part of the chapter, we note that any handicapping condition can be severe and that about 0.2 percent of the general population are severely/profoundly handicapped. The terms severely and profoundly handicapped refer to an extremely heterogeneous group that includes children who are organically impaired, retarded, emotionally disturbed, deaf, or blind.

Next we considered the definitions, classification, and characteristics of visually impaired persons. The most striking factors about the visually impaired is that most of them can see something; there are few totally blind individuals. Second, it is important to note that the visually impaired should be allowed, encouraged, and educated to use their residual vision. The assessment of blindness based on the Snellen Chart describes only the person's ability to see at a distance; it does not measure other important visual functions. Recently developed classification systems are attempting to describe visual functioning more completely.

There are many different kinds of visual impairment. Most common are the refractive errors of myopia (nearsightedness) and hyperopia (farsightedness). More handicapping conditions, such as visual impairments that result from glaucoma, cataracts, and diabetes were also described. Retrolental fibrophasia, now significantly reduced, is an example of a serious manmade disease, one that resulted from exposing premature infants to excessive concentrations of oxygen in incubators.

Visual impairments are the result of injury, disease, malfunctioning, and malformations. They can be due to events which occur prenatally, perinatally, or postnatally. About 47 percent of serious visual problems are related to events in the prenatal period.

There are several signs that might indicate that a child is having difficulty with vision. There are behavioral signs such as the avoidance of tasks requiring close vision as well as complaints about vision or eyes.

Properly educated, the blind do remarkably well when blindness is their only handicap. Measures of intelligence, language and speech, and personality do not indicate that the visually impaired differ significantly from sighted persons. The major problem they experienced is in social personal relationships. Sighted persons traditionally have reacted negatively to the blind, tending to treat them as dependent and helpless.

In planning educational strategies for the visually impaired, it is important to keep two points in mind: their main mode of learning is the tactile sense, and it is critical that their mobility be encouraged and taught. The teacher must augment the instructional program with meaningful language that helps the visually impaired child classify and discriminate objects and events. Visually impaired children learn to read either through braille or ink-print, which is sometimes enlarged. It is preferable for children to read through ink-print, and most legally blind persons seem to prefer to use whatever vision they have to do so. But the braille system is appropriate for those unable to read ink-print.

In the final section of this chapter, physical handicaps were discussed. As with visual impairments, the social impact of the handicap intensifies the child's problems. Physical handicaps, like other exceptionalities, can be mild or severe, congenital or adventitious. Some, however, are progressive, and others are not easily correctable. As a result, some are strictly medical problems, others are educational, and most require the services of an interdisciplinary team of physicians, teachers, speech therapists, physical therapists, and social workers. While we can define physical handicaps quite well, we seldom know their causes or cures.

Children's physical handicaps were divided into those related to brain damage and neurological dysfunction, those related to muscular and or skeletal malformations or diseases, congenital malformations and teratogens, and other health problems.

About half of the children with physical handicaps have cerebral palsy. Cerebral palsy carries with it a number of problems. The major one is that of motor disability, a disability that may affect different parts of the body, and one in which the motor system is differentially affected. The major types of motor problems are either spasticity or athetosis. Cerebral palsied children often have other handicapping conditions, including mental retardation, hearing problems, and speech difficulties. Intervention strategies thus often call for several types of specialties.

Epilepsy is another type of brain damage. The epileptic person's brain has abnormal discharges of electrical energy. The convulsion may be of the grand mal or petit mal variety. Epilepsy can occur as an isolated condition in otherwise normal persons or it may accompany other handicapping conditions such as mental retardation. Medication can control convulsions for most people, but very severe cases may require brain surgery.

Spina bifida is a condition in which the spinal column fails to close during fetal growth, often causing paralysis and loss of function of the body parts below the point where the column has failed to close. Surgery can relieve some cases.

Muscular dystrophy causes muscle fibers to degenerate. This is a very serious disease that results in early total disability or death. Other conditions that may cripple children include rheumatoid arthritis, club foot, and other congenital malformations. A particular point was made about teratogens, the development of misshapen fetuses. A pregnant woman and her fetus are vulnerable to damage from a host of external elements, many of which can be avoided. The thalidomide disaster is a prime example of how we can inadvertently create a handicapped child.

Finally, the impact of a physical handicap upon the social and psychological well-being of the child and family was discussed. In addition to the physical problems, a handicap brings rejection and stigma for both the child and the family. Nonhandicapped persons often feel uncomfortable interacting with disabled persons, and the result is that disabled children are likely to be considerably more isolated than nondisabled children.

REFERENCES

Barraga, N. C. Utilization of sensory-perceptual abilities. In B. Lowenfeld (Ed.), *The visually handicapped child in school*. New York: John Day, 1973.

Bateman, B. The modifiability of sighted adults' perception of blind children's abilities. *New Outlook for the Blind*, 1964, *58*, 133–135.

Bateman, B. D. Visually handicapped children. In N. G. Haring and R. L. Schiefelbusch (Eds.), *Methods in special education*. New York: McGraw-Hill Book Co., 1967, 257–301.

Brieland, D. M. A comparative study of the speech of blind and sighted children: *Speech of blind and sighted children. Speech Monographs*, 1950, *17*, 99–103.

Cruickshank, W. M., Hallahan, D. P., & Bice, H. V. The evaluation of intelligence. In W. M. Cruickshank (Ed.), *Cerebral palsy: A developmental disability* (3rd rev. ed.). Syracuse, N.Y.: Syracuse University Press, 1976.

Cutsforth, T. D. *The blind in school and society: A psychological study.* New York: American Foundation for the Blind, 1951.

DeMott, R. Visual impaired. In N. G. Haring (Ed.), *Behavior of exceptional children.* Columbus, O.: Charles E. Merrill, 1974, 529–563.

Dikmen, S., Matthews, C. G., & Harley, J. P. The effect of early versus late onset of major motor epilepsy upon cognitive-intellectual performance. *Epilepsia,* 1975, *16,* 73–81.

Dittman, A. T. The body movement-speech rhythm relationship as a cue to speech encoding. In A. W. Siegman and B. Pope (Eds.), *Studies in dyadic communication.* New York: Pergamon Press, 1972.

Dittman, A. T., & Llewellyn, L. G. Body movement and speech rhythm in social conversation. *Journal of Personality and Social Psychology,* 1969, *11,* 98–106.

Federal Register, Vol. 40, No. 35, Feb. 20, 1975, p. 7412.

Friedman, J., & Pasnak, R. Accelerated acquisition of classification skills by blind children. *Developmental Psychology,* 1973, *9,* 333–337.

Hall, J. A., Rosenthal, R., Archer, D., Dimatteo, M. R., & Rogers, P. L. The profile of nonverbal sensitivity. In P. McReynolds (Ed.), *Advances in personality assessment* (Vol. 4). San Francisco: Jossey-Bass Press, in press.

Hallahan, D. P., & Kauffman, J. M. *Exceptional children: Introduction to special education.* Englewood Cliffs, N.J.: Prentice-Hall, 1978.

Haring, N. G. Welcome address. Presented to the second annual meeting of the American Association for the Education of the Severely/Profoundly Handicapped, Kansas City, 1975.

Hatfield, E. M. Causes of blindness in school children. *The Sight-Saving Review,* 1963, *33,* 218–233.

Hewett, F. M., & Forness, S. R. *Education of exceptional learners.* Boston: Allyn & Bacon, Inc. 1977.

Jones J. W. *Blind children, degree of vision, mode of reading,* Bulletin 24. Washington, D.C.: U.S. Office of Education, 1961.

Kirk, S. A. *Educating exceptional children.* Boston: Houghton Mifflin, 1972.

Kleck, R., Ono, H., & Hastorf, A. H. The effects of physical deviance upon face-to-face interaction. *Human Relations,* 1966, *19,* 425–436.

L'Abate, L., & Curtis, L. T. *Teaching the exceptional child.* Philadelphia: W. R. Saunders Co., 1975.

Lawson, L. G. Ophthalmological factors in learning disabilities. In H. R. Myklebust (Ed.), *Progress in learning disabilities* (Vol. 1). New York: Grune & Stratton, 1968, 147–181.

Lerner, J. W. *Children with learning disabilities.* Boston: Houghton Mifflin, 1971.

Lowenfeld, B. Psychological problems of children with impaired vision. In W. Cruickshank (Ed.), *Psychology of exceptional children and youth* (2nd ed.). Englewood Cliffs, N.J.: Prentice-Hall, 1963, 226–310.

Mehrabian, A., & Williams, M. Nonverbal concomitants of perceived and intended persuasiveness. *Journal of Personality and Social Psychology,* 1969, *13,* 37–58.

National Medical Foundation for Eye Care. *Identification of children requiring eye care.* Washington, D.C.: American Association of Ophthalmology, 1959.

Park, G. E. Ophthalmological aspects of learning disabilities. *Journal of Learning Disabilities,* 1969, *2,* 189–198.

Pick, H. L., & Pick, A. D. Sensory and perceptual development. In Paul H. Mussen (Ed.), *Carmichael's Manual of Child Psychology* (Vol. 1). New York: John Wiley & Sons, 1970.

Richardson, S. A. The effect of physical disability on the socialization of a child. In D. A. Goslin (Ed.), *Handbook of socialization theory and research.* Chicago: Rand McNally & Co., 1969, 1047–1064.

Richardson, S. A., Hastorf, A. H., & Dornbusch, S. M. The effects of a physical disability on a child's description of himself. *Child Development,* 1964, *35,* 93–97.

Robinson, H. B., & Robinson, N. M. *The mentally retarded child: A psychological approach.* New York: McGraw-Hill Book Co., 1965.

Scholl, G. T. The education of children with visual impairments. In W. M. Cruickshank, & G. O. Johnson (Eds.), *Education of exceptional children and youth* (3rd ed.). Englewood Cliffs, N.J.: Prentice-Hall, 1975.

Scott, R. A. The socialization of blind children. In D. A. Goslin (Ed.), *Handbook of socialization theory and research.* Chicago: Rand McNally & Co., 1969, 1025–1045.

Smith, R. M., & Neisworth, J. T. *The exceptional child: A functional approach.* New York: McGraw-Hill, 1975.

Sontag, E., Smith, J., & Sailor, W. The severely/profoundly handicapped: Who are they? Where are we? *Journal of Special Education,* 1977, *11,* 5–11.

Strasser, H., & Sievert, G. Some psycho-social aspects of ectromelia: A preliminary report of a research study. Cited by S. A. Richardson in: The effect of a physical disability on the socialization of a child. In D. A. Goslin (Ed.), *Handbook of socialization theory and research.* Chicago, Ill.: Rand McNally & Co., 1969.

Suppes, P. A survey of cognition in handicapped children. *Review of Educational Research,* 1974, *44,* 145–175.

Sykes, K. Print reading for visually handicapped children. *Education of the Visually Handicapped,* 1972, *4,* 71–75.

Tanner, J. M. Physical growth. In Paul H. Mussen (Ed.), *Carmichael's manual of child psychology* (Vol. 1). New York: John Wiley & Sons, 1970.

Telford, C. W., & Sawrey, J. M. *The exceptional individual* (3rd ed.). Englewood Cliffs, N.J.: Prentice-Hall, 1977.

Underberg, R. *The relationship between parental understanding and child adjustment in the visually disabled adolescent.* Unpublished doctoral dissertation, University of Rochester, New York, 1958. Cited by Bateman, B., in N. G. Haring and R. L. Schiefelbusch (Eds.), *Methods in special education.* New York: McGraw-Hill, 1967, 257–301.

Wilson, M. I. Children with crippling and health disabilities. In L. M. Dunn (Ed.), *Exceptional children in the schools* (2nd ed.). New York: Holt, Rinehart & Winston, 1973, 467–532.

KEY TERMS

accommodation The process in which the ciliary muscles of the eye move to increase the curvature of the lens to focus on objects (that are closer than 20 feet).

astigmatism A defect of the optical system in which rays fail to meet at a focal point on the retina, resulting in a blurred image.

binocular vision The visual process involving coordination of the eyes so that the person views one focused image.

central vision A process of the visual system involving the detection and discrimination of objects.

hyperopia A condition in which visual images are focused behind the retina and vision is better for distant rather than near objects.

legal blindness A definition for services that includes two components:
(1) Corrected vision in the better eye is 20/200 or less.
(2) The widest diameter of the visual field includes an angle no greater than 20 degrees.

muscular dystrophy A hereditary disease characterized by a progressive deterioration of muscles.

myopia A condition in which visual images are focused in front of the retina, resulting in defective vision of distant objects.

partially sighted A legal definition that means an individual's corrected vision in the better eye is 20/70.

peripheral vision The ability to detect small amounts of light at the side extremes of the visual field.

Snellen Chart Screening chart that has eight rows of letters that vary in size. Used to assess visual acuity.

spina bifida Birth defect in which the bony elements of the spine have not completely fused together. Depending on extent and location of damage, there can be paralysis, hydrocephalus, or other effects.

teratogenic Having to do with agents that cause developmental malformations and monstrosities.

CHAPTER 10

The Gifted Child

Psychologists have long been interested in the nature of intelligence and, consequently, in the lives and heritage of individuals who demonstrate outstanding mental abilities. As early as 1883 Sir Francis Galton published a study of eminent men, and Terman began his studies of gifted children in 1921. National interest in the education and utilization of gifted persons, however, is relatively recent. It was inspired by the "cold war" between the United States and the Soviet Union. When the Soviets sent up Sputnik, the first space satellite, a public furor was raised in the United States over the evidence that Russia could outclass this country in science and technology. The specter of Russian superiority stimulated interest in and concern for our exceptionally able students. While the concern continues to this day, it appears to have waned somewhat.

In this chapter we discuss the gifted and the underachieving child. In addition, there is mention of the concept of assessment of creativity and its relationship to "giftedness." Definitions, characteristics, and some educational approaches considered useful for fostering the development of intellectual and creative prowess are also provided.

Definitions and Incidence Rates of Giftedness

As might be expected from our other discussions of individual differences, definitions of giftedness vary greatly. Some theorists use the intelligence test as the defining characteristic. Others prefer a broader definition that might include creativity, a wide band of talents, or a particular facility or outstanding achievement in one area of endeavor (Kirk, 1972). L'Abate and Curtis suggest that "the gifted, generally speaking, are individuals who deviate from the norm by having superior abilities which are typically viewed as intellectual in nature" (1975, p. 406). Hildreth (1966) suggested that giftedness is reflected by excellent performance in any socially useful endeavor. Terman (1925) defined genius as obtaining an IQ test score of 140 or above. The variations in defining giftedness are so numerous that Abraham (1958) was able to report finding 113 different ones. Thus, when people speak of giftedness, it is likely that they are referring to different concepts and different behaviors.

It should not be surprising that there are debates over the definition of giftedness. Underlying these attempts to delineate this concept are two major, albeit often implicit, goals. One is to include in the gifted category all individuals who would qualify. The second goal is to exclude those persons who would not qualify. Using a broad definition, one maximizes the likelihood that every child who might make a substantial contribution to society will be identified. But the use of a broad definition also increases the possibility that children will be erroneously identified as gifted. When narrow definitions of giftedness are used, the chances that children who might qualify will be excluded are increased, although the chances of erroneously labeling children are correspondingly minimized. Given the limited resources available for special programs for the gifted plus the great national need for the development of our human resources, one can understand the shifts in definitions of giftedness. In research studies that focus on gifted children, it is most probable that the definition used is primarily and most frequently based on intelligence test scores. But, even when researchers employ these scores to define high mental ability, there is debate and differences of opinion among them as to the intelligence quotient that should serve as the cutoff point to define it. For example, Ciha, Harris, Hoffman, and Potter (1970) used an intelligence test score of 120 as their criterion for giftedness, L'Abate and Curtis (1975) indicate than an intelligence test score of 130 is most commonly used, while Terman (1925) set his standard of giftedness at a test score of 140 or higher.

Estimates of the approximate incidence of giftedness among children vary according to the research worker's definition of giftedness. Most estimates indicate that about 2 to 3 percent of the children in the country should be considered gifted (Payne, 1974; Hewett and Forness, 1977). By almost any definition then, large numbers of children could be considered gifted.

Finding Gifted Children

One major problem in rendering services to gifted children is locating them. They do not step forward for identification. Unlike exceptional children, they are not causing severe problems for their parents or teachers, and thus school authorities have to initiate efforts to identify them. This costs time and money, so methods to detect the very able child have received a good deal of study.

The most frequently employed detective in the pursuit of the gifted is the classroom teacher. Several surveys of school districts' identification procedures indicated that the majority of districts use teachers as their major resource for identification of gifted children (Tannor, 1966; Marland, 1972). Other detection tools include group intelligence and achievement tests and tests of creativity. Although teacher nominations are the most common method used to identify gifted children, they are not considered the best one. Most respondents in surveys on this topic favor using the individual intelligence test as the primary identification method, but only 23 percent of districts reported doing so (Hewett and Forness, 1977). Like other methods, teacher identification of the gifted is subject to considerable error. Pegnato and Birch (1959) found that 31 percent of children identified as gifted by other methods were not considered gifted by teachers. These authors indicated that the use of group intelligence test scores was the best method for identification purposes. Through these test scores they found that the ratio of the number of referrals to the number of gifted children discovered tended to be low while the percentages of gifted children within the school setting who were identified was high. In effect, group tests did not miss identifying many gifted children, nor did they misclassify children of average intelligence as gifted.

While other methods of detection have been studied, they have not been studied sufficiently to warrant definitive statements as to their worthiness. However, they are a stimulant to thinking about alternatives to teacher nominations. One concern in any identification program is its cost efficiency. Any method that helps to reduce the cost of identification then frees resources for other purposes. One of the best predictors of the number of gifted children likely to be attending a particular school is the number of gifted children who were previously identified as gifted at that school (Anastisiow, 1964). Also, children have been studied as a source of identification. Pielstick (1963) presented children with a list of characteristics that are believed to be found in the gifted. The children were able to link the appropriate characteristics to the correct classmates. This accuracy was particularly pronounced among children in lower socioeconomic groups, groups where teachers may have difficulty spotting the gifted child. Parents have also been used as a source for identifying gifted children. Ciha et al. (1974) compared the abilities of teachers and parents to identify gifted children, children with high scores on an intelligence test. Parents were able to spot 76 percent while teachers identified only 22 percent of the gifted children. Unfortunately, the parents' high hit rate may have been attributable to the large numbers of children parents nominated for gifted status. If virtually all parents nominate their children for gifted status, it is not surprising that more of the gifted children would be spotted. Pride and hope seem to undermine the efficiency of parents as an identification source.

While definitions of giftedness and methods of detection vary, most educators prefer the individually administered intelligence test, even if they fail to use it. But, as you already know, the intelligence quotient varies for many children across time. In addition, certain forms of talent may not be detected through the use of the intelligence test. For example, intelligence tests are not likely to be sensitive to some forms of problem solving activities basic to creative efforts. Until definitions show some consensus and until methods to detect gifted children are better studied, it is likely that the identification of gifted children will be based upon a variety of techniques and intuitions with unknown costs and benefits.

CHARACTERISTICS OF GIFTED CHILDREN

Before we discuss physical, personal, and social characteristics of the gifted, a word is in order concerning common beliefs about genius or the exceptionally able person. Perhaps one of the most popular notions is that the products of the brilliant mind float out effortlessly (Ashby and Walker, 1968). The genius ponders briefly, a problem is solved, society benefits, and the public is awed—or so it is thought. The truth of this belief is difficult to establish because most geniuses are dead and biographical information is always suspect. But it can be argued that genius is the result of much work in a fairly narrow range of interests. Ashby and Walker write: "Newton, asked how he solved so many problems, replied simply, 'By always thinking about them'" (1968, p. 211). It appears that people who have made contributions to society that warrant their general recognition as geniuses have been extremely devoted to their pursuits, often to the neglect of many other aspects of life. It is probably a myth that one becomes a genius by virtue of some divine or genetic gift. A point we will return to later is that the educational programs designed for the gifted child will be affected by whether the creators of the program believe high accomplishment is the result of mystical gifts or concentrated efforts.

The major contributor to our knowledge of the personal and social characteristics of the gifted was Lewis Terman. In 1921, Terman initiated a longitudinal study of more than 1,500 children and adolescents, primarily from middle and upper socioeconomic status, who scored 140 or higher on individual intelligence tests. The results of his study of these individuals over the years provided a wealth of information that has been substantiated by other investigators using samples drawn from other parts of the country. Terman's contribution to our knowledge of the gifted child and adult cannot be overestimated.

Physical Status of the Gifted

Contrary to some myths, the gifted individual is likely to have superior physical development and general health. When compared with nongifted children, the gifted youngster is likely to be taller, stronger, and heavier (Terman, 1925). This does not mean that giftedness and physical development are both the result of identical genetic factors. When Laycock and Caylor (1974) studied the physical characteristics of the nongifted siblings of gifted children, the brothers and sisters also showed superior physical development. The gifted child is thus likely to come from home environments that provide the conditions necessary for excellent physical development.

Social Status of the Gifted

A second myth is that the gifted are withdrawn bookworms, interested primarily in scholarly activities, and rejected by their fellows. In fact, there is considerable evidence to indicate that the gifted child is likely to be quite popular

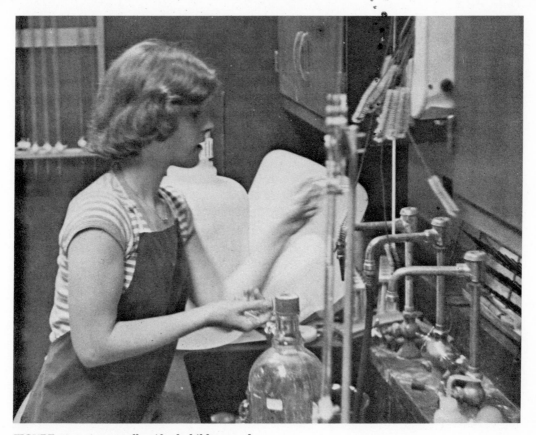

FIGURE 10-1 A mentally gifted child at work

with peers (Gallagher, 1975; Newland, 1976), and this is particularly true when the gifted male is athletically inclined. The intellectually able child is thus likely also to be well liked. However, if the child's intellectual abilities are markedly superior, the child may be unpopular with peers (French, 1967; Payne, 1974). There seems to be a curvilinear relationship between intelligence and peer popularity. Up to a certain point, intellectual abilities have a positive effect on peer acceptance. After some point, high intellectual skills lead to peer rejection.

Nor is it true that the gifted withdraw socially. Newland (1976) has reviewed the research on the social activities of the very bright. He reports that they are more interested and involved in extracurricular activities than nongifted children. They also tend to have a greater range of interests than less gifted peers (Hewett and Forness, 1977). There is little reason to assume that the gifted child is a social outcast, is withdrawn, or has narrow interests.

Personal Adjustment of the Gifted

Given the relatively successful social adaptiveness of the gifted, it is no surprise to find these children also apt to be well adjusted personally. They are less likely to manifest emotional and behavioral problems than less gifted persons (Terman, 1925). Interestingly, however, gifted youngsters often fail to recognize their unusual abilities (Werblo and Torrance, 1966). Whether this is due to the high value set on modesty in our culture, anti-intellectualism, failure to recognize their skills relative to others, or more personal reasons is not known. But gifted children do tend to underestimate their own abilities.

Midlife Status of the Gifted

While children verbally deny their capacities, their actions do not. Thanks to Terman's work, there is evidence on how the gifted fare as they enter adulthood. First, they are less likely to experience ill health, mental illness, or alcoholism than other people. Most report that they are active in political and social affairs that are not necessarily required or related to their occupations. It appears that gifted children maintain socially active lives as they age. Marital relationships appear to be adequate as most get married and their divorce rates are not greater than the rest of the adult population (Oden, 1968). The academic and vocational achievements of this group are impressive. They are more likely than the nongifted to graduate from college and to pursue their studies at a graduate level. In addition, most of them show excellent vocational adjustment. In 1950, for instance, Terman's gifted subjects had published 93 books; 2,000 scientific, technical, or professional articles; and about 375 short stories and plays. In addition, the group had patents on more than 230 inventions. This is not a bad productivity rate when you consider that these people entered college in the stressful years between 1930 and 1940 (Terman and Oden, 1959). Finally, it does seem that the gifted adult may have a wider range of interests than the less gifted (French, 1967).

The academically superior child, then, is likely to be better off physically, emotionally, and socially than less gifted classmates. Moreover, the gifted are likely to show superior personal, social, educational, and vocational adjustment as they continue through the life span. It is clear that high intellectual ability does not doom one to a life of social rejection and the status of misfit.

EDUCATIONAL APPROACHES FOR THE GIFTED

While there is little debate over the value of special education services for the handicapped, considerable controversy surrounds the provision of special programs for the gifted (L'Abate and Curtis, 1975). The proponents of special classes for the very bright suggest that these children learn more rapidly and have more knowledge; therefore they do not receive appropriate educations in regular classroom programs. To offer the best program for these children, these experts claim, special services are needed. Opponents of special classes for the gifted argue that such programs are not democratic, that gifted children should not be given resources that might be better employed for the handicapped, and that gifted children will prosper in any situation without such programs.

While differential treatment for the academically talented is apparently not popular with the majority of parents or teachers, there are special services and educational programs that have been established for gifted children (Hewett and Forness, 1977). In general, three types of programs have been implemented. These are special classes, acceleration of schooling, and enrichment programs. Let us review them.

Special Classes

One of the earlier methods to provide better educational experiences for gifted children was the establishment of segregated special classrooms. This parallels the type of programs developed for handicapped children. The child is removed from regular schoolrooms and placed with classmates whose skill levels and abilities are similar to his or hers. In the case of the gifted, the classroom instruction was broader than in the regular classroom and the materials were covered at a faster pace. There are other, less extreme, variations of segregated placement; for instance, in some cases the child might attend a special class for the gifted part of the day. Whether for part or all of the day, this classroom was designed to provide specially planned instruction for children with high abilities.

As with handicapped children, the special class or special school approach to educating the gifted did not meet with much favor (Kirk, 1972). Evidently school districts will not adopt segregated placements for gifted children for fear the community will disapprove. In addition, the research evidence on the educational effectiveness of special placement is rather contradictory, just as it is for handicapping conditions (Kirk, 1972; Payne, 1974). Perhaps this should not be surprising. What a child learns in school depends upon a host of factors unrelated to whether or not the youngsters' classmates are similar or dissimilar in ability. Teaching methods, relationship with teacher and peers, student motivation, and the time and effort devoted to studying are also important. French pointed out, "Narrowing the ability range does not result in consistently greater achievement without specifically designing varied academic programs for the various ability levels" (1967, p. 391). Nonetheless, there is evidence that children prefer to be in classrooms with students with ability levels similar to their own rather than classrooms in which children vary considerably in their skills. Since one important basis for people's being attracted to each other is their similarity, it may be that homogeneous groupings of children stimulate mutual acceptance (Byrne, 1974). As of now, there is little evidence that ability grouping has negative effects upon the personal or social characteristics of gifted children. The issues are more technological and political. The question is whether there is educational technology available that would provide the kind of learning programs that would enable these children to maximize their potential. Do we have gifted teachers and stimulating instruction for gifted children?

Politically, one reason for integrating handicapped children into regular classrooms is that these children will benefit from interaction with average children. Likewise, we might argue that it is better for average children to associate with gifted ones.

Enrichment

Enrichment usually refers to the provision of special educational opportunities to an individual or a small group within the regular classroom setting. Since there is a strong desire to individualize educational programs for all children, the notion that instruction should meet the particular needs of individual children is hardly revolutionary. When instructional material is altered for gifted children, the alteration is defined as enrichment. French (1967) describes two enrichment programs. One emphasizes providing increasing amounts of material similar to, but more difficult than, that already learned. The level of difficulty is increased across time while the topic being studied remains relatively narrow. In a second type of enrichment program, the level of difficulty remains rather constant, but the children study topics in greater depth. That is, they learn more information about a given topic. As French has indicated, it is likely that learning will involve varying difficulty levels irrespective of whether the topic is narrowly or broadly defined.

Enrichment programs are supposed to have benefits for the child that are not possible in segregated classrooms. By being allowed to remain in a heterogenous classroom while receiving the special attention needed for individual growth, the gifted child is expected to develop leadership skills, relate to contemporaries, stimulate the general intellectual atmosphere of the regular classroom, and reduce the costs of special education services (Kirk, 1972). Enrichment programs thus are presumed to provide the gifted child with many advantages while he or she maintains a normal life style.

The major difficulty in enrichment programs is teacher limitations. Many teachers may believe that children's education should progress in a lockstep fashion. Even when teachers are convinced that programs should be tailored to the individual child, this conviction is very difficult to implement. With 30 or more children in a classroom, all varying considerably in ability and temperament, enrichment programs for a few may require time, effort, and patience beyond most teachers' physical and emotional resources. In the absence of external support services, enrichment programs may place a heavy burden on the classroom teacher.

Acceleration

A third method of providing better educational opportunities to the gifted child is through acceleration. Acceleration can consist of early admission to kindergarten or first grade, allowing children to skip grades, and/or early admission to secondary schools or college (Kirk, 1972). In effect, the child is allowed to pass through school at a faster rate than is customary. Many individuals fear that allowing the child to pass through the educational system according to abilities and knowledge rather than age might have ill effects on the child. They worry about the child's social relationships with bigger, older classmates and the effects of physical and age incongruities upon subsequent personal development.

By and large, the evidence seems clear that most children who are accelerated do not experience the feared social and personal traumas. Justman (1953), for example, found that children who were moved ahead faster were less frequently rejected by classmates than children of comparable intelligence who were kept with their age groups. Similarly, Klausmeier (1963) and Klausmeier, Goodwin, and Ronda (1968) did not find that acceleration produced personal or social difficulties for children after a period of some years. Finally, Jones (1966) compared gifted children who had taken some college courses during their high school years with others who had not. The students who subsequently went to college were studied. In their adjustment to college, students who had been accelerated did not differ from those who had not been accelerated.

It seems then that moving the gifted child ahead faster is not likely to create many difficulties for him or her. Kirk (1972), however, has pointed out that most studies have focused on gifted children who were accelerated by one or two years rather than five or six. Since so few children are capable of being advanced more than a few years, evidence concerning greater acceleration is not readily available. It may be that great leaps forward might produce great stress on the precocious child whose physical, social, and personal maturity may lag considerably behind that of classmates. The point is that we do not know much about the effects of any educational program on extremely able youngsters. Finally, whether talking about the effectiveness of ability groupings or special classes, enrichment programs, or acceleration, it should be remembered that what is learned is heavily dependent upon the teacher, the curriculum, and student motivation. Special administrative arrangements are beneficial to the child only insofar as the classroom activities are geared to maximize learning.

UNDERACHIEVERS

There is a group of children who do not demonstrate the academic achievement predicted of them on the basis of their performance on intelligence or aptitude tests. While many gifted children do fulfill the potential these tests reveal, others fail to live up to their demonstrated promise. Definitions of the underachieving child are similar to those of learning disabled children. Indeed, it is not clear that there is a distinction between the learning disabled and underachieving child. The definitions of each group appear to be similar and many children from both groups appear to share common characteristics. However, there is a specific body of knowledge developed through investigations of children who have been called underachievers.

Personality and Family Characteristics

Most of the research on underachievement has been focused upon identification of family and personality characteristics that might underlie the lack of achievement. The evidence on the family characteristics that could be related to the child's underachievement appears to be mixed. Underachievers tend to have less educated parents whose values are less supportive of education than parents of high achievers. In addition, parents of achieving children are described as more "pushy," pressuring their children to do well in school and in other pursuits (French, 1967). There is, in addition, evidence that parents, at least fathers, of underachieving children, are somewhat more hostile toward their children than are parents of the achieving child (Gallagher, 1975). It remains to be determined whether parental hostility produces underachievement, the underachievement produces hostility, or whether hostility and underachievement are causally related at all. Finally, the underachieving child is probably more likely than the achieving child to have suffered a disruption in family life. For example, there is a higher incidence of broken homes among underachieving than achieving children (French, 1967).

What about the underachiever's social and personal adjustment? One question that has been studied concerns the aggressiveness of underachieving youngsters. There is some evidence to suggest that many underachieving youngsters may be generally more hostile toward others than their successful counterparts (French, 1967; Shaw and Grubb, 1958) and may have rather negative feelings about themselves (French, 1967). On the other hand, there is some indication that these children are more likely to blame themselves or not to assign blame in the event of a transgression than they are to blame others. High achievers are more likely to blame others that assume blame or avoid blaming altogether (Roth and Puri, 1967). It is not clear under which conditions the underachiever may be aggressive toward others, although it does appear that he or she may be more hostile in general than the achieving gifted student.

There is also some evidence that this child is significantly less popular with peers than the achieving child (Tringland, Winker, Munger, and Krangler, 1966). Additionally, there seem to be differences between achievers and underachievers in some activities that are particularly relevant to classroom conduct. Many achievers appear to be more sensitive to teacher criticism and more concerned with obtaining good grades than are underachievers. The latter group has also been found to have more difficulty than achievers in sustaining their attention, to suffer more anxiety about taking tests, to be more impatient while awaiting important instructions, and to need more external supports and help in meeting their academic responsibilities (Swift and Spivack, 1969).

The underachieving child seems to be more oriented than the achiever toward immediate gratifications rather than delaying them for greater rewards. They appear more concerned with the present than the future, at least more so than their successful counterparts (Davids and Sidman, 1962). Insofar as classroom schedules and activities often demand delays of gratification, the capacity to pay attention, and concern about achievement and grades, all of these factors may be important, singly or in combination, in limiting the accomplishments of gifted youngsters.

Finally, underachievement is not simply a transitory condition, here today and resolved tomorrow. There is evidence that a child not working to capacity today is likely to continue on the same path in the years to come (French, 1967). Thus, it is important to consider some of the educational approaches that might benefit such children.

Educating the Underachiever

Several investigators have experimented with procedures that might help the underachiever to realize his or her academic potential more fully. Engle, Davis, and Mazer (1968) attempted to influence the achievements of these children by manipulating the behaviors of teachers and peers toward them. Teachers were selected on the basis of their understanding and respect for students and were instructed to relate to the underachieving pupils in a warm manner. When underachievers in the program were compared with underachievers not taking part, it was found that the teacher's treatment had no effect upon achievement scores. What was discovered was that students exposed to the warm, understanding teacher showed more frequent and more severe discipline problems, more absenteeism, and more incidences of tardiness than did underachievers not receiving such treatment. These investigators also analyzed the effects of peers, selected for their leadership abilities, on underachievers' study habits and academic products. When the peers were the primary agents of intervention, underachieving children received better grades, committed milder discipline offenses, and were less frequently tardy than underachievers without peer intervention. Tutoring by competent and friendly peers may thus be one way to help the underachiever.

A study by Karnes, McCoy, Zehrbach, Wollersheim, and Clarizo (1963) suggests another approach to help the underachieving student. This team found that when these children were placed in a classroom with other high ability but achieving students, their achievements increased relative to underachievers who remained in a regular classroom with students of widely varying intellectual abilities. Whether the difference between the achievements of these two groups was due to the keener stimulation, greater teacher interest, or peer support in the special classroom was not determined.

While the research concerning educational approaches to the underachieving child are sparse, there is some suggestion that peer influence could be mobilized to play an important role in increasing the reluctant student's achievement.

CREATIVITY

As noted, gifted children are identified primarily by teachers' ratings and intelligence test results. These procedures may lead to equating giftedness with intelligence and school achievement. However, many believe that another factor should be considered in determining whether a particular child is gifted, and that is whether the child demonstrates creativity (Carroll and Laming, 1974; Guilford, 1975). Supporters of the approach argued that it is important to help children develop to their maximum potential and, insofar as creativity is a valued and valuable trait, special services should be provided to facilitate the development of creative children.

Definition

What is meant by the term creativity? When is a product considered to reflect the creative process? By and large there is no real agreement among investigators as to the definition, hypothesized processes, or measures of creativity (Dahlstrom, 1970). There are a number of definitions and hypotheses about creativity.

Hallman (1963) has suggested that creativity requires combinatorial activity on the part of the individual. The person must put disparate ideas or things together harmoniously. In addition, the product must be an original one; it has to be novel, unpredictable, and evoke surprise. Finally, Hallman suggested that the product reflect nonrationality or some unconscious operation.

Jackson and Messick (1968) suggested that there are four dimensions by which we judge creativity. The degree to which a product reflects these dimensions will be the degree to which it will be judged creative. They suggest that the creative product must be *original,* that is, it must be unique or rare. They also point out that creativity is not simply a matter of originality. A monkey's painting, the scribblings of a child and the ranting of a psychotic adult might all be original but few of us would feel that they meet our implicit standards for creativity. Thus, a second criterion for judging creativity is that of *appropriateness.* Does the product fit the producer's goal and the limitations of the situation? A third dimension in the evaluation of a creative product is the *degree of transformation* of materials or ideas. The question asked here is: How strong were the constraints that were overcome? Using a hot brick for a bed warmer would probably be judged less creative than arriving at the idea that human beings are not the center of the universe, or that they might be driven by other than conscious ideas. It is presumed that the forces that militate against arriving at the last two ideas are greater than those involving the use of a brick as a bed warmer, and hence the latter would be considered to be more creative. Finally, Jackson and Messick (1968) suggest that at the highest level of creativity, the product will show *condensation.* The meaning of the product might not be immediately apparent, but will be revealed on inspection. For example, a symphony which initially appears to be a complex production will subsequently be found to contain a few leading themes with lesser variations on those same themes.

Measurement

Creativity is often measured by having the individual suggest alternative uses of common objects; discuss the consequences or problems associated with unusual events; interpret lines, simple figures, or topics; and/or provide multiple definitions of a word or concept (Horn, 1972). One of the most frequent assessment techniques uses the notion and measurement of *divergent thinking*. This idea stems from Guilford's work on the nature of intelligence, which suggests that creativity requires, and is reflected by, the degree to which an individual can generate novel, experimental, and multiple answers to intellectual problems. It is thought that individuals who do well in this type of activity are likely to be creative people (Guilford and Christensen, 1973). A second method for assessing creativity is *audience judgments*. Sometimes teachers are asked to identify the creative students in their classes.

While there are several approaches to determining creativity, it appears that these various techniques are not correlated with one another (Horn, 1972; Tyler, 1972). Tests of verbal production are not necessarily predictive of teacher judgments of student creativity. Moreover, teachers' judgments of creativity often reflect the child's intellectual rather than creative abilities. It would be expected then that the results of studies of children's creativity might be highly dependent upon the methods used to measure it and that research efforts employing different techniques of assessment would not necessarily yield similar results.

Characteristics of Creative Children

One controversy that has characterized the work in creativity is that concerning the role of intelligence in this elusive ability. Is creativity really different from intelligence? If it is not different, why bother with the concept at all? In fact, both theoretical and empirical distinctions between these concepts have been drawn. Jackson and Messick suggest the following distinctions between these terms: "The adjectives *correct* and *good* apply differentially to *intelligent* and *creative* performances. Intelligent responses are correct, they satisfy objective criteria, they operate within the constraints of logic and reality and thus may be considered right or wrong, true or false. Creative responses, in contrast, are 'good,' they satisfy subjective criteria" (1968, p. 232).

Empirically, some of the tests designed to assess creativity do not appear to correlate closely with intelligence tests (Wallach and Kogan, 1965). Thus, tests of creativity using divergent thinking tasks do not show a very high correlation with the results of intelligence tests. This does not mean to say, however, that creativity is entirely independent of intelligence. Guilford and Christensen (1973) for example, tested fourth, fifth, and sixth grade students, all with IQ scores below 130. On their tests of divergent thinking, it was generally found that creativity increased with intelligence, but that many children who scored high on the intelligence test did not do as well on tests of divergent thinking. On the other hand, children who scored low on the intelligence tests were unlikely to perform much better on creativity tests. Essentially, then, children who score low on intelligence tests are unlikely to do well on creativity tests, but not all children who score high on intelligence tests will score high on tests of creativity. To make matters more complicated, Smith and Neisworth (1966) studied the relationship between intelligence test scores and 18 different types of measures of creativity. When creativity was assessed by means of verbal productions, gifted youngsters were more likely than nongifted ones to gain higher scores. When creativity was assessed by nonverbal tasks, there were no differences between the gifted and the nongifted. The bulk of the evidence suggests that creativity and intelligence are tied to each other, but the link is rather weak. High intelligence is probably necessary, but it is not sufficient by itself for creativity. Creativity and intelligence are closely correlated for children with intelligence test scores of about 120 or below, but not for children with scores above that figure (Gowan, 1967).

While creativity might be valued, it does not necessarily follow that the creative child is also held in high esteem. Getzels and Jackson (1960) studied two groups of children, one very intelligent, the other highly creative. The first group tended to have higher intelligence test scores than the second. In general, while both groups did equally well on achievement tests, the creative children were not as well liked by their teachers as the gifted children. This finding of the differences between teachers' reactions to the gifted and the creative child has been replicated by subsequent investigations.

Indeed, it has been found that "teachers have characterized creative students identified by test as less desirable pupils, less well known, less ambitious, expressive, asocial, given to erratic effort, playful, undependable, disturbing to the group and having more naughty ideas than their highly intelligent peers" (French, 1967, p. 404). It is likely that teachers' preference for the gifted over the creative mirrors the greater independence and nonconformity of the creative child. Creative activity may well be associated with other kinds of "deviant" or nonconforming behavior, and thus evoke peer and teacher disapproval.

EDUCATIONAL STRATEGIES FOR THE GIFTED

While we have mentioned the various administrative procedures for facilitating the education of the gifted child, we now turn to some specific suggestions and research concerning classroom activities.

Among these suggestions are the following:

1. Emphasize the basic structure or theoretical perspectives underlying the content matter, rather than simply teaching the child isolated facts (Kirk, 1972).
2. Emphasize activities that allow the child to discover the solutions

and that encourage him or her to think of unusual and unique solutions (Kirk, 1972; Hewett and Forness, 1977).

3. Stress the methods by which information is obtained, rather than simply the facts themselves (Kirk, 1972).

4. Call upon outside experts in specific subject matters, particularly those in which the teacher is relatively uninformed (Kirk, 1972).

5. Encourage independent activities that allow children to progress at their own rates of achievement (Torrance and Myers, 1970; Kirk, 1972; Payne, 1974).

6. Provide a classroom atmosphere where testing and other forms of evaluations are deemphasized while freedom to experiment without the fear of failure is the rule. Include brainstorming sessions where wild ideas, and many of them, are encouraged (French, 1967; Hewett and Forness, 1977).

7. Allow for some academic competition among students; this can be fun for them (Torrance, 1962).

8. The use of positive reinforcements should be considered carefully and critically. For example, the gifted child is often intrinsically motivated to master the curriculum and thus probably should not be exposed to immediate reinforcements contingent upon specific day-to-day accomplishments (Hobbs, 1960). On the other hand, insofar as originality is often antiestablishment and frequently subject to punishment in and out of school, creative children might well be reinforced in school for their creative products (Torrance, 1965).

By and large, these educated guesses stress an atmosphere where children are free to pursue their interests without anxiety over evaluations. Intellectual exploration, rather than rote memory, is the hallmark of the curriculum. Finally, there is an emphasis upon encouraging the child to be creative, to produce the novel and the unique. Not all persons, however, agree with the general thrust of these suggestions. Indeed, in a provocative chapter, Ashby and Walker (1968) put forth some of their informed guesses about educating the very bright student. For example, they suggest that teachers:

1. Define their goals for these students, these goals should not be abstractions but rather concrete events. Do not try to train creativity, originality, or abstract reasoning, but rather aim for concrete accomplishments that can be demonstrated and assessed. The focus of the educator should be to teach children how to select and discriminate important from irrelevant information.

2. Once the goal is defined, then "nothing remains but work and luck" (p. 217). This means, for both student and teacher, a lot of hard work. The student must be taught how to process the largest amount of information relevant to his or her goals and teachers

should use all possible emotional and intellectual stimulants to achieve this end.

3. Finally, let the child become obsessed with a particular topic, even to the neglect of others. Don't distract the child from his obsession. While this may not produce the "well-rounded" youth of many parental dreams, it may well produce a genius.

For the development of genius, Ashby and Walker might well reject notions that teacher warmth and permissiveness, focusing upon the production of novel ideas, or curriculum designed to produce the well-rounded person, would be helpful. Rather, they might argue that hard work, specific and concrete goals, intellectual obsessions stimulated by whatever means the teacher can devise, and a focus upon how to obtain and process information are the precursors of great intellectual accomplishments.

So far, we have focused upon matters of classroom activities and curriculum philosophy as they might affect the education of the gifted child. But it is clear that teachers play a critical role in the classroom, and the question can be asked: Who should be teaching the gifted child? Again, we do not know. There is little information concerning the characteristics of the teacher that might best promote the education of gifted children. But we do know something about the gifted students' preferences regarding their teachers. Pupils' views of the traits of the ideal teacher include, in order of importance:

1. knows the subject matter well
2. encourages students to think
3. makes the course interesting
4. gets the point across
5. makes you want to learn
6. keeps the class and course organized
7. maintains the respect of the students [French, 1967]

Interestingly, however, only one of the above traits was mentioned by the majority of the gifted children, and that was knowing the subject matter well. In effect, while gifted students generally disagree as to the most important teacher traits, they do agree that knowledge of the field is of importance to them.

Bishop (1968) studied the characteristics of teachers identified by gifted children as being good teachers. It was found that these teachers had high intelligence, superior verbal ability, high level literary and cultural interests, and a greater need to achieve than did teachers judged by the gifted as less competent. In addition, the preferred teachers were judged to have more favorable attitudes toward students and to be more inclined toward introspection about their motivations and those of their students than other teachers. Whether teachers preferred by the gifted are, in fact, better teachers than those less preferred is a moot point. As yet we do not know.

SUMMARY

The most neglected of all exceptional children are the gifted and the creative. They are neglected because they are not easily defined, do not present emotional or behavioral problems to parents or teachers, do not demand identification and treatment by virtue of aberrant behaviors. Yet the gifted and creative are the cornerstone of our future. While it may be more controversial and risky to demand resources for these children, who will do well personally without our help, our nation has great need for their fullest development. In the absence of external threat, as in the competition for technological superiority with other nations, we seem to have difficulty mustering support for our gifted.

In this chapter we discussed the incidence of giftedness and noted how the incidence rates vary according to the definition used. The consensus seems to be that about 2 or 3 percent of the school-aged population are gifted. In addition, we have seen that the identification of gifted children is no small problem. While most persons prefer to use the intelligence test score to pinpoint the extremely able child, the costs of this assessment have led to the more frequent use of teacher ratings to identify gifted children. Unfortunately, teachers tend to underrate children and many more of them would be identified as gifted if intelligence test data rather than teacher ratings were used.

Discussing the characteristics of gifted children, we find that there are a number of myths about these children. They are not gifted because of genetics alone or divine influence, they are not withdrawn bookworms with poor physical development. Indeed, the gifted appear to be gifted by virtue of both genes and hard work, their physical development and health are generally superior to the nongifted, and they are in addition social, active human beings as children and as adults. In general, they are not maladjusted or emotionally disturbed, but rather appear to be better off emotionally and socially than less gifted persons. In addition, it appears that they maintain their social status and high achievement throughout their middle life span.

Educational programs for the gifted have been primarily self-contained segregated classrooms, acceleration, and enrichment programs. The self-contained classroom for the gifted has met with the same public dislike as segregated settings for other exceptional children, but we have much to learn about the advantages and disadvantages of acceleration and enrichment programs. At this point, it appears that acceleration, at least of one or two years, does not hinder the child's social, personal, or academic achievements.

There is a special group of children who really merit our attention. These are the underachievers, youngsters who have the potential for giftedness based on intelligence and achievement tests, but who are not achieving it. The girl or boy who is very intelligent but doing poorly in school is the underachiever. The research on underachievers suggests that their parents tend to have less education, and may be more hostile toward the child. Also, their families are more apt to have suffered some disruption than families of achieving children.

As to their characteristics, many underachieving children are more likely than others to be hostile toward peers, to have negative feelings about themselves, and to blame themselves for transgressions. In addition, underachievers are more likely to have difficulty maintaining attention, to suffer anxiety about tests, to be impatient while waiting for instructions, and to need external supports. They are comparatively less able to delay gratification for rewards, less oriented toward the future and obtaining good grades. They also tend to be less sensitive to teacher criticism.

Efforts to help underachievers have had provocative results. Teacher warmth and support may not aid the underachiever, but friendly peer tutoring and peer competition in homogeneously grouped classes do appear to be helpful. Peer influence is thus a potential resource for bolstering the able but unwilling student.

Creativity was the chapter's next concern. There is no agreed upon definition of this quality, but the creative act does have to be unique, novel, and original while, at the same time, appropriate. Definitions of creativity also include how difficult it was for the person to devise the new product. Creative actions are thus original, appropriate, require transformation of ideas or materials, and will show condensation in that the complex are revealed to be not so complex.

Measurement of creativity have been developed using ideas of divergent thinking. Creativity then is judged by one's generation of novel and multiple answers to intellectual problems. The ability to generate multiple answers as well as other judgments of creativity have been used as assessment techniques. But, the various techniques for assessment are apparently not related to one another. We also have seen that there is a complex relationship between intelligence and creativity. The data suggest that in general children with low intelligence are not likely to be creative individuals, but neither are all children with high intelligence going to be creative. There is a relationship, but a weak one, between intelligence and creativity.

In reviewing educational strategies that are supposed to enhance the likelihood that creative children will become creative adults, we find two divergent approaches. On one hand, we have an approach that emphasizes freedom, free spirit, discovery, an atmosphere in which the child does not worry about tests or possible failure. On the other, we have a more "Protestant ethic" approach that emphasizes hard work. This approach does not seek to create the well-rounded individual, but recognizes that to become an expert or genius in some area requires concentrated and continuous effort in that area. While disagreeing on most characteristics of desirable teachers, many gifted children agree that the teacher should be knowledgeable in the subject matter.

Finally, it should be stressed that gifted children will eventually have an important positive impact upon our society and to neglect them reflects an unconscionable waste of a major national asset. As John Kennedy once stated: "If you scoff at intellectuals, harass scientists, and reward only athletic achievements, then the future is dark indeed."

REFERENCES

Abraham, W. *Common sense about gifted children*. New York: Harper & Row, 1958.

Anastosiow, N. J. Maximizing identification of the gifted. *The Journal of Educational Research*, 1964, *57*, 238–241.

Ashby, W. R., & Walker, C. C., Genius. In P. London and D. Rosenham (Eds.), *Foundations of abnormal psychology*. New York: Holt, Rinehart & Winston, 1968.

Bishop, W. E. Successful teachers of the gifted. *Exceptional Children*, 1968, *34*, 317–325.

Byrne, D. *An introduction to personality, research, theory and application*. Englewood Cliffs, N.J.: Prentice-Hall, Inc., 1974.

Carroll, J. L., & Laming, L. R. Giftedness and creativity: Recent attempts at definitions, a literature review. *The Gifted Child Quarterly*, 1974, *18*, 85–96.

Ciha, T. E., Harris, R., Hoffman, C., & Potter, M. Parents as identifiers of giftedness, ignored but accurate. *The Gifted Child Quarterly*, 1970, *14*, 191–195.

Dahlstrom, W. G. Personality. In P. Mussen and M. Rosenzweig (Eds.), *Annual review of psychology*. Palo Alto, Calif.: Annual Reviews, 1970.

Davids, A., & Sidman, J. A pilot study—impulsivity, time orientation, and delayed gratification in future scientists and in underachieving high school students. *Exceptional Children*, 1962, *29*, 170–174.

Engle, K. B., Davis, D., & Mazer, G. Interpersonal effects of underachievement. *Journal of Educational Research*, 1968, *61*, 208–210.

French, J. L. Research and educational practices with gifted children. In N. A. Haring & R. L. Schiefelbusch (Eds.), *Methods in special education*. New York: McGraw-Hill Book Co., 1967.

Gallagher, J. J. *Teaching the gifted child*. Boston: Allyn & Bacon, 1975.

Getzels, J. W., & Jackson, P. W. The study of giftedness: A multidimensional approach. *The Gifted Student*. Cooperative Research Monograph, 1960. *2*, 1–18. Washington, D.C.: U.S. Department of Health, Education and Welfare.

Gowan, J. C. What makes a gifted child creative?—Four theories. In J. C. Gowan, G. D. Demos, & E. P. Torrance (Eds.), *Creativity: Its educational implications*. New York: John Wiley & Sons, 1967.

Guilford, J. P. Varieties of creative giftedness, their measurement and development. *Gifted Child Quarterly*, 1975, *19*, 107–120.

Guilford, J. P., & Christensen, P. R. The one-way relation between creative potential and IQ. *Journal of Creative Behavior*, 1973, *7*, 247–252.

Hallman, R. J. The necessary and sufficient conditions for creativity. *Journal of Humanistic Psychology*, 1963, *3*, 1.

Hewett, R. M., & Forness, S. R. *Education of exceptional learners*. Boston: Allyn & Bacon, 1977.

Hildreth, G. H. *Introduction to the gifted*. New York: McGraw-Hill, 1966.

Hobbs, N. Motivation to high achievement. In B. Shertzer (Ed.), *Working with superior students: Theories and practices.* Chicago: Science Research Associates, 1960.

Horn, J. L. Human abilities: A review of research and theory in the early 1970s. In M. Rosenzweig and L. Porter (Eds.), *Annual review of psychology.* Palo Alto, Calif.: Annual Reviews, 1972.

Jackson, P. W., & Messick, S. Creativity. In P. London, & D. Rosenhan (Eds.), *Foundations of abnormal psychology.* New York: Holt, Rinehart & Winston, 1968.

Jones, R. L. The college adjustment of superior high school students who participate in a program of acceleration. *Exceptional Children,* 1966, *32,* 634–635.

Justman, J. Personal and social adjustment of intellectually gifted accelerants and non-accelerants in junior high schools. *The School Review,* 1953, *61,* 468–478.

Karnes, M. B., McCoy, G., Zehrbach, R. R., Wollersheim, J. P., & Clarizo, H. F. The efficiency of two organizational plans for underachieving intellectually gifted children. *Exceptional Children,* 1963, *29,* 438–446.

Kirk, S. A. *Educating exceptional children.* Boston: Houghton Mifflin Co., 1972.

Klausmeier, H. J. Effects of accelerating bright older elementary pupils: a follow-up. *Journal of Educational Psychology,* 1963, *54,* 165–171.

Klausmeier, H. J., Goodwin, W., & Ronda, T. Effect of accelerating bright, older elementary pupils: A record follow-up. *Journal of Educational Psychology,* 1968, *59,* 53–58.

L'Abate, L., & Curtis, L. T. *Teaching the exceptional child.* Philadelphia: W. B. Saunders Co., 1975.

Laycock, F., & Caylor, J. S. Physiques of gifted children and their less gifted siblings. *Child Development,* 1964, *35,* 63–74.

Marland, S. Education of the gifted and talented. Report to the Subcommittee on Education, Committee of Labor and Public Welfare, U.S. Senate, Washington, D.C., 1972.

Newland, E. T. *The gifted in socio-educational perspective.* Englewood Cliffs, N. J.: Prentice-Hall, 1976.

Oden, M. H. The fulfillment of promise: 40 years follow-up of the Terman gifted group. *Genetic Psychology Monographs,* 1968, *77,* 3–93.

Payne, J. The gifted. In N. G. Harding (Ed.), *Behavior of exceptional children: An introduction to special education.* Columbus, O.: Charles E. Merrill, 1974.

Pegnato, C. W., & Birch, J. W. Locating gifted children in junior high schools: A comparison of methods. *Exceptional Children,* 1959, *25,* 300–304.

Pielstick, W. Perception of mentally superior children by their classmates. *Perceptual Motor Skills,* 1963, *17,* 47–53.

Roth, R., & Puri, P. Direction of aggression and the non-achievement syndrome. *Journal of Counseling Psychology,* 1967, *14,* 277–281.

Shaw, M. C., & Grubb, J. Hostility and able high school underachievers. *Journal of Counseling Psychology,* 1958, *5,* 263–266.

Smith, R. M., & Neisworth, J. T. Creative thinking abilities of intellectually superior children in the regular grades. *Psychological Reports,* 1966, *18,* 335–341.

Swift, M., & Spivack, G. Clarifying the relationship between academic success and overt classroom behavior. *Exceptional Children,* 1969, *36,* 99–104.

Tannor, S. Survey on the gifted in cities over 250,000 population. *Exceptional Children,* 1966, *32,* 631–632.

Terman, L. M. Mental and physical traits of a thousand gifted children. *Genetic studies in genius* (Vol. 1). Stanford, Calif.: Stanford University Press, 1925.

Terman, L. M., & Oden, M. H. The gifted group at mid-life. *Genetic Studies of Genius* (Vol. 5). Stanford, Calif.: Stanford University Press, 1959.

Torrance, E. P. *Freeing the creative thinking abilities through teaching.* Paper presented to Classroom Teacher Work Conference, Athens, Ga., 1962.

Torrance, E. P. Psychology of gifted children and youth. In W. M. Cruickshank (Ed.), *Psychology of exceptional children and youth.* Englewood Cliffs, N.J.: Prentice-Hall, 1965.

Torrance, E. P., & Myers, R. E. *Creative learning and teaching.* New York: Dodd, Mead and Co., 1970.

Tringland, J. J., Winkler, R. C., Munger, P. F., & Krangler, G. D. Some concomitants of underachievement at the elementary school level. *Personal Guidance Journal,* 1966, *44,* 950–955.

Tyler, L. E. Human abilities. In P. Mussen and M. Rosenzweig (Eds.), *Annual Review of Psychology.* Palo Alto, Calif.: Annual Reviews, 1972.

Wallach, M. A., & Kogan, N. *Modes of thinking in young children.* New York: Holt, Rinehart & Winston, 1965.

Werblo, D., & Torrance, E. P. Experiences in historical research and changes in self-evaluation of gifted children. *Exceptional Children,* 1966, *33,* 131–141.

KEY TERM

enrichment Approach to education for gifted students in which a variety of supplemental, advanced experiences are offered within the regular school program.

CHAPTER 11

Prosocial Behavior

For many years, the chief preoccupation of special educators and mental health professionals has been the alleviation of people's personal misery or their social destructiveness. They have directed their efforts toward teaching the learning disabled to read, helping the phobic child overcome fears, helping the anti-social to participate cooperatively in society, and aiding the retarded to function at their best with whatever abilities they have. This reasonable and humane concern has led to considerable knowledge and some technology of behavior change.

Recently, however, psychologists have turned their attention to what are now called "prosocial behaviors." While no one has enumerated all of the behaviors that this conceptual umbrella might shelter, most of the time they are referring to altruistic, and to a lesser extent, cooperative behaviors. Several factors have piqued interest in prosocial behaviors. Events like the peace movement during the war in Viet Nam, student activism, and the apparently increasing brutality of many of our citizens toward themselves and others have been suggested as arousing this concern about prosocial behavior (Wispe, 1972). Moreover, the helping of another, the sacrifice of some comfort to produce a better distribution of resources between the haves and have-nots is a widely held value that often motivates the researcher. While arguments and debates might arise among citizens from differences as to how much to sacrifice and to whom, under what circumstances, and for how long, there is little question that most scientists as well as other citizens accept the Good Samaritan principle. Thus, interest is in part stirred by scientists' desire to make some contribution, however small, to the creation of a "better" society.

But there is another factor serving as a stimulus to such interest. For a rather long time psychologists have emphasized, and rightly so, the power of material and social rewards to affect and control behavior. Campbell has called this "skin-surface hedonism" (1965). The effects of what, when, and how rewards are given to a bird, rat, or a child have received widespread attention. Until recently, however, little thought has been given by researchers to the fact that adults and children often do sacrifice things that they value—money, time, and life itself—in order to benefit others. People do give up valued resources, run the risk of injury, and endure inconvenience even when neither material rewards nor social acclaim seems imminent or likely. By studying such prosocial behaviors, we also learn something about the limits and the nature of reinforcements.

The harvest of information yielded by these factors, though relatively new, is nonetheless rich. However, it has one limit that should be spelled out. Most categories of exceptionality have been devised because the child clearly demonstrates some characteristic across a variety of situations. The blind child is blind, irrespective of his or her location. The mentally retarded are likely to show their handicap in many different situations. It is not clear yet whether there is a large group of children who are exceptional because of their prosocial activities. There are, no doubt, some children who do show this exceptionality, but they have not been the object of much study. Knowledge of those events that contribute to inculcating prosocial behavior in most children will help us understand how such an unusual child develops. Understanding the causes of children's benevolence to those around them is, we believe, as important as understanding the concept of intelligence or methods of socialization.

As the Gallup Poll has recently documented, parents are extremely concerned about the teacher's role in the character training of our youth (*Chicago Sun Times*, 1977). Since the educational establishment has often asserted their collective belief that citizenship training is part of their professional obligation, it is reasonable to examine some of the behaviors often thought to reflect such citizenship. Finally, we believe that the mainstreaming of handicapped children into regular schools and classrooms mandates the development of a classroom atmosphere that is cooperative and benevolent rather than competitive. To focus on normal children and their willingness to behave in a prosocial fashion toward handicapped classmates who may be less skilled and competent seems important, both for the handicapped and the nonhandicapped child.

This chapter will present information concerning the development of cooperative, altruistic, and helping behaviors. We will also include a discussion of current views and data relating to children's honesty, and close with some recent theorizing on the development of moral judgments.

COOPERATION

So many of society's tasks and goals demand the sharing of expertise or coordinated actions between people that training children to cooperate is critical to their development. And, it is pretty obvious that a child who is generally uncooperative with peers or adults is likely to be seriously disruptive at home or in school, and to be treated as showing symptoms of personality or conduct disturbance. In this

FIGURE 11-1 An example of prosocial behavior

section, we present those conditions that appear to be important in eliciting cooperative behaviors from children.

Reinforcements

Much of the work concerning children's cooperation has been ad-
dressed to the role of reinforcement in affecting or altering it. Surely the reader will
not be surprised to learn that if children are given rewards for helping each other,
they will increase their cooperative behavior. Surprising or not, the relationship
between cooperation and reinforcement has been firmly established (Azrin and Lindsley, 1956; Mithaug, 1969; Mithaug and Burgess, 1968; Vogler, Masters, and Morrill,
1970). However, other findings may not seem so self-evident. For instance, the
question has been asked: will reinforcing the child for his or her achievements
produce different consequences than when the child is rewarded on the basis of the
group's accomplishments? Does reinforcing a child for what the entire class does
instead of for his or her own classroom performance make a difference in cooperation? Various sources indicate that the answer is yes. Bronfenbrenner (1970) has
written a very provocative and important book on the school systems in the USSR. He
reports that in most classrooms in the Soviet Union, children receive rewards for
group rather than individual performance. If the group does well, all persons in the
group benefit; if some members of the group perform poorly, all members suffer.
Bronfenbrenner suggests that such procedures are likely to be particularly powerful
in developing cooperation among children. While he fails to provide direct evidence
in support of this opinion, there are data that do confirm this idea. Several investigations using laboratory based experiments have found that group rewards are more
effective in increasing cooperativeness than individual ones, even when such a
procedure rewards the individual child less (Madsen, 1967; Madsen and Shapira,
1970; Nelson and Madsen, 1968; Richmond and Weiner, 1973; Shapira and Madsen,
1969). Indeed, in a most ingenious study, Fraser, Kelem, Diener, and Beaman (1973)
found that among college students, academic performance rose if grades were
assigned, not on individual merit, but on group performance!

While a system that ties an individual's fate to the actions of many
may offend our sense of justice (How would you like to get a C grade because of the
goof-offs in your class?), group administered rewards are likely to produce friend-
lier, more cooperative, and less antagonistic relationships among children. Why this
particular system of rewarding children appears so powerful in effecting cooperation has not been frequently studied and is certainly not clear. There are, however,
several hints of one factor that may underlie this process. For example, Shapira and
Madsen have shown that Israeli children, raised and living on a **kibbutz,** were more
cooperative with each other than children reared in an urban setting where rewards
were given individually. These authors felt that this superior teamwork was due to
the children's early and continuous training emphasizing cooperation and minimizing
competition and making them particularly resistant to the detrimental effects of
individually based rewards. Kagan and Madsen (1971) provide some experimental

evidence that individuals who are thinking of the group are more likely to be cooperative than those concentrating on themselves. One might suspect, then, that the administration of rewards based upon individual rather than coordinated group performance may produce a focus upon oneself and thus discourage children's cooperation. But whatever the reasons underlying this general finding, all individuals working with groups of children should give serious consideration to the idea of rewarding not only individual enterprise, but collective achievement as well.

Children's Characteristics and Cooperation

Do children who are older, belong to a particular social class, or who are bright behave more cooperatively than younger children who are less intelligent or from another social class? In this section we note which differences among children make a difference in their cooperation.

Developmental Factors

What are the developmental factors associated with teamwork? Do children as they mature become more or less cooperative? Unfortunately, there are no ready answers to this question. Some studies have concluded that older children are less cooperative than younger ones, while others report just the opposite findings (Kagan and Madsen, 1971; Friedrich and Stein, 1973). While these contradictory results await a final explanation, Bryan (1975) has suggested that it is likely that as children age, they may become both more competitive and more cooperative. In a situation in which a child is forced to choose between cooperating and competing, older children are more likely to choose competition than are younger ones. On the other hand, in situations that minimize the opportunities for competition, the older child may be more able and willing to enter into cooperative play and shared tasks than his or her younger counterparts.

Cultural Factors

A second question that has received some attention, particularly in the work of Madsen and colleagues, is: Are American children less cooperative than children from other cultures? There does seem to be evidence that Mexican-American children, when given a choice between competing or cooperating with another, are more likely to be less competitive than Anglo-American youngsters. Our culture does push, and even prides itself on inducing and maintaining a competitive spirit; it would not be surprising if American children were highly competitive in comparison with children from many other cultures.

Sex Factors

Are boys more competitive than girls? One might think so if one believes that part of the male sex role is to achieve, win, conquer; and that part of the female sex role is to be submissive, passive, and cooperative. While this stereotype may be held by many, there is little evidence of substantial differences between the sexes in their cooperation with others. Several studies have failed to find that boys and girls differed in their cooperation (Sampson and Kardush, 1965; Lindskold, Cullen, Gahagan, and Tedeschi, 1970; Richmond and Weiner, 1973). Occasionally it has been reported that boys were more cooperative than girls (Madsen, 1967; Wasik, Senn, and Epanchin, 1969; Friedrich and Stein, 1973). At this time, general statements concerning sex differences in competition or cooperation really cannot be made.

Social Class and Cooperation

Several reasonable notions have led investigators to study the question of the relationship between social class and children's cooperative activities. For example, McKee and Leader (1955) have argued that persons deprived of resources are more likely to pursue them vigorously than more affluent persons. Hence, children from lower social classes might well be exposed to models and direct training that induce a "competitive spirit." On the other hand, Richmond and Weiner (1973) argue that the likelihood of deprived children obtaining rewards is highly dependent upon their cooperation with others. Thus, poor children will demonstrate more cooperation than children from wealthier families. While the evidence is slight, what there is of it fails to indicate that children from the varying social classes differ in their cooperation with others (Brotsky and Thomas, 1967; Nelson and Madsen, 1968). Any number of reasonable assumptions would lead one to guess that social class differences would be reflected in children's cooperation, but these assumptions have not received empirical support.

With the current emphasis upon, and interest in, school integration, the lack of studies concerning cooperation among children of varying racial and ethnic backgrounds is puzzling. It would seem important to know whether black children and white children cooperate more with members of their own race or of another race, or fail to show any differences at all in working and playing together. The evidence that does exist demonstrates contradictory results. Some studies show that black children are less cooperative than white ones (Wasik et al., 1969); others indicate that black children are more cooperative than white ones (Sampson and Kardush, 1965), while others fail to find any differences at all (Nelson and Madsen, 1968). Moreover, some studies have found that children's cooperation does vary according to the race of the partner (Richmond and Weiner, 1973), while others fail to find any difference in cooperation because of the partner's race (Hartford and Cutter, 1966; Wasik et al., 1969).

In effect, we really do not know what personal differences matter in children's cooperation. The research into cooperation and its association with children's sex, race, and social class has not yielded a consistent picture. There does appear to be evidence that a child, particularly an older one, who has been reared in the United States may be more competitive than children raised in other cultures. Which personality characteristics of the child might be associated with cooperation is, as yet, undetermined.

Finally, we need to ask how children respond to the cooperation of others. Are helpful responses likely to be reinforced by the peer group, or are they signs to peers that future opportunities for exploitation are likely? There is evidence that children who have participated in a team enterprise will cooperate more readily with others, and that such team work strengthens the bonds of friendship between children (Altman, 1971; Blau and Rafferty, 1970; Gottheil, 1955; Sherif, Harvey, White, Hood, and Sherif, 1961). It does seem clear that cooperation increases interpersonal attraction and creates interpersonal relationships that are generally more benevolent than those produced by individualistic experiences.

There are several conclusions one can make concerning children's cooperation. First, children in the United States are likely to be trained in a competitive rather than cooperative style of behavior. Second, cooperation can be instilled by giving the child reinforcements for such behavior. When children are reinforced for their group's performance rather than for their own individual achievements, their cooperation is increased. Finally, it should be noted that while the socialization of children into a competitive style of behavior may well enhance achievement, skills mastery, and general success, it seems to have at least two negative consequences. First, competition may become an end in itself. It has been found that a child may well prefer to beat another child than to gain a reward through cooperation (Kagan and Madsen, 1971). Many children are apparently being taught to prefer interpersonal superiority to obtaining useful or pleasure-giving commodities. Additionally, training in competition may actually produce less cooperation and does apparently reduce the child's willingness to aid needy others (Barnett and Bryan, 1974).

CHILDREN'S HELPING AND ALTRUISTIC BEHAVIORS

The study of children's helping and altruistic behaviors has had a relatively brief but nonetheless productive history. There is a substantial body of knowledge concerning which children, under what circumstances, are likely to make personal sacrifices of time, money, or effort on behalf of another in distress. In this portion of the chapter, we present some of this information, addressing ourselves to the influence of models, moods and affects, personality, and social characteristics of children that are associated with altruism. Finally we will examine those socialization practices that might foster its development. First, a brief discussion of the definition of such behaviors and methods of studying them.

FIGURE 11-2 One child sharing with another

Many people think of altruistic behavior as helping another without any selfish motive, and this is in accord with standard dictionary definitions. However, such a definition of altruism is difficult for most social scientists to accept and still analyze acts of apparent self-sacrifice. The difficulty arises because this definition implies a person's actions on behalf of another stem from no personal motivation; that the act is unmotivated. In addition, if one defines altruism this way, the scientist is put in the position of having to prove the nonexistence of something, specifically, the nonexistence of any motives underlying the helpful act. Thus, psychologists define altruism in a somewhat different manner. Accordingly, Macaulay and Berkowitz have defined altruism as "behavior carried out to benefit another without anticipation of rewards from external sources" (1970, p. 73); while

Bryan and London suggest that such behaviors are those "intended to benefit another but which appear to have a high cost to the actor with little possibility of material or social reward" (1970, p. 200). These definitions allow for the possibility that some personal gratification, or some fulfilling of a motive, might result from altruistic actions.

Typically, rescue and donation are the two types of altruistic or helping behaviors that have been studied. When examining rescue behaviors, investigators arrange the situation so that the child is confronted with a person who is apparently hurt, but really is not. The researchers then observe how the child tries to help the "victim." For example, does the child try to help the person directly, seek out the experimenter, or simply not try to help at all? If he or she does help, how quickly is the help initiated? In studies involving donations, the child is typically given the option of contributing some of the prizes won during the experiment to some needy other. Experiments are usually arranged so that children believe that their donation will be unobserved. We now turn to some of the findings relevant to the development or elicitation of children's altruistic and helping behaviors.

Observing Others

Throughout this book we have emphasized the role of children's observations of the behavior of others as an important source of their learning. In the case of altruism, too, we must emphasize the role of models. If the child observes another person giving, the likelihood that the youngster will help is increased regardless of whether the giver is a peer or an adult, whether observed on videotape or in the flesh (Bryan, 1975). Children's imitation of a model's behavior has been demonstrated when the act involved rescuing a person in distress, donating money or gift certificates, giving candies or marbles (Rosenhan and White, 1967; Bryan and Walbek, 1970a,b; Harris, 1971: Schwartz and Bryan, 1971a,b; Staub, 1971; White, 1972). Moreover, there is evidence that the effects upon children of observing altruistic behavior may be relatively enduring. Thus, Rushton (1975) found that children who watched an altruistic model were more likely to donate their winnings to a needy other after a lapse of two months than were children who did not view such a model. Similar effects were found by Midlarsky and Bryan (1972) and White (1972) after a lapse of 10 days between the child's observing the model and being tested for generosity. Altruistic models are effective then in increasing the child's own benevolence towards others.

Model Characteristics

While it is known that altruistic models increase the generosity of observing children, questions have been raised as to whether certain characteristics of the model affect imitation. Does the model's personal warmth or cordiality make a difference? Does the model's own affective responses to his or her behavior alter the likelihood of the person's being imitated? What are the effects of inconsistency between the model's preachings and practices? Let us look at some research into these questions.

Interpersonal warmth has been a central notion in theories of imitation and identification (Mowrer, 1950; Bandura, 1969) and has been demonstrated to be important in imitative behavior (Hetherington and Frankie, 1967). A warm or cordial model is more likely to be imitated than one who is cold and indifferent to the child. The results of model warmth upon helping behavior, however, are somewhat complicated. First, it has generally been found that the warmth of the model either has no effect on or, in fact, decreases the child's willingness to make anonymous donations (Grusec, 1971; Weissbrod, 1976). By contrast, model warmth increases children's rescue behavior (Staub, 1971; Yarrow, Scott, and Waxler, 1973). These apparently contradictory results might be explained on the basis of the differences between helping by donating and helping by rescuing. Staub (1971) has suggested that an important motive for the child in a rescue situation is to reduce his or her distress brought about by an emergency. That is, seeing another in pain or anguish is likely to disturb the child. The child's motive then is to reduce the anxiety, to turn off the emergency. One way to do this is to render help. Rendering help, however, often requires the child to act in an unusual manner, to do something not explicitly permitted. In effect, it requires a bit of courage to give aid, to do things that may well not be acceptable to the authorities. The reason the warm model may induce greater rescue behavior than the cold one is that such a model may be less frightening to the child. The child might feel that if rescuing should prove to be an act of transgression, the warm model is less likely to punish than the cold one.

In the donation situation, the motivations of the child might be quite different. It is reasonable to assume that most youngsters really do not wish to give up their rewards and are reluctant to do so. It is also probable that most children realize that it is good to give to the needy, and hence are under some moral pressure to do so (Bryan and Walbek, 1970a). An act of courage, then, does not involve donating. If the model is warm, the child may well expect that a selfish act will lead to less punishment than if the model is cold or indifferent. Whatever the explanations for the differences produced in the child's donation and rescue activities by the model's warmth toward the child, it is important to recognize that such differences do exist.

Another model charactistic greatly influencing the child's imitative altruism is the model's reactions to his or her own behavior. It has been suggested that if the model seems happy or sad after committing a particular behavior, these displays of emotion will have an important effect upon the child's imitation of him or her. In fact, there is evidence to support this idea (Bryan, 1971; Midlarsky and Bryan, 1972). Children are more likely to imitate models who appear happy about what they have done, whether this is donating or keeping their winnings, than models who show little emotion about their actions.

Hypocrisy

Very likely parents, educators, or friends are often inconsistent in matching their verbalized morality with their actual behaviors. Our behavior often falls short of our moral preachings and many times contradicts them. It is likely then that children are frequently confronted by models who are hypocrites. Most people probably feel that moral hypocrisy will have detrimental effects upon observing children. Several investigations have focused on the impact of discrepancies in a model's words and deeds of altruism upon youngsters who see them. Are children's actions more likely to follow the preachings or the practices of the model, and do these discrepancies affect his or her attractiveness for the child? What effects will discrepant inputs have upon the child's own preachment? In fact, there is little evidence that the hypocrisy of the model directly affects the child. What seems to occur is this: When it comes to altruistic acts, the child will imitate the actions of the model and will not be immediately affected by the person's preaching. The model's preachings as well as actions do affect that person's appeal for the child, the one who preaches generosity is better liked than the one who preaches greed. Additionally, the model's preaching may affect the child's preachings to other children. A child who observes a model preach generosity but practice selfishness is likely to follow suit in both. A child exposed to this hypocritical model is likely then to demonstrate hypocrisy to others (Bryan and Walbek, 1970a,b; Bryan, Redfield, and Mader, 1971; Midlarsky and Bryan, 1972; Schwartz and Bryan, 1971a). Finally, there is some evidence that models who are inconsistent in their preaching and practice of generosity might lose their ability to influence the child's actions by means of their social approval. Indeed, evidence suggests that when a hypocritical model approves the child's altruisms, the child's generous actions will decrease rather than increase (Midlarsky, Bryan, and Brickman, 1973).

So far, we have seen that helping models are likely to be imitated by observing children and that a model's warmth toward the child may have complex effects upon helping, depending on whether the helping involves rescuing or giving to others. Additionally, it does appear that the model's own affective responses to his or her actions influence imitation so that the model who is "trying it and liking it" is more likely to be imitated than one who is "trying it but not liking it." Moreover, there is evidence that a hypocritical model may well produce similar behavior by the child, and that children do like a generous person more than a selfish one. But there are other factors that shape children's helping behavior. These include the child's moods, some personal or social characteristics, and the manner in which the child has been reared. We now turn our attention to these influential factors.

Personal Characteristics

Within the United States, there are various norms and values dictating a variety of actions, many of which contradict each other (Darley and Latané, 1970). Thus we should be helpful, but we should also mind our own business. We should help the needy, but people also ought to get what they deserve. Given these contradictory norms, it may be that moods and emotions are particularly important in directing acts of altruism. There have been several notions about the relationship between mood states and helping actions. One idea is that positive moods are likely to increase helping, that pleasant affect allows children to focus on their assets rather than their liabilities and upon others rather than themselves (Moore, Underwood, and Rosenhan, 1973). The second theory about moods and helping is that negative affects, such as guilt, serve as a basic motive for aiding others. It is believed that altruistic acts might serve as a redemptive device and thus reduce the negative feelings associated with guilt. The evidence concerning children generally supports the idea that happy children are more likely to be generous than sorrowful ones (Aronfreed, 1968; Midlarsky and Bryan, 1967; Moore et al., 1973). On the other hand, there is little reason to assume that children's negative affect or feelings of guilt are likely to increase their helpfulness toward others (Silverman, 1967; Test, 1969; Moore et al., 1973). Apparently, the happy child is also the generous one.

Age

What are the other social or personal characteristics associated with helping? First is age. By and large, as children age, they become more generous, at least through the first 10 years of their lives (Bryan, 1975; Rushton, 1976). However, the picture is not entirely clear. While this strong relationship is found when children are studied within a laboratory setting, it may not be apparent in the child's real life setting. While the evidence is sparse, it suggests that children may become less altruistic with age when altruism is measured in day-to-day situations (Severy and Davis, 1971). One possible explanation of these contradictory findings is that children not only learn to become more generous but also more competitive as they get older. When the situation allows for competition, the child is more likely to compete with, than aid, a peer. In the laboratory settings, however, competition is rarely possible, and thus the child will opt to be altruistic. It is probably safe to say that in settings where competition is stressed or stimulated, children will become less altruistic as they develop.

Sex, Economic Status

Are girls more nurturant or more generous with their bounty than boys? Are children from affluent families more altruistic than those from families with few resources? That is, will children who probably have more money and advantages be more likely to give them up than children who have little to give? The answer to the first question is yes; to the second no. By and large, girls do seem to be more generous than boys, especially when it comes to giving up money (Midlarsky and Bryan, 1972; Moore et al., 1973; Rosenhan, 1969a; White, 1972). Not only are girls more apt than boys to be generous in the immediate situation, but their donation behavior shows more stability in the long run than does that of boys (White, 1972). Apparently, however, children with the most resources are not necessarily the most likely to give them up. The economic status of the child's family appears to bear little relationship to the child's helping (Madsen, 1967; Rosenhan, 1969b; DePalma and Olejnik, 1973).

Personality

What kind of people are children who are helpful? This question is really two questions. First, are children who are helpful on one task likely to be helpful in other ways as well? Second, are there particular personality characteristics associated with helpfulness? Let us look at the evidence.

Several studies have demonstrated that children who are helpful in one way, or in one setting, are likely to be so in other ways and in other settings. For example, Friedrich and Stein (1973) found that preschool children who were nurturant toward others were also cooperative with others. Dlugokinski and Firestone (1974) in their study of fifth to eighth graders discovered that children viewed by their peers as kind were also likely to be generous with their money and to have some concept of the meaning of kindness. Finally, Baumrind (1971) found that preschool children who were sympathetic to others were also likely to be helpful, thoughtful, nurturant, and less insulting to their peers than children who were not sympathetic to others. Behaviors were related in a way that suggests an underlying disposition by the child to be considerate to his or her peers. Thus, there does seem to be some evidence that various forms of helpfulness may be related to one another.

A number of attempts have been made to discover the relationship between children's acts of compassion or helping and various personality traits. By and large, most of these studies have not yielded significant findings, and those that have require further study before statements of this relationship can be made with confidence. There are hints, however, that the child's need for social approval, his or her sense of social responsibility, and some forms of aggression are correlated with children's helping.

Parental Practices

Finally, parental training practices appear to affect the development of altruism in children. Throughout this section a number of studies have been reviewed that provide cues as to training techniques that might be helpful in developing a considerate and cooperative child. Certainly, one technique is that of providing the child with a model of helpfulness. Whether your interactions with the child take place in the home or classroom, your own helpfulness will provide a training experience for the development of the child's compassion for others. This is particularly true when you are helping and at the same time showing the child that you also like doing so. It also seems likely that the happy child is more likely to be generous than the unhappy youngster. By implication, the environment that fosters such a mood in the child is conducive to the development of the child's generosity. But this should not be interpreted as recommending an environment of child indulgence. Indeed, one investigator concerned with parental discipline techniques and the development of kindness has written that parents who specified "aims and methods of discipline, promoted their own code of behavior, could not be coerced by the child and set standards of excellence for the child" were those most likely to produce friendly and cooperative children (Baumrind, 1971, p. 62). In addition, Staub (1970) has argued that prosocial behavior is facilitated by assigning responsibility to children.

While indulgence is not likely to increase the helping behavior of children, neither are certain forms of discipline. Parents and teachers who rely on their power over the child, who resort to physical or verbal assaults as a technique of control, are less likely to raise helpful children than those teachers and parents who employ reasoning and who point out to the child the consequences of his or her transgression upon others when imposing discipline (Midlarsky and Bryan, 1972; Staub, 1973). In effect, firm discipline policies that include explanations of just and fair standards of behavior are likely to be helpful in developing a prosocial child (Baumrind, 1971; Staub, 1973).

We have reviewed some of the evidence concerning those experiences and situations that may affect the helping and altruistic behavior of children. But there is yet another form of behavior of critical concern in the development of prosocial behavior and that is honesty. What are the factors that contribute to developing a child who will not cheat or lie?

HONESTY

Is there such a thing as an honest child? Are children who are honest in one situation likely to be so in other situations with other demands and with different goals and gains at stake? Is there a trait of honesty, or are we honest only occasionally? And if we are dishonest occasionally, why are we?

This section reviews some analyses of these questions. As you will see, there are many factors that do affect honesty in children so that there can be no quick answers to these questions.

Honesty as a General Trait

Probably most people assume that individuals who are honest in one situation are likely to be honest in others. We suspect that honesty, in the face of temptation, is generally considered to be an underlying personality trait. Interestingly, however, psychologists have long debated this question. In a classic study, Hartshorne and May (1928) gave 33 different tests to schoolchildren to measure various forms of dishonesty such as lying, cheating, and stealing. They found that there was little correlation between a child's deceitfulness on one type of task and such behavior on another task. Hartshorne and May concluded that, in general, there was little evidence that honesty is an overall trait but rather that children will be honest in some tasks and dishonest in others. One might conclude from these findings that it is not possible to call any child "honest." This emphasis on the specificity of honesty has been challenged, however, and blanket statements about this trait or its lack cannot be made. Burton (1976) points out that when different tests were given within the *same general context,* as in a classroom, and the *form of the deception* was the same, like copying on an examination, children did show consistency in their responses. Thus, while all forms of dishonesty were not highly correlated, some forms were if the methods of deception and the context in which they might occur were similar. Indeed, Burton (1963), using the original data provided by Hartshorne and May, did find evidence for a limited degree of children's consistency in honesty. In a later study, Burton uncovered additional evidence of this limited consistency (Burton, 1976).

There are other ways to look at moral consistency. For example, are moral values or knowledge of accepted standards of honesty correlated with honest behavior? Let us look briefly at the evidence.

Verbal and Behavioral Consistencies in Honesty

The reader may recall from our discussion about altruism that children can readily be taught to be hypocrites, preaching one thing about self-sacrifice, but practicing quite another (Bryan and Walbek, 1970a). This finding suggests that such might also be the case when not altruism, but cheating, lying, and stealing are involved. A variety of studies have been conducted to examine this premise. The usual procedure is to administer a test of moral knowledge or values to the child and then observe how the child actually behaves when tempted to cheat. Other studies obtain peer or teacher ratings of the child's moral conduct and knowledge and then observe the child's actual behavior. What is generally found is an association between moral knowledge and moral conduct, but a very weak one. As Burton writes: "The evidence indicates that there is certainly not a strong relationship between overt behavior and verbal measures such as more judgment, moral knowledge, and values, although the relationship reported tends to be positive" (1976, p. 177). The association between actual behavior and peer and teacher ratings is also positive but very low.

There are many factors tending to divide "lip service" morality and actual behavior. Preaching morality is probably less costly than practicing it (Brown, 1973; Bryan, 1973). It is one thing to verbally condemn cheating on an examination; it is quite another to refrain from doing so when the stakes may be parental or peer disapproval or refusal of admission into college. In effect, talking a moral game is a lot easier than practicing one in the face of temptations. It is perhaps not so surprising either that teacher ratings may not be highly correlated with children's actual conduct since teacher ratings are subject to a variety of biasing effects. For example, Walsh (1967) found that active and curious children who did not cheat were likely to be rated by their teachers as having little self-control. Furthermore, Dion (1972) found that undergraduate females' judgments of young children's honesty were affected by the physical attractiveness of the particular child. While teacher and perhaps peer ratings of a child's honesty are somewhat correlated with the child's conduct, the correlation is not high and the margin of error in judgments is great. If one wished to predict a child's honesty in behavior it would not be desirable to give much weight to the child's statements concerning values, his or her knowledge concerning moral rules, or the opinions of teachers or peers. Perhaps the best way to determine a child's honesty is to observe that youngster's behavior in the face of temptation. Some predictions can then be made concerning whether he or she is likely to be dishonest in a similar situation requiring a similar response.

To sum up the question of consistency in honesty, there is no easy or simple answer. Now we look at situational and personal characteristics that are associated with honesty.

Situational Influences on Honesty

Several situational factors affect children's honesty, including incentives, risks, group norms, and models.

Most people believe that honesty is more difficult when the incentives to cheat are high. Thus, many professors think that college students seeking admission to graduate programs like medicine and law are more likely to cheat in their examinations than students without these aspirations. The incentive to cheat may include a variety of things, such as money or saving face. By and large, common sense is correct. The hitch, though, is understanding the nature of the incentives. For young children material rewards like money or prizes may well induce cheating. For older persons, however, material gains might be less compelling than the temptation to do well on some task. If the individual has some "ego" or "face" at stake in the task, temptations to cheat are greater than if he or she personally has little to gain in mastering the task at hand (Burton, 1976).

A second common sense notion is that deception is more likely when it can be easily concealed. Common sense is right again. Several studies have shown that the greater the risk of discovery, the less likely the cheating (Hartshorne and May, 1928; Canning, 1956).

A third and very important determinant of dishonesty are the norms, or standards, of the individuals with whom the child or young adult is associated. Apparently, a child can hang around with the "wrong crowd" and suffer for it. For example, if one sibling cheats, it is more likely that the other one will than if there were no dishonest siblings (Hartshorne and May, 1928). And the same is true of close friends (Hartshorne and May, 1928). Likewise, cheating among members of a particular organization, such as a fraternity or sorority, increases the likelihood of any group member's cheating. Indeed, Burton (1976) has presented information that leads to the conclusion that group membership may be a better method for predicting deception than extensive information on personality or personal background.

Finally, children's observations of others cheating or deviating is likely to increase their transgressions. For example, Ross (1971) found that children who observed a peer steal were also likely to steal. Wolf and Cheyne (1972) found that children who were in contact with a peer who played with a forbidden toy were more willing also to violate the rules; and this was true not only after immediate exposure to the model but as long as one month later. Finally, Stein and Bryan (1972) found that youngsters exposed to a model who either preached or actually demonstrated rule transgression were more likely to misbehave than those exposed to a model who both advocated and practiced rule adherence. The results of this study suggest that any hints by the model that would endorse transgression are likely to be effective in eliciting cheating, even when the child is aware that it is wrong.

We have seen that models, norms, risks, and incentives, all of which may vary from situation to situation, will play a key part in affecting whether we have an "honest" or "dishonest" child. Given that such factors are often outside the child's control, it is perhaps not so surprising that children are not entirely consistent in their honesty. But which characteristics of the child appear to determine whether behaviors in the classroom or laboratory will be honest or dishonest?

Personal Characteristics Associated with Honesty

Many studies have attempted to tie certain personal characteristics of children to their honesty. Perhaps one of the most frequently studied is that of sex differences in cheating. Interest in such differences was initially stimulated by the theorizing of Sigmund Freud (1933). Showing a bit of male chauvinism, Freud suggested that women have weaker superegos, or senses of values, than men and, therefore, are more likely to be deceitful (Rieff, 1959). On the other hand, many feel that girls are more likely to obey the rules, to be trustworthy, less likely to be dishonest. Evidently many people believe that there are sex differences in children's honesty. Abundant evidence has been gathered showing that girls are more dishonest than boys and, conversely, that boys are more dishonest than girls (Burton, 1976). In fact, the most that can be said about sex differences in honesty is that there are none, and whether girls or boys are the most dishonest depends upon their age, the task, and no doubt a raft of undetermined factors.

A second area of investigation is whether children become more honest with age. It is clear that older children have more sophisticated and complex moral judgments. However, there is not much evidence that their scruples increase with age. Indeed, the correlation between age and honesty is typically found to be rather low. Thus, neither sex nor age seems to be a good predictor of honest conduct.

A third field of study is the relationship between intellectual or academic abilities and honest conduct. There seems to be a good deal of evidence indicating that intelligence and academic ability do accompany children's honesty. By and large, bright and academically successful children do not appear to be dishonest. However, like most things, there is a hook to this generalization. Apparently, bright, achieving students do not cheat on tasks in which they think they will do well. Thus, such children are not likely to cheat on academic tasks, but apparently will on tasks in which they have had little experience or in which they believe they will not perform adequately. The relationship between intelligence and honesty may also be affected by the bright child's more accurate judgment of the risk the deception carries. Intelligent children may not cheat as much as their less able counterparts because they better detect the potential for being discovered. When the probability of detection is very slight, the bright child's dishonesty is increased (Burton, 1976).

It is quite likely that most children try to deceive because of their fear of failure and their strivings to achieve. Children who know that others have done well on a task, that their own performance may become known to others, and who have a strong need to achieve are more likely to cheat than children with other needs and in other circumstances. Indeed, Gilligan (1963) found that youngsters with both a high need to achieve and a great fear of failure cheated the most on an achievement game. Finally, there is evidence that children who show the ability to delay gratification, who are willing to give up a small but immediate reward for a larger reward in the future, are most likely to demonstrate honest behavior when tempted by low risks of detection or strong incentives (Mischel and Gilligan, 1964). Apparently, children's self-control is an important ingredient in maintaining their honesty.

Burton summarizes the literature with the following statement: "Functional relations between moral conduct and certain experimental treatments such as the manipulation of norms, risk, incentive, or modeling and the functional relations between conduct and some motivational measures such as knowledge of others' performance and fear of failure are consistently produced. Many different measures of honesty have been used, and various measures of these independent variables have also been employed; yet the consistency of these functional relationships is impressive" (1976, p. 187). Honesty does not entirely rest within the soul of the individual child but is, in fact, determined by both motives and situational influences.

MORAL JUDGMENTS AND BEHAVIOR

There are several reasons for looking into contemporary views of moral judgments and their relationship to behavior. A firmly entrenched notion is that values or principles so dictate our behavior in many situations that we become relatively immune to immediate pressures within those situations. Values allow us to resist temptation, to spurn positive reinforcements the environment may offer, while we pursue other goals. Values and principles are also thought to facilitate greatly our obstinance in the face of punishment from the environment. Values are thought to be significant in allowing us to become autonomous from the immediate rewards and punishments of our environment.

Many assume that conduct is a simple outgrowth of a person's values or morals, that moral behavior is directly traceable to moral values. It is believed that moral thought dictates moral action. One particular theory of moral development, that proposed by Lawrence Kohlberg, appears to be increasingly influential in dictating classroom practices designed to develop greater moral maturity among the nation's youth. As educators have become more concerned with the moral conduct of students, they have turned to Kohlberg's theory for guidance in curriculum development. Parents and teachers should be familiar with developments in this field, as these developments may well have a direct effect upon them or their offspring.

Assumptions

Kohlberg (1964, 1969, 1976) advanced the notion that understanding moral conduct requires the understanding of moral decision making. He has encouraged research and theorizing concerning the general principles that children use to arrive at moral judgments. He suggests that underlying moral principles are greatly affected by the general cognitive abilities of the child, and that such principles will show predictable changes as the child matures. He thus refers to his approach as cognitive-developmental in nature. While many theorists emphasize the effect of reinforcements, punishments, and models on moral conduct, Kohlberg focuses upon the cognitive, rather than the affective, components of moral training. Moral development is not simply a conditioning process, but is a development that is intimately tied to the child's intellectual development. Kohlberg proposes that children pass through various stages of moral development, depending on the child's use of very different principles in arriving at moral judgments. He argues that the stages are qualitatively different from one another, that they appear in an invariant sequence, and that they are universal. Thus principles at a given stage are not simply extensions of previously held ideas concerning justice or morality, but rather are new principles resulting from the development of new intellectual abilities. Additionally, he believes that moral development proceeds in the same sequence for all people, whether they reside in New Guinea or New York. All people who reach a particular stage must have passed through all the previous stages, and in the proper order.

What are the forces that support this development? First, it is assumed that general improvements in intellectual abilities will provide the foundation for moral change. Second, it is assumed that the motivation for such changes does not reside in fear or anxiety but in motives for acceptance, self-realization, or self-esteem. Third, certain environmental events are thought to be important given the intellectual foundation and the motives for change. One event that is particularly emphasized is the opportunity for role-taking (Kohlberg, 1976). Practice in taking the perspective of another, assuming another person's difficulties, needs, and views, is thought to be an important force in evoking moral change. It is presumed that the child's participation in various groups will provide such role-taking opportunities. Additionally, Kohlberg suggests that moral dialogues between teacher and student, parent and offspring, may facilitate more advanced moral reasoning.

Stages

Kohlberg (1976) indicates that there are six developmental stages of moral judgment. Individuals at Stage 1 of development define what is correct as an avoidance of breaking rules and act properly in order to avoid punishment. Their moral judgments are based upon a principle of punishment avoidance and reinforcement gains, rather than in terms of abstract conceptions of justice, social reciprocity, or caring for others.

Stage 2 morality involves principles revolving around following rules only when it is to your immediate advantage and allowing others to act in a similar manner. What is right depends upon a particular person's self-interests. The rationale for doing right boils down to acting appropriately because it will serve an individual's immediate needs, not because it will enhance the state of humanity or society.

Stage 3 morality has sometimes been referred to as "good boy morality" (Kohlberg, 1969). At this stage, moral judgments are based upon the idea that one should live up to other people's expectations. Being good, maintaining good relationships with authorities one must deal with, and maintaining trust, loyalty, and interpersonal harmony are the principles of individuals demonstrating Stage 3 morality.

While the first three stages are generally limited to those individuals within the immediate environment, Stage 4 morality introduces a more abstract audience. Now the moral principle revolves around the notion that one ought to maintain the social order, to support society's institutions, to keep the system going. The individual takes the point of view of the system and its definition of an individual's duties and obligations.

Stage 5 morality involves a realization that laws are social contracts among people derived for their mutual benefit, and thus they should be supported. There is an emphasis upon the social use of laws and a realization that they may be changed with social consensus. Some values are held to be nonrelative, however, for Stage 5 individuals are said to insist upon the values of life and liberty regardless of majority opinion.

In Stage 6, individuals hold "universal ethical principles." Laws and values are judged upon a set of principles, such as justice, equality of human rights, and respect for others. The principles that determine customs, laws, and values are logically integrated and ultimately reflect the belief that persons are ends in themselves and must be so treated.

Kohlberg writes that "the claim we make is that anyone who interviews children about moral dilemmas and who follows them longitudinally in time would come to our six stages and not others" (1976, p. 47). These stages are thought to capture the entire span of moral development throughout an individual's development. This does not mean to say, however, that all children eventually reach Stage 6. As far as can be determined, most individuals do not advance beyond Stage 4 (Kohlberg, 1969).

Criticisms

In spite of the popularity of Kohlberg's theory of moral development, it has received important criticism. First, there is considerable variation in the applications of principles by any single individual. Individuals are not "pure" stage types. Thus, the same individual may demonstrate a number of Stage 3 and Stage 5 responses even though the majority of responses are at Stage 4 (Mischel and Mischel, 1976). Second, while various verbal measures of judgments correlate reasonably well with one another (Rest, 1976), close correlation between such judgments and actual conduct are infrequent (Mischel and Mischel, 1976). There seems to be considerable evidence that a variety of factors influence behavior other than moral judgments. For example, Bryan and Walbek (1970a) found that children's preachings to others to be generous were virtually uncorrelated with their own generosity. Mischel and Mischel (1976) have argued that moral behavior is dependent upon the rules of conduct or standards held by the child, the anticipated consequences resulting from obtaining these goals, subtle actions, such as a child's instructions to himself, the object and duration of the child's attention within the situation, and the child's plans in the event of confronting positive support or obstacles within the environment. All of these features may well be independent of a particular stage of moral development, and thus a close relationship between moral levels and moral conduct would not be expected. Knowledge of a person's stage of moral judgment does not seem to enable very accurate predictions concerning actual conduct. Indeed, Aronfreed says that there are "some very serious questions about whether any significant amount of moral decision making enters into the internalized control of conduct for most human beings (despite the fact that various states of moral knowledge may be available to them)" (1976, p. 56). We might be overly optimistic to think that just because we train our youth in moral judgment such judgments will consequently govern much of their behavior.

Kohlberg's theory has been attacked on several other grounds as well. One implication of the theory is that moral changes, grounded as they are in cognitive changes and complex social relationships, might be highly resistant to rapid change. It has been demonstrated, however, that changes in moral judgments can be swiftly enacted by group pressures or by observing models with a moral orientation different from that of the observer (Bandura and McDonald, 1963;

Aronfreed, 1968). It is clear that a variety of situational stresses may significantly alter moral conduct in spite of the moral level of the individuals exposed to them (Mischel and Mischel, 1976). Finally, Kohlberg's position has been attacked because of errors of omission. He has neglected the role of affect and conditioning in affecting moral conduct (Aronfreed, 1976), his own theory being too cognitive in orientation.

In spite of these criticisms, we do not believe that moral judgment training of youngsters is worthless. While verbalization of social proprieties, and by inference moral principles, may not be correlated with actual behavior, studies have demonstrated that such statements are important in determining how children view each other (Bryan and Walbek, 1970a,b). Appropriate moral judgments may be an important determinant in affecting children's interpersonal attraction and may even play some role in governing conduct.

SUMMARY

One of the main concerns of parents of both handicapped and non-handicapped children is their socialization, the development of a person who adheres to the rules, laws, and mores of our society. While rhetoric supports the notion that we must turn our children into good citizens, moral education is not usually a formal component of the American public school curriculum. Nonetheless, teachers certainly have to maintain discipline and control in the classroom, and thus do have some investment in the deportment of their charges. In light of current policies favoring the mainstreaming of handicapped children, we introduce an additional note on the need for moral training in the classroom as the degree to which normal children treat handicapped children with compassion, acceptance, and helpfulness is of great import. The integration of handicapped children into regular schools and classrooms seems to us to dictate concern for the humane atmosphere and moral principles being promoted within the home and classroom. Developing children who are helpful and empathic, as well as rule abiding citizens, seems to be a reasonable and desirable goal.

The development of prosocial behavior in children is a complex process. While, in general, some children behave in an honest, cooperative, or altruistic fashion much of the time, they probably do not do so all of the time. Likewise, although some children may be generally dishonest, they are not always so. It is clear that a variety of situational and motivational factors determine much of prosocial behavior. Models, their affect and their power, the nature of the reinforcements, and the competitiveness of the situation may all greatly affect whether the child acts like a saint or a sinner.

But motives are also important, and the need to achieve, to get ahead, to perform well, the risk involved, as well as previous experiences will all shape that child's ability to follow a straight and narrow path. Awareness of these factors and an appreciation of the complexity of the forces affecting moral and prosocial behaviors will, it is hoped, allow us to better implement our programs of moral education for all children, handicapped or not.

Kohlberg has advanced a theory of the development of moral judgment that relates moral judgement to general cognitive development and to the child's motivations for acceptance, self-esteem, or self-realization. Kohlberg has suggested that individuals go through an invariant sequence of moral stages, the highest, or most mature, stage of moral thought being Stage 6. His theory has been criticized on the grounds that most individuals make moral judgments that reflect more than one stage of moral thought, that the theory fails to consider the important influence of immediate environmental influences upon moral judgment and behavior, and that moral judgments do not appear to be highly correlated with moral actions.

REFERENCES

Altman, K. Effects of cooperative response acquisition on social behavior during free play. *Journal of Experimental Child Psychology,* 1971, *12,* 387–395.

Aronfreed, J. *Conduct and conscience: The socialization of internalized control over behavior.* New York: Academic Press, 1968.

Aronfreed, J. Moral development from the standpoint of a general psychological theory. In T. Licona (Ed.), *Moral development and behavior: Theory, research and social issues.* New York: Holt, Rinehart & Winston, 1976.

Azrin, N. H., & Lindsley, O. R. The reinforcement of cooperation between children. *Journal of Abnormal and Social Psychology,* 1956, *52,* 100–102.

Bandura, A. Social-learning theory of identificatory processes. In D. A. Goslin (Ed.), *Handbook of socialization theory and research.* Chicago: Rand McNally and Co., 1969.

Bandura, A., & McDonald, F. J. The influence of social reinforcement in shaping children's moral judgments. *Journal of Abnormal and Social Psychology,* 1963, *67,* 274–281.

Barnett, M., & Bryan, J. H. The effects of competition with outcome feedback on children's helping behaviors. *Developmental Psychology,* 1974, *10,* 838–842.

Baumrind, D. Current patterns of parental authority. *Developmental Psychology Monograph,* 1971, *4,* 1–103.

Blau, B., & Rafferty, I. Changes in friendship status as a function of reinforcement. *Child Development,* 1970, *41,* 113–121.

Bronfenbrenner, U. *Two worlds of childhood: U.S. and U.S.S.R.* New York: Russell Sage Foundation, 1970.

Brotsky, S. J., & Thomas, K. Cooperative behavior in preschool children. *Psychonomic Science,* 1967, *9,* 337–338.

Brown, R. Schizophrenia, language and reality. *American Psychologist,* 1973, *28,* 395–403.

Bryan, J. H. Model affect and children's imitative behavior. *Child Development,* 1971, *42,* 2061–2065.

Bryan, J. H. *You will be well advised to watch what we do instead of what we say.* Paper delivered to the Symposium on Contemporary Issues of Moral Development, Loyola University, Chicago, 1973.

Bryan, J. H. Children's cooperation and helping behaviors. In M. E. Hetherington (Ed.), *Review of child development research* (Vol. 5). Chicago: University of Chicago Press, 1975.

Bryan, J. H., & London, P. Altruistic behavior by children. *Psychological Bulletin,* 1970, *73,* 200–211.

Bryan, J. H., Redfield, J., & Mader, S. Words and deeds about altruism and the subsequent reinforcement power of the model. *Child Development,* 1971, *42,* 1501–1508.

Bryan, J., & Walbek, N. Preaching and practicing sacrifice: Children's actions and reactions. *Child Development,* 1970a, *41,* 329–353.

Bryan, J. H., & Walbek, N. H. The impact of words and deeds concerning altruism upon children. *Child Development,* 1970b, *41,* 747–757.

Burton, R. U. Generality of honesty reconsidered. *Psychological Review,* 1963, *70,* 481–499.

Burton, R. U. Honesty and dishonesty. In T. Lickona (Ed.), *Moral development and behavior: Theory, research and social issues.* New York: Holt, Rinehart & Winston, 1976.

Campbell, D. T. Ethnocentric and other altruistic motives. In D. Levine (Ed.), *Nebraska Symposium on Motivation: 1965.* Lincoln, Neb.: University of Nebrask Press, 1965.

Canning, R. Does an honor system reduce classroom cheating? An experimental answer. *Journal of Experimental Education,* 1956, *24,* 291–296.

Chicago Sun Times. May 24, 1977.

Darley, J. M., & Latané, B. Norms and normative behavior: Field studies of social interdependence. In J. Macauley & L. Berkowitz (Eds.), *Altruism and helping behavior.* New York: Academic Press, 1970.

DePalma, D. J., & Olejnik, A. B. *Effects of social class, moral orientation, and severity of punishment in boys' generosity.* Unpublished manuscript, Loyola University, 1973.

Dion, K. K. Physical attractiveness and evaluation of children's transgressions. *Journal of Personality and Social Psychology,* 1972, *24,* 207–213.

Dlugokinski, B. L., & Firestone, I. J. Other centeredness and susceptibility to charitable appeals: Effects of perceived discipline. *Developmental Psychology,* 1974, *10,* 21–28.

Fraser, S. C., Kelem, R. T., Diener, E., & Beaman, A. L. Two, three or four heads are better than one: Modification of college performance by peer monitoring. Unpublished manuscript, University of Southern California, 1973.

Freud, S. *New introductory lectures on psychoanalysis* (W. J. H. Sproutt, trans.) New York: Norton, 1933.

Friedrich, L. K., & Stein, A. H. Aggressive and prosocial television programs and the natural behavior of preschool children. *Monographs of the Society for Research in Child Development,* 1973, *38* (No. 4), 1–64.

Gilligan, C. F. *Responses to temptation: an analysis of motives.* Unpublished doctoral dissertation, Howard University, 1963.

Gottheil, E. Changes in social perceptions contingent upon competing or cooperating. *Sociometry*, 1955, *18*, 132–137.

Grusec, J. E. Power and the internalization of self-denial. *Child Development*, 1971, *42*, 93–105.

Harford, T., & Cutter, H. S. G. Cooperation among Negro and white boys and girls. *Psychological Reports*, 1966, *18*, 818.

Harris, M. B. Models, norms and sharing. *Psychological Reports*, 1971, *29*, 147–153.

Hartshorne, H., & May, M. A. *Studies in the nature of character.* Vol. 1: Studies in deceit. New York: The Macmillan Co., 1928.

Hetherington, E. M., & Frankie, G. Effects of parental dominance, warmth and conflict on imitation in children. *Journal of Personality and Social Psychology*, 1967, *6*, 119–125.

Kagan, S., & Madsen, M. C. Cooperation and competition of Mexican, Mexican-American, and Anglo-American children of two ages under four instructional sets. *Developmental Psychology*, 1971, *5*, 32–39.

Kohlberg, L. Development of moral character and moral ideology. In M. L. Hoffman & L. W. Hoffman (Eds.), *Review of Child Development Research* (Vol. 1). New York: Russell Sage Foundation, 1964.

Kohlberg, L. Stage and sequence: The cognitive-developmental approach to socialization. In D. A. Goslin (Ed.), *Handbook of socialization theory and research.* Chicago: Rand McNally & Co., 1969.

Kohlberg, L. Moral stages and moralization: The cognitive-developmental approach. In T. Lickona (Ed.), *Moral development and behavior: Theory, research and social issues.* New York: Holt, Rinehart & Winston, 1976.

Lindskold, S., Cullen, P., Gahagan, J., & Tedeschi, J. T. Developmental aspects of reaction to positive inducements. *Developmental Psychology*, 1970, *3*, 277–284.

Macaulay, J., & Berkowitz, L. (Eds.), *Altruism and helping behavior.* New York: Academic Press, 1970.

Madsen, M. C. Cooperative and competitive motivation of children in three Mexican sub-cultures. *Psychological Reports*, 1967, *20*, 1307–1320.

Madsen, M. C., & Shapira, A. Cooperative and competitive behavior of urban Afro-American, Anglo-American, Mexican-American, and Mexican village children. *Developmental Psychology*, 1970, *3*, 16–20.

McKee, J. P., & Leader, F. B. The relationship of socioeconomic status and aggression to the competitive behavior of preschool children. *Child Development*, 1955, *26*, 135–142.

Midlarsky, E., & Bryan, J. H. Training charity in children. *Journal of Personality and Social Psychology*, 1967, *5*, 408–415.

Midlarsky, E., & Bryan, J. H. Affect expressions and children's imitative altruism. *Journal of Experimental Research in Personality*, 1972, *6*, 195–203.

Midlarsky, E., Bryan, J. H., & Brickman, P. Aversive approval: Interactive effects of modeling and reinforcement on altruistic behavior. *Child Development*, 1973, *44*, 321–328.

Mischel, W., & Gilligan, C. Delay of gratification, motivation for the prohibited gratification, and response to temptation. *Journal of Abnormal and Social Psychology*, 1964, *69*, 411–417.

Mischel, W., & Mischel, H. N. A cognitive social-learning approach to morality and self-regulation. In T. Lickona (Ed.), *Moral development and behavior: Theory, research and social issues.* New York: Holt, Rinehart & Winston, 1976.

Mithaug, D. E. The development of cooperation in alternative task situations. *Journal of Experimental Child Psychology,* 1969, *8,* 443–460.

Mithaug, D. E., & Burgess, R. L. The effects of different reinforcement contingencies in the development of social cooperation. *Journal of Experimental Child Psychology,* 1968, *6,* 402–426.

Moore, B. S., Underwood, B., & Rosenhan, D. L. Affect and altruism. *Developmental Psychology,* 1973, *8,* 99–104.

Mowrer, O. H. *Learning theory and personality dynamics.* New York: Ronald Press, 1950.

Nelson, L., & Madsen, M. C. Cooperation and competition in four-year-olds as a function of reward contingency and subculture. *Developmental Psychology,* 1968, *1,* 340–344.

Richmond, B. O., & Weiner, G. P. Cooperation and competition among young children as a function of ethnic grouping, grade, sex, and reward condition. *Journal of Educational Psychology,* 1973, *64,* 329–334.

Rieff, P. *Freud: The mind of the moralist.* New York: The Viking Press, 1959.

Rosenhan, D. L. *Studies in altruistic behavior: Developmental and naturalistic variables associated with charitability.* Paper presented at the meeting of the Society for Research in Child Development, Santa Monica, Calif., 1969 (a).

Rosenhan, D. L. *Determinants of altruism: Observations for a theory of altruistic development.* Paper presented at the meeting of the American Psychological Association, Washington, D.C., 1969 (b).

Rosenhan, D. L., & White, G. M. Observation and rehearsal as determinants of prosocial behavior. *Journal of Personality and Social Psychology,* 1967, *5,* 424–431.

Ross, S. A. A test of the generality of the effects of deviant preschool models. *Developmental Psychology,* 1971, *4,* 262–267.

Rushton, J. P. Generosity in children: Immediate and long-term effects of modeling, preaching and moral judgment. *Journal of Personality and Social Psychology,* 1975, *31,* 459–466.

Rushton, J. P. Socialization and the altruistic behavior of children. *Psychological Bulletin,* 1976, *83,* 898–913.

Sampson, G. G., & Kardush, M. Age, sex, class and race differences in response to a two-person non-zero-zum game. *Journal of Conflict Resolution,* 1965, 212–220.

Schwartz, T., & Bryan, J. H. Imitation and judgments of children with language deficits. *Exceptional Children,* 1971, *38,* 157–158 (a).

Schwartz, T., & Bryan, J. H. Imitative altruism by deaf children. *Journal of Speech and Hearing Research,* 1971, *14,* 453–461. (b).

Severy, L. J., & Davis, K. E. Helping behavior among normal and retarded children. *Child Development,* 1971, *42,* 1017–1031.

Shapira, A., & Madsen, M. C. Cooperative and competitive behavior of kibbutz and urban children in Israel. *Child Development,* 1969, *40,* 609–617.

Sherif, M., Harvey, O. H., White, B. J., Hood, W. R., & Sherif, C. W. *Intergroup conflict and cooperation: The Robbers Cave experiment.* Norman, Okla.: Institute of Group Relations, The University of Oklahoma, 1961.

Silverman, I. W. Incidence of guilt reactions in children. *Journal of Personality and Social Psychology,* 1967, *7,* 338–340.

Staub, E. A child in distress: The influence of nurturance and modeling on children's attempts to help. *Developmental Psychology,* 1971, *5,* 124–132.

Staub, E. *To rear a prosocial child: Reasoning, learning by doing, and learning to teach others.* Paper presented at the conference on Contemporary Issues in Moral Development, Loyola University, Chicago, 1973.

Staub, G. A child in distress: The influence of age and number of witnesses on children's attempts to help. *Journal of Personality and Social Psychology,* 1970, *14,* 130–140.

Stein, G. M., & Bryan, J. H. The effect of a televised model upon rule adoption behavior of children. *Child Development,* 1972, *43,* 268–273.

Vogler, R. E., Masters, W. M., & Morrill, G. S. Shaping cooperative behavior in young children. *Journal of Psychology,* 1970, *74,* 181–186.

Test, M. A. *Children's responses to harm-doing: A behavioral study.* Unpublished dissertation, Northwestern University, 1969.

Walsh, R. P. Sex, age, and temptation. *Psychological Reports,* 1967, *21,* 625–629.

Wasik, B. H., Senn, S. K., & Epanchin, A. Cooperation and sharing behavior among culturally deprived preschool children. *Psychonomic Sciences,* 1969, *17,* 371–372.

Weissbrod, C. S. Noncontingent warmth induction, cognitive style, and children's imitative devotion and rescue effort behaviors. *Journal of Personality and Social Psychology,* 1976, *34,* 274–281.

White, G. M. Immediate and deferred effect of model observation and guided and unguided rehearsal on donating and stealing. *Journal of Personality and Social Psychology,* 1972, *21,* 139–148.

Wispe, L. G. Positive forms of social behavior: An overview. *Journal of Social Issues,* 1972, *28,* 1–19.

Wolf, T. M., & Cheyne, J. A. Persistence of effects of live behavioral, televised behavioral, and live verbal models on resistance to deviation. *Child Development,* 1972, *43,* 1429–1436.

Yarrow, M. R., Scott, P. M., & Waxler, C. Z. Learning concern for others. *Developmental Psychology,* 1973, *8,* 240–260.

KEY TERM

kibbutz A collective farm or settlement in Israel.

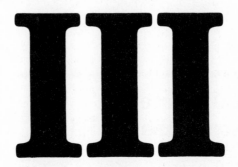

REMEDIATION

**EDUCATIONAL STRATEGIES
FOR THE EXCEPTIONAL CHILD**

PSYCHOLOGICAL REMEDIATION

CHAPTER 12

Educational Strategies for the Exceptional Child

We have described many types of handicapping conditions, conditions that vary in severity, in how they may affect the child and at what age, and in the types of help they demand. So it is that the field of special education has evolved to provide teaching programs for children with such disparate characteristics and learning needs. In this chapter we will introduce the reader to some of the ways in which the field of special education is organized and the methods its workers use in helping handicapped children.

We start with a review of programs developed for preschool exceptional children, following this with a description of the service delivery system for school-aged children: who delivers what services and where. In this connection, we will scan controversies in assessment practices and the relationship of assessment to the design of educational programs for children. Following the description of the service delivery system, we will examine three different areas special education programs cover. The first area to be considered is language intervention. Although designed to meet rather narrow and well-defined educational needs, language intervention programs are appropriate for many different exceptional children. Next, we describe some of the ideas developed within the field of learning disabilities. There is also a discussion of programs for trainable retarded children, those who are in regular schools but segregated classrooms. Finally, we discuss the activities and considerations demanded of regular and special education teachers to facilitate the growth and learning of exceptional children.

EARLY CHILDHOOD EDUCATION

For many years, people have been interested in early childhood education. Programs for children from birth to 8 years of age have been on the scene for centuries. What is new, however, is the considerable interest of the government in early childhood education. Since 1965, with the initiation of the Head Start programs, the government has been providing legislation and funds establishing programs for the very young child that were hoped to have a broad impact upon children's lives (Peters, 1977). Since then the government has been attempting to circumvent the vicious and destructive cycle of poverty leading to educational, physical, and social deprivation that, in turn, locks the disadvantaged child into a life of poverty. While large-scale federal intervention was originally prompted by the desire to help the child of poverty-stricken parents to obtain adequate nourishment and intellectual stimulation, the government's concern has been extended to trying to help all preschool age children whose personal or social circumstances require it.

Before going into a discussion of programs for the disadvantaged and the exceptional child, a discussion of some of the basic assumptions underlying these programs is warranted. It is commonly assumed that the earlier problems can be identified and treated, the more the child will benefit. The benefits are derived from alleviation of the debilitating condition and from the prevention of the secondary stresses it brings. A secondary assumption is that children go through critical developmental periods during which they are particularly able to develop various skills. If the child passes through the critical periods without acquiring the skills, it is thought, the more difficult it will be to acquire them later. For example, motor and language development may be subject to some kinds of critical period effects. A third and related assumption is that children are relatively susceptible to remediation efforts and that early intervention is likely to be more effective in mitigating the difficulty than later attempts.

We will now turn to some of the general approaches used to help the disadvantaged or poor child, and then look at more recent special education practices for the preschool youngster.

TYPES OF EARLY CHILDHOOD EDUCATION PROGRAMS

Early childhood education has been defined as a "pragmatic effort in which an agent, operating within a context, uses some means, according to some plan to bring about changes in the behavior of children between birth and age eight in terms of some definable criteria" (Peters, 1977, p. 2). It is clear from the definition that various early childhood education programs can take very different theoretical forms. In the following sections, we will discuss some of the philosophies and personnel guiding these programs.

Perspectives and People

There are at least three different philosophical approaches that guide workers and programs in early childhood education. One perspective can be termed the **maturationalist-socialization** approach wherein it is believed that the school program should provide an atmosphere in which the child's kindness and skills can "naturally unfold." The curriculum accompanying this somewhat Rousseau-like perspective is often unstructured, allowing the child to do pretty much his or her "own thing." The curriculum may consist primarily of activities emphasizing role-playing, drama, and creative arts. What appears important to those who believe in the "unfolding" approach is providing the child with a warm, nonthreatening environment so that his or her development will not be inhibited by interpersonal fears and constraints.

A second approach often reflected in early childhood education programs can be termed the **behavioristic approach.** In these programs, care is taken to define the behaviors that should be instilled and the specific nature of the reinforcements that will be used. The curriculum is likely to be highly structured and focus upon teaching the child skills that will be important in subsequent academic and social life.

A third perspective is the **cognitive-developmental** one, a viewpoint that has been influenced by Piaget's theory of intellectual and cognitive development. This perspective is likely to focus upon the child's abilities to conceptualize the world and to provide stimulation for encouraging these abilities. Curricula might involve many tasks in which the child would code and classify objects.

The personnel employed in early childhood education programs include professional teachers (that is, certified teachers), paraprofessionals, and parents. There are several major differences between regular school and early education programs with regard to personnel. One is that early education teachers are not necessarily certified. Thus, their educational experiences and skills may vary considerably in breadth and depth from those of a regular schoolteacher. A second difference involves the parents. Parents are more frequently included in the activities of the early childhood education program than they are in regular public school programs. Thus, there are early childhood programs in which the teacher sets up a plan for the child that is implemented in the home. That is, the teacher helps the parent become a teacher. Other programs give parents the opportunity to meet in groups where they discuss and receive training in child-rearing and their children's educational program. In other instances the parents observe activities in the classroom and assist in curriculum development. Finally, assorted combinations of parental involvements may be implemented.

Effectiveness of Early Childhood Programs

While the specific impact of early childhood education programs is still a matter of some debate, there is evidence that they benefit the children who participate. Reviewing studies of the effectiveness of home based early childhood educational programs, Peters (1977) suggests that children who attend these programs have shown gains in their intelligence test scores, more responsiveness to people, greater social maturity, and fewer school problems than would have been expected had they not participated in such programs. Interestingly, even mothers and siblings of participating children may undergo changes as a result of a child's early schooling. Peters (1977) cites studies that indicate that mothers are likely to emphasize communication and success more, are more accepting and accessible to their children, show greater sensitivity and responsiveness to their children's requests, use more reasoning and praise, and show an increase in verbal interactions with their children than would be expected if their children were not in the program. Moreover, Peters indicates that the mothers of children in a home based program apparently change their behaviors in other ways as well. These mothers are more likely to enroll in courses designed to improve their own skills, become more interested in the community, and express a greater desire to improve their living conditions than mothers not involved in educational programs. Peters writes: "In general, mothers who participate in the programs gain a sense of environmental mastery. They gain confidence in their own abilities and become hopeful instead of hopeless" (pp. 13–14).

That early intervention might offset the debilitating effects of early deprivation is illustrated by a study conducted by Campbell and Ramey (1977). These investigators assessed disadvantaged children at ages 6, 12, 18, 24, and 36 months. When first tested, children attending the early education program did not differ in their test scores from children outside the program. By 18 months of age, however, the two groups of children began to achieve very different test scores, with participating children showing superiority to nonparticipating ones. The group attending the intervention program thereafter maintained their intellectual levels, while the nonparticipating children demonstrated a sharp decline in test scores beginning about their second year of life. The latter group of children never did match the participating children in test scores. The differences between these groups of children were most marked in assessments of language and perceptual-motor skills.

The early childhood programs we have discussed have involved children from poverty-stricken families. We now turn to programs designed for the handicapped child.

Early Childhood Special Education Programs

With the advent of early childhood programs came a shift away from institutionalizing the handicapped child to that of providing community based programs. The movement toward community programs is warranted by beliefs and data about the effects of institutionalization upon children. For example, there seems to be little doubt that institutional life is likely to hamper seriously the mentally retarded youngster's subsequent intellectual development (Kirk, 1958; Heber and Dever, 1970). Preschool education for the exceptional child is now becoming a major area of community, parental, and professional investment. This means that education, or some kind of intervention, is likely to be initiated the instant the child comes to the attention of professionals who provide care. The emphasis is no longer simply on physical care for the handicapped preschooler, but rather includes a focus upon the child's educational needs as well.

FIGURE 12-1 Child taking part in an early childhood special education program

Program of Infant Intervention

Perhaps the most extensive evaluation of infant intervention programs is that conducted by Heber and his colleagues in Milwaukee. In this study,
training was provided to very poor mothers, all with intelligence test scores below
75, and their children. The likely inheritance of low intelligence and poverty put
these children at risk for handicaps, in particular, mental retardation. Hence the
program was one of preventive intervention. To determine if an intervention program
would be effective in preventing mental retardation, another comparable group of
mothers did not take part in an intervention program, but were observed during the
same period. From the child's birth to about 3 months of age, a teacher would come
daily to the house and work with the mother and baby. During this period the
teacher would instruct the mother in how to interact verbally and physically with
the infant. After the infant reached about 3 months of age, the mother and child
attended a program at a center during which time the child was stimulated with
verbal interactions and play activities. At about 2 years of age, the child entered an

all-day program in which several adults worked with small groups of children. Language stimulation, problem solving activities, science and art, free play, Sesame Street, field trips, and food were part of the curriculum. Meanwhile, mothers were given various forms of vocational training.

Effectiveness of Infant Intervention

The impact of the treatment program was assessed by measuring the child's language and intellectual development; these skills were evaluated every six weeks, from the time the children reached 18 months of age until they were 3 years old. When participating and nonparticipating children were compared, it was found that the former group were more advanced than the latter in both language and intellectual development. Most striking were group differences in intelligence. By the time the children were 3 years and 7 months old, the treated group had, on the average, intelligence test scores 33 points higher than those obtained by children who were not in the education program (Garber and Heber, 1973). In a later study, the intelligence test scores of the two groups were compared when they reached 9 years of age. The children who had participated in the educational program still had intelligence test scores that were more than 20 points higher on the average than those obtained by nonparticipating children.

Heber and his colleagues have not been the only ones to try to help the handicapped preschool youngster. For example, Diane and William Bricker have devised a program designed to aid children with severe, profound, and multiple handicaps. Their plan serves to illustrate how an early intervention program for young handicapped children might function.

The Infant, Toddler, and Preschool Research and Intervention Project

Bricker and Bricker (1973) developed an extensive and intensive program for serving handicapped children. The children being served, at the time of this 1973 report, were from 4 months to 6 years of age, and were suffering from a variety of handicaps. These ranged from minor delays in their physical and/or mental development to severe deficits. While one-half of the children within the program were developmentally disabled, the remaining children were not. Thus, the inclusion of "normal" children constituted a part of the intervention program.

This approach to intervention attempts to integrate the best of various theories concerning human development. While Piagetian influence can be seen in the delineation of the behavior to be assessed, operant conditioning techniques serve as intervention tools. From one-half day to four days a week the children in the project take part in programs based on a test-teach cycle. Using a developmental screening technique, the point at which the child begins to fail defines the point where the intervention program begins. For example, the infant's visual tracking and search capacities are assessed by 12 actions, ranging from fixating on an object to following an object visually as it falls. The point at which the child fails to respond correctly defines the point where treatments will be designed and initiated to overcome this failure.

Parents are also brought into the program. They are trained in small groups to use behavior management techniques and apply them to the areas of motor, language, and social development. In addition, they are given training in consumer education as well as in techniques for dealing with school officials in order to obtain programs for their children. Parents are also asked to specify what they want their children to learn as well as to assist in the development of the program, monitor its effects, and subsequently to evaluate it.

There are several notable features of this program. First, the Brickers attempt to establish the developmental level of the child with reference to these levels described in Piagetian terms. A second point concerns the involvement of parents. Parents' involvement is necessary for a variety of reasons. First, there simply are not enough trained professionals to go around. Parents thus become professional substitutes. Additionally, the Brickers believe that the parent is the person with the most opportunity and power to administer reinforcements to the child.

The final noteworthy feature of the program is its inclusion of non-handicapped children. The rationale for this integration is that it provides the disabled child the opportunity to observe the behavior of nondisabled peers. Adaptive imitation by the disabled child is therefore a possibility that might well be denied him or her in many other settings. The integrated program provides parents of the handicapped with the opportunity to educate the parents of normal children to their goals as well as to the difficulties and stresses burdening them and their other family members. Given the current goals of maintaining handicapped children in their home communities, virtually any form of raising the consciousness of the parents of sound children should be helpful to handicapped children and their families.

We have, to this point, described some research and programs related to relatively severe handicapping conditions, that is, poverty and developmental difficulties. We now turn our attention to early educational efforts for high risk children, those who give us reason to assume that they will have academic deficiencies but who do not show visible or severe sensory, motor, or intellectual losses.

The Mildly Handicapped

There is increasing concern in the United States for the detection and treatment of children who appear likely candidates for future academic failure, even though they suffer no obvious impairment. Indeed, in the past few years there has been a great proliferation of testing instruments designed to detect such children even in the preschool years. As is often the case, society's concern has preceded the development of adequate technology.

Problems in Early Detection and Intervention

Efforts to detect and help children for whom future academic difficulties are predicted are accompanied by some rather unique problems. First, it is not clear how such predictions can be made. Just which tools, what procedures, and which rate of false negative and false positive diagnoses should be employed in the detection procedures? Secondly, there is the problem of labeling the child as high risk and so producing a self-fulfilling prophesy. Once a child is diagnosed as being at high risk, will that diagnosis produce reactions from others that increase the likelihood the child will become an academic failure?

Parents and teachers should be alert to both the possible dangers and the benefits to the child from this new emphasis upon the early detection and remediation of high risk children (Keogh & Becker, 1973). As Wolfensberger writes: "Early diagnosis is desirable when it leads to prevention, early treatment, or constructive counseling; it is irrelevant if it is purely academic and does not change the course of events; it is harmful if, in balance, child or family reap more disadvantages than benefits" (1965, p. 65).

There are some indications that given a fairly precise identification of the type of problem, and an intervention procedure addressed to that problem, early treatment programs for high risk children might be beneficial. For example, Luick and Feshbach (1974) provided high risk first and second grade children with training in a task requiring them to remember visual stimuli in proper sequence and found that the training so increased the children's performance that they were on a par with "normal" children. In another instance, Friar (1972) categorized children at high risk in two groups. One group was found to have difficulty with perceptual discrimination, while the other appeared to have behavior and attention problems. Half of each group were provided attentional training, while the other half were given exercises in perceptual discrimination. The children received only 15 minutes of training in two days. Following this they were administered a learning task and a discrimination task. The group weak in perceptual discrimination who received training in that ability did best on the perceptual discrimination task; while the behavior/attention group that received attention training on the vigilance task performed best on the learning task. The data did support the notion that intervention designed to meet the needs of the individual deficit could have benefits for the child, even when the intervention is of short duration.

Integrating Mothers into Intervention Programs

A study of preschool children identified as being at high risk for school failure underscores the possible benefits of integrating mothers into the training program. Abbott and Sabatino (1975) identified children who, on a test of visual-motor development, were at least 1½ years below the level indicated by their age. Each child's mother volunteered to work 20 minutes a day with her child on a program of visual motor development. The mothers participated in parent training, then administered daily training exercises to the child while continuing to attend weekly in-service training sessions. After 10 weeks it was found that the children who received help from their mothers made significantly greater gains on a test of visual motor development than a group of children who did not receive such assistance. In addition it was found that the more time the mothers and children spent on the daily exercises, the more progress the child made.

Teacher's Influences

When we reviewed the programs for preschool children, it was clear that the influence of the mother's interactions with the child can be critical. In the same vein the influence of the first teachers with whom the young child interacts in school may be quite critical in determining whether the child becomes a potential school failure. This is not to say that teachers cause children's developmental problems. Sometimes this is the case, but most likely the complex interactions 'between teacher and child are critical in exacerbating or alleviating the child's problem. For example, in a very extensive study conducted by Feshbach, Adelman, and Feller (1974) concerning the prediction of reading problems, it was found that of the many measures used for forecasting, one significant predictor was the amount of time the teacher spent teaching small groups and individuals relative to total class instruction. The greater the time in small group and individual instruction, the greater the child's subsequent reading achievements. Additionally, Feshbach et al. reported that the students of first grade teachers who value reading skills attain higher levels of reading in the second grade than those students of teachers who do not prize reading as highly. Certainly the next decade should bring more knowledge about the early detection and intervention strategies relevant to those children who are likely to be school failures.

SPECIAL EDUCATION STRATEGIES FOR SCHOOL-AGE CHILDREN

We often assume that differential learning programs for exceptional children are the core of special education, an assumption implying that special education has a technology different from that used to teach nonhandicapped children. There are certain characteristics of special education intervention that should be mentioned at the outset. First, educational technology is more advanced for some types of exceptionalities than for others. While teaching methods are still controversial, there is probably less controversy about dealing with physical and sensory handicaps than about dealing with learning disabilities and mental retardation.

Second, Public Law 94-142 not only requires us to develop an educational technology that specifies the child's strengths and deficits, but also compels us to provide intervention plans that reflect the academic curriculum of the school, say, in social studies, science, and library use. Because of this, special education is in a state of flux, the shift in policy is beginning to produce changes in diagnostic procedures and, we hope, improvements and advances in educational technology for exceptional children.

Since any education program can be no stronger than the people carrying it out, a good place to begin our discussion of intervention programs for exceptional children of school age is with a look at the types of professionals likely to provide the diagnosis, educational planning, and intervention these children need.

Special Education Services

Among the many professionals helping the handicapped, the special education teacher is likely to have the most extensive contact with the exceptional child. These teachers give instruction to individuals or small groups of children whose educational needs cannot be met by a regular teacher within the regular classroom context. They are expected to provide diagnostic and instructional help to exceptional children. With growing numbers of exceptional children participating in regular school programs, the role of the special education teacher is expanding. In addition to giving direct services to some children, the special education person is expected to function as a resource for the classroom teacher by providing additional materials, restructuring classroom exercises and activities, and giving the child extra time. Special education teachers are typically trained in universities and colleges and certified by the state as expert in a particular handicap, for example, mental retardation or deafness.

Speech and Language Specialists

Another important group of professionals provide speech and language training. Speech and language pathologists conduct screening programs to determine which children in the primary grades might require help. They deal directly with the children in correcting speech and language problems; they also provide materials to regular and special education classroom teachers and consult with them. Therapeutic services are rendered to children who have difficulty understanding what is told to them (language comprehension) or articulating what they wish to say (stutterers) and to those with voice problems such as excessive hoarseness. Currently, the trend in educational requirements for professionals is to obtain a master's degree, although this varies from state to state.

Psychologists

The school psychologist provides a number of evaluative and assistance services. The children with whom the psychologist typically interacts are referred because their teachers suspect they have serious psychological problems.

Although serving primarily as a diagnostician, spending much time administering and interpreting psychological tests, the school psychologist also counsels both children and parents as well as regular classroom teachers. By and large, most school psychologists are required to have a master's degree and many have earned their doctorates.

Social Workers

Not infrequently school districts employ a school social worker. The social worker's function includes the identification of children having problems, the development and sometimes coordination of a case study involving an individual child, and liaison work between the family and other services available outside of the school. In addition, they often counsel parents, coordinate community resources for the child, and locate nonschool services for which the child might be eligible. Social workers usually possess a master's degree.

Other Specialists

Additional specialists are often available as needed. Specialists are provided by schools for children with physical and sensory handicaps, but since these problems are rare, several school districts are likely to share the financial costs and services of such specialists. For children with visual problems, school districts retain persons who will read to the child, teachers of braille, typists to produce material in either braille or large type. In effect, personnel are provided to translate educational materials into a form that the visually impaired or the blind child might utilize. Physical and occupational therapists are provided for the child whose physical difficulties require therapeutic attention in addition to an educational program. Similarly, there are professionals who specialize in helping hearing impaired persons. There are audiologists trained to assess hearing impairments, and teachers trained to develop and implement programs that take into account the special problems faced by hearing impaired children.

Psychiatric and medical consultants are also available on demand. If needed in the diagnostic assessment of a child, medical and psychiatric examinations can be obtained at the expense of the school district. Long-term psychiatric and medical treatments, however, are not the responsibility of the school district and cost of such procedures will not be paid entirely by the district.

Decisions

Before the specialists described above can bring their expertise into play for the benefit of a particular child, there must be a decision making process to bring expert and child together. Let us trace the steps in this decision making process. The exact nature of decision making differs somewhat from district to district depending on who is responsible for what in the particular school system. In addition, the process varies with the nature of the problem. Many sensory defects and physical impairments are likely to be detected before the child is enrolled in school as many school districts conduct screening programs for preschoolers and school-aged children in order to detect these defects as well as learning and behavior problems. However, many children with learning disabilities, educable mental retardation, and behavior disorders are likely to have problems that are noticed and treated only after the child has entered school.

Screening

The flow of services for special education evaluations and placement might be something like this. First, school districts sometimes have district-wide programs in which the public is alerted to the problem of exceptional children, especially very young preschool children. The goal is to find preschoolers and screen them for existing or potential problems. Some districts provide preschool programs for those children deemed likely to have academic difficulties. These public information programs, screenings, and services are often the first step in the school district's special education services to the child.

Referral

The second step is the referral process. Referrals can be initiated by anyone—parents, teachers, social workers, or the court. The age, socio-economic level and race of the child, plus the severity of the problem may affect the who, when, and why of referrals. Age, socioeconomic level, and race are probably more significant for the less visible types of handicaps such as learning disabilities, educable mental retardation, and behavior disorders than they are for sensory deficits and physical impairments. It should be stressed that the referral process is a complex one. For instance, some kinds of children in some communities are over-referred for special services. As discussed in Chapter 5, minority group children, Black or with Spanish surnames, have been overreferred for placement in classes for the retarded (Mercer, 1973). On the other hand, affluent and/or well-educated families are more likely to seek and demand services for their children than poorer, less-educated families (Rowitz, 1973). The distribution of resources, therefore, seems related to several factors external to the specific problems of the child. The bias in the distribution of resources and referrals is a factor that teachers and others should consider when dealing with a problem child.

Evaluation

Once the referral process is initiated, conferences occur among the teacher and principal and/or special educator. Discussions center around the nature of the specific problem as well as any other information that might be relevant to the child's personality, academic progress, and social development. Additionally, these educators may analyze the particular curriculum and learning styles of the child, and consider how these might be changed to improve school performance. If then it is assumed that extensive special educational services are required, the school district must obtain the approval of the child's parents before either testing the child or altering his or her educational program. It is the school district's responsibility to inform the parents, in their native language, of the results of the school's evaluation of the child and of the proposed plans for remediation. Should parental consent not be forthcoming, the school district's personnel can either drop plans to provide special services to the child or initiate action, in accordance with PL 94-142, to override the parents' objection.

Specialists

If further evaluation and special plans are to be implemented, several specialists may become involved. A psychologist or social worker may interview the child and observe the child's classroom behaviors. The school nurse, social worker, or psychologist may obtain the child's medical and developmental history through interviews with the parents. Questions concerning these histories can be far-ranging. Medical information may include the child's past illnesses, accidents, and operations. Questions for a developmental history will focus on the mother's health during pregnancy, and the ages of the child's early developmental milestones such as sitting, walking, talking, and toilet training. Information is also obtained concerning the child's visual and hearing competencies.

The Task of the Psychologist

The most extensive part of the evaluation concerns the child's psychological status. The school psychologist is typically the person responsible for evaluating the child's academic and emotional status. Based on a variety of standardized tests and observations of the child, the psychologist may designate the diagnostic category that best describes the child, the nature of the most promising treatment, and perhaps make some predictions about the child's future academic performance.

Assessments

There is considerable concern and some controversy over the evaluation of the child's psychological and academic status. The controversy stems from two sources: the discriminatory nature of psychological tests and the type and relevance of information yielded by standardized tests. With respect to the former, Public Law 94-142 mandates that assessment not be such that children from disadvantaged or minority culture populations are overidentified as handicapped. The law states that school districts in the states must develop:

> Procedures to assure that testing and evaluation materials and procedures utilized for the purposes of evaluation and placement of handicapped children will be selected and administered so as not to be racially or culturally discriminatory. Such materials or procedures shall be provided and administered in the child's native language or mode of communication, unless it clearly is not feasible to do so, and no single procedure shall be the sole criterion for determining an appropriate educational program for the child. (Sec. 615-5c)

Psychologists have not been able to identify tests that are culture-fair; they have yet to agree even on what constitutes fairness (Ysseldyke, 1977). Since there is evidence that pupil characteristics of race, sex, socioeconomic status, and physical attractiveness influence decisions made about children, we are under considerable pressure to mend our decision making ways. In the absence of culture-fair assessment devices, school personnel are being very conscientious in trying to reduce or eliminate human bias in assessment.

The second source of controversy arises from the instruments used to measure disabilities. Assessment is the first step in the development of an intervention program; thus, the techniques used often serve as the foundation for decisions about curriculum. When tests are used for clinical assessments, several goals underlie their use. Ysseldyke (1977) has outlined five purposes of assessment:

1. to identify those children who need further evaluation
2. to classify children properly and indicate the degree and nature of their handicaps
3. to plan the educational program for the child; to delineate the skills that the child can be expected to acquire
4. to evaluate the child's progress within a particular program
5. to evaluate the school program's adequacy in providing an education to students

Controversy over Assessments

Disagreements about assessment revolve around the second and third uses of testing: the means whereby classification and placement decisions are made and the manner in which the educational curriculum is developed. To make classification and placement decisions, psychologists typically administer tests of intelligence and achievement that are norm-referenced. That is, they compare the child's performance with that of many other children of the same age from various sections of the country. Even when the assessments employed are of adequate reliability and validity, the number of false positives and false negatives possible in their clinical use may be rather high. This is a legitimate concern. On the other hand, others may be equally concerned that the failure to use such tests in making decisions will open the way for less reliable and less valid procedures.

There is also controversy as to which assessments should be used in planning a particular child's educational program. Some believe that evaluation should analyze the child's abilities; others argue that such procedures should detect the child's academic strengths and weaknesses (Ysseldyke and Salvia, 1974).

The argument advanced for ability assessment is that certain faculties are a prerequisite for sufficient academic performance, that we know what some of these are, and that they can be adequately assessed. Ability training programs are based upon the idea that the inadequacies in ability have been identified, that they can be altered, and that such improvements will enhance academic achievement.

According to Ysseldyke (1977), the task analysis focuses on remediation of the academic skills the child does not demonstrate. In this case standardized tests are not used; rather the intervention program is built on the academic achievement area in which the child is failing. The assumption is made that the child's success or failure is related to an interaction between characteristics of the child and characteristics of the task. The task analysis process is a test-teach-retest model in which the child is repeatedly tested in order to assess frequently the efficacy of the intervention strategies. In this approach, the teaching is tied to the testing in a continuous recycling of assessment and instruction. This is a data-based approach to teaching that is very attractive to those concerned with the development of educational programs and the assessment of the value of these programs. However, measurements of task performance under these conditions can also be unreliable and yield misleading information. For instance, how often does a child have to be tested on a particular skill before one can assume that the child has mastered the material? If the testing is too infrequent, the reliability is reduced. What cut-off point marks acceptable progress? Should the child obtain 80 percent, 90 percent, or 60 percent correct responses before the child can move on to another skill level? If the child's educational pacing is determined solely by his or her responses, the teacher can lose sight of where other children have progressed and set standards that are too low or too high, even for that child. While the task analysis approach helps us solve some of the problems encountered in other approaches, we cannot forget that the assessment in it may also have limited reliability and validity.

Finally, it is noteworthy that while the psychological assessment procedures for classification and placement have been of central importance in the evaluation of children, their role may be diminishing. First, those involved in classroom instruction often do not obtain information from psychologists that could aid them in developing educational curricula. Additionally, Public Law 94-142 mandates that children be maintained in the least restrictive educational environment and that an individual education plan for each child be developed. With increasing emphasis on maintaining children in regular classrooms, there is less need for placement decisions and ever-increasing need for the development of good educational plans. Third, the law dictates that the use of standardized psychological tests cannot be the sole source of information about children; that observations in the classroom must be employed and that decisions must be made on the basis of multiple measures. Hence, professionals in addition to the school psychologist must take part in the decision making process regarding special services for the particular child.

The Individual Education Plan

This brings us to Public Law 94-142's mandate for individual education plans (IEP). The IEP is defined as

> A written statement of each handicapped child developed in any meeting by a representative of the local educational agency or an intermediate educational unit who shall be qualified to provide, or supervise the provision of, specially designed instruction to meet the unique needs of handicapped children, the teacher, the parents or the guardian of such child, and, whenever appropriate, such child, which statement shall include (A) a statement of the present levels of educational performance of such child, (B) a statement of annual goals, including short-term instructional objectives, (C) a statement of the specific educational services to be provided to such child, and the extent to which such child will be able to participate in regular educational programs, (D) the projected date for initiation and anticipated duration of such services, and appropriate objective criteria and evaluation procedures and schedules for determining, on at least an annual basis, whether instructional objectives are being achieved [P. L. 94-142, 1975, Sec. 4, a, 19].

To develop an IEP some assumptions have to be made concerning the nature of the child's problem.

Assessment Requirements of an IEP

The requirements of an IEP may significantly alter the means of assessing youngsters. For example, the first stipulation is a statement of the present levels of the child's educational performance. While one can argue that standardized achievement and ability tests might well serve to provide such information, others involved in special education believe that assessments for this purpose should be directed toward the current classroom behaviors of the child being evaluated. The critical elements in suggested revisions of assessment are that the assessment should (1) simulate actual instruction and learning, (2) focus on academic products (for example, reading skills) and processes of learning (such as memory, attention) that are relevant to classroom activities, and (3) include an evaluation of the conditions under which the child learns successfully (for example, instructional method, curriculum). Kratochwill (1977) provides an example of how assessments might be altered to meet these goals. He suggests we use diagnostic teaching, which is essentially the task analysis approach. This involves teaching the child the curriculum under different conditions and then deciding which conditions foster the greatest increase in learning. For instance, if the child is to learn new vocabulary words, some of the words may be presented orally and others visually, with the child responding orally, in writing, by pointing to pictures, and/or by generating sentences with the new vocabulary. Assessment would consist of short sessions of trial teaching. The steps followed are to determine what the child already knows, how he or she learns new information, how the child's rate of learning may be affected by the way the information is presented, and the influence upon learning of various child and teacher responses.

Short- and Long-term Goals Specified

The second requirement of the IEP is that short- and long-term instructional goals be specified. "Short-term instructional goals" can be construed as a synonym for improved methods of presenting lesson plans. Teachers traditionally are expected to develop lesson plans and these lesson plans are supposed to reflect the daily goals of instruction. Specifying short-term instructional goals should not be difficult and should permit us to evaluate the program's effectiveness more easily and more systematically.

It is noteworthy, however, that there are frequently a number of shortcomings in traditional lesson plans. One problem has been that they have been written in "shorthand"; that is, teachers often list page numbers in workbooks on which children are to work. A second problem is that they are often phrased in jargon ("The child shall work on visual-motor skills") rather than in language describing the actual activity ("The child shall practice cursive writing"). Specifying short-term instructional goals should force us to be more specific in stating what the child will work on and what will be the expected outcome.

A statement of long-term goals is going to be risky unless the teacher and special education staff have a data base upon which to predict the child's rate of progress through the curriculum. The danger in requiring statements of long-term goals that can be understood by parents and others is that their developers will tend to be very conservative in their long-range estimates. It is not likely that they will "shoot for the moon" when they might be liable to a lawsuit for failure to deliver the promised results. In addition, the statement of goals may reflect only what the staff are sure they can improve and fail to outline goals for difficult problems. For instance, the child's main problem may be maladaptive behavior, but the stated aims may be limited to academic objectives.

The IEP mandates that a statement indicate the where and who of educating the child. Many types of professionals, offering many kinds of educational services, may be involved in the assessment and intervention plan for the exceptional child. Speech therapists, social workers, psychologists, reading teachers, learning disability specialists, and other special educators are among the types of professionals who might be called in to assist the child. The point is that the educational plan, the IEP, must state who shall provide services. In addition, the plan must specify whether the child will be receiving the education in a regular classroom or a self-contained special education facility, and how much time and service the child shall receive from other professionals.

To specify the educational services and the projected date at which the child will begin and finish a special education program requires changes in educational planning, as in assessment procedures. To comply with these two requirements, special education teachers and regular classroom teachers must become data-oriented. Both groups of teachers have to be able to specify daily instructional target behaviors, revise their instruction on the basis of these data, and demonstrate through the accumulation of such information exactly what has been accomplished through the intervention program. It is not known to what extent a data-based orientation toward teaching prevails in this country; but it is believed that once both regular and special education teachers become facile and comfortable with data-based educational planning and evaluation, they will be able to contribute to the development of better educational technology.

Technical Assistance

To comply with Public Law 94-142, to cope with heterogeneous groups of children, to provide adequate education simultaneously for children with different needs and to manage the work load places a heavy burden upon the classroom teacher. This burden has been increasingly recognized and there has been speculation as to how it might be lightened. For example, Lance (1977) has suggested that computer technology may be of considerable aid to the teacher as it can facilitate matching the child's educational needs to curriculum, help find educational materials, and simplify the evaluation and reporting of the educational outcomes of the program. Indeed, there have been a number of computer programs designed to help teachers plan and provide instruction. The Wisconsin System of Instructional Management (CMI) is a system in which tests and observational data are stored and through which achievement profiles, educational needs, and information about needed materials are available.

A less technical form of professional assistance is available to teachers through the resource centers established around the country. There are about 800 special education learning resource centers around the United States, staffed by personnel who are well acquainted with educational materials, media, and technological advances being made for intervention strategies (Lance, 1977). Certainly, teachers should avail themselves of these free services.

Additionally, there have been, and will continue to be, technological innovations to help the sensorily impaired child. For example, there are a number of devices to help visually impaired persons. Video tape systems can now be used to present materials in enlarged formats through closed circuit television. It is also possible to design this system as an interactive video system so that the student can call up the material when it is convenient. The Kurzweil Reading Machine, now under development, is being designed to convert printed words into synthetic speech. To help hearing impaired persons, there are call-type telephones and calculators that have a speech output.

By and large it appears that most teachers are not keeping abreast of the various technical advances made in education. Indeed, classroom teachers spend less than one percent of their working day in selecting instructional materials, suggesting an overwhelming lack of interest in such tasks (Lance, 1977). Moreover, it is unlikely that school administrators are forcing teachers to address themselves to educational advances. Perhaps administrators are unwilling to spend money for what they may see as unproven gadgetry or are concerned about burdening any further their teachers. It may be that teachers feel threatened by technology, or that they are simply too busy or indifferent to such advances. Whatever the reason, teachers do not take full advantage of the opportunities to learn about recent developments and to use them in their everyday classroom work.

Placements

Once it has been decided that the child's problems require special attention, considerations of educational placement become paramount. There are several different settings and procedures that can meet the child's educational needs.

One possibility is that the child be enrolled in a special facility designed to help youngsters with a particular handicap. Thus, vision or hearing impaired children may be placed in a school setting planned for children with their handicaps. A second possibility is that the child's formal education take place primarily in a special class conducted in a regular school by a teacher specially trained in the child's problem area. Thus, the child may be placed in a classroom for educable mentally retarded, learning disabled, or the emotionally disturbed.

Mainstreaming

Currently, there is considerable emphasis upon integrating the exceptional child into the regular school classroom; that is, mainstreaming the exceptional child. When exceptional children are mainstreamed, they may receive their formal education either totally or partially in a classroom of their nonhandicapped peers. The child's problems may then be dealt with by the specialist consulting with the teacher and providing that teacher with advice and materials needed to manage the child in the classroom. Frequently the child who needs special help remains in the classroom but receives supplementary aid periodically from a special teacher.

Such help is typically given in a setting other than the regular classroom, a setting usually referred to as a **resource room**. Resource rooms are primarily utilized by speech pathologists, reading teachers, and learning disability specialists.

It is important to realize that successful mainstreaming of exceptional children into regular school classrooms, or even into regular school programs part-time, requires careful planning that goes beyond selecting appropriate curricular materials. The regular school classroom is a complex place where teachers are busy and the pace of activities rapid. The facilitation of mainstreaming requires that a number of strategies be implemented. Regular and special educators have to structure the classroom, as well as the individualized program, for the exceptional learner. The nondisabled children have to be accepting, compassionate, and helpful to their classmates who have special problems. Figure 12-2 shows the kinds of decisions and planning that regular and special educators have to undertake in designing an educational program suitable for mainstreaming the exceptional.

Facilitating Mainstreaming

In this figure, Heron (1978) points out a number of processes that might facilitate the integration of the exceptional child into the regular classroom. Since nondisabled peers tend to reject the exceptional child, it is particularly necessary to help normal children in their relationships with the handicapped child. Teachers can work directly to increase awareness and acceptance of individual differences. They can arrange working conditions so that the exceptional child becomes an active participant in the classroom activities. Nonhandicapped children may serve as tutors to the exceptional child, a procedure that has been shown to decrease inappropriate behavior, while increasing appropriate activities (Csapo, 1972) and promoting academic performance (Hamblin and Hamblin, 1972). Aditionally, concerns about reinforcements and modeling and consideration of both the children's and the teacher's conduct are evidenced. These techniques may serve to increase the sensitivity and consideration of nondisabled children for their handicapped classmates.

For classroom teachers to accept the exceptional learner into the classroom, they must understand the child's problems. In-service and preservice training have been instituted in many school districts to help teachers in this respect. Classroom teachers need to work with other members of the special services staff to plan the educational program for the child. Academic and social management plans should be drawn up, and the classroom teacher should have support and direct help from special services in implementing them. If classroom teachers have experience in diagnostic teaching and in putting learning theory into practice and if they feel comfortable with exceptional children they are more likely to be accepting of them and will structure the classroom so that the child who is different is accepted by other children.

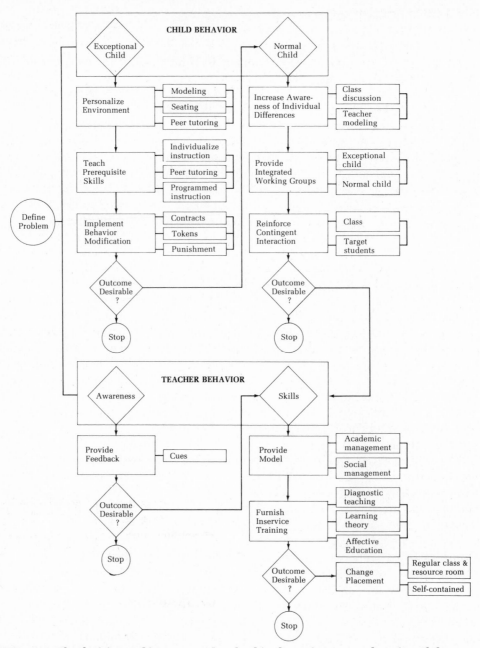

FIGURE 12–2 The decision making process involved in the mainstream education of the exceptional child

Source: Journal of Learning Disabilities, Volume 11, Maintaining the Mainstreamed Child in the Regular Classroom: The Decisionmaking Process, T. E. Heron, p. 213, figure 1. Copyright by the Professional Press, Inc. and reprinted by special permission.

The Teacher

Irrespective of the class placement or technical advances, the teacher is still that person who has the most influence and effect upon the child within the classroom. If there is to be intervention, the teacher will serve as the agent of change. Interestingly, as important as she or he is, we still know relatively little concerning the behavior and attributes that might distinguish the competent classroom teacher from the incompetent. Nonetheless, the role of teachers and special educators is now so expanded that they have greater responsibility in the assessment, planning, and delivery of intervention services to the exceptional child.

Recently there have been attempts to specify what teachers are expected to do and then train them to do these things. One offspring of such attempts has been competency based teacher training programs; university or college programs that specify exactly what the teacher in training must be able to accomplish by the end of training. The orientation of these programs is very behavioristic. Competencies are judged according to whether the teacher has skills that can be demonstrated behaviorally, skills that he or she can actually perform. These skills are systematically evaluated through observations of these behaviors. Further stipulations of the standards of behavior expected of the teacher and further methods to evaluate systematically the degree to which the teacher is performing competently will probably emerge in the future. Increasingly, teachers will be forced to become more active in evaluation, to bring parents of exceptional children into the program goals, and to produce an educational result visible to all who wish to see it.

Forms of Intervention

To this point we have discussed how help is delivered to individual children. Let us now turn to some forms of educational intervention that have been developed to help school-aged exceptional children. While the educational programs that have been devised often integrate behavior modification principles, discussed in the following chapter, we present remediation programs here in terms of how they are structured for academic achievement areas. Since language and speech difficulties are common to so many types of exceptionalities, we begin with a review of the assessment and intervention strategies employed for such problems.

Before discussing the characteristics of language interventions, the reader should be aware that these programs have not been based upon significant amounts of data (Vellutino, 1977). That is, they have not been subjected to much empirical analysis, so that we do not know if the programs are effective, if one program is more effective than another, or if their effectiveness varies for different kinds of children.

A number of methods and related materials to facilitate language development skills in learning disabled children have recently been developed. One program is noteworthy, that developed by Lee, Koenigsknect, and Mulhern (1975).

Interactive Language Development Program

Lee and her colleagues have developed a language teaching method, the Interactive Language Development Program, that can be used with children in their early elementary school years who have delayed language development. It can be employed with either small groups or individuals. There are specific programs for helping the child acquire basic sentence structures and/or more advanced grammatical structures. In the Interactive Language Development Program, the teacher tells a story and then asks the children specific questions about it. Rather than being fantasy based, the stories deal with everyday events likely to be familiar to the child. The teacher is guided in implementing the program as each lesson's concepts and vocabulary, necessary materials, and particular grammatical structures to be emphasized are specified. The system also outlines instructional techniques that authors feel will facilitate the children's performances. For example, in responding to a child's errors, it is recommended that the teachers both repeat the sentence correctly for the child and then repeat those parts of the sentence that the child omitted. Other techniques include asking the child to expand an incomplete response, having the child correct a wrong answer without the teacher's presenting the right one, and repeating an incorrect response by the child in order to elicit a correction from him or her. In addition to providing explicit lessons, the program includes methods for monitoring the program's effectiveness. This is done by means of the Developmental Sentence Score, described in Chapter 4.

Lee and her associates (1975) have attempted to demonstrate empirically the effectiveness of this program in facilitating language development. They report that 25 language delayed children, ages 3 to 5, who had received approximately eight months of intervention, showed significant gains on a variety of language tests. While one swallow doesn't make a summer, the fact that this intervention program is being systematically assessed is encouraging. No doubt further research will show both its merits and limitations, but unlike so many corrective programs, further research should be forthcoming, adding to our knowledge about this particular intervention method.

Peabody Language Development Kit

The Peabody Language Development Kit (Dunn and Smith, 1966) contains a rather well-known language program designed to stimulate expressive language through a variety of lessons. The course actually has four levels, suitable for testing children with mental ages between 3 and 9½ years. At each level, there are 180 lessons. One program, suitable for children with a mental age between 4½ and 6½ years, contains 180 daily lessons, 430 colored cards, colored plastic chips, two hand puppets, and six recorded fairy tales. Using auditory and visual presentations, those carrying out this program expect that the oral language of slow, disadvantaged first graders, upper primary educable mentally retarded, intermediate trainable mentally retarded, and average and above average kindergarten children will improve. The Peabody program can be used with individual children as well as with large groups. Teachers are encouraged to make this a talking time for children that is fun for them and for which they are heavily rewarded (hence, the plastic chips). Some studies have indicated that this program does stimulate children's language; others have found negative results (Bartel, 1975). It is likely that individual differences in teacher use of the kits are a factor in how effective this type of program is.

Other Language Development Programs

In contrast to the Peabody language program, there are a number of highly structured language development techniques. One is the Fitzgerald approach, presented in *Straight Language for the Deaf* (Fitzgerald, 1949). This method was designed for deaf children, but can be used with "all children who have linguistic deficits manifested by an inability to formulate sentences" (Bartel, 1975, p. 189). In this system the Fitzgerald Key is used to show children how to classify words and then how to arrange them into syntactically correct sentences. The Key is a chart subdivided into a series of sequential headings. Children are taught to group words under the proper heading. For instance, children are initially taught to categorize words under the headings "Who" and "What," which are often the first two words in a sentence. Once children begin to classify "who" and "what" correctly, they move to grouping words under the headings "How many" and "What color." When they can classify single words under the proper headings, they can use these headings to guide them in constructing sentences. Fitzgerald presents a variety of lessons and tips for teachers to promote children's language development.

A second highly structured language program is the DISTAR Language Program (Engelmann and Osborn, 1970). This was developed for use with preschoolers, kindergarteners, primary graders, or older children, depending on the child's language skills. The program, whose instructions are highly structured for the teacher, is administered to small groups of children in one 30-minute lesson each day. There are two parts. In the first part, the teacher presents lessons on "identity statements, polars, prepositions, pronouns, multiple attributes, comparative-superlatives, location, same-different, only, action, categories, plurals, why, verbs of the senses, verb tense, if-then, before-after, oral, one, some, all, none, colors, patterns, shapes, and comprehension. The second part covers questioning skills, materials, description, opposites, following instructions, synonyms, classifications, left-right, analogies, statements, synonyms-opposites, definition, information, function, problem solving, vocabulary review, and deductions" (Bartel, 1975, p. 193). According to Bartel the effectiveness of DISTAR has been compared with other programs on populations of normal and handicapped children with favorable results.

While the language development programs focus on particular approaches to helping children improve their speech and other communication skills, there have been rather unique forms of educational programs developed in response to the needs of school-aged children with learning disabilities and reading problems. While these approaches include techniques of behavior modification, they are increasingly becoming more classroom oriented and provide alternative hypotheses concerning the remediation of problems like those found in reading deficits.

Perceptual-Motor and Information Processing Dysfunctions

A major assumption is that some children suffer an information processing dysfunction that prevents them from learning as other children do. In this perspective, learning is seen as requiring the perception, comprehension, storage, retrieval, and integration of information through the sense modalities. In analyzing learning problems the auditory and visual modalities are emphasized. For many years, for instance, it was believed that reading required primarily visual information processing; more recently, there has been interest in the role of auditory information processing in affecting reading and in the role of the ability to integrate auditory and visual information. Learning to read is thus viewed as the composite of several skills in action, skills related to auditory and visual discriminations. When a child fails to learn to read, the assumption is made that he or she has not developed the ability to process information through one or more of the sensory modalities, or, can process the information through each modality but cannot integrate the information received from them.

The process deficit attracting the greatest interest has been perceptual-motor dysfunctions. When specialists observed that a child having difficulty learning to read also made errors in writing letters in the proper order, and frequently reversed their order, they believed that either the youngster was not perceiving the letters as other children do, or that he or she was perceiving them correctly, but could not match the perception with the writing movements. Many intervention programs were developed based upon the belief that visual perceptions and perceptual-motor integration are primary skills necessary for the child to acquire reading proficiencies. The intervention program was aimed at training the child's perceptual-motor skills. For example, Kephart (1963) and Frostig and Horne (1964) developed assessment and intervention programs based upon perceptual motor skills. Kephart's program focused on motor skills in particular, and included observations, ratings, and interventions for five areas of perceptual-motor skills: balance and posture (the child's walking and jumping are assessed); body image and differentiation (identification of body parts); perceptual-motor match (rhythmic writing on a chalkboard); ocular control (visually following a moving object); and form perception (the child copies geometric forms). Frostig and Horne developed the Developmental Test of Visual Perception (1964) which assessed five aspects of motor functioning: eye-motor coordination; figure-ground skills; form constancy; position in space and the ability to assess spatial relationships. For example, the child is asked to draw a straight line between two parallel lines (eye-hand coordination), discover hidden figures within a larger figure (figure-ground skills), recognize and trace a square or circle (form constancy). If the child demonstrates inadequacies in any of these skills, interventions consist of having the child practice mastering the area of deficiency.

An extension of the perceptual-motor perspective is an emphasis upon information processing. This refers to the brain's capacity to integrate information arriving through the various sense modalities, for example, hearing and sight. Information processing is seen as critical to academic performance, and learning problems are viewed as a result of a breakdown in integrating such information. Assessment procedures consist of determining how well the child deals with information presented within particular modalities. Intervention procedures are then designed to train the child within the modality in which he or she appears most competent, as well as helping the child to develop skill in handling information through the modality that is evidently the weakest.

Example of Remediation Approach in Information Processing

An example of a remediation approach emphasizing information processing is that proposed by Johnson and Myklebust (1967). They developed a program that distinguishes between the child's ability to receive information and to express it. A youngster may have difficulty in understanding others or in expressing his own ideas. Johnson and Myklebust incorporate into their program the notion that the child may be able to understand information when it is presented auditorily but have difficulty when it is given visually. Conversely, the child may function well visually but not cope well with auditory information. The assessment of the child is to determine under which modality of presentation the child learns, and with which combination he or she fails to learn. Interventions are then designed to build up the child's deficit areas, while using the child's intact skills to learn new skills. If the child learns well visually, unfamiliar material is presented in a visual format. If the child learns well auditorily, unaccustomed tasks are presented through sounds. The child who has difficulty in writing is asked to verbalize answers, and written assignments are tape recorded. The basic idea is avoid penalizing the child by forcing him or her to deal with new material under the most difficult instructional format. Separate instruction is provided with the intention of building up deficit skills.

Investigations of Information Processing Approach

There have been a number of studies to investigate whether the information processing approach to assessment and intervention facilitates children's learning. Bruininks (1970), for instance, studied the relationship between auditory and visual competence in the child and the effectiveness of teaching through one or the other modality. In this study, the subjects were disadvantaged boys. One group was identified as having auditory strengths and visual weakness, while in a second group the strengths and weaknesses were reversed. Each child was taught 30 words he did not know; 15 through a phonetic method and 15 through a whole-word approach. The results failed to find that matching the auditory and visual strengths of the boy to an auditory or visual method of instruction resulted in more effective learning.

The link between sensory modality skills and learning to read has not been established (Arter and Jenkins, 1977). The challenge remains to determine what subskills and processes are required in reading or other learning tasks so that programs can be devised to help the child. At this time the correct skills have apparently not been adequately identified or defined. Neither perceptual-motor nor information processing analogs of learning have been demonstrated to predict a child's performance on academic achievement, and interventions based on these approaches have not been found to improve school performance. It is probably fair to say at this point that some young children who have difficulty on tasks evaluated by these approaches might derive some benefit from training. We do not know, however, which child, when, or through what method will benefit (Hammill, 1972).

While the perceptual deficit and information processing approaches have failed to explain, predict, or cure poor academic achievement, challenges to these perspectives have led to research which holds promise for understanding children's academic failures.

Language Processing

Accumulated data from various research efforts support the idea that academic failure, reading in particular, may be related to problems in developing and using language. What seemed to be visual-perceptual problems like the reversals of b and d and "saw" and "was" now appear to be related to deficits in language processing (Hammill, 1972; Vellutino, 1977). Children failing to learn to read have difficulties labeling the symbols correctly, that is, making the connection between the written notation and the spoken word it represents. Their grouping (chunking) these written, or spoken, symbols for later use is not as efficient as that of children who readily learn to read. The breakdown in language that prevents the child from connecting symbol and label, and from chunking information for storage and retrieval, may stem from a breakdown in any or all of the various components of language. The child with difficulties in phonology, syntax, or semantics will be at a disadvantage in learning. Poor readers are apt to have a developmental history of language delay (Lyle, 1970), they make more errors on tasks that require quick automatic verbal responses (Denckla & Rudel, 1976), and they take longer to respond (Perfetti & Hogaboam, 1975) when a task requires rapid naming. Summarizing the results of many studies, Vellutino states: "Severely impaired readers are not as proficient as other readers in their knowledge of words, syntactic facility, and verbal fluency in general. . . . The evidence suggests that both difficulties appear at an early age and may have a common source" (1977, p. 345). Reviewing the data on phonological differences between good and poor readers, Vellutino (1977) indicates that there is also strong evidence that reading disabled children have phonological deficits that limit their ability to use the phonetic structure of spoken and written language. This does not mean that poor readers are unable to hear that words sound the same or different; they can hear the differences. What it does mean is that poor readers do not hear the single segments of a word; rather, they hear the word as a whole. They apparently do not realize that words consist of separate sounds. As a result they are not able to analyze the components of words and so do not connect the parts of words with their written symbols; they are at a loss in deciphering the written representation of words that they do not know. In sum, children who have difficulty learning to read are probably poor in using language phonology, syntax, and semantics. They are likely to have particular problems in associating visual symbols with their verbal referents, organizing information for purposes of learning it, and consequently have difficulty in retrieving words as needed. They appear not to use language to process the information they are receiving, nor to organize the information in order to learn and remember it.

What sort of intervention would evolve from this kind of information about children deficient in reading? It is too soon to say because the viewing of reading problems through language skills is a quite recent development.

Curricula for Trainable Retarded Children

As a final example of the types of approaches and programs for exceptional children, we look at some curricula for trainable retarded children. These children are less likely to be completely mainstreamed in regular school classrooms than to be housed in special classrooms in conventional public schools. The assumption that underlies developing an educational program for them is that they will not be independent as adults but will always require supervised work and living centers. However, this assumption may not be warranted (MacMillan, 1977).

Like any other educational plan, the goal of these programs is to develop the skills and social deportment that will allow the child a productive life without undue dependence upon others. It is hoped that the trainable mentally retarded child will mature so as to be able to work and to live, if not entirely independently, at least with some autonomy from, and in harmony with, others. At the very least, such an eventuality requires that the trainable mentally retarded (TMR) be able to take care of his or her own personal needs, behave in proper social fashion, and help with routine housekeeping chores. An examination of the TMR curriculum in Figure 12-3 shows that the school's activities are designed to develop these skills. The program can be divided into four main components. One type of schooling is related to self-help and independent living skills. Health habits, physical education, and grooming are categories of skill development in this area of learning. A second category includes communication, oral language, and cognitive development skills. In this category are the typical academic achievement areas, but designed for the TMR. The third category is socialization and personality development. Here, specific activities are focused on helping the child play with others, providing a range of experiences in which the youngster can practice various social skills. The fourth category of the curriculum covers vocational, recreational, and leisure skills. The young student starts with learning to follow instructions, and the training ends with participation in a sheltered workshop. Children are organized primarily according to age, into primary, intermediate, and advanced levels. Since

FIGURE 12-3 Curricular content areas by organization levels in TMR programs

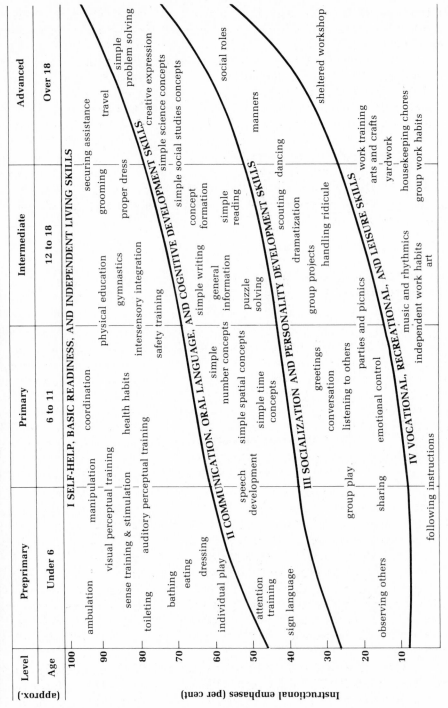

Level	Preprimary	Primary	Intermediate	Advanced
Age	Under 6	6 to 11	12 to 18	Over 18

I SELF-HELP, BASIC READINESS, AND INDEPENDENT LIVING SKILLS

ambulation
manipulation
coordination
securing assistance
visual perceptual training
physical education
grooming
travel
sense training & stimulation
health habits
gymnastics
proper dress
simple problem solving
toileting
auditory perceptual training
intersensory integration
creative expression
bathing
safety training
simple science concepts
eating
dressing
simple social studies concepts
individual play

II COMMUNICATION, ORAL LANGUAGE, AND COGNITIVE DEVELOPMENT SKILLS

speech development
simple number concepts
simple writing
concept formation
social roles
attention training
simple spatial concepts
general information
simple reading
sign language
simple time concepts
puzzle solving

III SOCIALIZATION AND PERSONALITY DEVELOPMENT SKILLS

group play
greetings
conversation
group projects
dramatization
scouting
dancing
manners
sharing
listening to others
handling ridicule
observing others
emotional control
parties and picnics

IV VOCATIONAL, RECREATIONAL, AND LEISURE SKILLS

independent work habits
music and rhythmics
art
work training
arts and crafts
yardwork
sheltered workshop
housekeeping chores
group work habits
following instructions

Instructional emphases (per cent)

100
90
80
70
60
50
40
30
20
10

Source: L. W. Campbell, Study of Curriculum Planning, 1968.

376

TMR children are likely to be identified during their preschool years, there are preschool programs for them. Sheltered workshops are facilities for young adult and adult TMR persons in which their work is closely supervised.

Before closing this section, a note of caution is in order. It is far too soon for professionals to place much confidence in their estimates of the limits to the potential of the TMR. First, educational technology is improving. Indeed, it was not long ago that many would have laughed at the notion of severely retarded non-verbal adults learning to assemble bicycle brakes, an activity that involves learning a complex motor task. Yet Marc Gold (1973) has demonstrated that this is possible. As new methods of helping the handicapped are developed, the prospects of a more productive, happier, and autonomous life might well increase for the trainable mentally retarded child. After all, an individual's achievements are partly the results of educational experiences, and if these experiences are improved, so may his or her accomplishments.

SUMMARY

In this chapter we reviewed the intervention programs for preschool handicapped children. We saw that while early childhood education has been in existence for a long time, it is only recently that the government has actively developed policies and provided funds to support early childhood education for disadvantaged and handicapped children. The assumptions underlying early childhood programs for the handicapped are: The child derives greater benefits from programs initiated early than from later ones, that additional problems can be avoided by early intervention, and that children go through critical periods of development during which corrective measures should be initiated.

Three perspectives that guide the implementation of early childhood programs are the maturationalist-socialization approach, in which the child's activities are fairly unstructured and natural development is emphasized; the behavioristic approach, which involves the defining of behavior and skills to be trained and the nature of reinforcements to be used; and the cognitive-developmental perspective, which has been greatly influenced by Piaget's theories of cognitive development.

There are differences in the personnel employed in many preschool programs. Unlike teachers in public elementary and high school levels, teachers in early childhood programs may or may not be certified by their respective states, and paraprofessionals and parents play rather important roles. In some programs the parent is designated as the primary teacher, with the professional staff guiding the parents' activities.

There is a good deal of evidence that preschool programs are beneficial to children. Peters (1977) indicates that the children who have participated in such programs show gains in intelligence and social development and have fewer than expected school problems in the following years. In addition, there is evidence that the mothers and even the siblings of the participating children also benefit from the program.

Reviewing early childhood programs for handicapped children, we see a development of programs to educate the youngster; no longer is concern limited to physical well-being. Early childhood education for the handicapped is now likely to be initiated as soon as the child comes to the attention of persons who provide the programs.

We also discussed the problems inherent in providing special preschool programs for children at risk of becoming school failures. The dangers associated with early detection programs include the lack of precise tools and procedures, the possibility of having many false positive and false negative identifications, and the danger of labeling the child and producing a self-fulfilling prophecy of failure for the child.

Nevertheless, there can be benefits derived from preschool training for potentially disabled children. It is necessary, however, to be very specific about the behavior to be trained, and to match the training to that behavior. If the child has a perceptual discrimination problem, then training should be specific to perceptual discrimination. It was also found that, given training, mothers could provide the needed educational treatment.

In describing services for school-aged exceptional children, we reviewed the types of professionals likely to conduct the assessment and intervention process. Special education teachers, regular classroom teachers, psychologists, social workers, speech and language therapists, occupational and physical therapists, as well as physicians and psychiatrists may be called upon for assistance in diagnosing a problem or in helping to alleviate it. The flow of services may be initiated with a school district's preschool screening of the community to find children in need of help, or the services may be initiated by referrals for help from teachers, parents, or even the courts. Most school districts have agreed upon practices for assessing the child who is referred for help. We see that parents' permission and parent participation are increasing. Since the most extensive part of an evaluation is the assessment of the child's academic and psychological status, we reviewed some of the issues related to assessment. The use of standardized versus criterion referenced tests, the adoption of an abilities assessment versus a task analytic approach are considered. Assessment must be nondiscriminatory to disadvantaged and minority culture children and must yield an individualized education plan (IEP).

The IEP is a statement of the child's present level of functioning and an outline of short- and long-term educational goals for the exceptional child. Mandated by Public Law 94-142, the IEP provides an instructional strategy that should lead to data-based educational interventions. Using a test-teach-retest cycle, the special education and regular classroom teachers should be able to develop an appropriate education plan and demonstrate that it has indeed been effective.

The idea of an IEP is likely to be considered appropriate for all children, not just the exceptional. For special education and regular classroom teachers to undertake individualized instruction requires the teacher to cope with hetero-geneous groups of children simultaneously. There have been efforts to provide teachers with technical assistance, in the form of computer technology, and also to provide them with readily accessible regional resource centers. Making it possible for teachers to obtain materials and information should greatly lighten their burden of implementing individualized programs.

Once it is determined that a child requires special education, deci-sions are made about where the services shall be delivered. Segregated residential institutions, separate day schools, and regular public schools are all places where services are provided. Increasingly, exceptional children are being mainstreamed, given all or most of their education within conventional school classrooms.

To mainstream exceptional children successfully demands that the special educator and classroom teacher work together to provide the best possible curriculum. But it also requires that the teacher structure the classroom so that exceptional children are accepted by nondisabled classmates. Teachers can actively work to develop acceptance and to integrate the child into classroom activities. Nondisabled children can help their exceptional classmate through peer tutoring, and also by serving as models and sources of reinforcement for the child.

It was also pointed out that the teacher is the person who has the most influence and effect upon the child within the classroom. The classroom teacher has to understand the handicap, know how to construct effective educa-tional programs that sidestep the obstacles presented by the handicap, accept the child, and help others accept the child. The teacher's compassion and tolerance for individual differences can be communicated to nondisabled children. We believe that this will improve the life of the exceptional child; it will greatly enhance the life of the nonhandicapped as well.

Intervention strategies boil down to the teacher. Unfortunately, we have not yet established the attributes of a good teacher. Current directions in teacher training are toward competency based programs in which the skills to be acquired by the teacher in training are specified. The teacher in training must demonstrate his or her acquisition of these skills prior to completion of the program. The standards of behavior expected of the teacher and the methods to evaluate systematically the degree to which he or she is competently performing seem to be the wave of the future.

In the section concerned with educational programs, three different areas were described. First, a number of language intervention programs were reviewed. Language problems are found in many handicapping conditions; hence, a specific language program is likely to be desirable for most exceptional children. Second, we discussed how notions concerning learning disabilities evolved into training programs specific to information processing deficits. Third, we reviewed the content of a curriculum for trainable mentally retarded persons. By focusing on three rather different areas of special education, the reader sees how disparate needs have yielded rather disparate assumptions, assessments, and teaching pro-grams for the education of exceptional children.

REFERENCES

Abbott, J. C., & Sabatino, D. A. Teacher-mom intervention with academic high-risk preschool children. *Exceptional Children*, 1975, *41*, 267–268.

Arter, J. A., & Jenkins, J. R. Examining the benefits and prevalence of modality considerations in special education. *Journal of Special Education*, 1977, *11*, 281–298.

Bartel, N. R. Assessing and remediating problems in language development. In D. D. Hamill & N. R. Bartel, *Teaching children with learning and behavior problems*. Boston: Allyn & Bacon, 1975, 155–202.

Bricker, W. A., & Bricker, D. D. *Early language intervention*. Paper presented at the NICHD Conference of Language Intervention with the Mentally Retarded, Wisconsin Dells, June 1973.

Bruininks, R. Teaching word recognition to disadvantaged boys. *Journal of Learning Disabilities*, 1970, *3*, 28–35.

Campbell, F., & Ramey, C. *The effects of early intervention on intellectual development*. Paper presented at the Conference of the Society for Research in Child Development, New Orleans, April 1977.

Csapo, M. Peer models reverse the one bad apple spoils the barrel theory. *Teaching Exceptional Children*, 1972, *5*, 20–24.

Denckla, M., & Rudel, R. Naming of object drawings by dyslexic and other learning disabled children. *Brain and Language*, 1976, *3*, 1–16.

Dunn, L., & Smith, J. O. *Peabody language development kits*. Circle Pines, Minn.: American Guidance Services, Inc., 1966.

Engelmann, S., & Osborn, J. *Distar: An instructional system*. Chicago: Science Research Associates, 1970.

Feshbach, S., Adelman, H., & Feller, W. Early identification of children with high risk of reading failure. *Journal of Learning Disabilities*, 1974, *7*, 639–644.

Fitzgerald, E. *Straight language for the deaf*. Washington, D.C.: Volta Bureau, 1949.

Friar, J. *Factors of predicted learning disorders and their interaction with attentional and perceptual training procedures*. Unpublished dissertation, University of California at Los Angeles, 1972.

Frostig, M., & Horne, D. *The Frostig program for the development of visual perception*. Chicago: Ill.: Follett Publishing Co., 1964.

Garber, H., & Heber, R. *The Milwaukee Project: Early intervention as a technique to prevent mental retardation*. Storrs: The University of Connecticut National Leadership Institute, Teacher Education/Early Education, 1973.

Gold, M. W. Research on the vocational habilitation of the retarded: The present, the future. In N. R. Ellis *International review of research in mental retardation*. New York: Academic Press, 1973, 97–147.

Hamblin, J. A., & Hamblin, R. L. On teaching disadvantaged preschoolers to read: A successful experiment. *American Education Research Journal*, 1972, *9*, 209–216.

Hammill, D. Training visual perceptual processes. *Journal of Learning Disabilities*, 1972, *5*, 552–559.

Heber, R. F., & Dever, R. B. Research on education and habilitation of the mentally retarded. In H. C. Haywood (Ed.), *Social-cultural aspects of mental retardation.* New York: Appleton-Century Crofts, 1970, 395–427.

Heron, T. E. Maintaining the mainstreamed child in the regular classroom: The decision-making process. *Journal of Learning Disabilities,* 1978, *11,* 210–216.

Johnson, D. J., & Myklebust, H. *Learning disabilities: Educational principles and practices.* New York: Grune & Stratton, 1967.

Keogh, B. K., & Becker, L. D. Early identification of learning problems: Questions, cautions and guidelines. *Exceptional Children,* 1973, *40,* 5–11.

Kephart, N. C. *The brain-injured child in the classroom.* Chicago: National Society for Crippled Children and Adults, 1963.

Kirk, S. A. *Early education of the mentally retarded: An experimental study.* Urbana, Ill.: University of Illinois Press, 1958.

Kratochwill, T. R. The movement of psychological extras into ability assessment. *Journal of Special Education,* 1977, *11,* 299–311.

Lance, W. D. Technology and media for exceptional learners: Looking ahead. *Exceptional Children,* 1977, *44,* 92–97.

Lee, L. L., Koenigsknect, R. A., & Mulhern, S. T. *Interactive language development teaching.* Evanston, Ill.: Northwestern University Press, 1975.

Luick, A., & Feshbach, S. *Visual sequential memory deficit in children with learning disorders: An investigation of a remedial program utilizing sequence training and color coding.* Unpublished manuscript, University of California at Los Angeles, 1974.

Lyle, J. G. Certain antenatal, perinatal, and developmental variables and reading retardation in middle class boys. *Child Development,* 1970, *41,* 481–491.

MacMillan, D. L. *Mental retardation in school and society.* Boston: Little, Brown & Co., 1977.

Mercer, J. R. *Labeling the mentally retarded.* Berkeley: University of California Press, 1973.

Perfetti, C. A., & Hogaboam, T. The relationship between single word decoding and reading comprehension skill. *Journal of Educational Psychology,* 1975, *67,* 461–469.

Peters, D. L. Early childhood education: An overview and evaluation. In H. L. Hom, & P. A. Robinson (Eds.), *Psychological processes in early education.* New York: Academic Press, 1977, 1–21.

Rowitz, L. Socioepidemiological analysis of admissions to a state-operated out-patient clinic. *American Journal of Mental Deficiency,* 1973, *78,* 300–307.

Wolfensberger, W. Diagnosis diagnosed. *Mental Subnormality,* 1965, *11,* 62–70.

Vellutino, F. R. Alternative conceptualizations of dyslexia: Evidence in support of a verbal-deficit hypothesis. *Harvard Educational Review,* 1977, *47,* 334–354.

Ysseldyke, J. E. *Current issues in the assessment of learning disabled children and some proposed approaches to appropriate use of assessment information.* Paper presented at the Conference on Assessment in Learning Disabilities, Atlanta, Georgia, 1977.

Ysseldyke, J. E., & Salvia, J. A. Diagnostic-prescriptive teaching: Two models. *Exceptional Children*, 1974, *41*, 181–186.

KEY TERMS

behavioristic approach A perspective in psychology that emphasizes the study of overt, objectively measurable behavior and the relationships between these behaviors and specific events in the environment.

cognitive-developmental approach A perspective of psychology that focuses on creating learning environments that stress the acquisition of cognitive abilities. The curriculum consists of providing active experiences that will enhance skills appropriate for the developmental level of the students.

maturational-socialization approach A perspective of psychology that emphasizes creating learning environments that are supportive of the natural maturational processes. The curriculum also focuses on developing appropriate social interaction skills.

resource room A classroom, separate from the regular classroom, staffed by a special educator who provides small-group instruction to children with similar learning problems and serves as a consultant to the regular teacher.

CHAPTER 13

Psychological Remediation

Many teachers and parents are confronted with children who are too shy, disruptive, incoherent, inattentive, or show other problems that limit their opportunities to enjoy living. These children are likely to receive psychological treatment, an intervention program based upon psychology's current ideas about human behavior.

Insight Therapy

For many years children needing help were likely to undergo some form of **insight therapy**. Although the settings for administering insight therapy varied from the psychiatrist's easy chair to the social worker's playroom, there are some common assumptions about this form of therapy. One assumption is that the child's motives play an important role in producing the unwelcome behavior. Since these motives are viewed as the source of the problem, the source of the problem is within the child. To help the child it is necessary to focus upon motives, which often are obscure, rather than upon the child's behavior or upon environmental factors possibly affecting that behavior. The idea is that by gaining insight, or self-awareness, as to motives, the child is better able to control the symptomatic behaviors. The route to symptom removal, and perhaps happiness, is through awareness, particularly awareness of one's motives. In addition, insight therapists believe that if the symptom is removed in the absence of insight, two untoward effects are likely to occur. First, the symptom will return, making the cure transitory. Second, other symptoms may develop, with the cure possibly proving to be worse than the disease. Thus, they warn about *symptom substitution*. Symptom removal without insight is considered poor therapeutic practice.

As a rule, insight therapies have not been remarkable for their success. The children receiving this type of intervention often show little personal gain while their parents show great economic loss. The combination of low effectiveness and high cost has led many to seek other forms of intervention that would produce high effectiveness at low cost.

Behavior Therapy

During the last twenty years or so, quite different approaches to resolving children's personal problems have evolved. They are often referred to as *behavior therapy* or *behavior modification* and interest in them appears to grow each year. These methods emphasize treating children's behavior, rather than their motives. As in insight therapy, practitioners using behavior modification techniques make certain assumptions about the causes and solutions for a child's aberrant behaviors. But the assumptions in behavior modification are different from those underlying insight therapies. In behavior modification approaches, the first and foremost postulate is that the child's problems should be attacked at the behavioral, not the motivational, level. The goal of treatment is to remove the symptom, to change the child's behavior. Intervention is addressed directly to the symptom rather than hypothetical motives. The patient is cured if the symptom is removed. A second assumption is that the most efficient way to remove the symptom is found in psychological literature on children's learning. When we know how to facilitate a child's learning, we can help the child unlearn maladaptive behaviors and adopt adaptive ones. In effect, behaviors are defined as habits that are susceptible to change through techniques designed to facilitate learning. Finally, behavior modifiers point out that there is no evidence to suggest that if a child drops one maladaptive behavior another will be adopted. They claim that the whole notion of substituting one symptom for another is so vague it is virtually untestable (Bootzin, 1975).

This chapter is focused on various behavior therapy techniques that have been used to help children extinguish old habits and learn new ones. For several reasons insight therapies are not reviewed. First, there is considerable evidence that behavior modification techniques are the most effective means to help many children with many different kinds of problems. Although behavior modification techniques have not been effective for all the kinds of problems children experience, they have worked often enough to be considered a viable technology for helping children struggling with various difficulties. Second, behavior modification is likely to be the dominant therapeutic approach in the forthcoming years, if it has not already achieved this status. The different methods used by behavior modifiers are most likely to interest teachers and parents.

There are three basic forces that shape children's behavior. First, children act in a particular way because they have an *incentive* to do so. Children learn to escape, to avoid unpleasant feelings and experiences, and they learn to act so as to maximize their pleasures. Their actions are thus affected by reinforcement and punishment. Second, children learn a great deal by *watching* the behaviors of others, and the consequences to others of their actions. That is, children learn through observation and modeling. Third, children learn through *instructions*, verbal tutoring from others. Most of the behavior modification literature deals with the use of reinforcement and punishment to help disturbed children. The reason these have been stressed is that they have powerful impact on children's behavior; many actually believe that reinforcement and punishment are the foundation for modeling and tutorial effects. While the literature on learning through observation and modeling is not as vast as that on reinforcement techniques, it is nevertheless substantial. This type of learning also appears to be powerful in shaping children's behavior. There is not much information as to the effects of verbal instruction upon the behavior of disturbed children. This gap in knowledge appears reasonable as it is likely that most children with problems receive an abundance of advice, exhortations, and instructions, probably to no avail. Thus, the remainder of this chapter will present behavior therapy techniques that use reinforcement, punishment, and modeling to help children with personal difficulties.

CONTINGENCY MANAGEMENT

"Contingency management refers to the process of changing the frequency of a response by controlling the consequences of that response" (Bootzin, 1975, p. 12). **Contingency management** may include positive reinforcements and punishment. We will consider first the use of positive reinforcements as an intervention technique.

Extinction Procedures

One important intervention technique makes use of extinction procedures, the practice of withdrawing the reinforcements gained by the child through undesirable behavior. There are no attempts to suppress the undesirable behavior through punishment. But when the unwanted behavior occurs, it is hoped that there will be no environmental responses to reinforce it. This is frequently difficult to arrange as many forms of children's undesirable behaviors produce professional and parental attention and concern that in fact may serve as a reward for those actions. For instance, children may develop physical or psychological problems that gain attention, sympathy, and other forms of positive reinforcement. A good illustration of such a problem and the extinction procedures that eliminate it is seen in Williams's (1959) case report of a young boy who displayed excessive crying, temper tantrums, and demandingness. The boy had been ill for several months during his infancy and received considerable, necessary attention from his parents. When he recovered, his parents gave him somewhat less attention. It was then that he developed his "symptoms," which were most likely to occur at bedtime. Following intervention instructions, the parents put the child to bed, refrained from punishing him, and ignored his screaming. The boy cried for about 45 minutes the first night the extinction procedures were begun. The crying ceased on the second night, but returned on the subsequent four nights for periods of about ten, five, and three minutes, ending with one minute. Finally, the boy's crying behavior at bedtime was extinguished altogether.

One major difficulty in the use of interventions based upon extinction methods and other forms of contingency management is making sure that the procedure is carried out by all those individuals who have important or on-going interactions with the child. If another person appears on the scene and reinstates the reinforcements for the child's deviant behavior, a "relapse" might well occur. This is, in fact, what happened to the boy treated by Williams. An aunt was on the scene who alternated with the parents in putting the boy to bed. When the aunt subsequently reinforced the boy for his temper tantrums and crying, he reverted to these behaviors. A second extinction program was initiated and the uproar again eliminated.

Extinction procedures have been employed to eliminate a variety of disruptive and even bizarre behaviors in both children and adults (Bandura, 1969). Several considerations concerning these procedures should be mentioned. The first, already discussed, is that some uniformity in the responses of individuals to the child's deviant actions must be maintained. The second involves the course the deviant behavior may take as the treatment progresses. During the initial stages of the extinction procedure, the child's undesirable behavior will probably increase in frequency as he or she attempts to regain the reinforcements associated with it. Thus, during the initial stages of treatment, the concerned parent or professional may have some very rough moments. The third consideration concerns those behaviors that evolve as the undesirable actions decrease. If the child does not have acceptable alternative responses, other offensive behaviors may develop. These would then require yet further extinction procedures. To prevent this possibility, extinction procedures are often accompanied by training alternative and more desirable actions through reinforcements. Let us now look at the use of positive reinforcements as a treatment program.

Positive Reinforcements

As explained in Chapter 3, a positive reinforcement is an object or event that increases the probability of the reoccurrence of a response that immediately precedes it. Knowing that behavior can be altered through such events has provided psychologists, teachers, and parents with a tool to help the needy child. This tool is particularly popular since it seems to help children and its application seems more humane and therefore more acceptable than alternative techniques using punishments or other aversive methods. Furthermore, if positive reinforcements have side effects, they seem less undesirable than those apt to accompany aversion and punishment procedures. There seems little question that, other things being equal, the use of positive reinforcement to help the child should be the treatment of choice.

What Is Reinforcing?

In employing positive reinforcements to help the child, one must make several important determinations. The first is: Which event or events serve as reinforcement for that particular child? Often praise, smiles, head nods, money, and candies may serve as reinforcements. Sometimes they will not, as a particular child may not care about being liked, having money, or eating sweets. One interesting and practical idea has been offered by Premack (1965). He suggests that any behavior that has a high probability of occurring, for example, watching television, may serve as a reinforcement for any behavior less likely to occur, such as eating spinach. Bootzin (1975) has pointed out the practical advantages associated with the Premack principle. One can fathom the appropriate reinforcer for a particular child by observing what he or she does when given a choice. In addition, the means of providing the reinforcements are located within the child's immediate environment, and giving them is not only possible but probably convenient. Thus, the disruptive child who loves to play ball may be significantly and conveniently quieted by making ball-playing contingent upon acceptable behaviors.

While reinforcements can be bestowed directly, sometimes it is more convenient and efficient to give symbols of reinforcements. The symbols most frequently used are tokens, objects the child knows can be exchanged for reinforcements (called *back-up reinforcements*) at a later time. The use of tokens is especially prevalent when reinforcing a large number of individuals, as in the classroom or a mental hospital. As discussed in chapter 3, this use of tokens as symbols applied to groups of individuals is called a *token economy*. What are the advantages of token economies? First, tokens may be more easily administered than direct reinforcements. They are easier to dispense than, for example, melting ice cream, the chance to watch television, or a ride on a horse. Second, tokens provide the child with a visible and nonconsumable sign of progress. Third, it is often easier to control the timing of the reinforcement. This is to say that giving the child a token immediately following the desired behavior is considerably simpler than giving him or her an opportunity to play ball during classroom hours. Fourth, a wider variety of reinforcements can be made available to the participating children (Bootzin, 1975). Just imagine trying to provide, on a moment-to-moment basis, the array of reinforcements that might appeal to several children in a program. It is not surprising that the use of token economies has gained in popularity during the recent years. They do have many advantages over other techniques of controlling behavior through positive reinforcements.

Reinforcements for Unwanted Behavior

Another important determination is: Just which reinforcements are sustaining the child's undesirable behavior? This is significant since it affects the efficacy of the procedures to change habits. If the offensive behavior is frequently reinforced—wittingly or unwittingly—by parents, teachers, or peers, or if the behavior is intrinsically highly gratifying, the duration, frequency and amount of reinforcements given the child for more appropriate actions may have to be adjusted accordingly.

Specifying Behavior to be Reinforced

A third consideration involves deciding just which behavior is required before the reinforcement will be given. Since the administrations of reinforcement must be consistent for a particular behavior and omitted in the face of other behaviors, it is critically important to specify concretely the behavior to be reinforced. It is more effective to reinforce such behaviors as sitting still, being quiet, focusing upon a particular problem, than indicating that "attention" should be reinforced. Additionally, it must be remembered that for a behavior to be reinforced, it has to occur. If standards of conduct are set too high for the reinforcement to be earned, then little will be accomplished since the behavior never will have occurred. When a child only very infrequently displays the behavior ultimately sought, several procedures might be used to elicit the desired activity. One is the use of *shaping* procedures. In this case, behavior that resembles the desired behavior is reinforced. Reinforcements then become increasingly contingent upon ever-finer approximations of the targeted acts. Often, however, shaping procedures are time consuming. A second method of eliciting the behavior is through *modeling,* by motorically demonstrating the behavior to be reinforced. Additionally, *verbal instructions* explaining the desired behavior and the means by which to exhibit it can be tried. Finally, the behavior might be elicited by *physically guiding* the child in doing it (Bandura, 1969).

It is also important to monitor the effects of the treatment. One cannot assume a priori that any particular reinforcement, or for that matter any particular treatment, will have the hoped-for impact. Thus, one must consider just how and when monitoring will be accomplished. The preferred monitoring procedure is actually observing and counting the number of times the behavior being sought occurs.

Power of Reinforcement

While there is still some debate over the mechanisms that underlie the power of positive reinforcements to affect behavior, there is absolutely no debate concerning their power (Bandura, 1969). Positive reinforcements, when made contingent upon the display of some behavior, are very likely to affect that behavior. This really is not a new revelation since countless teachers and parents, past and present, have recognized that giving praise, stars, and hugs are likely to have an important influence upon the child. However, our knowledge of the specific nuances in the timing, amount, and duration of reinforcement practices is relatively recent. As Bandura (1969) has pointed out, behavior control by the layperson is likely to suffer from that person's insufficient awareness of these nuances. For example, positive reinforcements are often available to a child on essentially an ad lib basis; that is, positive reinforcements are often there for the taking. While such affluence is laudatory in general, it does put the parent or teacher in the position of having to use other forms of behavior control, mostly aversive in nature, to affect the child's actions.

Given the appropriate programming of positive reinforcements, their applications to the problems experienced by many exceptional children have been well documented. It really seems as if positive reinforcements affect virtually all types of children and their various weaknesses. For example, Staats, Minke, Finley, Wolf, and Brooks (1964) found that by giving 4-year-old-children toys as back-up reinforcers for attending to a reading lesson, their attentiveness increased. Becker, Madsen, Arnold, and Thomas (1967) discovered that reinforcing children's classroom behaviors that facilitate learning significantly reduced the frequency of classroom disruptions. Along the same line, Zimmerman and Zimmerman (1962) found that if a teacher withheld attention from an emotionally disturbed child in the midst of a temper tantrum and noticed the child when engaged in appropriate activities, the temper tantrums were extinguished in a relatively brief time. Hall, Panyon, Rabin, and Broden (1968) were able to increase the percentage of time a class of students spent studying by increasing the teacher's attention to those pupils who were studying. These results are particularly striking in light of the findings that teachers' commands to sit down will increase the probability that children will stand up! (Madsen, Becker, Thomas, Koser, and Plager, 1968).

The benefits of systematic positive reinforcements to individuals have not been limited to relatively nondisturbed children within the classroom. Kazdin (1973) found that nonverbal behavior of a teacher, such as smiles and physical contact, served as positive reinforcements for a classroom of mentally retarded children and influenced the children's attentiveness. Indeed, the use of positive reinforcements has alleviated problems like severe withdrawal, extreme passivity, aggressiveness, feelings of depression, and overdependency. The control of behavior through positive reinforcements has been demonstrated with a wide number of behavioral problems of varying severity (Bandura, 1969).

Effectiveness of Token Economies

The greatest extension of behavior modification principles into the classroom has been through the introduction of the token economy. Many of the children displaying learning problems in school are those who have not responded to the usual techniques teachers use to control classroom behavior. Some children are unaffected by praise or reproof, stars or grades, peer or parent pressures. To meet this challenge, investigators instituted the now-prevalent token economy program. These programs capitalize on the fact that children will behave in a manner that gets them something they want. If teachers provide desirable rewards, most children will "shape up" and perform in accordance with the teacher's desires.

Can the judicious use of a token economy program ameliorate problems found with exceptional children? The answer seems to be yes. For example, the reinforcement of nondisruptive behaviors has been demonstrated to reduce greatly disruptive behavior while increasing studiousness and academic achievement (Kazdin and Bootzin, 1972; O'Leary and Drabman, 1971). It might be predicted that academic skills would be immune to alteration by tokens because of the new learning demanded; nonetheless, gains have been reported through the use of token economy systems. Wolf, Giles, and Hall (1968) introduced such a system into a remedial program for low achieving elementary schoolchildren. The youngsters were given tokens contingent upon correct academic performance in reading, language, and arithmetic. Gains were made in all areas of performance that had been reinforced. Hewett, Taylor, and Artuso (1969) found that the arithmetic of 8- to 11-year-old emotionally disturbed children could be improved when they took part in a token economy program. However, their reading was unaffected. Token economy programs have been effective in controlling aversive behaviors and in improving academic performances.

There is every reason to be optimistic about remediation efforts that are based upon principles of behavior modification. Children do have to sit in their seats or at least pay attention in order to learn, and they are, by and large, well motivated to do so by means of incentives. Numerous studies reviewed by O'Leary and Drabman (1971), Kazdin and Bootzin (1972), and Bootzin (1975) amply documented the utility and power of the appropriate use of reinforcements in the classroom setting. Of course, teachers, adults, and even children have long recognized the power of a carrot; yet their use of the carrot often appears to be less than optimal. The token economists have given us many useful suggestions for making full use of the power of the carrot.

Limits to Positive Reinforcements

While the systematic use of positive reinforcements is a powerful tool in affecting behavior change, it has its limits and problems. As mentioned in Chapter 3, a potential difficulty with positive reinforcements is that they may lessen the child's intrinsic interest in the task. Therefore, positive reinforcements should probably not be given to children who are already engrossed in the task or demonstrating the behaviors being demanded. But the recipient of systematic positive reinforcement programs is probably only rarely interested in the task at hand. While one should be alert to the negative effects positive reinforcements may have upon intrinsic interests, negative consequences are unlikely to result from systematic use of positive reinforcements for children with behavioral or attentional problems.

There is a second limitation in the use of positive reinforcements that should be mentioned, and that pertains to its applicability. There are instances when desired behavior is never displayed, or when maladaptive behavior is so strongly reinforced by virtue of its commission (for example, stealing and eating cookies), or when the maladaptive action is so life-threatening (such as running into the street) that the systematic use of positive reinforcements, *in isolation from the use of other techniques,* may be to little avail.

A third limitation is in the durability of the effects produced by positive reinforcements. By and large, when a behavior is sustained with positive reinforcement alone, the behavior stops when the reinforcement does. While the therapist may start the program with the message to the child, "No behavior, no reward," it appears that the child will end the treatment with a message to the therapist, "No reward, no behavior" (Bootzin, 1975; O'Leary and Drabman, 1971).

This particular problem of maintaining the behavior once the reinforcements have been withdrawn is relevant to yet another issue, the generalization of the behavior across situations. By and large, behaviors being reinforced in a situation, for example, the classroom, do not generalize to other classrooms or social contexts. O'Leary and Drabman sum up the situation when they write: "Those investigators who have assessed the generalization of behaviors reinforced in the token programs to those same behaviors when the token program is not in effect, in different situations and at different times, have not found generalization" (1971, p. 394). Most individuals administering and studying control through positive reinforcements believe that the lack of generalization is at least partially attributable to the fact that children are not reinforced appropriately for their conduct in other situations. It is assumed that if the child can experience the appropriate reinforcements in different settings from a number of people, then the reinforced behavior might generalize to other situations. There is currently much greater concern for planning programs that will facilitate the generalization and durability of appropriate behaviors.

Other problems have been noted, if not systematically studied. One common concern of the public regarding the implementation of behavior modification procedures has revolved around the concept of bribery. Some people feel that in programs like token economies, children are being bribed to behave in an appropriate manner. The implicit notion is that youngsters should behave properly irrespective of possible pay-offs. Although this concern is not usually elaborated further, it reflects an interest in the impact of programs using positive reinforcement on the attitudes and expectancies of the child. It would be naïve to assume that such programs do not affect attitudes and expectancies, although, surprisingly, these effects have not been systematically scrutinized. On the basis of anecdotal evidence, it seems that children will model the "if-then" position of the token economist. Bushell, Wrobel, and Michaelis (1968) reported that children taking part in this type of program would negotiate contracts with their peers and friends in which pay-offs accompany compliance with a requested behavior. These behaviors might have taken place on a nonreciprocating basis before the children experienced the token economy. Similarly, Meichenbaum, Bowers, and Ross (1969) reported that adolescent female delinquents turned the tables on the investigators. The girls were on a part-time token economy and blackmailed the investigators to extend the token periods. They refused to work unless there was a pay-off.

In spite of some of these limitations, it is our belief that the systematic use of positive reinforcements offers teacher and parent considerable power of control over children's behavior. The fact that such techniques lead to little generalization of the desired behavior to other teachers, classrooms, or settings is not a devastating criticism. Many studies of generalization have focused upon social behaviors or deportment. They have not evaluated the durability of the academic skills produced through the wise use of positive reinforcements. Social behaviors are most likely to be affected by the power of the reinforcement contingencies within the child's immediate environment, such as watching television or playing ball. If such is the case, then generalization may well be expected not to occur. However, it is quite another matter to believe that academic skills obtained under positively rein-forcing circumstances will be lost when reinforcement ends. The motivation to continue to achieve may cease, the behaviors necessary for achieving more may not be evidenced, but it is highly unlikely that past learning will somehow disappear from the child's repertoire because reinforcements have been stopped. It would cer-tainly be desirable if procedures could be developed whose application would result in a generalization of their effects to other situations. But to criticize current pro-grams, such as the token economies, on the grounds of their failure to produce generalizable effects seems quite unjust. Parents and educators attempt to train children's "character," to develop a human being who will show desirable behav-iors across a variety of situations for an extended period of time. But the factors that promote such development are not really well known. To criticize the positive control of behavior because of this limitation is to criticize all known techniques used to influence children. That control of behavior can be obtained on a predict-able basis within the classroom and the home is an achievement of considerable magnitude. As to the effects of such programs on children's attitudes and expec-tancies toward reward for effort, little can now be said concerning the program's nature or desirability. Perhaps the direction taken in research on positive reinforce-ments in the future will be to systematically study and evaluate their effects upon attitudes. In the meantime, anecdotal reports do not indicate that such effects warrant discontinuing these procedures. Even if these programs produce a recipro-cal orientation toward interpersonal and academic relations, one must ask whether these effects are worse than those produced by continuing school and personal failures.

Punishments

A great deal of human behavior is controlled and moderated through the use of punishments. Children are usually taught not to touch hot stoves, stick their fingers into an electrical socket, run into the street, jump off high places, or fight with a stronger and bigger peer because of the unpleasant consequences that result from such activities. People do learn to suppress behavior because of their previous experiences with aversive or painful consequences.

For a long time many psychologists believed that punishment was an ineffective way to suppress behavior. As indicated in Chapter 3, this belief is no longer tenable. There is little question that punishment produces behavioral suppression, although this may be accompanied by undesirable side effects. In this section we discuss two forms of punishment: the use of aversive stimulation to suppress a behavior, and the removal of positive reinforcements. First, we discuss the use of **aversive stimulation** for therapeutic purposes.

Aversive Stimulation

Before aversive stimulation, such as physical punishment or scolding, should be contemplated in treating children's problems, there are several important considerations. First and foremost is whether such stimulation is really necessary. Are there no other effective treatment techniques? If there are no alternatives, there are several other problems to ponder. As with positive reinforcements, the amount, duration, and frequency of aversive stimulation has to be established. The reinforcements that maintain the behavior have to be defined, and the manner in which the treatment is to be monitored has to be established. The intensity of the aversive stimulation and the way the undesirable behavior is maintained are particularly important. As suggested in Chapter 3, one must be sure that the aversive stimulation is intense enough to suppress the undesirable behavior. If the punishment is too weak, the punishment may signal the child to repeat the unwanted behavior. Ethical and practical problems make it probable that aversive stimulation will be effectively used only rarely for therapy. Punishments, such as public scoldings, administered by teachers are not very likely to be effective.

Indeed, teacher punishments may serve as positive reinforcements for just that behavior the teacher is trying to eliminate. In most situations in which children and teachers interact, the effective use of aversive stimulation is impossible.

Although punishment procedures are probably not worth using often in the classroom, there are a number of instances in which they might help exceptional children. Their use might be warranted when children are autistic or engage in self-mutilation behaviors. Bucher and Lovaas (1968) used punishment to eliminate children's self-mutilation, including frequent and destructive head-banging. They report that while improvements can be obtained by removing positive reinforcements that may be supporting the self-mutilation, the process is long and painful for the child. They found that self-mutilation could be suppressed faster by the adult saying "No" loudly, painful spankings, and the use of electric shocks. Electric shocks, spankings, and scoldings may sound brutal, but it should be remembered that many children who try to mutilate themselves seriously are otherwise kept from self-destruction by the use of physical restraints. These restraints are no less brutal than aversive stimulation, which might have the benefit of eliminating the self-mutilating behavior.

Lang and Melamed (1969) report another example of punishment used as a therapeutic technique. These therapists were confronted with an infant who chronically vomited. As a result, the child weighed only 12 pounds at 9 months of age. Clearly, the baby's life was in danger. After ruling out the possibility that the vomiting was caused by some medical disorder, Lang and Melamed instituted an electric shock treatment. Through the use of electrical recordings of throat muscle movements, they were able to determine when the child was beginning to vomit. At this moment an electric shock was applied to the child's leg. The results of the treatment are pictured in the following illustrations. Figure 13-1 shows the child at 9 months of age; in Figure 13-2 we see the child after two weeks of treatment, while Figure 13-3 shows the child five months after treatment had ended. It was found that the child ceased vomiting after six electric shock treatments, given once a day. The baby had a slight relapse after the termination of treatment, received three more treatments, and then showed no further vomiting. When the treatments were over, the child had gained 16 pounds, and during the next five months he gained an additional 10 pounds.

The application of aversive stimulation has been of value in altering other behaviors. It has been successfully applied in such problems as motor dysfunctions, tics, sexual deviations, and alcoholism.

To this point we have discussed the application of aversive stimulation, physical punishment, for remedial purposes. It would be worthwhile to reiterate some of the dangers associated with these procedures that were mentioned in Chapter 3. First, the child may learn that aggressive actions are appropriate for resolving conflict. He or she may model aggression. Second, the child may become alienated from the punitive agent. These two dangers can probably be offset if the child understands that the punishment is not arbitrary, that it is based upon the commission of particular misdeeds and not all actions, and that it does not reflect the sentiments of the punishing agent toward the child (Bandura, 1969).

A third danger associated with physical punishment is that the child may become generally inhibited, fearing to commit even many acceptable behaviors. This danger can be offset if the punishing agent helps the child distinguish between what is and is not punished. The adult should provide positive reinforcements for positive behaviors, and punishment for unacceptable actions.

We now turn to another form of punishment: removing positive reinforcements.

Removing Positive Reinforcements

It is common practice for parents and teachers to attempt to control children's behavior through the removal of privileges, allowances, recesses, candy and ice cream, and other things or events that make the child's life joyous. The responsible adult may deprive the child of a particular reinforcement or of an opportunity to gain any reinforcements. While both procedures involve **response costs,** the latter condition is referred to as a **time-out** procedure. The effectiveness of these procedures depends upon the usual factors, such as the reinforcements sustaining the inappropriate behavior, the consistency with which the positive

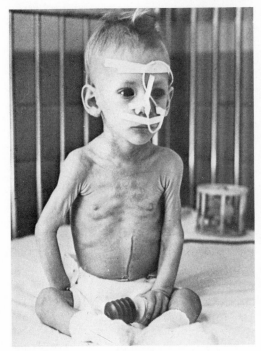

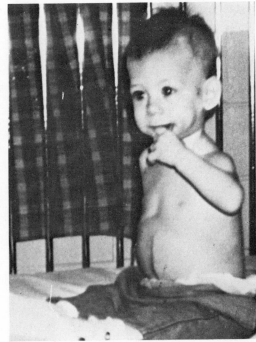

FIGURE 13-1   FIGURE 13-2

reinforcements are removed when the behavior occurs, and the reinforcement of alternate behaviors.

When appropriately administered, the removal of positive reinforcements or the use of a time-out procedure can have beneficial results. Kazdin (1971), for example, reported treating a mentally retarded adult female whose problem was inappropriate speech. This woman would blurt out statements that led many to believe that she was not only retarded but might be psychotic as well. To eliminate her inappropriate comments, Kazdin fined her a token from her earnings in a token economy. The vocalizations decreased in frequency almost immediately. After about two weeks they were infrequent. A month following the termination of the punishment, the frequency of the woman's inappropriate talk was still very low.

In time-out procedures the child is excluded from social interactions, which deprives him or her of the opportunity to obtain positive reinforcements. Upon displaying unacceptable behavior, the child is physically removed from the setting and placed in "isolation." Wolf, Risley, and Mees (1964) report treating an autistic 3-year-old boy by means of a time-out procedure. The child threw temper tantrums, tried to mutilate himself, and threw food. The treatment consisted of placing the boy

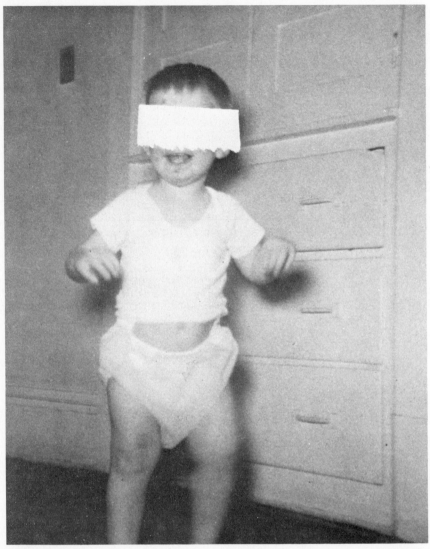

Source: Journal of Abnormal Psychology, 1969, vol. 74—1–8, Lang, P. J., and B. Melamed, ''Case Report: Avoidance conditioning therapy of an infant with chronic ruminative vomiting''; figures 1 and 7.

FIGURE 13-3

in a room devoid of interesting material for a 10-minute period. If the child continued to have a temper tantrum or otherwise misbehaved during his stay in isolation, he was forced to stay in the room for a longer time. Through the use of the time-out procedure and the administration of positive reinforcements for appropriate behaviors the boy's behavior in the hospital improved. His parents were also trained to control his behavior. He was subsequently discharged from the hospital and, through an extensive application of reinforcement procedures during his nursery school years, was able to be enrolled in a public school (Risley and Wolf, 1966; Wolf, Risley, Johnston, Harris, and Allen, 1967).

Response cost procedures can be effective. They appear to have at least one advantage over physical punishment: They are not as likely to evoke the strong emotional responses from the child that physical punishment does. Certain circumstances, however, will undermine their effectiveness. First, one must make sure that the child is being removed from a reinforcing situation. To remove a disruptive child from a classroom or home the child detests may reinforce the child's disruptive actions. Secondly, it is important not to give positive reinforcements during the time-out procedure. Thus, lengthy explanations of the reasons for the time out, expressions of sympathy, or any personal attention following the child's inappropriate behavior may well serve as a positive reinforcement (Wolf et al., 1964). Finally, it is important in response cost procedures, whether the child is deprived of candy or freedom, that the punishment not be terminated until the child has demonstrated appropriate behaviors.

While most of the direct applications of the behavior modification approach to the classroom have made use of reinforcements, particularly token economies, studies focused on modeling have appeared that have relevance to the remediation of the exceptional child. We now turn to the use of models as a form of therapy.

MODELS

One of the most commonly stated justifications for mainstreaming handicapped children into regular school classrooms is that the children will imitate and learn from their nonhandicapped peers (Snyder, Appolloni, and Cooke, 1977). Unfortunately, special educators have not really examined whether handicapped children imitate the nonhandicapped, or indeed, whether the reverse is true. Nor have they analyzed those circumstances in which imitation might be facilitated or retarded. It is clear, however, that exceptional children do imitate others. For example, Schwartz and Bryan (1971; 1974) found that learning disabled and deaf children would imitate a model's altruistic behavior. Likewise, Mercer, Cullinan, Hallahan, and LaFleur (1975) and Mercer, Hallahan, and Ball (1977) found that learning disabled children do imitate others. Additionally, a number of studies of the imitative behaviors of autistic children and children with pronounced fears have also demonstrated the power of a model in affecting their behavior (Bandura, 1969). It appears that children with many different handicapping conditions are susceptible to the influence of models.

In Chapter 3 we discussed the theory and research relevant to children's imitation of persons they observe. It is clear that the actions of others can have a controlling influence on the behavior of the observing child. It is, therefore, not surprising that techniques making use of models have become part of the armory of therapists working with children.

Eliciting New Behaviors

As Bandura (1969) has indicated, a very important function of models is to elicit new behaviors from the child. Without the commission of the modeled behavior, other forms of behavior control, like positive reinforcements, cannot be employed. Modeling, then, provides the therapist with the opportunity to elicit, in a relatively efficient way, the desired behavior from the child so that it can be appropriately reinforced.

Overcoming Fear

There are several conditions in which the child demonstrates a deficiency in responding that, theoretically at least, could be remedied through the use of models. One condition is fearfulness; the child will not commit an appropriate action because of extreme fear.

There is no doubt that children who observe the courageous behaviors of others toward an object they fear will imitate the courageous model. Bandura, Grusec, and Menlove (1967) were able to reduce children's fear of dogs by having them observe a model who interacted with a dog with increasing fearlessness. While the Bandura, Grusec, and Menlove study employed a live model for the remediation, it is also possible to eliminate some children's fears by means of film. Weissbrod and Bryan (1973) were able to reduce children's fears of snakes, and Bandura, Blanchard, and Ritter (1968) their fear of dogs, by showing them films of brave models. In an important study O'Connor (1969) showed preschool children who were extremely withdrawn a film that depicted a child who was initially hesitant but eventually joined and participated with peers. The children who viewed this film were subsequently found to be more socially interactive than other children who had seen a neutral film. Thus, children's fears of snakes, dogs, and of each other have been reduced through exposure to courageous models.

Teaching the Autistic to Speak

Because autistic children show gross deficiencies in their responses, intervention programs employing positive reinforcement procedures exclusively are likely to be quite inefficient. Modeling, in conjunction with other techniques, might be particularly useful as a remediation technique with autistic children. Ivar Lovaas and his colleagues (Lovaas, 1968; Lovaas, Berberich, Perloff, and Schaffer, 1966) employed both modeling and reinforcement procedures in attempts to train autistic children to talk. In the program the child was initially reinforced every time he or she made a sound or looked at the teacher's (model's) mouth. In the initial period the

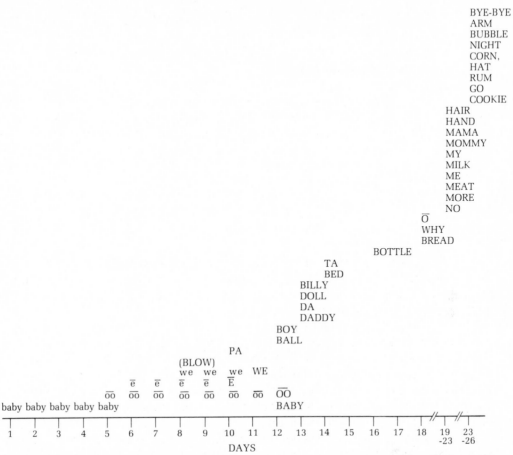

FIGURE 13–4 The rate of verbal imitation by an autistic child under modeling and reinforcement procedures

Source: "Acquisition of Imitative Speech by Schizophrenic Children," Lovaas, I. O. et al., *Science,* Vol. 151, pp. 705–707, Fig. I, II, February, 1966, used by permission.

object of training was to encourage the child's vocalization and attention to the model. During the second phase of the training, the model would say a sound and reinforce the child for any vocalization within a six-second period.

   During the third stage of the program, the model again said a sound but this time gave the child a reinforcement only if the child produced a similar one. When the child mastered the sound, the model would introduce a new sound. Figure 13-4 depicts the rate of verbal imitation by an autistic boy under this program. The sounds and words are printed in lower-case letters on the days they were introduced and in capital letters on the days they were mastered.

   It is clear that speech training of autistic children is a very slow, laborious task. It is also clear that less handicapped children can learn appropriate speech through the influence of models (Bandura, 1969).

Inculcating Prosocial Behaviors

Finally, mention should be made of the instilling of prosocial behaviors through the influence of models. While exceptional children often have worse problems than lack of consideration, poor social poise, or meanness to others, it is also true that prosocial behaviors are likely to bring important benefits to persons who demonstrate them. There is a good deal of evidence that models who show consideration or cooperation with others are likely to affect the child's kindness to peers or to less fortunate others (Bryan, 1975). Certainly, a deficiency in prosocial activities might well be eliminated through the judicious use of models presented on film or live in the home or classroom.

There is, then, little doubt that models may be an important tool in eliciting responses that the observing child would not otherwise display. Modeling actions may prompt the desired behavior, which then can be sustained by positive reinforcements. The combination of rewards and models may provide an especially powerful procedure for gaining control over the child's behavior.

Inhibiting Undesirable Behaviors

Treatments based upon social learning theory have also been shown to be effective in inhibiting behaviors. Children who behave poorly can be helped through treatment techniques employing models. For example, children who witnessed a model act aggressively and suffer punishment for it were less likely to exhibit aggression than were children who viewed the model's aggressive behavior without any negative consequences (Bandura, 1965). Likewise, children who saw another child punished for playing with a forbidden toy were more likely to resist their own temptation to play with the toy than were children who had not seen the sequence (Walters, Leat, and Mezel, 1963). Moreover, it is noteworthy that the model's own evaluation of the act, depending upon its nature, may serve as a deterrent or a reinforcement (Bandura, 1969; Midlarsky and Bryan, 1972). That is, if children witness a model express positive or negative affect or make self-approving or self-critical statements, the child's subsequent imitation of the model will be affected. Positive affect and self-approval increase the likelihood of imitative behavior; negative affect and self-criticism decrease it.

Use of Modeling in the Classroom

That modeling treatments may have important implications for the classroom is suggested by the work of Csapo (1972). This investigator enlisted socially mature peer models to demonstrate appropriate behaviors to six emotionally disturbed children. The goal was to decrease the children's disruptive classroom behavior. To do this, Csapo asked the peer model to sit next to the emotionally disturbed student throughout the school day for 15 days. The model's job was to demonstrate appropriate classroom behavior. The emotionally disturbed child was told that the socially mature peer wanted to help him in the classroom and that he should try to act like the model. The deviant youngster was also told that the peer would indicate when a response was correct by giving him a token (with no exchange value) that would indicate his progress. The results showed a decrease in the number of inappropriate behaviors by the disturbed children. Csapo also reports that the effects of the treatment seemed to generalize to other situations, and that the attitudes of the peer models toward the problem students were extremely positive. Indeed, the models became concerned for and protective of their "charges." Because of the lack of certain control groups, one cannot tell whether the results of the treatment were due to the models, to peers' sudden concern for the disturbed child, to increased status and/or attention from the teacher, to the models' behaviors plus the instructions and/or tokens from the teachers and models, or to a combination of some or all of these factors. However, the study does suggest that peer modeling might have beneficial effects for both the observing emotionally disturbed child and for the model.

Limits to Use of Models

What are some of the limiting conditions in the use of models as a therapeutic instrument? These are suggested by Bandura's theory and were outlined in Chapter 3. First, the child must be able to attend. The reader will have noted that Ivar Lovaas in his work with autistic children initially had to train these children to focus visually upon the model's mouth. Additionally, studies by Mercer, Cullinan, Hallahan, and LaFleur (1975) and Mercer, Hallahan, and Ball (1977) have found that modeling by learning disabled children is positively correlated with their ability to attend to stimuli. Thus children with severe attentional problems may require training in paying attention to a model. Additionally, the child must be able to organize what has been seen in such a way as to recall the model's actions. This may be the reason that children's impulsivity has not been found to be affected by simply observing a model's behavior. If the child is shown a deliberate model, one who is slow in making correct decisions about difficult choices, the child will also show greater hesitancy and "deliberation" in decision making. However, the number of correct decisions will not increase following the deliberation (Messer, 1976). It is likely that the child does not notice, or cannot organize, the strategies necessary for making "correct" choices simply by viewing the model's actions. As will be seen in the next section, however, appropriate modeling and certain forms of instruction can be successfully combined to reduce children's impulsivity. Third, the child must have the motor capabilities to perform the actions. If the model's behavior exceeds the motor abilities of the child, the child obviously cannot imitate it. Finally, the impact of the model upon the child will be greatly affected by the reinforcements available for imitation, either as implied by the consequences experienced by the model, or through direct reward by others.

While the applications of social learning theory to the treatment of exceptional children is relatively new, we believe it holds great promise. Several considerations prompt this bias. First, models have been shown to affect a wide variety of conduct by both normal and exceptional children. Second, this method of treatment can be implemented with relatively little cost, either of money or of effort. If children learn violence from television, if they learn about nature from nature films, they certainly can learn social, and perhaps cognitive, behaviors from films about people. Moreover, unlike such individualized remediation techniques as counseling and one-to-one tutoring, films can reach large numbers of children simultaneously. Canned television therapy is a real possibility.

COGNITIVE BEHAVIOR MODIFICATION

So far our discussion of psychological remediation has focused upon the roles of incentives and models in affecting behavior. Recently, considerable work has been undertaken on the effectiveness of instructions, in combination with models and reinforcements, in helping the problem child. **Cognitive Behavior Modification** (CBM) refers to the remediation method that carefully integrates reinforcements, models, and appropriate verbal instructions. An important goal in this form of treatment is to teach the child to "think," that is, to provide direct training in the processes important for problem solving.

Procedure: Verbalization by Model

Just what are the steps involved in CBM? Typically, the child is shown a model who is not only trying to overcome a difficult problem or situation, but is also speaking aloud his or her thoughts and feelings while trying to master the difficulty. Rather than simply giving instructions to the child as to the correct way to proceed, the model is programmed so that the child can observe how that model thinks and feels about the task. For example, in a study involving hyperactive children, Douglass, Parry, Martin, and Garson (cited in Meichenbaum, 1977) had children listen to a model say such things as "I must stop and think before I begin." "What plans could I try?" "How would it work out if I did that?" "What shall I try next?" "Have I got it right so far?" "Gee, I made a mistake there—I'll try to erase it." "Now, let's see, have I tried everything I can think of?" "I've done a pretty good job" (pp. 4–5).

Verbalization by Child

A second step in the procedure is to allow the child to try coping with an analogous situation with the instructions that he or she also think aloud. During this period, further displays of "thinking" by the model may take place. This phase is referred to as having the child practice **overt rehearsal** of the thinking that might facilitate his or her performance. Finally, the child is asked to solve the problem while silently thinking about the appropriate strategies. This phase is referred to as **covert rehearsal.**

It is obvious that the content of the model's verbalizations to the child will vary considerably. For example, when trying to help a child with strong fears, the model might speak about his or her fears and hesitations concerning the feared object or circumstance. Or the model might approach the situation with no signs of any anxiety. The former instance is often referred to as a *coping model,* while the latter is termed a *mastery model.* It is now believed that the mastery model may be the most effective type for helping children with severe fears (Bandura, 1969; Meichenbaum, 1977).

Reinforcement

It is also beneficial to provide reinforcements for the child's adequate performance following cognitive training. As the child verbalizes the right problem solving activities, or performs the task at hand correctly, the effects of the regimen are likely to be enhanced by the use of social approval (Kennedy and Miller, 1976). It is also important to note that approval statements can be self-generated by the child and that with proper instructions, children will show the effects of self-generated approval or positive affect. For example, Masters and Santrock (1976) found that when children were instructed to call the work "fun" rather than "no fun," "easy" instead of "difficult," and when they expressed approval of their work, they were likely to persist for a longer period on a dull task than they would have without the self-instructions.

There seems to be a good deal of evidence that this complex treatment in which instructions, models, and reinforcements are employed will help children with various problems. Children who have been experiencing social isolation have been shown to benefit from a form of this program. Jabichuk and Smeriglio (1975) have studied the remediation effects of providing children with models of vicarious self-reinforcement and direct tutoring in social behavior. One group of preschool children, who were characterized as socially unresponsive to others, were shown films of an isolated child. Initially, the young actor was seen playing alone. The scenario then depicts the boy approaching peers and then finally playing happily with his peers in a variety of situations. Accompanying the film was a soundtrack that expressed the child's feelings of isolation, coping responses to the stressful events, and then self-praise for his actions. When the group of preschool children who viewed this scenario was compared with control groups, it was found that the former group showed more social responsiveness to others and that these improvements were maintained for at least three weeks. More recently, Gottman, Gonso, and Schuler (1976) found that through a complicated treatment procedure employing a model's coping self-statements and role-playing, socially isolated children became more popular with their peers, as assessed by sociometric techniques, than children not receiving the treatment.

CBM and Pupil Performance

But social skills have not been the only ones shown to be affected by CBM approaches. As the reader may recall, simply exposing a child to a "deliberate" model does not appear to have much effect upon the youngster's impulsivity. However, several studies have indicated that exposing the impulsive child to a thoughtful model, along with self-instructional training, will produce not only a more deliberate approach but also more correct judgments by the impulsive child. For example, Kendall and Finch (1976) found that 10-year-old emotionally disturbed boys, when shown by a model how to use verbal self-instructions, were less likely to demonstrate impulsive behavior on the Matching Familiar Figures Test and more likely to show improved classroom performance than children who were trained on the task under a response cost reinforcement procedure alone. Nelson (cited in Miechenbaum, 1977) also found that children receiving cognitive training plus response cost reinforcements during the training were less likely to demonstrate impulsive behavior on the Matching Familiar Figures Test than were children receiving other forms of treatment. Finally, Cullinan (1976) found that mentally retarded boys who received a treatment consisting of a model plus overt and covert rehearsal opportunities were better able to match various samples to a standard than similar children who just viewed a model or those who obtained feedback and social reinforcements during their training trials.

CBM Durability

Aside from the range of applicability of this form of treatment, there is also evidence that the effects of these procedures may be lasting. Kendall and Finch (1976) found that children exposed to self-instructional training by a model were less impulsive after a two-month period than those who did not receive the training. Nelson (cited in Meichenbaum, 1977) found treatment effects on children's impulsivity evidenced after a six-week interval. While effects of the program are likely to show some durability, they are also apt to show generalization to other tasks, particularly when care is taken to train the generalization. Alkus (cited in Meichenbaum, 1977) tested various procedures on second and third graders who were having difficulty in their schoolwork. The group that received self-instructional training for problem solving, plus coping models (that is, models who expressed their own frustrations and feelings about failure) were those most likely to show the benefits of training on tasks not covered in the original treatment-training. Alkus suggests that children's generalization of skills learned through self-instructional training are enhanced when the children also are taught how to cope with their fears and frustrations.

It appears that CBM effects important changes in children's social and cognitive skills, skills that are often critical to their academic success. The results of studies concerning this training, and the convenience of its administration, make it appear to have considerable usefulness for both parents and teachers. Teachers and parents do indeed model behavior to children, and it takes perhaps but a little loss of pride to verbalize in front of the child the various problem solving strategies, the frustrations and failures involved in coping with life. The combination of self-instruction, modeling, and the use of reinforcements can be an important and even powerful tool for helping the exceptional child.

SUMMARY

In this chapter we reviewed several methods used in changing children's behavior. We see that the least effective method is that of insight therapy, an approach focusing on the child's motives as the path to improved behavior. Insight therapies are costly and children treated in this way show little improvement.

More successful are behavior therapy and behavior modification techniques that concentrate on changing the child's behavior. Using principles found to govern the way we learn, behavior modification techniques have succeeded in eliminating maladaptive behaviors and in eliciting adaptive behaviors in children.

There are two basic forms of behavior modification. One is through the experience of reinforcement or punishment, which in turn increases or decreases the likelihood a child will repeat a behavior. The second method is through the observation and imitation of models. Reinforcement strategies have been widely used because they have been so effective; modeling techniques are also effective, but have not been as widely employed.

Contingency management is a form of behavior modification. In this method the behavior is changed by controlling its consequences. Within the framework of contingency management, behavior modifiers have used positive and negative reinforcement and punishment.

The removal of positive reinforcement when a child commits an undesired behavior is referred to as an extinction procedure. There is no attempt to suppress the undesirable behavior; the child simply loses whatever might have been gained through the maladaptive response. This treatment can be very effective in some cases, such as tantrums and excessive crying. It is not effective when the child does not have alternative behaviors, or when all adults in the child's environment do not subscribe to it.

Positive reinforcements can be given to increase the likelihood that a behavior will reoccur. This is an acceptable, humane approach to eliciting behavior change. For positive reinforcements to help a child, the reinforcing events, their amount and duration have to be defined. One possible technique is to use the Premack principle in which some activity the child may particularly like serves as a reinforcement for behavior that is desired but less likely to occur.

The administration of individual reinforcements to groups is cumbersome; the use of token economies, however, allows a teacher more convenience in managing the administration of reinforcements to groups of children. In a token economy the child earns symbols of the reinforcement, which are then exchanged for reinforcements at a later date. The advantage is that individual children may opt for different rewards while still receiving a visible acknowledgment of appropriate behavior.

Several points of concern in using reinforcements to shape children's behavior were noted. It is important to know what represents an effective positive reinforcement for the child just as it is important to determine what reinforces maladaptive behavior. The parent and teacher must also be very specific in defining what behavior will be reinforced. They must also recognize that if the desired behavior is not among the child's skills, other steps will have to be taken to train the child. Shaping, modeling, verbal instructions, and physical guidance are a number of techniques used when the behaviors are not in the child's repertoire of skills. While there are certain limitations to the use of positive reinforcements, this method provides a powerful tool for teachers and parents.

The use of punishment was then described. We saw that punishment can be very effective in suppressing undesirable behavior. One type, referred to as aversive stimulation, has worked very well in helping exceptional children to stop self-mutilation. A loud "No," spanking, and the use of electric shock may actually be more humane than physical restraints that fail to eliminate the self-destructive, even life threatening behaviors. Aside from our personal reluctance to use of aversive stimulation unless absolutely necessary, there are some practical disadvantages to physical punishment. Children may learn aggression by being aggressed against, become alienated from the punitive agent, or become very fearful and inhibited.

Removing positive reinforcements is another form of punishment, one that is more likely to be used by parents and teachers. Stopping the payment of a child's allowance or not allowing the child to go to recess are common forms of punishment. Another way to remove positive reinforcements is through time-out procedures. In this method the child is placed in isolation when exhibiting the undesired behavior. The idea is that the isolated youngster cannot receive any positive reinforcements from anyone. The child may not leave the time-out area until the maladaptive behavior ceases. It is important that the child be removed from a situation he or she prefers; when the child behaves appropriately, positive reinforcements are given.

Observation and modeling patterns have also been used to increase the likelihood a child will learn and engage in particular behaviors, and to decrease the likelihood of various other actions. Models are very important because they give the child the opportunity to learn unfamiliar, useful behaviors. Special educators have not fully explored the use of models to help exceptional children, but it appears that many types of problems may be alleviated through their use. Learning disabled children; children with strong fears; children who are deaf, very socially withdrawn, or autistic have all been found susceptible to the influence of models. The use of models who are punished can inhibit children's undesirable behaviors. Children will be less aggressive or more likely to resist temptation following the observation of a model whose aggressive or forbidden behavior leads to aversive consequences.

For models to be effective with exceptional children, it is necessary that the child attend to the model, organize what has been seen so that it can be recalled, have the motor capabilities to imitate the behavior, and be motivated to do so. We suggest that models could fill a much wider role in the education of exceptional children if steps were taken to ensure attention, organization and retrieval, motor capacities, and motivation.

Cognitive behavior modification (CBM) is a technique in which the use of models and reinforcements are combined with verbal instruction in order to teach the child how to think, how to solve problems. The model demonstrates the activity, speaking aloud of ideas and feelings that the activity arouses, and commends himself or herself. The child then is instructed to perform the same task while thinking aloud. Finally, the child performs the task with the instruction to think silently. While performing the task, the child engages in overt rehearsal (talking aloud) and covert rehearsal (thinking silently). The model presented the child may be a coping model expressing fears and hesitations about performing the task, or the model may assume a mastery posture and voice self-assurance. The mastery model appears to be the most effective.

A good deal of evidence is rapidly accumulating that indicates that this complex combination of instructions, models, and reinforcements is very effective in helping children with many different kinds of problems. Very isolated, withdrawn children; very impulsive, hyperactive children; mentally retarded children, and emotionally disturbed children have all responded positively to this method.

REFERENCES

Bandura, A. Influence of model's reinforcement contingencies on the acquisition of imitative responses. *Journal of Personality and Social Psychology,* 1965, *1,* 589–595.

Bandura, A., *Principles of behavior modification.* New York: Holt, Rinehart & Winston, Inc. 1969.

Bandura, A., Blanchard, E. B., & Ritter, B., The relative efficacy of desensitization and modeling approaches for inducing behavioral, affective, and attitudinal changes. *Journal of Personality and Social Psychology,* 1969, *13,* 173–199.

Bandura, A., Grusec, J. E., & Menlove, F. L., Vicarious extinction of avoidance behavior. *Journal of Personality and Social Psychology,* 1967, *5,* 16–23.

Becker, W. C., Madsen, C. H., Arnold, C. & Thomas, D. R., The contingent use of teacher attention and praise in reducing classroom behavior problems. *Journal of Special Education,* 1967, *1,* 287–307.

Bootzin, R. R., *Behavior modification and therapy: An introduction.* Cambridge, Mass.: Winthrop Publications, 1975.

Bryan, J. H., Children's cooperation and helping behaviors. In M. Hetherington (Ed.), *Review of child development research* (Vol. 5). Chicago: University of Chicago Press, 1975.

Bucher, B., & Lovaas, O. I., Use of aversive stimulation in behavior modification. In M. R. Jones (Ed.), *Miami symposium on the prediction of behavior, 1967: Aversive stimulation.* Coral Gables, Fla.: University of Miami Press, 1968.

Bushell, D., Wrobel, P. A., & Michaelis, M. L., Applying "group" contingencies to the classroom behavior of pre-school children. *Journal of Applied Behavior Analysis,* 1968, *1,* 55–63.

Csapo, M., Peer models reverse the one bad apple spoils the barrel theory. *Teaching Exceptional Children,* 1972, *5,* 20–24.

Cullinan, D., Verbalizatoin in EMR children's observational learning. *American Journal of Mental Deficiency,* 1976, *81,* 65–72.

Gottman, J., Gonso, J., & Schuler, P., Teaching social skills to isolated children. *Journal of Abnormal Child Psychology,* 1976, *4,* 179–196.

Hall, R. V., Panyon, M., Rabin, D., & Broden, M., Instructing beginning teachers in reinforcement procedures which improve classroom control. *Journal of Applied Behavior Analysis,* 1968, *1,* 315–322.

Hewett, F. M., Taylor, F. D., & Artuso, A. A., The Santa Monica Project: Evaluation of an engineered classroom design with emotionally disturbed children. *Exceptional Children,* 1969, *35,* 523–529.

Jabichuk, Z., & Smeriglio, U., *The influence of symbolic modeling on the social behavior of pre-school children with low levels of social responsiveness.* Unpublished Manuscript, University of Western Ontario, 1975.

Kazdin, A. E., The effect of response cost in suppressing behavior in a prepsychotic retardate. *Journal of Behavior Therapy and Experimental Psychiatry,* 1971, *2,* 137–141.

Kazdin, A. E., The effect of nonverbal teacher approval on student attentive behavior. *Journal of Applied Behavior Analysis,* 1973, *6,* 643–654.

Kazdin, A. E., & Bootzin, R. R., The token economy: An evaluative review. *Journal of Applied Behavior Analysis,* 1972, *5,* 343–372.

Kendall, P., & Finch, A., *A cognitive behavioral treatment for impulsivity: A group comparison study.* Unpublished manuscript, Virginia Treatment Center for Children, Richmond, Va., 1976.

Kennedy, B., & Miller, D., Persistent use of verbal refusal as a function of information about its value. *Child Development,* 1976, *47,* 566–569.

Lang, P. J., & Melamed, B., Case Report: Avoidance conditioning therapy of an infant with chronic ruminative vomiting. *Journal of Abnormal Psychology,* 1969, *74,* 1–8.

Lovaas, O. I., Some studies on the treatment of childhood schizophrenia. In J. M. Schlien (Ed.), *Research in psychotherapy* (Vol. 3). Washington, D.C.: American Psychological Association, 1968.

Lovaas, O. I., Berberich, J. P., Perloff, B. F., & Schaeffer, B., Acquisition of initiative speech by schizophrenic children. *Science,* 1966, *151,* 705–707.

Madsen, C. H., Jr., Becker, W. C., Thomas, D. R., Koser, L., and Plager, E., An analysis of the reinforcing function of "sit down" commands. In R. K. Parker (Ed.), *Readings in educational psychology.* Boston: Allyn & Bacon, 1968.

Masters, V., & Santrock, J., Studies in self-regulation of behavior: Effects of contingent cognitive and affective events. *Developmental Psychology,* 1976, *12,* 334–348.

Meichenbaum, D., *Cognitive-Behavior Modification Newsletter,* 1977, No. 3.

Meichenbaum, D. H., Bowers, K. S., & Ross, R. R., A behavioral analysis of teacher expectancy effect. *Journal of Personality & Social Psychology*, 1969, *13*, 306–316.

Mercer, C. D., Hallahan, D. P., & Ball, D. W., *Modeling and attention of mentally retarded, learning disabled and normal boys.* Unpublished manuscript, 1977.

Mercer, C. D., Cullinan, D., Hallahan, D. P., & LaFleur, N. K., Modeling and attention-retention in learning disabled children. *Journal of Learning Disabilities*, 1975, *8*, 444–450.

Messer, S. B., Reflection-impulsivity: A review. *Psychological Bulletin*, 1976, *83*, 1026–1052.

Midlarsky, E., & Bryan, J. H., Affect expressions and children's imitative altruism. *Journal of Experimental Research in Personality*, 1972, *6*, 195–203.

O'Conner, R. D., Modification of social withdrawal through symbolic modeling. *Journal of Applied Behavior Analysis*, 1969, *2*, 15–22.

O'Leary, K. D., & Drabman, R., Token reinforcement programs in the classroom: A review. *Psychological Bulletin*, 1971, *75*, 379–398.

Premack, D., Reinforcement theory. In D. LeVine (Ed.), *Nebraska Symposium on Motivation: 1965.* Lincoln: University of Nebraska Press, 1965.

Risley, T., & Wolf, M. M., Experimental manipulation of autistic behavior and generalization into the home. In R. Ulrich, T. Stachnik, and J. Mabry (Eds.), *Control of human behavior.* Glenview, Ill.: Scott, Foresman, 1966.

Schwartz, T., & Bryan, J. H., Imitation and judgments of children with language deficits. *Exceptional Children*, 1971, *38*, 157–158.

Schwartz, T., & Bryan, J. H. Imitative altruism of deaf children. *Journal of Speech and Hearing Research*, 1974, *14*, 453–461.

Snyder, L., Apolloni, T., & Cooke, T. P., Integrated settings at the early childhood level: The role of nonretarded peers. *Exceptional Children*, 1977, *43*, 262-269.

Staats, A. W., Minke, K. A., Finley, J. R., Wolf, M., & Brooks, L. O., A reinforcer system and experimental procedure for the laboratory study of reading acquisition. *Child Development*, 1964, *35*, 209–231.

Walters, R. H., Leat, M., & Mezei, L., Inhibition and disinhibition of responses through empathic learning. *Canadian Journal of Psychology*, 1963, *17*, 235–243.

Weisbrod, C., & Bryan, J. H., Film treatment as an effective fear reduction technique. *Journal of Abnormal Child Psychology*, 1973, *1*, 196–201.

Williams, C. D., The elimination of tantrum behavior by extinction procedures. *Journal of Abnormal and Social Psychology*, 1959, *59*, 269.

Wolf, M. M., Giles, D. K., & Hall, R. V., Experiments with token reinforcement in a remedial classroom. *Behavior Research and Therapy*, 1968, *8*, 51–54.

Wolf, M. M., Risley, T., Johnston, M., Harris, F., & Allen, E., Application of operant conditioning procedures to the behavior problems of an autistic child: A follow-up and extension. *Behavior Research and Therapy*, 1967, *5*, 103–312.

Wolf, M. M., Risley, T., & Mees, H. L., Application of operant conditioning procedures to the behavior problems of an autistic child. *Behavior Research and Therapy*, 1964, *1*, 305–312.

Zimmerman, J., & Zimmerman, E. The alteration of behavior in a special classroom situation. *Journal of the Experimental Analysis of Behavior,* 1962, 5, 59–60.

KEY TERMS

aversive stimulation Any action or event that evokes extremely negative reactions.

cognitive behavior modification An approach to behavior change that focuses on both the central and motor processes related to the task or problem solving skills.

contingency management A technique of behavior change in which new consequences for a target behavior are introduced. Rewards are made contingent on more appropriate behavior, while reinforcement for undesirable behavior is withdrawn.

covert rehearsal Problem solving activity in which the person is directed to silently think about selecting successful strategies.

insight therapy Approach to behavior change in which persons are directed by a therapist toward becoming aware of the underlying reasons for their inappropriate behavior. Once this point is reached, it is assumed that the person will make adaptive changes in their behavior.

overt rehearsal Problem solving activity in which the person is instructed to talk aloud about the selection of effective strategies.

response cost Behavior change techniques that involve the removal of positive reinforcement after an episode of inappropriate or unacceptable behavior.

time-out procedure The removal of a person from a potentially positively reinforcing environment. Typically involves isolation.

Subject Index

Acceleration, 306–7
  effects of, upon gifted, 306
Adaptive Behavior Scale, 149–50
Aggressive behavior, 185–93, 209. *See also* Emotional disorders
  definitions of, 185–86
  parental effects upon, 191–93
  sex differences in, 189
  social class differences in, 189–90
  theories of, 186–89
Altruism, 326–33. *See also* Prosocial behavior
  affected by hypocrisy, 330
  defined, 327–28
  parental practices affecting, 332–33
  personal characteristics affecting, 330–33
  as a result of models, 328–29
American Association of Mental Deficiency, 147, 148, 149–50, 152, 153
  Adaptive Behavior Scale of, 149–50
  classification system of, 152
American Foundation for the Blind, 16
American Psychiatric Association, 183–84, 208
American Standard Association, classification system of, 221–23, 238
Ameslan (American Sign Language), 233
Aphasia, 261, 269

Articulation disorders, 248–49, 251–52. *See also* Speech disorders
Assessment, 6, 150, 360–63, 364–65
  controversy over, 361–62
  purposes of, 361
  required for EIP, 363–64
Association for Retarded Children, 22
Audiometer, 218–19, 242
Auditory Discrimination Test, 120, 251
Auditory perception, 114–16, 372–74
  and hearing acuity, 114
  and reading problems, 126
  remediation for disability in, 372–74
  tests of, 114–15
Autism, 25, 204, 206, 213, 398–99
Aversive stimulation, 393–94, 410

Bandura, Albert, 72–73, 89–93, 185–86, 199, 388, 398, 401
Bayley Scale of Infant Development, 42–43
Behavior modification, 71, 73, 77, 97, 208, 265, 384–407. *See also* Punishment; Reinforcement; Skinner, B. F.
  as remediation for emotional disorders, 385
Bell, Alexander Graham, 215
Bender Visual Motor Gestalt Test, 111
Binet, Alfred, 33–35, 36, 38–39, 57

Author Index